DENNIS SWANN

THE ECONOMICS OF THE COMMON MARKET

INTEGRATION IN THE EUROPEAN UNION

Eighth Edition

PENGUIN BOOKS

PENGUIN BOOKS

Published by the Penguin Group
Penguin Books Ltd, 27 Wrights Lane, London W8 5TZ, England
Penguin Books USA Inc., 375 Hudson Street, New York, New York 10014, USA
Penguin Books Australia Ltd, Ringwood, Victoria, Australia
Penguin Books Canada Ltd, 10 Alcorn Avenue, Toronto, Ontario, Canada M4V 3B2
Penguin Books (NZ) Ltd, 182–190 Wairau Road, Auckland 10, New Zealand

Penguin Books Ltd, Registered Offices: Harmondsworth, Middlesex, England

First published 1970
Second edition 1972
Third edition 1975
Fourth edition 1978
Reprinted with revisions and Addendum 1981
Fifth edition, published in Pelican Books, 1984
Sixth edition 1988
Reprinted in Penguin Books 1990
Seventh edition 1992
Eighth edition 1995
10 9 8 7 6 5 4 3 2

Typeset by Datix International Limited, Bungay, Suffolk
Filmset in $9\frac{1}{2}/11\frac{1}{2}$ pt Times (Monotype Lasercomp)
Printed in England by Clays Ltd, St Ives plc

TO BARBARA CLAIRE

CONTENTS

PREFACE TO EIGHTH EDITION

On 25 March 1957 the governments of France, West Germany, Italy, the Netherlands, Belgium and Luxembourg signed the Rome Treaty. In so doing they agreed to create what came to be known as the Common Market or, more accurately, the European Economic Community. That institution has remained the centrepiece of the movement towards closer union and economic integration in Europe. It was of course accompanied by the creation of Euratom and had indeed been preceded by the European Coal and Steel Community of 1951. Both these bodies are dealt with in this book but the main focus is on the Common Market and Monetary Union aspects of the European story. The Common Market has of course evolved and is evolving both in terms of membership and scope. The key developments were the Single European Act of 1986 and the Maastricht Treaty on European Union of 1992. The Single Act set the Community the basic task of completing the creation of a Single European Market. The Maastricht Treaty transformed the relationship in a variety of ways. First, the European Economic Community is now referred to as the European Community since it covers social and cultural as well as economic matters. Second, the process of economic integration has now been pointed towards the ultimate destination of Economic and Monetary Union. Third, the whole complex of relationships has been given the title of the European Union. The Union's task is not only economic, social and cultural integration; it also takes in the Common Foreign and Security Policy and Cooperation on Justice and Home Affairs. In short, integration has spilled over from economic to broadly political affairs.

The purpose of this book is to present a picture of the European Union in the second half of the nineteen nineties. The central focus is on the economic principles underlying the decision to create, and extend the scope of, the Common Market or European Community and on the economic policies which the Community has been following since its inception. An understanding of economic policy also requires us to discuss the decision-making system and the means by which the Union finances its operations. These are covered in chapters 2 and 3.

In writing this book I have been greatly assisted by my wife Beryl, who has been closely involved in vetting the final manuscript and in proofreading. I am also extremely grateful to Lorraine Whittington who, with her customary efficiency, has helped to get the manuscript into a fit state for publication. The presentation of much of the argument has been greatly facilitated by having to present it to successive groups of British and foreign civil servants at the Civil Service College, and I am grateful to John Eastmead, Annette Morgan, Katrina Morris and Adrian Rossiter for invitations to speak.

1

THE EVOLUTION OF THE EUROPEAN UNION

European unity in history

Although the actual steps which have been taken to achieve economic and political unity in Europe are mostly, if not all, post 1945 in origin, the idea of such a coming together is not unique to the last fifty or so years. Quite the contrary: history is littered with proposals and arrangements which were designed to foster European unity.

As early as the fourteenth century the idea of a united Christendom prompted Pierre Dubois to propose a European confederation to be governed by a European Council of 'wise, expert, and faithful men'. In the seventeenth century Sully proposed to keep the peace in Europe by means of a European army. In 1693, William Penn, the English Quaker, suggested 'a European Diet, Parliament, or State' in his *Essay towards the Present and Future Peace of Europe*. In the nineteenth century Proudhon was strongly in favour of European federation. He foresaw the twentieth century as opening an era of federations and prophesied disaster if such developments did not occur. It was only after the 1914–18 war that statesmen began to give serious attention to the idea of European unity. Aristide Briand – a Prime Minister of France – declared that part of his political programme was the building of a United States of Europe.

The achievement of a lasting peace has been the chief motivating factor behind the drive for unity. However, economic advantage also played a role. The free-trade tradition, and Adam Smith's dictum that 'the division of labour is limited by the extent of the market', was a contributing element. The idea that European nation states were no longer large enough to hold their own in world markets was put forward by the German thinker Friedrich Naumann in 1915.

Despite the fact that there was no shortage of plans to create a united Europe, it was nevertheless not until after 1945 that there occurred a combination of new forces together with an intensification of old ones, compelling action. In the first place, Europe had been the centre of yet another devastating war arising out of the unbridled ambitions of nation states. Those who sought, and still seek, a united Europe, have always had at the forefront of their minds the desire to prevent any further outbreak of war in Europe. By bringing the nations of Europe closer together it has always been hoped that such a contingency would be rendered unthinkable. The 1939–45 war also left Europe economically exhausted. This engendered the view that if Europe were to recover, it would require a joint effort on the part of European states. The war also soon revealed that for a long time Western Europe would have to face not only a powerful and politically alien USSR, but also a group of European states firmly anchored within the Eastern bloc. An exhausted and divided Europe (since the West embraced co-belligerents) presented both a power-vacuum and a temptation to the USSR to fill it. Then the ending of the war soon revealed that the wartime Allies were in fact divided, with the two major powers – the US and the USSR – confronting each other in a bid for world supremacy. It was therefore not surprising that 'Europeans'[1] should feel the need for a third force – the voice of Europe. The latter would represent the Western European viewpoint and could also act as a bridge between the Eastern and Western extremities.

Europe – the East–West division

The Economic Commission for Europe (ECE) was one of the first experiments in European regional action. It was set up in Geneva in 1947 as a regional organization of the United Nations (UN), and was to be concerned with initiating and participating in concerted measures aimed at securing the economic reconstruction of Europe. The aim was to create an instrument of cooperation between all the states of Europe – Eastern, Central and Western. Unfortunately, by the time it began to operate, the Cold War had become a reality

1. 'Europeans' – members of the 'European movement' – sought to break away from systems of inter-governmental cooperation and to create institutions in Europe which would lead to a federal arrangement in which some national sovereignty would be given up.

and the world had been divided into two camps. In the light of future developments in Europe, this was a turning-point. Economic cooperation over the whole of Europe was doomed. Thereafter, Western Europe followed its own path of economic and political unity, and Eastern Europe likewise pursued an independent course. This in due course led to two blocs in Europe – the Common Market or European Economic Community (EEC) and the European Free Trade Association (EFTA) on the one hand, and the Council for Mutual Economic Assistance (Comecon) on the other.

The political division of Europe was further revealed in 1948 by the emergence of the Brussels Treaty Organization. The Brussels Treaty was signed by the UK, France, Belgium, the Netherlands and Luxembourg, and was designed to establish a system of mutual assistance in time of attack in Europe. Clearly the Western European states had the USSR and its satellites in mind. This organization in turn took on an Atlantic shape in 1949 when, in order to provide a military defence organization, the North Atlantic Treaty Organization (NATO) was created by the five states just mentioned, together with the US, Canada, Denmark, Norway, Portugal, Iceland and, significantly, Italy, which had been an Axis power.[1]

Division in Western Europe – the beginning

The creation of the Organization for European Economic Cooperation (OEEC) in 1948 and the Council of Europe in 1949 marked the beginning of a division between the UK and some of the countries later to become members of EFTA, and the Six[2] who subsequently founded the EEC.

The division was founded in large measure on the fact that the UK was less committed to Europe as the main area of policy than the six Continental powers. During the second half of the 1950s the UK was still a world power. She had after all been on the victorious

1. Greece and Turkey joined in 1952 and West Germany in 1955.
2. The Six were, of course. France, West Germany, Italy, the Netherlands, Belgium and Luxembourg. In discussing divisions between Western and Eastern Europe, and within Western Europe, it should be remembered that the Six were also members of the European Coal and Steel Community (ECSC) and members of the European Atomic Energy Community (Euratom).

side and had been a major participant in some of the fateful geopolitical decision-making meetings such as Yalta. Moreover, she still had the Empire to dispose of. British foreign policy was therefore bound to be based on wide horizons. Relations with Europe had to compete with Commonwealth (and Empire) ties and with the 'special relationship' with the US. In addition, the idea of a politically united Europe (in some eyes the goal was a United States of Europe) was strongly held on the Continent – particularly in France and the Benelux countries[1] – but despite the encouraging noises made by Winston Churchill both during the 1939–45 war and after, it was not a concept which excited British hearts.

The difference between British and Continental thinking about the political nature of European institutions was revealed in the discussions and negotiations leading up to the establishment of the OEEC and the Council of Europe.

The war had left Europe devastated. The year 1947 was particularly bleak. Bad harvests in the previous summer led to rising food prices, whilst the severe winter of 1946–7 led to a fuel crisis. The Continental countries were producing relatively little, and what was produced tended to be retained rather than exported, whilst import needs were booming. Foreign exchange reserves were therefore running out and it was at this point that the US entered upon the scene and presented the Marshall Plan. General George Marshall proposed that the US make aid available to help the European economy to find its feet and that European governments get together to decide how much assistance was needed. The US did not feel it fitting that it should unilaterally decide on the programmes necessary to achieve this end. Although it seemed possible that this aid programme could be elaborated within the ECE framework, the USSR felt otherwise. Russian reluctance was no doubt based on the fear that if her satellites participated, this would open the door to Western influence.

A conference was therefore convened, and a Committee for European Economic Cooperation (CEEC) was established. The attitude of the US was that the CEEC should not just provide the US with a list of needs. The latter had in mind that the aid it was to

1. Belgium, the Netherlands and Luxembourg agreed to form a customs union in 1944; it came into effect in 1948 and was called Benelux.

give should be linked with progress towards European unification. This is a particularly important point since it indicates that from the very beginning the 'European movement' has enjoyed the encouragement and support of the US.

The CEEC led in turn to the creation of an aid agency – the OEEC. Here the conflict between Britain and other Western European countries, particularly France, came to a head over the issue of supra-nationalism. France in particular – and she was supported by the US – wanted to inject a supra-national element into the new organization.[1] We should perhaps at this point pause to define what is meant by supra-nationalism. It can refer to a situation in which international administrative institutions exercise power over, for example, the economies of the nation states. Thus the High Authority of the European Coal and Steel Community (ECSC)[2] was endowed with powers over the economies of the Six and these powers were exercised independently of the Council of Ministers. Alternatively, it can refer to a situation in which ministerial bodies, when taking decisions (to be implemented by international administrations), work on a majority voting system rather than by insisting on unanimity.

The French view was not shared by the British. The latter favoured a body which was under the control of a ministerial council in which decisions should be taken on a unanimity basis. The French, on the other hand, favoured an arrangement in which an international secretariat would be presided over by a Secretary General who would be empowered to take policy initiatives on major issues. Significantly, the organization which emerged was substantially in line with the UK's wish for a unanimity rule. This was undoubtedly a reflection of the UK's relatively powerful position in Europe at the time. In the light of subsequent events it is also interesting to note that the US encouraged the European countries to consider the creation of a customs union. Although this was of considerable interest to some Continental countries, it did not attract the UK. In the upshot the OEEC Convention merely recorded the intention to continue the study of this proposal.

1. It is, of course, ironic that whereas France was then in the vanguard of the supra-national movement she subsequently became a dedicated opponent.
2. Created under the Paris Treaty of 1951.

For a variety of reasons, one of which was the opposition of the UK, the matter was not pursued further.

The creation of the Council of Europe also threw into high relief fundamental differences in approach between the countries which later formed the Common Market on the one hand, and the British and Scandinavians on the other. The creation of the Council was preceded by the Congress of Europe at The Hague in May 1948. The latter was a grand rally of 'Europeans' which was attended by leading European statesmen including Winston Churchill. The Congress adopted a resolution which called for the giving up of some national sovereignty prior to the accomplishment of economic and political union in Europe. Subsequently a proposal was put forward, with the support of the Belgian and French Governments, calling for the creation of a European Parliamentary Assembly in which resolutions would be passed by majority vote. This was, of course, contrary to the unanimity rule which was then characteristic of international organizations. A Committee of Ministers was to prepare and implement these resolutions. Needless to say, the UK was opposed to this form of supra-nationalism and in the end the British view largely prevailed. The Committee of Ministers, which is the executive organ of the Council of Europe, alone has power of decision and generally decisions are taken on the unanimity principle. The Consultative Assembly which came into existence is a forum – its critics would call it a debating society – and not a European legislature. In short, the British and Scandinavian functionalists, who believed that European unity, in so far as it was to be achieved, was to be attained by inter-governmental cooperation, triumphed over the federalists who sought unity by the more radical method of creating European institutions to which national governments would surrender some of their sovereignty. The final disillusionment of the federalists with the Council of Europe as an instrument of federal unity in Europe was almost certainly marked by the resignation of Paul-Henri Spaak from the Presidency of the Consultative Assembly in 1951.

The Six set forth – success and failure

The next step in the economic and political unification of Europe was taken without the British and Scandinavians. It took the form of the creation in 1951 of the ECSC by the Six, and this creation marks a parting of the ways in postwar Europe – a parting which by 1959 was to lead to the creation of two trading blocs.

The immediate precipitating factor was the revival of the West German economy. The passage of time, the efforts of the German people and the aid made available by the US all contributed to the recovery of the German economy. Indeed the 'Economic Miracle' was about to unfold. It was recognized that the German economy would have to be allowed to regain its position in the world, and that Allied control of coal and steel under the International Ruhr Authority could not last indefinitely. The fundamental question was how the German economy in the sectors of iron, steel and coal (the basic materials of a war effort) could be allowed to re-attain its former powerful position without endangering the future peace of Europe. The answer was a French plan, elaborated by Jean Monnet and put forward by Robert Schuman in May 1950. The Schuman Plan was essentially political in character. It sought to end the historic rivalry of France and Germany and to do this by making a war between France and West Germany not only 'unthinkable but materially impossible'. This was to be done in a way which ultimately would have the result of bringing about that 'European federation which is indispensable to peace'. The answer was not to nationalize nor indeed to internationalize the ownership of the means of production in coal, iron and steel, but to create, by the removal of customs duties, quotas and so forth, a common market in these products. Every participant in the common market would have equal access to the products of these industries wherever they might be located, and, to reinforce this, discrimination on grounds of nationality was to be forbidden.

The plan had a number of attractive features. It provided an excellent basis for solving the Saar problem. The handing back of the Saar to West Germany was more likely to be palatable to the French if West Germany was firmly locked in such a coal and steel community. It was also extremely attractive to the Germans since membership of the Community was a passport to international respectability – it was the best way of speeding up the ending of occupation and of avoiding the imposition of dampers on German economic expansion. It was also attractive to the federalists who had found the OEEC as inadequate to their aspirations as the

Council of Europe. The OEEC unanimity rule, and the fact that no powers could be delegated to an independent commission or commissariat, were extremely frustrating. Not only that, but the prospects for the OEEC were not good, since by 1952 the four-year period of the Marshall Plan would be over, and the UK attitude was that thereafter its budget should be cut and some of its functions passed over to NATO. As it emerged, however, the Community was much more to the federalists' taste since, as already indicated, the High Authority was endowed with substantial direct powers which could be exerted without the prior approval of the Council of Ministers.

The Schuman Plan met with a favourable response from West Germany, France, Italy, the Netherlands, Belgium and Luxembourg. The UK was invited to join but refused. The Prime Minister, Clement Attlee, told the House of Commons:

We on this side are not prepared to accept the principle that the most vital economic forces of this country should be handed over to an authority that is utterly undemocratic and is responsible to nobody. (Quoted in Palmer *et al.*, 1968, p. 258)

However, the Six were undeterred, and in April 1951 the Treaty of Paris was signed. The ECSC was brought into existence and the Community embarked on an experiment in limited economic integration.

The next episode in the development of European unity was also connected with West Germany. When the Korean War broke out in 1950 the response of the US was to suggest that West Germany be rearmed. However, this proposal was opposed by France, which was equally opposed to West Germany becoming a member of NATO. But the French approach to this problem was not a negative one. Instead, the French Prime Minister – René Pléven – put forward a plan. This envisaged that there would be no German army as such but there would be a European army to which each participating state, including West Germany, could contribute.

The UK was not opposed to the idea but did not itself wish to be involved. The Six were positively enthusiastic and discussion began in 1951 with a view to creating a European Defence Community. It was envisaged that there would be a Joint Defence Commission and a Council of Ministers. In addition, there was to be a Parliamentary Assembly and a Court of Justice parallel to those created in connection with the ECSC. The Six made rapid progress in the negotiations and European Defence Community Treaty was signed in May 1952.

Having gone so far, there seemed to be a number of good reasons for proceeding yet further. The pooling of defensive and offensive capabilities inevitably reduced the possibility of independent foreign policies. It was therefore logical to follow integration in the field of defence with measures which would serve to achieve political integration as well. Other forces were also at work. One was the desirability of establishing a system whereby effective democratic control could be exercised over the proposed European army. The other was the Dutch desire that progress in the military field should be paralleled by more integration in the economic sphere. The foreign ministers of the Six therefore asked the ECSC Assembly, in conjunction with coopted members from the Consultative Assembly of the Council of Europe, to study the possibilities of creating a European Political Authority. In 1953 a draft of a European Political Community was produced. It proposed that, after a transition period, the institutions of the ECSC and the proposed European Defence Community be subsumed within a new framework. There would then be one European Executive responsible to a European Parliament (the later would consist of a People's Chamber elected by direct universal suffrage, and a Senate elected by National Parliaments). In addition, there would be one Council of Ministers and one European Court to replace the parallel bodies created under the ECSC and European Defence Community Treaties.

This was undoubtedly a high-water mark in the history of the 'European movement'. The Six had already successfully experimented in limited economic integration in the fields of coal and steel. They had now signed a treaty to integrate defence and were about to go further and create a Community for the purpose of securing political unity. Not only that; the draft treaty proposed to push economic integration still further since it called for the establishment of a general common market based on the free movement of goods and factors of production.

However, on this occasion the success which had attended the Six in the case of coal and steel was not repeated. Five national Parliaments approved the European Defence Community Treaty, but successive French Governments felt unable to guarantee success in asking the French Assembly to ratify. Finally, the Mendès-France Government attempted to water down the Treaty but failed to persuade the Five. The Treaty as it stood was therefore submitted to the French Assembly. The latter refused to consider it and in so doing killed the European Political Community also.

An amalgam of motives lay behind the refusal of the French Assembly to consider the Treaty. One was opposition to the supra-national element which it contained. Another was the refusal by the French Left to countenance the re-armament of West Germany and the refusal of the French Right to have the French army placed under foreign control. British aloofness was also a contributory factor. One of the arguments employed by those who were against the Treaty was that France could not take part in the formation of a European army with West Germany if Britain was not a member.

It is perhaps worth noting that the failure of the European Defence Community was followed by a British initiative also aimed at dealing with the problem of rearming West Germany in a way acceptable to the French. A series of agreements was reached in 1954 between the US, UK, Canada and the Six. Under these agreements, the Brussels Treaty Organization was modified and extended. West Germany and Italy were brought in and a new inter-governmental organization – Western European Union (WEU) – was formed. The agreements also related to the termination of the occupation of West Germany and the admission of the latter into NATO. As a counterbalance to the West German army, the UK agreed to maintain specified forces on the Continent. As has been pointed out, the main purpose of the agreement

was to provide a European framework in which Germany could be re-armed and become a member of NATO, while providing also for British military participation to relieve French fears that there would be no check or balance to possible German predominance. (Palmer *et al.*, 1968, p. 32)

It should also be noted that the response of Eastern Europe to those agreements was a further hardening of the East-West division in the shape of the formation of the Warsaw Pact.

The *relance*

1954 had been a bad year for European unity. The supra-nationalist cause had suffered a reverse and the creation of WEU – an organization cast more in the traditional inter-government mould – had thereafter held the centre of the stage. However, such then was the strength of the 'European movement' that by 1955 new ideas were again being put forward. The relaunching initiative came from the Benelux states. They produced a memorandum calling for the establishment of a general common market and for specific action in the fields of energy and transport. The basic idea behind the Benelux approach was that political unity was likely to prove difficult to achieve. It was the ultimate objective but it was one which could only be realized in the longer run. In the short and medium term the objective should be overall economic integration. Experience gained in working closely together would then pave the way for the achievement of the political goal. The memorandum called for the creation of institutions which would enable a European Economic Community to be established. These ideas were considered at the meeting of the foreign ministers of the Six at Messina in June 1955. They met with a favourable response. The six governments resolved that work should begin with a view to establishing a general common market and an atomic energy pool. Moreover, a committee should be formed which would not merely study the problems involved but should also prepare the texts of the treaties necessary in order to carry out the agreed objectives. An inter-governmental committee, presided over by Paul-Henri Spaak, was therefore created. The Messina resolution recorded that since the UK was a member of WEU and was associated with the ECSC,[1] it should be invited to participate in the work of the committee. The position of other OEEC countries was not so clear – the question of whether they should be allowed to participate was in fact left for later decision by the foreign ministers.

The Spaak committee held its first meeting in July 1955. British representatives were present and subsequently played an active part in the deliberations. However, as the committee's probing progressed, differences between the Six and the UK became evident. The latter was in favour of a free trade area arrangement, whilst the Six were agreed upon the formation of a customs union – the Messina resolution had explicitly called for this kind of arrangement. Then again the UK felt that little extra machinery was

1. The UK signed an 'Agreement of Association' with the ECSC in 1954.

needed to put the new arrangement into effect. The OEEC, perhaps somewhat strengthened, would suffice. This view was bound to antagonize the federalists, who laid stress on the creation of supranational institutions which would help to achieve more than mere economic integration. These differences culminated in the withdrawal of the UK representatives from the discussions in November 1955. Meanwhile, the Spaak committee forged ahead, although not without internal differences. The French, for example, were anxious about the transition period allowed for dismantling the tariff system, about escape clauses and about harmonization of social charges, and they desired a high tariff round the union whilst the Benelux states were in favour of a low one. In April 1956 the committee reported (Spaak, 1956) and its conclusions were considered by the foreign ministers of the Six at Venice in May of that year. Attitudes among the six governments were not uniform. The French liked the idea of an atomic energy community, but were cooler on the idea of a general common market. The other governments held reverse views. However, despite all this, the governments agreed that the drafting of two Treaties, one to create the general common market and one to create an atomic energy community, should begin. Intensive negotiations followed and the two Treaties were subsequently signed in Rome on 25 March 1957. These were duly ratified by the national parliaments. The EEC (and Euratom) came into being on 1 January 1958.

The development of the EEC

1958–69

In practice by far the more important of these two Treaties was that which called for the creation of the EEC. This committed the Six to a far-reaching exercise in economic integration which was to be accomplished within a transition period of twelve years. Economic integration can take various forms and these can be ranged in a spectrum in which the degree of involvement of the participating economies, one with another, becomes greater and greater. The *free trade area* is the least onerous in terms of involvement. It consists of an arrangement between states in which they agree to remove all customs duties and quotas on trade passing between them. Each party is free, however, to determine unilaterally the level of customs duties on imports coming from outside the area. The next stage is the *customs union*. Here tariffs and quotas on trade between the members are also removed but in addition the members agree to apply a *common* level of duty on goods entering the union from without. The latter is called the common customs, or common external, tariff. Next comes the *common market* and this technical term implies that to the free movement of *goods* within the customs union is added the free movement of the *factors of production* – labour, capital and enterprise. Finally there is the *economic union*. This is a common market in which there is also a complete unification of monetary and fiscal policy. There would be a common currency which would be controlled by a central authority and in effect the member states would become regions within the union.

The *original* Rome Treaty quite clearly provided for the creation of a common market. This is apparent from the contents of Article 3 which lays down the key objectives of the EEC. Article 3(a) calls for the elimination of internal trade barriers, Article 3(b) provides for the creation of a common external tariff whilst Article 3(c) requires the member states to abolish obstacles to the free movement of factors. In order to facilitate this free movement of goods, services and factors of production, Article 3(h) provides for any necessary harmonization of member state laws and Article 3(f) supplies yet further underpinning by calling for the institution of a system which will ensure that competition in the common market is not distorted. The latter Article is of great significance because it clearly indicates that the integration of national markets is to be accomplished not by planning but through the agency of free and competitive trade interpenetration. The Treaty, however, went beyond a commitment merely to create a common market. Common policies were to be established in agriculture and transport – this was provided for under Articles 3(d) and 3(e) respectively. The Treaty also envisaged the establishment of institutions designed to improve the standard of living of workers and the development of the less developed regions of the Community. Hence the European Social Fund (ESF) and the European Investment Bank (EIB), to which Articles 3(i) and 3(j) respectively refer. The Community was also required to develop a common commercial policy *vis-à-vis* the rest of the world (Article 3(b)), and in particular to make special trade and development arrangements for the colonial and ex-colonial dependencies of the member states (Article 3(k)). Without those special arrangements the dependencies would have suffered from the automatic discrimination inherent in the common external tariff. The Treaty also recognized that the greater the degree of economic integration the greater would be the impact of national macroeconomic policies on the other member states. This would be particularly the case when a member state took action to rectify a balance of payments deficit. Article 3(g) addresses this problem but does so in terms of cooperation and coordination rather than the unification and centralization which would be required in an economic and monetary union.

From 1958 to 1969 (when the transition period came to an end) the Six proceeded to construct the kind of economic community envisaged in the Rome Treaty. We shall not attempt to describe all the various measures – they are discussed in detail in the subsequent chapters. Suffice it to say that the basic ingredients of the customs union – internal tariff and quota dismantling and the establishment of the common external tariff – were established ahead of schedule. Initial steps were taken and measures proposed to deal with the many non-tariff barriers to the free movement of goods and services. Steps were also taken and measures proposed in respect of the free movement of factors of production so that by 1969 a recognizably common market could be said to exist. In the sphere of common policies variable progress was evident. Thanks in particular to French insistence and indeed threats, the Common Agricultural Policy (CAP) was virtually fully operational by 1969 – the Common Transport Policy was, however, slow to evolve. The ESF and the EIB were duly established and were fully operational at an early stage. Steps were taken on the road to the creation of a common commercial policy, and the Six devised appropriate trade and aid arrangements in respect of their colonial and increasingly ex-colonial dependencies. A rudimentary system of macro-economic coordination was also devised. Although during this period progress was evident and optimism about the success of the European venture was very much in the ascendant, there were disappointments. Perhaps the greatest was the French refusal to accept the supra-national element in the Rome Treaty decision-making system. More will be said about that later and in Chapter 2.

1969–79

When in 1969 the transition period came to an end it would have been possible for the Six to have called a halt. Having said that, it is important to emphasize that a total cessation of activity at the Community level would not have been possible or appropriate. First, having established policies in areas such as agriculture and competition, it would have been necessary to have continued to operate them. Thus decisions about agricultural prices would have had to be taken season by season and markets would have had to be continuously manipulated in order that those prices were obtained by farmers. Then again, the activities of businessmen and governments would have had to be monitored continuously in order that factors which could otherwise prevent, restrict or distort competitive trade were rooted out. Secondly, although substantial progress had been made in achieving the objectives listed in Article 3, when the transition period drew to a close it had to be admitted that substantial policy gaps still remained to be filled before it could be said that a truly common market existed.

Nevertheless it would have been possible for the member states to conclude that, subject to the need to operate existing policies and to fill obvious policy gaps, no further economic integration or institutional development should be attempted. In fact the Community decided quite the contrary.

First, new areas of economic policy were opened up and old ones substantially recast. In 1969 the Heads of State and of Government of the Six held a summit meeting at The Hague. On that occasion they decided that the EEC should progressively transform itself into an Economic and Monetary Union (EMU). Although important measures were subsequently introduced in order to achieve that end, the enterprise ultimately failed. Nevertheless the idea did not go away, and in the late seventies a more modest scheme in the shape of the European Monetary System (EMS) was successfully introduced. The EMU proposal was only one of a succession of new policy initiatives during the period 1969 to 1972. Indeed this period can be described as a second *relance*. In 1970 the Six achieved a common position on the development of a fisheries policy although total agreement was not to be achieved until 1983. At the Paris Summit of 1972 agreement was reached on the development of new policies in relation to both industry and science and research. The summit also envisaged a more active role for the Community in the sphere of regional policy. A European Regional Development Fund (ERDF) was to be established to channel Community resources into the development of backward regions. The summit also called for a new initiative in the fields of social policy and the environment. Later in the seventies the relationship between the Community and its ex-colonial dependencies was significantly reshaped in the form of the Lomé Conventions.

Secondly, there was a series of institutional developments. We have already noted the role of summit meetings. These were not new, but in the period from 1969 they became much more obviously the vehicle for the identification of new areas of Community activity, and the meetings of the Heads of State and of Government were later formalized and given the title of the European Council. It is evident from what has gone before that the Community needs financial resources not only to pay for the day-to-day running of the Community but also to feed the various funds. We have already referred to the ESF and the ERDF and later, in Chapter 8, we shall be discussing the most important one of all, the European Agricultural Guidance and Guarantee Fund (EAGGF). In 1970 the Community took an important step forward by agreeing to introduce a system which would provide the Community, and specifically the Community budget, with its own source of income. These are referred to as own resources. Another step of great importance was the decision that the European Parliament should be elected by the people and not by the national parliaments. In addition the Community decided to grant the Parliament significant powers over the Community budget – this was to prove to be a very significant development! Finally, but by no means least, was the development of the political cooperation mechanism. Although this book is concerned with matters economic it is important not to forget that ardent Europeans had always hoped that the habit of cooperation in the economic sphere would spill over into the political arena – that is to say into foreign policy matters. That indeed happened. European Political Cooperation (EPC) as it came to be known can be said to date from the Hague Summit of 1969 and was formally inaugurated in 1970. More will be said about political cooperation in Chapter 2 and Chapter 12.

Whilst there was abundant evidence of institutional change during the post-1969 period, it has to be acknowledged that by then the relationship between member states within the Community had undergone a significant change. In signing and ratifying the Rome Treaty the member states had opted for a system of decision-making that centred on the Community's own Council of Ministers, which could take decisions on the basis of a supra-national majority voting system. That, as we noted earlier, was knocked on the head by the French at a fairly early stage and instead the Six regressed to a system in which any member state could insist that nothing should happen unless it agreed that it should happen. In addition, and most notably after 1969, the centre of gravity in decision-making within the Community began to shift in favour of the European Council. The latter was a body which was not envisaged in the Rome Treaty and whose method of operation was cast in the traditional inter-governmental mould. The development of what we may term inter-governmentalism might have been expected to slow down the pace of development within the Community. In other words, the unanimity principle would always force the Community to adopt the lowest common denominator and that might mean little or even zero change. But certainly that was not the case in the early seventies. As we have seen, a host of new initiatives was launched and in the main those initiatives were designed to further the process of integration. Inter-governmentalism still held sway in the eighties but the performance of the inter-governmental Community of the eighties was markedly less dynamic than that of the early seventies. There was a notable absence of policy initiatives at a time when big problems called for imaginative and collective solutions. A good deal of activity within the Community centred on wrangles over such matters as the reform of the CAP, the reform of the Community budget and, as we shall see below, over the vexed question of the UK[1] contribution to the budget.

There is one other interesting development which we must note. The ebullient Paris Summit of 1972 also envisaged the establishment by the end of the decade of a European Union. The exact nature of the arrangement was not indicated. In due course Leo Tindemans, then Prime Minister of Belgium, was charged with the task of

1. The UK had joined in 1973.

producing a report on this development, and in 1975 he duly presented his ideas (EC Commission, 1976a). We shall not attempt to summarize that report. One topic was, however, of considerable interest. The report laid emphasis on the need to relaunch EMU which by that time had run into the ground. Tindemans also entertained the interesting possibility of a two-tier Community. Those who had the will and ability to forge ahead with such a union should do so – the others could lag behind but would not be released from the need to achieve the ultimate goal. Interpreted pessimistically, the fact that such an idea was entertained suggested that cohesion was becoming more difficult to achieve. The idea could, however, also be viewed optimistically, since it meant that even in the absence of majority voting some could progress even if all did not wish to do so. In fact, the EMS was launched in 1979 on such a basis since the UK refused to participate in the exchange rate aspect of the scheme.

The emergence of the Single European Act

Altogether more important was the decision of the first directly elected European Parliament of 1979 to take up the European Union issue again and indeed to produce a *draft* European Union Treaty (EUT). This was adopted by the European Parliament in 1984. More or less simultaneously the European Council had been exploring similar territory. In 1981 the German and Italian Governments had submitted to the member states a draft European Act designed to further European integration. This was remitted to the foreign ministers and the results of their labours were presented at the Stuttgart Summit in 1983. The Heads of State and of Government were aware that the Community had been increasingly paralysed by internal disputes and that a new initiative was needed which might help to relaunch the Community. Whilst those disputes were not yet resolved, a better atmosphere was desirable, and it was against this background that they received the report of the foreign ministers and adopted what was called the Solemn Declaration of European Union. They returned to the subject at the Fontainebleau Summit in 1984 and set up two committees. The Adonnino Committee was to examine ways of making the European Community more of a reality to its citizens (a People's Europe), while the Dooge

Committee, the more important in practice, was to investigate institutional reform and related matters. Dooge reported at the Brussels Summit in 1985 and also recommended in favour of an inter-governmental conference (IGC) to negotiate a European Union Treaty. This was agreed at the Milan Summit later in the year.

Before we proceed any further, it is important to recognize that the European Parliament and the European Council initiatives were not by any means identical. The Parliament's EUT, if agreed, would have radically altered the Community's decision-making structure. This the Parliament felt was essential, since, as we noted above, the Community was failing to take essential decisions, particularly in the light of the need to respond imaginatively to problems such as the recession and competition from countries such as the US and Japan. This failure was at least in part due to the kind of institutional blockages to which we referred earlier.[1] The EUT would have (a) brought both economic and foreign policy matters within the ambit of the Union decision-making machinery, (b) strengthened the position of the Commission, (c) progressively phased out national vetoes, and (d) given the European Parliament an enhanced legislative (as opposed to a largely consultative) role similar to that which exists in national political systems. By contrast, the Solemn Declaration was to a large extent a set of laudable aspirations concerning the need for closer unity which even the most cautious member state could adopt without actually committing itself to any immediate change. This difference was also reflected in the Dooge report which opted for streamlining the institutional system rather than radical change. It also called for a number of policy changes. In fairness these were important – particularly the need to create a true internal market.

The IGC was duly convened and the Commission and Parliament were also represented. Spain and Portugal also took part as they were about to join. The Commission made an extremely important contribution, notably the Cockfield Report or White Paper *Completing the Internal Market* (EC Commission, 1985a). It specified some 300 measures which would have to be introduced before the single

---

1. These blockages had been identified by the 'Three Wise Men' – a committee set up by the European Council in 1978.

internal market could be said to be completed. The report of the IGC was submitted to the Luxembourg Summit in December 1985, which agreed a compromise. The terms of the agreement were embodied in the Single European Act (SEA), which was signed by all the member states in 1986 and duly ratified. The SEA came into force on 1 July 1987.

The Single European Act

Whilst the SEA disappointed the Parliament, and it certainly did not achieve a European Union, it did constitute a highly significant act of consolidation, contained commitments to carry integration forward and provided for improvements in the way the Community was to be run. The full import of these observations will become clearer in later chapters.

The Act formally placed the three European Communities and EPC at the centre of the search for European Unity, and the European Council was clearly recognized as the supreme overall body. The role and institutional arrangements concerning EPC were spelled out in detail and are discussed in the next chapter.

The Act also reformed the decision-making processes of the three founding treaties. The three main changes related to the Rome (EEC) Treaty. (a) The voting arrangements in the Council of Ministers both in respect of the provisions relating to the completion of the single market and in respect of other policies, such as economic and social cohesion and research and technology, were re-cast so as to allow for majority voting. (b) The legislative relationship between the Council of Ministers and the European Parliament was also reformed by including a cooperation mechanism and powers to approve trade treaties and the admission of new members. (c) An additional court was to be grafted on to the Court of Justice. These changes are discussed in the next chapter.

The Single Act declared that the Community should aim to complete the internal market by 31 December 1992. It also specified that the EEC internal market should compromise an area *without internal frontiers*.

The Act inserted into the Rome (EEC) Treaty new provisions on macro-economic policy. These implied that the need to ensure convergence of economic and monetary policy was a key aim. In so doing member states should take account of experience in the European Monetary System (EMS) and with the development of the European Currency Unit. These had not featured previously in the treaty. Perhaps more significant was the fact that the preamble to the Act recollected that in 1972 the Paris Summit had committed itself to the goal of EMU. Whilst not committing members to full membership of the EMS, as an instrument deriving its authority from the Rome Treaty, these provisions did help to move matters forward in that direction.

The Act modified the provisions concerning social policy. Member states should pay particular attention to encouraging improvements in the working environment. The key point is that while the original Rome Treaty placed no compulsion on member states, the Act subjected such social improvement proposals to majority voting. The Act also required the Commission to seek a dialogue between labour and management at the European level. The Social Charter stems in part from provisions contained in the preamble to the SEA.

The Act also gave rise to innovations in respect of what is called economic and social cohesion. Most interestingly, the aspiration of the Community to reduce disparities between the various regions and backwardness of the least favoured regions, *which had only been in the preamble to the old treaty*, was shifted into the main body of the amended treaty. The Act also required that expenditures under the Community budget be directed to these ends. This was acted upon in 1988 when the Community budget was reformed – increased provision was made for the so-called structural funds (notably the ESF and ERDF).

New provisions were also added to the Rome Treaty which declared that the Community's aim should be to strengthen the scientific and technological basis of European industry to encourage it to become more competitive at the international level. A clutch of new articles designed to facilitate this was also provided. Finally, the Act added to the treaty powers which quite explicitly provided for a Community competence in matters concerning the environment and health and safety at work.

Beyond the Single Act

The ink was not long dry on the Single Act when thoughts began to turn to the idea of pressing the process of European Union yet further. At the Hanover Summit in June 1988 the European Council, recalling the 1972 Paris Summit commitment to EMU contained in the preamble to the Single Act, asked the President of the Commission, Jacques Delors, together with the central bank governors and others, to examine the progressive realization of EMU. They were to report back to the Madrid Summit in June 1989. At that the now-famous Delors Report (EC Commission, 1988a) was considered. It recommended a three-stage approach to EMU culminating in a single currency. The summit agreed to proceed to stage one and that preparatory work should begin for the organization of another IGC to determine the subsequent stages.

Stage one required members to participate in the Exchange Rate Mechanism (ERM) of the EMS – which the UK had not done. The UK was far from happy about the prospect of EMU but agreed to meet the ERM requirement when certain conditions were satisfied. These included a reduction of the UK inflation rate, the abolition of exchange controls by other member states and the completion of the internal market. In fact the UK jumped the gun and joined the ERM in October 1990 whilst its actual inflation was still high.

A series of other factors was also propelling the Community yet further. One was connected with the social dimension of integration. Concern was expressed about the possible impact of the intensified competition which would emerge as a result of the removal of the final barriers to cross-frontier trade as part of the 1992 single market programme. Some felt that competitive pressures could lead throughout the Community to an erosion of social standards. Others feared social dumping – i.e. that footloose investment would gravitate to countries with the lowest social standards where labour costs were consequentially low. The preamble to the Single Act had itself affirmed the Community's support for the Council of Europe's *Convention for the Protection of Human Rights and Fundamental Freedoms* and the *European Social Charter*. In 1988 the European Council asked Jacques Delors, himself an enthusiast for a balance between economic and social progress, to explore the implications of the preamble aspiration. The result was the Social Charter involving a whole raft of social rights and freedoms for Community citizens – in particular for workers whether employed or self-employed. This was endorsed by eleven member states – the UK dissenting. It was, however, clear that the Rome Treaty did not provide the powers necessary to implement the Charter. A revision of the Rome Treaty was called for and hopefully the UK might be coaxed on board.

Another propelling factor was concern about the 'democratic deficit' in the Community. At one point Jacques Delors let slip the speculation that by the mid-1990s perhaps 80 per cent of economic legislation would derive from Brussels. If only half-true, it pointed to the emergence of a democratic gap. Since Community law is supreme, national parliaments would necessarily be consigned to rubber-stamping the actions of the Council of Ministers. The European Parliament, on the other hand, was largely consultative. It did not provide a substitute for national parliaments in that the Council of Ministers did not legislate through it and was not accountable to it in the way which is typical of representative democracies. Some change, possibly a re-defined role for the Parliament in relation to the Council of Ministers, would be needed. Not surprisingly, all kinds of ideas began to be canvassed.

Another quite major factor was external. The changes in Eastern Europe and in the general international atmosphere had several implications. The changes were of such a magnitude that it was increasingly felt that the EPC mechanism was inadequate to bear the weight of the new challenge. The changes also carried with them the possibility of new members. But in the absence of institutional reform a larger Community would slow down decision-making. The increasing prospect of German reunification was a powerful influence. The rest of the Community felt that German unity would be a safer and more acceptable prospect if it was to take place within a Europe which was more united. The Germans, too, were increasingly warm to European unity. Whereas previously there was always the fear that it would cut them off from reunification with East Germany, this was now no longer a concern. They were in fact anxious to obtain approval for reunion and their support for EMU was partly designed to underline their commitment to Europe and thus to induce the rest of the Community to support the reunion proposal. At the Strasbourg Summit in December 1990 the need for more rapid progress led the European Council to conclude that the IGC on EMU should start in December 1990.

Early in 1990 Jacques Delors expressed some ideas on constitutional reform in which he maintained that the subject justified its own IGC. This won the support of both the French President and the German Chancellor. In April 1990 the two issued a joint appeal for European Union. The two Dublin Summits that followed in fact decided that a parallel IGC devoted to Political Union should be convened in December 1990. There was, however, disagreement on what this meant. The UK was cool. Prime Minister Margaret Thatcher, in her Bruges speech in 1988, declared that her first guiding principle was that 'willing and active cooperation between independent sovereign states' was the best way to build a European Community. While federalism was not mentioned in her critique of Europe's future, she made her feelings plain when she expressed her opposition to the suppression of nationhood and to the fitting of British customs and traditions into an 'identikit European personality'. The IGCs on EMU and Political Union were duly convened in December 1990 in Rome.

The Maastricht Treaty on European Union

Intensive negotiations ensued which reached their culmination at a European Council meeting at Maastricht in December 1991. The Council tied up the loose ends, the treaty was signed in February 1992 and then came the prolonged process of parliamentary ratification which in some cases had to wait upon referenda and court actions. Matters were further delayed by the failure of the Danish government to secure approval on the first referendum. Only after accommodations had been made did the Danish government finally secure referendum support. All twelve parliaments then having ratified, the treaty entered into operation on 1st November 1993.

The negotiations revealed considerable differences of opinion. Pressure was exerted notably by Germany, Italy, Belgium and the Netherlands, for the treaty to embody a federal vocation, but the UK adamantly refused to accept this. EMU was particularly enthusiastically supported by Germany but also by France, the Netherlands and Belgium. However, it was opposed by the UK. The latter obtained an opt-out and the Danes were similarly treated as part of their referendum accommodation. The democratic deficit signalled by Jacques Delors and the idea of granting greater powers to the European Parliament were strongly supported by Germany, Italy, Belgium and the Netherlands. France was less keen but was prepared, once assured that the predominant role of the European Council would be strengthened, to rebalance the system in favour of Parliament as a means of securing German commitment to EMU. The UK was unenthusiastic and whilst not totally opposed nevertheless aimed to tightly circumscribe concessions. Its preference was to give Parliament more power to act as a financial watchdog – notably in relation to Commission spending – and to approach the democratic deficit problem by giving national parliaments a more effective role in the Community law-making process. New policy competences and beefed-up decision-making powers in the Council of Ministers was another area where the UK was at odds with its partners. The UK was also deeply at odds over the proposal to provide powers to implement the Social Charter. The idea of a Common Foreign and Security Policy (to replace EPC) and Cooperation on Justice and Home Affairs were both supported by the UK and France provided they were based on inter-governmental cooperation and did not embody the Rome Treaty majority voting system. The security and defence dimension did however cause divisions because of the fear, notably of Italy, the Netherlands and the UK, that the approach proposed by Germany and France might undermine NATO and the US commitment to Europe. The poorer countries led by Spain placed great emphasis on the need for them to enjoy a further transfer of resources.

The Maastricht Treaty is best viewed as an edifice supported on three principal pillars. The three pillars support what is now referred to as the European Union and this is the collective name for them. The European Union confers Union citizenship rights additional to those enjoyed at member-state level. Union citizens can take up residence in any other member state and can stand as a candidate or vote in municipal and European elections in that state. Abroad they are entitled to protection from any member state when their own government is not represented. They have a right to petition the European Parliament and can make applications to the EC

Ombudsman in respect of maladministration by Community institutions.

The first pillar relates to the economic, social and cultural competences of the Union. The Maastricht Treaty modified all three of the treaties setting up the founding communities (i.e. ECSC, EEC and Euratom) but the modifications to the ECSC and Euratom treaties were of no great significance. By contrast the modifications to the Rome (EEC) Treaty were of enormous significance. In the first place, because the Rome Treaty now covers social and cultural as well as economic affairs, it was felt appropriate to retitle the European Economic Community simply as the European Community. New and confirmed policy competences were added. The key new competence is that which provides for a process whereby the Common Market would be transformed into an EMU. It envisages a process of economic convergence leading to a single currency controlled by a European System of Central Banks (ESCB). This arrangement refers to the relationship between the national central banks and the envisaged European Central Bank (ECB). The UK and Denmark were granted opt-outs from this commitment. On all this see Chapter 7. Other policy competences were either formally new – e.g. industrial policy which did not feature in the Rome Treaty – or were confirmations of competences which had in the past crept in peripherally – e.g. education, culture and consumer protection. Social policy was dealt with in an untidy fashion. The UK refused to accept the incorporation of the Social Charter in the treaty. The result was the Protocol on Social Policy in which the rest of the Community agreed to introduce social measures on a majority voting or unanimity basis but the UK would not participate in this law-making activity or be bound by it.

Two other features are relevant at this point. The first is the incorporation, clearly a behest of the UK in particular, of the principle of subsidiarity. This was conceived by the UK as a means by which it would be possible to set limits to the ability of the Community to invade national sovereignty. The principle asserts that member states retain a general competence to make laws and that the Community law-making process should only supervene when it can be shown that an objective identified by the Community can only be achieved by Community action or can demonstrably be more effectively achieved by Community action. The second feature of the Maastricht Treaty was the conferment of additional powers notably on the European Parliament – this will be dealt with in more detail in Chapter 2.

The second pillar of the treaty involved the introduction of the Common Foreign and Security Policy (CFSP) in replacement of the old EPC mechanism. In due course it was anticipated that this would lead to a common defence policy and a common defence. The third pillar was concerned with the introduction of a system of Cooperation on Justice and Home Affairs (CJHA). Both these arrangements were essentially inter-governmental in character and did not, except marginally, incorporate any majority voting. They are dealt with in more detail in Chapters 2 and 6.

A protocol was attached to the treaty incorporating a commitment to set up a Cohesion Fund to assist the poorer countries. This would provide financial support for environmental and Trans-European Networks (TENs) projects. The latter was a new area of Community activity. The role of the Cohesion Fund and TENs is discussed in Chapter 3.

A Committee of the Regions was established in order to create closer cooperation and contact between the Community institutions and representatives of regional and local bodies.

Before we leave the subject of the Maastricht Treaty it is important to stress that that treaty does not replace the Rome Treaty. Quite the contrary; much of it is designed to modify the founding Rome Treaty although the two provisions relating to the two inter-governmental pillars do stand separately from the Rome Treaty.

The enlargement issue

We now come to another important development of the post-transition period. The creation of the common market in the period up to 1969 was the work of the Six alone. But at quite an early stage other states began to knock on the door and ask for admission. One of the significant achievements of the post-1969 period was that the Community was able to take new members into its midst and still survive. The first enlargement occurred in 1973 when the UK, Ireland and Denmark joined the Community. They were followed in 1981 by Greece, in 1986 by Spain and Portugal and in 1995 by former members of EFTA. The approach to the first enlargement was a long, drawn-out affair, and in order to understand fully how it came about we have to go back in time to 1955 when the Six were engaged in the discussions which led to the formation of the EEC and Euratom.

The UK and the free trade area proposal

As we saw earlier (see p. 12), at the end of 1955 Britain's attitude towards the Six cooled to such an extent that she withdrew from the Spaak committee. However, as the Six pressed ahead, the UK began to realize that it had severely underestimated the determination which lay behind the *relance*. As a result, a reappraisal of policy took place. In July 1956 the OEEC, under British stimulus, embarked on a study of the proposal that the OEEC states should create a free trade area which would embrace the customs union of the Six. The British hoped that the negotiations for the free trade area, and those relating to the Common Market, could take place simultaneously, but the Six refused. The OEEC report was completed in December 1956 and published in January 1957. Its conclusions were that a free trade area with the common market as an element was feasible. The UK took this as a signal to take the initiative and proposed that discussions should begin in earnest with a view to creating a European Industrial Free Trade Area. Detailed negotiations on the terms of a Treaty began in March 1957 and continued from October 1957 in an inter-government committee under the chairmanship of Reginald Maudling. These negotiations dragged on until the end of 1958 when they finally broke down.

The negotiations were extremely complex, and the reasons for their failure are equally complicated. However, basically the problems were as follows. On the political side, the 'Europeans' were suspicious of the UK's intentions. They suspected that the UK, after it had realized that it had underestimated the impetus behind the *relance*, had decided to take the offensive by proposing a free trade area as a means of wrecking the common market. Furthermore, it was recognized that while the path to the achievement of a common market (and what lay beyond) was bound to be hard, a free trade area would confer somewhat similar benefits and yet would involve a relatively less onerous régime. Because of this, some members of the Six might lose heart and decide to follow the easier course.

From the economic standpoint, the major difficulty was the UK's insistence on a free trade arrangement for industrial goods. Under such a system she would remain autonomous in respect of tariffs on goods emanating from outside the free trade area. This would enable her to go on enjoying her tariff preferences on exports of industrial goods to Commonwealth markets. Agriculture would also be excluded – this was certainly the basis of the earliest British proposals. This left the UK open to the criticism that she wanted the advantage of free access to West European industrial markets without giving a reciprocal concession to Continental food producers. The Commonwealth Preference system also meant that the UK would be guaranteed a continuing supply of food at low world prices. If, on the other hand, agriculture was brought within the free trade area framework, this low-priced supply of food could be in jeopardy. Indeed, if the agricultural protection systems of the Six were adopted, cheap Commonwealth food would be excluded. The UK would have to buy food at price levels approximating to those paid to farmers in the Six, and the traditional British deficiency payments system would have to be abandoned. It did not escape the attention of the Six that cheap food could have an effect on industrial wages, conferring an artificial advantage on British industries when competing in the industrial markets of the free trade area.

Another source of difficulty was the degree to which harmonization of such things as social security charges was necessary. The French, particularly, tended to play this up, much as they did in the Common Market negotiations.

Undoubtedly one of the greatest bones of contention was the problem of the origin of imports and the possibility of deflections of trade. In a customs union, since there is a common tariff level on the imports of, for example, raw materials coming from outside, competitive strength tends to depend on the ability of member states to transform such inputs into industrial (and agricultural) outputs. In a free trade area, however, member states are free to decide the tariffs on such imports. These tariffs can therefore differ from state to state, and imports of raw materials are therefore likely to be deflected through the low tariff countries. Methods of dealing with this problem gave rise to much technical discussion, but a unanimously acceptable solution was never achieved.

The failure of the negotiations was also in considerable degree due to diplomatic postures, particularly those of the British and the French. The latter left an impression of a certain deviousness. It was difficult to know whether, when they took a stand on a point of principle, it was because they really believed what they said, or whether it was because they found it useful as a means of opposing progress along a particular path. For its part, the UK exhibited some diplomatic weakness. The British undoubtedly underestimated the enthusiasm of the Six for their kind of arrangement. There was a failure to appreciate what the 'Europeans' hoped to achieve in the political sphere. Also there was a tendency to frame British proposals in too stark and provocative a fashion, as for example when the UK declared that agriculture should be totally excluded from the free trade arrangement.

The inter-governmental discussion at least served to create an identity of interest between the 'Other Six' – the UK, Norway, Sweden, Denmark, Austria and Switzerland. It was therefore decided early in 1959 that they should press ahead with a free trade area, and in this they were encouraged by their industrial federations. Portugal joined the discussions in February 1959 and on 4 January 1960 the Stockholm Convention establishing EFTA was signed.[1] Western Europe was now divided into two trade blocs.

The EFTA

The EFTA arrangement was one which admirably suited British interests. The institutional machinery was minimal. There was nothing to match the majority voting in the EEC Council of Ministers or the ECSC High Authority's[2] powers of independent action. There were absolutely no signs that EFTA was a stepping-stone to political unity – basically it was a commercial arrangement. The emphasis was on free trade in industrial goods; in a limited number of cases agricultural goods were treated as industrial goods and

1. Finland, Iceland and Liechtenstein joined EFTA at a later date
2. In 1967 the Commissions of the EEC and Euratom and the High Authority were merged into one Commission located in Brussels – see Chapter 2.

therefore tariff reductions were applied to them. In the main, agriculture was left out of the arrangement, each member being free to decide its own method and degree of support. There was absolutely no question of the agricultural systems of the member states being organized within the framework of a common agricultural policy. Members were free to determine the level of protection applied to goods coming from outside. This enabled the UK to maintain Commonwealth Preference not only on industrial but also on agricultural commodities. The latter implied the continuance of a supply of cheap food and the deficiency payments system of agricultural support.

UK reappraisal and entry bids

The ink of the Stockholm Convention had not long been dry before the UK began a major reappraisal of policy. Until quite late in the 1950s various British Ministers went on record as saying that the UK could never become a full member of the Community. A number of factors were adduced in support of this view. The first was the effect upon the Commonwealth. Commonwealth Preference would have to give way to the Community common tariff on imports (the Common External Tariff). This would harm Commonwealth members at a time when the idea of a multi-lingual, multi-racial Commonwealth was still on the lips of most politicians and was still regarded as an important vehicle of British influence. Also, the elimination of Commonwealth countries' preferences in the British market was almost certainly likely to lead to a loss of British preferences in Commonwealth markets. There were also some specific problems. One was that New Zealand relied heavily on the UK as an outlet for her butter production. The other was the British import of sugar from low-income Commonwealth countries under the Commonwealth Sugar Agreement. Secondly, there was the British agricultural system. It was supported in a radically different way from that adopted on the Continent. The level of farm incomes and the participation of farmers in price determination were at stake. Also the adoption of a Community system was bound to raise prices and the food import bill. Thirdly, the formation of EFTA raised the problem that British membership of the Community would require that adequate arrangements be made for the

EFTA partners. Then, finally, there was the critical point of supra-nationalism. The need to give up sovereignty was not welcomed then and it has remained a subject about which British politicians still tend to be wary.

However, it was apparent by 1960 that the Conservative Government was beginning to change its tune, and in the House of Commons on 31 July 1961 Mr Harold Macmillan,[1] the Prime Minister, formally announced that the UK had decided to apply for full membership. A letter to this effect was sent on 9 August 1961. The Irish Republic despatched its request before the UK – on the day of the House of Commons announcement. Denmark's application was despatched the day after the UK's. Norway, however, waited until 1962 before applying. Subsequently Austria, Sweden and Switzerland made separate applications for association. Portugal also applied, though no clear indication was given of the arrangement sought. The Council of Ministers decided to accept the British application on 26 September 1961 and on 10 October of the same year the UK, through Mr Edward Heath, made a comprehensive statement of its position at a Ministerial Conference in Paris. The negotiations which subsequently followed dragged on until 14 January 1963 when General de Gaulle at a Paris press conference declared that Britain was not ripe for membership and it was left to M. Maurice Couve de Murville, the French Foreign Minister, to deliver a *coup de grâce* on 29 January at Brussels by securing the indefinite adjournment of negotiations.

The change of government in the UK did not, however, change the course of British policy, as the Labour Party itself became convinced of the need for the UK to join the Community. On 10 November 1966 the Prime Minister, Harold Wilson, announced to the House of Commons plans for a high-level approach to the Six with the intention of becoming a full member of the Community. This was followed between January and March 1967 by visits to the capitals of the Six. Having judged the prospects to be satisfactory, the Prime Minister announced to the House of Commons on 2 May that the UK would submit its second application. This was made on 11 May and was followed by applications from Ireland, Denmark and Norway. However, in November 1967 General de Gaulle delivered another of his famous press conferences which effectively

1. The late Earl of Stockton.

closed the door to entry. The General took the view that full membership for Britain would lead to the destruction of the Community. Some form of association would, however, be acceptable. Great play was made of the British balance-of-payments deficit which was said to indicate a permanent state of disequilibrium. The restrictions on the export of capital by the UK were contrasted with free movement within the Six. Then there was the sterling system with its large and vulnerable liabilities. At the Ministerial meeting on 19 December 1967, the Five expressed themselves in favour of commencing negotiations, but France took the view that enlargement would profoundly modify the nature and ways of administering the Community. In addition, the UK economy had to be restored to health before its application could be considered. No vote was taken. The Community once more agreed to disagree and the application remained on the agenda.

Subsequently, various member states put forward proposals to bring the UK closer to the Community and prepare her for membership. The Commission lent a hand by proposing a preferential trade arrangement with the states seeking membership, together with closer consultation and collaboration on scientific and technological matters. No progress was made. However, the events of May 1968 and the resignation of General de Gaulle in 1969 brought the subject of British membership back into the foreground. This was followed by the accession to power of President Pompidou, and at the Hague Summit of December 1969 the Six agreed to open negotiations with the applicant countries 'in the most positive spirit'. The Six were therefore agreeing to take up the British application which had lain on the table since the Labour Government's previous bid. Britain was accompanied by three other applicants – the Irish Republic, Denmark and Norway.

UK negotiations and terms

In June 1970 Anthony Barber was charged with the conduct of the British negotiations, but following the tragic death of Iain Macleod and the translation of Mr Barber to the role of Chancellor of the Exchequer the negotiating role was passed to Geoffrey Rippon. The negotiations were conducted relatively expeditiously as compared with 1961–3. Mr Barber made his opening statement at a meeting between the Six and the UK at Luxembourg on 30 June 1970 and the Six replied. A series of ministerial meetings then took place at roughly six-weekly intervals in the second half of 1970 and the first half of 1971. (There were of course more frequent meetings between the Permanent Representatives of the six states and a British team led by Sir Con O'Neill, and there was continuous study of the problems arising by all the parties involved, including the Commission.) Although considerable progress was made, it became apparent by the beginning of 1971 that some political impetus was needed if certain particularly knotty problems were to be solved, and that in practice it was necessary that Britain and France should come to a clear understanding. The Heath–Pompidou meeting of 20 and 21 May 1971 served this purpose. The discussions were centred on the difficult problems of EEC membership which still remained to be solved, in particular those concerning New Zealand, sugar, the role of sterling and the UK contribution to the Community budget (for an explanation of the latter see below). The available evidence suggests that the two leaders achieved at least a close identity of view, and political commentators noted the relatively rapid pace of the negotiations after the summit. The final ministerial round was completed in Luxembourg on 23 June – the entry talks had been completed successfully. The terms were embodied in a White Paper, *The United Kingdom and the European Communities* (HMSO, 1971), which was presented to Parliament in July 1971. Parliament had a 'take note' debate in July during which the terms were considered. Then in October both Houses debated the issue again with the intention that a final vote for or against entry should be taken. This vote occurred on 28 October. The House of Commons voted 356 to 244 in favour. The House of Lords majority was even greater – 451 to 58. The problem of getting the subsequent enabling legislation through both Houses still remained but was eventually surmounted.

With respect to the actual conduct of the negotiations, the British attitude was again to reduce the number of issues to manageable proportions. Membership of Euratom and the ECSC would not pose major problems and the UK would seek only a short transitional period. The EEC would, however, throw up more difficult problems. These related to agricultural policy, the UK contribution to the Community budget, Commonwealth sugar exports, New Zealand dairy exports, and certain other Commonwealth issues.

There was also a new problem – fisheries policy. Undoubtedly, of all these the major obstacles were bound to be encountered in negotiating an acceptable UK contribution to the budget. The length of the transitional period before the barriers to free movement of industrial and agricultural goods were removed was also capable of causing some difficulty, as was the role of sterling.

It is not intended in this account to list in detail all the terms of the final settlement. The reader can find these laid out in the 1971 White Paper. This account will only be concerned with major issues.

One of the early matters to be settled was the length of the transitional period. The UK originally asked for three years for industry and six for agriculture. A solution was finally hammered out. The UK and the Six compromised on a transition period of five years for both agricultural and industrial goods. On the assumption that the UK joined on 1 January 1973 (which it did) industrial tariffs on trade between the Six and Britain would be removed in five stages, consisting of five cuts of 20 per cent, one in each of the five years 1973 to 1977. The UK would also adopt the common external tariff in four movements, one in each of the four years 1974 to 1977. In the case of agriculture the UK would in the first year of membership introduce the Community system of support. Prices for agricultural products would be set which at first would be lower than those in the Community, but they would be gradually increased to Community levels in six steps over the five-year period. From a negotiating point of view as long a transition period as possible was desirable in the case of agriculture, since this would put back the day when the full weight of the Community agricultural policy would be felt. Weight in this sense relates not only to the effect on the price of food but also to the contribution which the UK would have to make to the Community budget.

At this point we must remind ourselves of the role of the Community budget. Its function is to finance not only the administration of the Community but also the various funds concerned with particular aspects of Community policy. In practice the biggest drain on the budget has been the cost of financing the CAP (financing the sale of surpluses at a loss, etc.). The longer the transition period the longer the UK could delay paying a full contribution to the financing of the expensive farm policy.

At the time the UK was negotiating its way into the Community, the Six were on their way to fully implementing a new system for financing the budget. In its final form this would involve the member states paying 90 per cent of the proceeds of the common external tariff (10 per cent being allowed for collection expenses), 90 per cent of the proceeds of levies on agricultural imports (the UK is a big importer of food), and if necessary the proceeds of up to a 1 per cent VAT rate on a common assessment base. All these would constitute the Community's own resources to which we referred earlier.

The UK proposal on the budget was that its initial contribution to it should be 3 per cent, rising to 15 per cent by the end of the transition period. This was a highly provocative proposal since the Commission envisaged two possibilities which both involved a much more onerous régime. One envisaged an initial contribution level of 21.5 per cent and the second involved a progressive rise in contributions from between 10 and 15 per cent in the first year to 20 to 25 per cent in the final year of the transition period. There was then the question of what would happen thereafter – as we have seen the Community had agreed on a final solution to the financing of the budget.

In the event the negotiated settlement involved the UK in paying the following percentage costs of the budget – 1973 8.64, 1974 10.85, 1975 13.34, 1976 16.03, 1977 18.92. From the UK point of view this was certainly better than the Commission had originally proposed, but worse than it had initially hoped for. In 1978 and 1979 the UK would normally have been subject to the Community budgetary system. It was, however, agreed that in 1978 the UK contribution should not increase above the 1977 level by more than two fifths of the difference between the 1977 level and what the level should be under the new system. Likewise in 1979 the increased contribution over the 1978 level would be similarly determined. Then there was the question of what would happen in 1980 and beyond – in other words what would the permanent as opposed to the transitional system be? The answer was that the UK would be subject to the Community budgetary finance system and 90 per cent of levies and customs duties would be paid into the Community budget, together with the proceeds of up to a 1 per cent rate of the VAT. In other words, the UK accepted the Community system as it stood. The 1971 White Paper pointed out that the size of the commitments so arising was not susceptible to valid estimation nor was the size of any possible benefits. Because of this the White Paper went on to point out that the Community had declared in the course of the negotiations that if unacceptable situations should arise 'the very survival of the Community would demand that the institutions find equitable solutions'.

New Zealand was a particularly difficult problem. Butter and cheese represented about 15 per cent of her exports, and 85 per cent of her dairy export receipts came from sales to the UK. The problem was therefore one of attempting to guarantee New Zealand access to the UK market after membership. The solutions devised were as follows. In the case of butter the guaranteed quantity would be reduced over the first five years by 4 per cent per annum. Thus in the fifth year she would still be able to sell at least 80 per cent of her 1971 entitlement in the UK. She would also enjoy a guaranteed price at a level equal to the average of prices in the UK in the four years 1969 to 1972. In the third year after the UK accession the Community would look again at the position and would decide 'on suitable measures for ensuring beyond 1977 the continuation of special arrangements for New Zealand butter' (1971 White Paper). For cheese, access would be reduced so that in the fifth year it would be able to market 20 per cent of its 1971 level of sales. No guarantee was held out after 1977 in the case of cheese, but substantial sales were expected to continue because New Zealand cheese did not compete directly with Community production. According to the 1971 White Paper, New Zealand described the agreement as highly satisfactory. In the case of lamb no common organization existed within the Six. A common external tariff of 20 per cent was therefore agreed. The White Paper stated that the UK and New Zealand believed that an acceptable level of trade in lamb would continue to flow over such a tariff.

In the case of sugar, Mr Rippon sought what he termed 'bankable assurances'. The UK's contractual obligations under the Commonwealth Sugar Agreement, which required it to buy agreed quantities until the end of 1974, would be fulfilled. Thereafter it was agreed that the arrangements for sugar imports from developing Commonwealth sugar producers would be made within the framework of an association or trading agreement with the enlarged Community. It was further agreed 'that the enlarged Community will have as its firm purpose the safeguarding of the interests of the developing countries concerned whose economies depend to a considerable extent on the export of primary products and in particular of sugar' (1971 White Paper). The countries concerned expressed the view that this solution was satisfactory.

One of the important issues which seems to have concerned France in particular was the role of sterling and indeed the whole question of how in monetary terms the UK could be fitted into the Community. In the weeks before the Heath–Pompidou meeting the French built the subject up into a major negotiating issue. But more or less immediately after the meeting the French did a *volte-face* by agreeing without demur to the British proposals to discuss sterling's role after her entry. However, the UK agreed to stabilize the size of the sterling balances and in the longer term to run them down. But no agreement was reached about how they would be run down or how long the process would take.

The UK also had to deal with the market-access problems of developing countries in the Commonwealth. The details of the position of various countries will not be discussed here. Basically the solution was that a variety of arrangements would be brought to bear. Independent Commonwealth countries in Africa, the Caribbean, the Indian Ocean and the Pacific could choose between the renewed Yaoundé Convention, some other form of association, or a commercial agreement. All British dependent territories (except Gibraltar and Hong Kong) would be offered association under Part Four of the Rome Treaty. Hong Kong would be included within the scope of the Community's Generalized Preference Scheme (see Chapter 11). In the case of India, Pakistan, Ceylon, Malaysia and Singapore the Community was willing to examine with them trade problems which might arise, taking account of the Generalized Preference Scheme which would benefit them considerably. One specific problem which the Community expressed its willingness to discuss was India's sugar exports to the enlarged Community. The continued suspension of the tariff on tea would help India and Ceylon. Malta concluded a trade agreement. Arrangements would be made for Cyprus and Gibraltar.

On the matter of fisheries policy the UK indicated that the existing policy was not satisfactory. The Community agreed that the arrangements would have to be reconsidered in the light of enlargement.

The successful conclusion of negotiations for UK entry was also accompanied by successful conclusions in respect of the Irish Republic, Denmark[1] and Norway. However, the latter did not ultimately join – a national referendum did not produce the necessary votes for membership. The Irish and Danish negotiations were not as complicated as those relating to the UK. Their terms were similar to those obtained by the British but a number of special accommodations were provided and are detailed in the Community's *Fifth General Report* (EC Commission, 1972b, pp. 49–57). A link with those EFTA states who had not become full members was provided by means of industrial free trade arrangements. Countries benefiting from these agreements were Austria, Finland, Iceland, Portugal, Sweden, Switzerland and Norway. (Austria, with the agreement of EFTA, had been seeking association with the Community for a number of years. Under the State Treaty of 1955 Article 4 precluded any form of economic union with West Germany and the best that Austria could hope for was some form of association.)

UK renegotiation

The entry terms were those obtained by the then Conservative Government. The opposition Labour Party expressed itself willing to enter the EEC if the terms were right but concluded that the settlement actually obtained was unacceptable – in the words of Labour leader Harold Wilson it involved 'an intolerable and disproportionate burden on every family in the land and, equally, on Britain's balance of payments'. In the subsequent election the Labour Party committed itself to a renegotiation of the terms of entry. The Labour Party was indeed returned to power in February 1974 and very quickly set in hand a process of renegotiation, indicating that if the settlement obtained was acceptable it would put it to the people for approval, either by referendum or general election.[2]

1. Greenland gained home rule from Denmark in 1979. It decided by a referendum in 1982 to leave the Community. This took effect in 1984.
2. Whether the Government would commend the terms to the people was at that stage not made clear.

The negotiations which then ensued were finally brought to an end at the Dublin Summit in March 1975. It finally resolved some major outstanding issues. The British Government then pronounced itself satisfied with the new terms[1] and it declared that it would commend them to the electorate in a referendum which would be the final determining factor. On 5 June 1975 the first nationwide referendum in British history took place. The electorate was asked 'Do you think that the United Kingdom should stay in the European Community (the Common Market)?' Seventeen million voted 'Yes' and eight million voted 'No'.

The reader will obviously wish to know what exactly were the terms which the UK Government secured and which it successfully commended to the UK electorate. It should be said that they consisted partly of accommodations made by the Community and partly of a realization by the UK Government that on some issues its fears were groundless.

The concern over EMU proved to be a damp squib. Quite simply Foreign Secretary Callaghan found out from his opposite numbers that such a union by 1980 was not on the cards. Indeed, as we noted earlier, the scheme had run out of steam – more will be said on this issue in Chapter 7.[2]

On the issue of the Community budget the UK did make what it thought was progress. The Dublin Summit of 1975 endorsed a correction mechanism which enabled not just the UK but any member which was unfairly treated to secure a refund.

On the question of the CAP the British were able to claim that they had helped to institute a full-scale reappraisal of the policy – this was referred to as a stocktaking. In addition it was claimed that farm prices had been held down, that the British had managed to persuade the Community to adopt more flexible arrangements (i.e. surplus beef had been dealt with by subsidies designed to cheapen it and extend demand) and financial control had been tightened up

---

1. The statement of Prime Minister Harold Wilson commending the new terms is to be found in *Membership of the European Community*, Cmnd 5999 (HMSO, 1975a), and a report of the negotiated terms is to be found in *Membership of the European Community: Report on Renegotiation*, Cmnd 6003 (HMSO, 1975b).
2. In fairness it should be pointed out that the original UK position on monetary union was quite judicious. It did not oppose such a union but emphasized the danger of fixing parities before there was a convergence of price movements, etc.

(this included the taking of steps to prevent fraudulent use of agricultural support funds).

The concern over VAT also proved to be a damp squib. By the time the renegotiation was in process the Community was considering proposals as to the nature of the common base for VAT and these provided for zero rating.

The UK concern about the possibly adverse impact of membership on regional policy was wholly misconceived. In the first place one of the results of the 1972 Paris Summit was the decision to create the ERDF. This was a wholly new departure. Prior to that, Community policy was largely devoted to seeing that regional aids did not distort competition in the Common Market. The new Fund now meant that the Community would be actively engaged in giving aid. It should be added that the UK was undoubtedly interested in this Fund because she saw herself as a major beneficiary from it – this was one way of securing a *juste retour*, a flow of receipts to balance her payments into the Community budget! There was some concern over the fact that the European Communities Commission (ECC) was responsible for vetting aid but this was clearly likely to assist countries such as the UK since it was intended to be operated in a way which prevented extravagant and unnecessary aid-giving in the central regions of the Community. The UK had everything to gain by such control, and if the Community had broken up Britain would have been hard pressed to compete with the more prosperous economies of West Germany and France in attracting footloose investment. In 1975 the Commission issued a Communication relating to regional policy which indicated that the control of aid-giving would leave British policy intact.

On the question of protecting the interests of Commonwealth countries, progress was made. In the case of New Zealand the original terms did not contain satisfactory provisions for a continuing relationship between New Zealand and the Community after 1977. The Dublin Summit in fact provided for imports of New Zealand butter in 1978–80 to remain close to deliveries in 1974–5. It was also accepted that there was a need for a periodic review and, as necessary, an adjustment of the prices paid to New Zealand. The Dublin Summit invited the Commission to produce as soon as practicable special import arrangements for butter after 1977. It was also agreed that the position in respect of imports of New Zealand cheese after 1977 should be urgently considered. In respect of Commonwealth sugar the Community offered access for up to 1.4 million tons of sugar per annum from the Commonwealth developing countries for an indefinite period – prices would be negotiated annually and would be related to prices paid to Community producers. As for trade and aid generally in respect of developing countries, the British position was overtaken by events. For example, the new Lomé Convention, discussed below in Chapter 11, was greeted with little short of ecstasy by the then Minister of Overseas Development, who was not known for her enthusiasm for the European cause.

The capital movements issue was yet another damp squib. Quite simply the British Government discovered that without special agreement governments could act to control capital movements when it was necessary to do so.

Greek, Mediterranean and EFTA membership

The relationship between Greece and the Community goes back to the early sixties. A Treaty of Association came into operation in 1962 and provided for the eventual formation of a customs union between Greece and the Six. However, following the *coup d'état* in 1967, the Greek association agreement was frozen but was reactivated in 1974 as a result of the restoration of democracy. In 1975 Greece applied for membership and became a full member on 1 January 1981. A transition period of five years was allowed for the progressive alignment of Greek protection of industrial goods and a similar period was allowed for the accommodation of Greek agriculture to the CAP although for a few products the period was extended to seven.

The relationship of Spain and Portugal to the Community had also been clouded by dictatorship, but following the restoration of democracy they too became eligible. Unfortunately their applications, lodged in 1977, became bogged down as the Community struggled with its own mounting internal problems – budgetary, agricultural, fishing, etc. The agricultural impact of Iberian membership was a source of growing concern as existing Mediterranean producers within the Community considered the effect of adding two more Mediterranean competitors. This gave rise to strong reservations, notably on the part of the French. It should be added that the newest member, Greece, was also opposed to further enlargement until adequate measures had been agreed which would help to insulate the Mediterranean region from its impact. It was only after (a) the Common Fisheries Policy had been agreed in 1983, (b) the Fontainebleau Summit of 1984 had settled the budget issues and had made a start on cutting CAP spending, and (c) integrated Mediterranean spending programmes had been agreed at the Brussels Summit of 1985 that the way was cleared for Iberian membership.

Both countries were allowed seven-year transition periods (from their accession date of 1986) for adjusting industrial tariffs. In the case of agriculture different arrangements were made. For Portugal, a programme of two five-year periods was agreed. The first stage was to be devoted to preparing for the introduction of the CAP system of market organization. The second would see them introduced. Spain was allowed a seven-year agricultural transition with a ten-year exception in a few cases. Both countries were involved in the Single European Act negotiations and successfully pressed for a transfer of resources to poorer countries.

Turkey has had a long-standing trade agreement with the Community and we shall discuss this and the applications of Malta and Cyprus and the membership aspirations of the countries of Central and Eastern Europe in Chapter 11.

Whilst it is true to say that the EFTA countries enjoyed a comparatively privileged status *vis-à-vis* the Community in that they were involved in reciprocal *bilateral* free trade arrangements from 1973 onwards, they were not entirely satisfied with the relationship. They began to press for closer ties. This process began in 1984 as a result of a joint meeting between EFTA and the EC in Luxembourg. This gave rise to the Luxembourg Declaration and the so-called Luxembourg Process. Twenty-five working groups were established. They were charged with the task of injecting into the EFTA–EC relationship three basic principles – multilateralism (without new institutions); a political commitment to the special nature of the relationship; the introduction of elements of Common Market integration into the free trade system – i.e. to create a European Economic Space (EES).

Some progress was made but it seemed insufficient when compared with the dynamic process initiated in the EC following the Single Act of 1986. Moreover in 1989 Commission President Jacques Delors, when addressing the European Parliament, expressed some doubts as to whether the existing framework was adequate and the EFTA Heads of State expressed similar sentiments in the subsequent Oslo Declaration of 15 March 1989. This in turn led to exploratory negotiations and to the signing on 2 May 1992 in Porto of an agreement creating the European Economic Area (EEA).

The main features of the agreement were as follows. First, the four freedoms of the single market were to apply throughout the EEA. This implied free movement of goods, services, capital and persons. Second, an EEA competition regime, based on the existing EC competition rules, would aim to ensure competition throughout the EEA. Third, there would be closer cooperation between the EC and EFTA in a number of important areas including R&D, education and the environment. Fourth, EFTA would set up a new fund to assist some of the poorer regions of the EC. Fifth, new institutions would be set up to administer the agreement and ensure that both sides complied with the rules. Finally, the EEA would be based on a dynamic agreement in that EFTA would take on new single market measures as they were adopted and would have an opportunity to influence new proposals.

The free movement of goods involved the removal of non-tariff barriers (NTBs), further tariff reductions and a simplification of trading procedures. The NTB aspect required the EFTA countries to adopt most EC legislation concerned with technical and safety regulations. However this did not mean that standards would be the same for all states. Thus the EFTA countries could specify higher standards for their own manufacturers but would not be able to exclude products from other EEA states. The NTB aspect also involved a ban on discriminatory taxation and an open public purchasing policy. State monopolies would no longer be able to pursue marketing and purchasing policies which discriminated against products emanating from other EEA states. The tariff reductions involved the abolition of protection (including quotas) on a range of manufactured food and drink products not included in the old bilateral free trade agreements. Tariffs on imports of fish and fish products were also to be abolished or gradually phased out. The CAP of course remained inviolate!

The free movement of services meant that the provisions of the Second Banking Directive (see Chapter 6) would apply throughout the EEA. Professional, commercial, telecommunication and transport services would also be liberalized.

A common market element would be introduced in that the EEA agreement introduced a right of establishment for EEA nationals throughout the area. Free movement of persons was also provided for – EC and EFTA nationals had the right to work throughout the EEA. They would be free to accept offers of employment in any EEA country, could stay in that country to work and, subject to status, could remain there afterwards. The EEA agreement also removed restrictions on the movement of capital belonging to EEA companies and individuals.

The agreement aimed to achieve a common approach to competition by extending the EC competition rules to the whole of the EEA. This covered cartels, abuses of dominant positions, mergers and state aids. Parallel to the European Commission and European Court of Justice, an EFTA Surveillance Authority (ESA) was to be established in order to guarantee that the rules were enforced in the EFTA. A division of labour was prescribed that decided which authorities dealt with cartels, dominant firms and state aids, but all merger cases fell to the European Commission.

Fisheries were bound to be a difficult problem largely because of Norway's interest in the matter. In the final agreement EFTA undertook to give the EC greater access to its fishing opportunities. The EC share of the total allowable catch for North Norway cod was to increase from 2.15 per cent to 2.9 per cent. This in turn was allocated to various EC states. On top of this some additional Norwegian cod was to be made available to the poorer countries in the EC – specifically Spain, Portugal and Ireland.

An EEA Financial Mechanism which provided funds for the less favoured regions of the EC was established. Over five years EFTA was required to provide 500 million ECUs by way of grants and an interest rate subsidy of 3 per cent on 1.5 billion ECUs of loans. Northern Ireland was a potential beneficiary.

Apart from the competition institutions already referred to, the agreement also set up an EEA Council where ministers from the member states of the EC and EFTA could meet in order to give political direction whilst day-to-day matters would be under the direction of an EEA Joint Committee. Originally it had been decided to create a joint EEA panel of judges to resolve disputes over the interpretation of EEA laws. However the whole EEA accord was thrown into doubt when the EC Court of Justice declared against the joint panel arrangements on the grounds that it would undermine its autonomy as the Community's supreme court. The EEA Joint Committee was therefore substituted at the last moment. This was cleared by the EC Court on the basis of an understanding that the committee's decisions were not contrary to its own rulings.

Many of the economic arrangements outlined above are reminiscent of the kind of system which had existed in the European Community. However, the EEA was based on a free trade area and not a customs union. EFTA did not participate in the CAP. Nor was it involved in the EMS or committed to the EMU. It was also outside the Community budget, played only a limited role in the shaping of EC legislation and was excluded from participation in the CFSP.

This could have been regarded as an ideal arrangement. EFTA enjoyed the benefits of the larger market and retained some independence in areas such as monetary and foreign and security policy. Why then did the larger EFTA states quickly decide to apply for full membership of the European Union? Three reasons suggest themselves. First, whilst the larger market was attractive to the EFTA states, there was an economic and political cost in not fully participating in the process whereby internal market rules were set. A second reason is connected with neutrality. Austria had been precluded from economic union with Germany as part of the 1955 State Treaty. The ending of the Cold War lifted this inhibition. Thirdly it could be argued that neutrality was particularly significant in a polarized Europe, but participation in the CFSP was less of a challenge when the Cold War threat had largely evaporated. For countries such as Finland the ending of the Cold War did not totally extinguish concerns about Russian intentions and the future direction of its political system. The EC was valuable to Finland because of the safe haven which it afforded.

The arrangements in respect of membership of the EC customs union were quite simple. As a result of the reciprocal free trade agreements, tariffs, etc. between the EFTA countries and the Community had already been removed. In respect of the common external tariff, the EFTA countries were, with some minor exceptions, required to introduce it by the time they became full members.

The negotiations between the EFTA Four and the EC did however throw up a number of problems. Neutrality, which had always been seen as a stumbling block, certainly in the case of Sweden, Finland and Austria, proved not to be a problem – no doubt for the kind of reasons outlined above. The CFSP (and also CJHA) were quite easily taken on board. In connection with the free movement of goods one of the major concerns of the applicant countries was the need to maintain a high level of health, safety and environmental protection after accession. However closer inspection revealed that these fears were largely groundless, but for a limited range of cases, acceding countries could maintain their own rules for four years. All Four had specific rules regarding the purchase of holiday homes (secondary residences) by foreigners. They were allowed to retain these rules for five years. The Nordic alcohol monopolies were a matter of some concern. The Four agreed to modify their rules regarding import and wholesale monopolies. Given that the Court of Justice had not pronounced on retail monopolies, they were allowed to continue provided that they did not discriminate against the products of other member states.

Road transit was a major issue for Austria – i.e. the environmental impact. Whereas in the Community heavy goods vehicles normally enjoy unrestricted passage (provided certain rules are satisfied), the danger to Alpine passes and the narrow valleys leading to them had led the Community to conclude a bilateral agreement with Austria. This involved an 'ecopoint' system of transit licences. It was therefore agreed to continue with the plan for a target reduction of 60 per cent by 2003 in the pollution from heavy lorries in transit through Austria. To help achieve this, extra rail capacity and a new tunnel under the Brenner Pass were identified as supportive ways forward.

Agriculture was bound to cause problems since the national

systems of the Four had to deal with difficult natural conditions, were important for environmental reasons and enjoyed price and support levels above those of the EC. The Four wanted transitional periods for prices and adaptations of the CAP which would take account of their particular problems. The EC, for its part, wanted to maintain a single market and insisted that the Four should adopt common prices immediately. This latter point was finally accepted together with compensation payments to cover price reductions. These would be degressive but there would be a safeguard mechanism in case of market disruption. The mountain and less favoured areas, to be designated in the Four, would also be able to benefit from income-support programmes designed to help farmers coping with difficult climates and terrain.

Fishing proved to be one of the most difficult problems being, as we have already noted, of particular concern to Norway. Norway's initial position was quite firm – the Norwegian fisheries minister declared that Oslo 'had no fish to give away', a view not to the liking of the Spanish. Eventually a solution was found which involved the agreement of Norway to consolidate the fishing possibilities it had allocated to the Union in the context of the EEA agreement and the granting of certain additional fishing possibilities.

The acceding countries attached considerable importance to being able to continue their regional policies since, whilst generally prosperous, they do have areas of low income and high unemployment together with problems stemming from low density populations in remote northern regions. It was possible to envisage Burgenland in Austria as an Objective 1 (i.e. low income) region. It was also decided to create a new Objective 6, which would permit the designation of areas with very low population densities.

In respect of the Community budget the Four were expected in due course to be net contributors but, whilst accepting the *acquis* in full, they won a temporary budget rebate (disguised as a farm adjustment payment) which together with other sweeteners was worth 3.6 billion ECUs over four years.

The necessary institutional adjustments were made (in the case of majority voting against some British objections) which included adding four more commissioners to the existing body of seventeen.

All four countries conducted referenda but only the electorates of

Austria, Finland and Sweden approved. They became full members at the beginning of 1995. Norway remained in the EEA arrangement and Switzerland continued with its EFTA agreement but sought special arrangements with the European Union.[1] Iceland and Liechtenstein also remain in the EEA.

Conclusion

By 1995 the Community had expanded to Fifteen and was surrounded by countries which wished to join it and to enjoy closer economic ties with it. The Community had indeed become the major economic force on the European continent and in that capacity was spearheading programmes of assistance to the weaker liberalizing economies of Eastern Europe. The Community had a population in excess of 368 million – a population greater than that of the old USSR. Its collective Gross Domestic Product was significantly greater than that of the USA. These facts, conjoined with the cohesion that sprang from the Community relationships, were bound to confer upon the Fifteen considerable leverage in world economic affairs. It should be added that the process of integration had spilled over into the foreign-policy field, so that here too the Community could increasingly speak as one in the international political arena. All this was a far cry from the devastation and division which existed in Europe in the early postwar period.

Note to the reader

From this point forward the European Economic Community will be referred to as the European Community (the term adopted in the 1992 Maastricht Treaty on European Union) and will be abbreviated as the EC or simply the Community. The European Coal and Steel Community and the European Atomic Energy Community will respectively be referred to as the ECSC and Euratom and collectively all three economic communities will be referred to as the European Communities. The term European Union (the Union for short) unfortunately tends to be used indiscriminately in the

1. By a referendum Switzerland had rejected the EEA agreement.

media but correctly used it refers either to the three economic communities, CFSP and CJHA *as a collectivity* or to activities under the inter-governmental CFSP and CJHA, and these usages are employed in this book.

2

THE UNION DECISION-MAKING INSTITUTIONS

Since what we are primarily concerned with in this book is the economic policy of the EC, it is clearly important that we should appreciate how that policy is formulated. It was of course the hope of those who set up the Community that economic unity would give rise to political unity, and that has happened to a significant degree in the shape of EPC and its successor CFSP. In the first part of this chapter we shall be concerned with how decisions are made in the EC (there is considerable institutional overlap with the ECSC and Euratom but we will focus on the EC) and in the second part we will take a look at EPC, the CFSP and the relatively new CJHA.

As we saw in Chapter 1, one of the institutions which has been notably important in the development of the Community has been the summit meeting. The Hague Summit of 1969, the Paris Summit of 1972 and the Fontainebleau Summit of 1984 are outstanding instances. At the 1974 Paris Summit it was resolved that these meetings should henceforth be dignified with the title of the European Council. It was decided that the Heads of State and of Government, together with their foreign ministers, would meet three times a year (and, where necessary, in the Council of Ministers of the European Communities and in the context of EPC). The President of the European Communities Commission also attended these meetings. It should be noted that the Paris Summit communiqué was careful to emphasize that the European Council procedure in no way affected the rules and procedures of the European Community Treaties and of EPC. All this was very much the brainchild of the then French President Valéry Giscard d'Estaing.

The Council came to play several roles. First, it was a forum where new initiatives were identified. Here we are thinking of developments which were consistent with the stated objectives of the existing Rome Treaty. It is essential to recognize that the Council would not normally be involved in the finer detail of

Community law-making – that task would be remitted to the decision-making system which we discuss below. Second, it was essential that the Rome Treaty should not be a static document since otherwise, as time passed, new problems and opportunities would emerge but the Community would be saddled with Treaty objectives and associated powers which were only relevant to the mid-1950s. Hence the importance of Article 236 (we return to it below), which enabled the Treaty to be modified by means of an IGC. The convening of such a conference and the wrapping up of the final details were roles discharged by the European Council. The Single European Act and the Maastricht Treaty were both products of this process. Third, the Council was a forum to which the Council of Ministers and Commission (see below) could resort when the Community decision-making system was locked in disagreement. Finally, the Council might conclude agreements outside the scope of the Rome Treaty. Thus in 1979 it entered into a convention which led to the creation of an EMS. This did not stem from the treaty but was confined to Community members.

Part of the importance of the Single European Act was that it quite explicitly and formally recognized the supreme position of the European Council, and the Maastricht Treaty on European Union has re-emphasized the Council's leading role. The Maastricht Treaty declared that the Council will provide the Union with the necessary impetus for its future development and will define the general political guidelines of that development. In this context the European Council continues to consist of the Heads of State and Government together with the President of the European Commission. They are to be assisted by the Ministers of Foreign Affairs and a member of the Commission. The European Council will meet at least twice a year.

The European Community

The six main bodies which have an influence on policy-making and implementation under the Rome Treaty are the European Commission, the Council of Ministers of the European Union, the Court of Justice, the Court of Auditors, the European Parliament and the Economic and Social Committee. The above order of listing does not reflect an order of influence on policy formation – there can, however, be no doubt that the Commission, the Council of Ministers and, to an increasing extent, the European Parliament are the most important bodies.

Before we proceed to discuss the role of the six main bodies, there are a number of preliminary issues which need to be dealt with. In the first place in this book we are dealing with economic policies which are founded on treaties. The Rome Treaty places a constraint upon the policies which the Community institutions can adopt, and it is always open to the Court of Justice to declare that this or that action or decision is not in accordance with the treaty. It must be admitted that this constraining factor has been variable in its impact. In some instances, such as EC Transport Policy, the treaty said little more than there should be a common policy. As a result it was left to the Commission, working through the other Community organs, to make the policy. On the other hand, there are branches of EC policy where the Rome Treaty is quite explicit. For example, Articles 85 and 86 enunciate the basic approach which has to be adopted in dealing with cartels and dominant firms. Nevertheless, even in these cases, this clear specification has not precluded Community institutions – here primarily we would think of the Commission and the Court of Justice – from putting a lot of policy flesh on basic treaty bones.

We should not, however, make too much of the constraint imposed by the original provisions of the treaty. Article 235 provides that:

If action by the Community should prove necessary to attain, in the course of the operation of the common market, one of the objectives of the Community and this Treaty has not provided the necessary powers, the Council shall, acting unanimously on a proposal from the Commission and after consulting the Assembly, take the appropriate measures.

Additionally, as we implied earlier, Article 236 declares that:

The Government of any member state or the Commission may submit to the Council proposals for the amendment of this Treaty.

If the Council, after consulting the Assembly and, where appropriate, the Commission, delivers an opinion in favour of calling a conference of representatives of the Governments of the member states, the conference shall be convened by the President of the Council for the purpose of determining by common accord the amendments to be made to this Treaty.

Between them these two provisions enable existing powers to be supplemented and new objectives to be set. They therefore provide for the possibility of considerable expansion and change in the economic policies falling within the Community ambit.

The European Commission

The Commission is in effect the civil service of the Community. Originally there were three civil services – one for each Community. In the case of the ECSC it was the High Authority, whilst the EC and Euratom each had a Commission. However, by virtue of a treaty signed in Brussels on 8 April 1965 it was agreed that these three executives should be merged as from 1 July 1967. It is perhaps worth mentioning that the three treaties remained separate (whether they will in due course be fused only the future will tell). The merged Commission was therefore left with the task of administering the provisions of three separate founding treaties.

Originally there were nine EC Commissioners. This number was raised to fourteen in 1967 when the executives were merged but in 1970 was slimmed back down to nine. As a result of the accession of nine states the number of Commissioners has been raised, and currently there are twenty. The United Kingdom, West Germany, France, Italy and Spain each designate two Commissioners, while the other ten countries provide one each.

The Commissioners are appointed for five-year renewable terms. One of the Commissioners is President of the Commission and the Commission is empowered to choose one or two Vice-Presidents. Each Commissioner is responsible for a portfolio which will primarily be concerned with a policy area. For example, under the new Commission presided over by Jacques Santer, one Commissioner was to be responsible for agriculture, another for the internal market, another for transport, yet another for competition policy and so on. The need to find jobs for all the members of the Commission seems to have influenced the shape of the external relations portfolio since it was divided into three. One Commissioner was to look after multilateral trade issues, another was to take charge of the Central and Eastern European portfolio whilst another was to be concerned with relations with developing countries.

Originally the Commissioners were appointed by common accord by the governments of the member states. However, following pressure to confer greater powers upon the European Parliament, the Maastricht Treaty modified the system. Governments now nominate by common accord the person they intend to appoint as President – Parliament is merely consulted on this issue. Then the governments in consultation with the nominee President nominate the other persons to be Commissioners. Then the President and the other Commissioners are as a body subject to a vote of approval by Parliament. Assuming Parliament approves, they are then by common accord appointed by the member state governments.

Each Commissioner has a private office or *cabinet*, the appointments to which are his or her private prerogative. Usually, but not invariably, the members of the *cabinet* are of the same nationality as the Commissioner. If the Commissioner is away the *chef de cabinet* will act in his or her stead at the weekly meeting of the Commission which is usually held on a Wednesday. Beneath each Commissioner there is usually at least one Director General in charge of a Directorate General, i.e. a broad *policy* area. A Directorate General will in turn be split into areas relating to various aspects of the broad policy problem. They are presided over by Directors and below them are Heads of Division.

It is most important to note that Article 157 of the Rome Treaty requires that Commissioners 'shall neither seek nor take instruction from any Government or from any other body'. In other words Commissioners are *supposed* to act with complete independence.

The role of the Commission

To the Commission fell the task of taking steps to see that the Community, as envisaged by the Rome Treaty, was established. In short, action was needed if the aspirations of Article 3 – that there should be common policies in agriculture and transport, that competition should not be distorted, that a customs union should be established and so forth – were to be turned into concrete realities. To this end the Rome Treaty conferred upon the Commission an important power – the right of initiative. It is the task of the Commission to draft proposals (for regulations, etc.) which the Council of Ministers (representing the member state governments) has to consider. The Council of Ministers has to decide whether to accept the draft or not. In some cases there must be unanimity (for example on the subject of new members) while in others a qualified majority (see below) or a simple majority may suffice. If the Council accepts the draft proposal it is promulgated in the Official Journal and becomes law. However the Commission may experience difficulty in securing agreement in which case it has to take the proposal back and come up with some alternative that will command support. This brings us to the second role of the Commission – it acts as a mediator, trying by means of negotiations to find an acceptable compromise which at the same time, hopefully, does not mean that the overall Community interest has been sacrificed by the horse-trading which may have to take place.

In approaching the Council of Ministers, the Commission feeds it with draft proposals which in due course emerge as Directives, Decisions, Regulations and Recommendations.[1] Only the first three have the force of law. Directives do not apply directly to individuals and companies.[2] They are aimed at the member states and require them to modify national laws. For example, it may be that national laws concerning the design and composition of goods vary from state to state, and as a result trade cannot flow across frontiers. One solution has been to harmonize such laws. The Directive will require member states to amend their national laws and then individuals and companies have to obey the appropriately modified (harmonized) national law. Decisions and Regulations are directly binding on individuals, companies or governments. A Decision will name a person, company or state to which it specifically applies. A Regulation will be general in its application – for example, all companies rather than just one will be bound by it. It is essential to remember that when Community and national law conflict, the requirements of Community law must be regarded as paramount.

The Commission, having secured the Council's agreement to a

1. This terminology refers to the Rome Treaty.
2. The idea that Directives are not directly binding is not always true. If, for example, the Community introduced a Directive which required action to be taken on an aspect of the environment it would fall to each member state to introduce laws which gave effect to it. But if a member state had not acted within the time-limit set down it would be open to an individual to engage in legal action to force the state to act. This applies vertically – i.e. individual versus state but not horizontally – i.e. individual versus individual.

particular line of policy, has to see that it is carried out. Here there is an administrative task. For example, the Council of Ministers, on a proposal of the Commission, fixes the prices of farm products for the coming agricultural year. These prices have to be achieved by various devices such as protection at the common frontier and support buying. This is a task which involves the Commission but it is not one that it discharges alone. In practice a large proportion of the staff of national ministries of agriculture have become effectively the agents of the Community, operating the CAP in cooperation with intervention agencies set up in each country. However, the Commission is involved in that the functioning of the CAP is supervised by Management Committees staffed by both national and Commission officials. Since the Commission staff totals only about 16,500,[1] while a larger ministry in the UK may employ upwards of 12,000 it is not difficult to see that the Commission could not hope to be solely responsible for the administration of all the policies which it helps to initiate.

Finally the Commission discharges a very important policing task. It has to see that individuals, companies and member states do not act in ways which clearly run counter to the Treaty or to specific policies laid down by the Council. For example, groups of firms may enter into agreements which restrict competition and are clearly contrary to Article 3(g) (which calls for the achievement of conditions of undistorted competition) and Article 85 (which prohibits agreements, subject to exceptions in clearly defined circumstances). The Commission may begin by seeking a voluntary termination of such an agreement, but if necessary it has the power to issue a formal Decision prohibiting the agreement. By a Decision it can also inflict fines on parties to an agreement. Equally the Commission can take member states to task. In the case of state aids, for example, it will usually ask a state to voluntarily terminate an infringement, but if the state refuses the Commission can take the matter to the Court of Justice for a final determination and the latter can now impose fines (see below).

---

1. This figure relates to 1993. It covers both permanent and temporary staff and includes research appointments, the publications office and two associated institutes.

The Council of Ministers of the European Union

The Council is a body which represents the member state govern-ments.[1] It is clearly the ultimate controlling authority since draft regulations and draft directives (perhaps inspired by European Council communiques) only become the law of the Community if the Council agrees.

The Council is not a fixed group of individuals in the way that the Commission is. Where matters of agriculture are under discus-sion it will be the ministers of agriculture of the member states who will meet as the Council, and when transport is under discussion it will be the ministers of transport and so on. The chairmanship or presidency of the Council rotates – each member state holds it in turn for a period of six months.

The original Rome Treaty laid down important rules concerning voting procedure within the Council. Generally in the early stages (the transition period was divided into three four-year stages) deci-sions required a unanimous vote. However, in certain areas, such as agriculture, it was provided that subsequently a qualified majority of the votes in Council was adequate for a measure to be adopted. For this purpose France, West Germany and Italy had four votes each, Netherlands and Belgium two votes and Luxembourg one. Twelve votes were necessary for a measure to be passed. It was this which constituted much of the supra-national element of the EC Treaty. Unlike the normal system of international organizations where unanimity is necessary, it was possible to evolve policy if only a qualified majority of the votes had been cast in its favour. This was a protection for the Commission since in its task of setting up the various Community policies it did not indefinitely face the prospect of having to achieve a unanimity among the member states.

Three observations are now necessary. First, not all subjects were ones in which qualified majority voting was in due course envisaged. The admission of new members was one exception – hence the possibility that the French could, had they chosen, have blocked the admission of the UK indefinitely. Secondly, where the Council was acting on a proposal not initiated by the Commission, in addition

1. It has a secretariat of 2,170 (1993).

to the twelve-vote requirement four states also had to agree to the measure. This was a protection against the smaller Benelux states being overridden by the three bigger ones. Thirdly, in practice qualified majority voting after 1966 ceased to have the significance which had been envisaged earlier. The issue arose in 1965 in connection with the Commission's proposals to tie into one package three elements: the completion of the farm finance regulations (desired by France), the independent financing of the Community out of its own resources (strongly desired by the Commission), and the granting of greater budgetary powers to the Parliament (desired by both the European Parliament and the Netherlands). France strongly disliked parts of this package and virtually absented itself from the Council for seven months. Much of the wrath of the French was directed against the Commission, which in their eyes was getting ideas above its station, and against qualified majority, due to apply amongst other things to agriculture in 1966, which France apparently feared might be used against it. The upshot was the famous Luxembourg compromise of January 1966. There was also an agreement to modify the status of the Commission, although the changes were not really of great significance. In respect of Council voting the Six agreed as follows:

I Where, in the case of decisions which may be taken by majority vote on a proposal of the Commission, very important interests of one or more partners are at stake, the members of the Council will endeavour, within a reasonable time, to reach solutions which can be adopted by all the members of the Council while respecting their mutual interests and those of the Community, in accordance with Article 2 of the Treaty.
II With regard to the preceding paragraph, the French delegation considers that where very important interests are at stake the discussion must be continued until unanimous agreement is reached.

The effect of this was that by tacit agreement Council hardly ever took decisions by majority vote despite the fact that the Rome Treaty provided for such a procedure on a wide range of issues.

In the light of this significant change in procedure it is interesting to note that at the Paris Summit of 1974 the Heads of State and of Government stated in their communiqué:

In order to improve the functioning of the Council of the Community they consider that it is necessary to renounce the practice which consists of making agreement on all questions conditional on the unanimous consent of the member states whatever their respective positions may be regarding the conclusions reached at Luxembourg on 28 January 1966.

It is not too clear what this entailed in practice. The Heads did not formally renounce the Luxembourg agreement. Rather the communiqué seemed to be more a statement of what was desirable. Nevertheless it seemed to have the effect of relaxing the post-Luxembourg system. Thus the Commission's *Ninth General Report* (EC Commission, 1975a, p. 20), *Tenth General Report* (1976b, p. 34) and *Eleventh General Report* (1977a, p. 23) noted a tendency for decisions to be taken by majority rule. Nevertheless some members, notably the UK, continued to insist on the right to veto acts which they deemed affected vital national interests. Such was the case in 1982 when the UK withheld its support for farm price increases because of the lack of progress on its budget problem. In the end the Council decided that the vital matter of increasing the price of farm products could no longer be held up and took a decision on a majority basis – much to the disgust of the UK! The Commission noted this development with approval. However, in observing: 'There is, of course, not likely to be any sudden change from former practice' (*Sixteenth General Report*, 1982, p. 299) it clearly indicated that the spirit of Luxembourg 1966 was by no means dead.

The gravely unsatisfactory nature of this reluctance to employ the majority voting possibility was frequently criticized. As we noted in Chapter 1, the European Council set up a committee (the Three Wise Men) in 1978 to consider what adjustments in machinery and procedures would make the Community more effective. Most of the criticism of the Three was in fact directed at the Council of Ministers, which was seen as being too inter-governmental in character – the supra-national element had been lost sight of and much more use needed to be made of majority votes. We have in Chapter 1 also seen that the European Parliament, in drafting its European Union Treaty, was conscious of this deficiency and of the increased paralysis which was likely to ensue if the enlarged and more diverse Community of Twelve continued to require unanimity before anything could be agreed. The heightened consciousness of this deficiency was instrumental in influencing the content of the Single European Act of 1986. Significantly, it has led to revisions of certain articles relating to the completion of the internal common market by requiring qualified majority voting to be substituted for unanimity. The articles in question were 28, 57(2), 59, 70(1), 84(2) and 100. Modified Article 100 was particularly significant since it related to the power to harmonize national laws which by virtue of their diversity impeded the creation of a true internal common market. It should, however, be noted that not all harmonization activity was shifted to a majority voting basis. The British were anxious to set limits to majority voting and it was almost certainly because of this that some areas were exempt from the application of majority voting in the harmonization process. These areas related to fiscal matters, the free movement of persons and the rights and interests of employed persons. The relatively slow progress subsequently made in respect of fiscal matters under the 1992 single market programme was almost certainly due to this exception. As we noted in Chapter 1 the pressure for more majority voting continued to be exerted in the lead up to the Maastricht Treaty. Further progress was indeed made at Maastricht. Two examples will no doubt suffice. Thus in the 1986 Single European Act environmental protection measures required unanimity but in the Union Treaty of 1992 mainstream environmental measures were shifted to a qualified majority basis. Also in respect of new competences, such as consumer protection *per se*, qualified majority voting decisions became possible.

Following the admission of new members in 1973, 1981 and 1986 the voting system was successively changed. From 1986 Germany, France, Italy and the UK had ten votes each, Spain had eight votes, Belgium, the Netherlands, Greece and Portugal had five votes each, Denmark and Ireland had three votes each and Luxembourg had two. This gave a total of seventy-six votes and fifty-four represented a qualified majority. When the Council acted on a proposal that did not emanate from the Commission, fifty-four votes and the support of eight states were both necessary. An important point was that twenty-three votes represented a blocking minority. When in 1994 the voting formula was being recast to deal with the four expected new members, the proposal was to raise the total vote to ninety. It was also proposed to raise the blocking minority to twenty-seven. This was however opposed by the UK and Spain who wanted to keep it at twenty-three. Eventually they had to climb down. As a concession it was agreed that a delay would occur in taking decisions opposed by countries mustering between twenty-three and twenty-six votes. The total Council vote will of course fall because of Norway's eventual decision not to join.

Thus far we have presented the legislative process as one in which the Commission proposes and the Council of Ministers disposes. However, it is important to recognize that from the beginning two other bodies had in particular to be consulted – the European Parliament and the Economic and Social Committee (see below for both). The Rome Treaty indicated the issues upon which the opinion of these two bodies had to be obtained. If, for example, the Rome Treaty said that on a particular kind of proposal the Parliament had to be consulted, but the legislators had failed to consult, then the proposal adopted by the Council would have been invalid. It is crucial to recognize that while the views of the Economic and Social Committee and Parliament had to be sought, the Commission and Council were not in general required to agree to what they said. Here we see a crucial difference between national parliaments and the European Parliament. Generally speaking, the Council of Ministers could make laws even if the European Parliament disagreed with them, whereas under national systems ministers can usually only make laws if they command a majority vote in parliament.

The reader will not be surprised to learn that in due course this situation changed. In Chapter 1 we noted continued pressure both from within and from without Parliament for a move towards a situation in which it becomes a legislature and not just a body to be consulted (and possibly ignored). Whilst under Maastricht there are some issues where Parliament is merely consulted, the general trend has been for it to progressively acquire additional and widened powers. As we shall see in Chapter 3, when we discuss the development of the Community budget in the 1970s, Parliament was granted significant financial powers. Then in 1986 under the Single Act its power to approve – the so-called Positive Assent procedure – was extended to trade treaties under Article 238 and the admission of new members to the Community and its power to put pressure on Council was extended via the Cooperation Mechanism. Finally, under Maastricht, the Positive Assent procedure was extended to other topics as was the Cooperation Mechanism. Additionally, it came to dispose of the Negative Assent procedure whereby if it finally failed to agree with the Council of Ministers on an issue it could block the measure. These and other powers are discussed below.

When approaching the Council with draft proposals, the Commission proceeds by way of a number of committees[1] of which one of the more important is the Committee of Permanent Representatives – known as Coreper, which is an abbreviation of its French title. Coreper is located in Brussels. Proposals are discussed in Coreper and its sub-committees before they arrive on the Council table. If Coreper reaches full agreement the matter can pass through the Council without debate. In other cases it may be possible for the permanent representatives to agree on large sections of a draft proposal, but areas of disagreement (either as between states or between states and the Commission) are placed in square brackets and left to be settled around the Council table. In some cases little headway may be made by Coreper and the matter is then left to the ministers themselves to thrash out.

The Court of Justice

Whereas the Commission is located in Brussels, in and around the Berlaymont building, and the Council meets in the Charlemagne building close by, the Court of Justice has its seat in Luxembourg in a five-storey building on the Kirchberg.

The Court of Justice originally came into being in connection with the ECSC, but it now dispenses a legal function for each of the three communities. There are currently sixteen judges, each appointed for a six-year term. Like the members of the Commission they are not representatives of national interests but are required to act as independent judicial officers. They are protected from pressure from member state governments by two procedural arrangements. First, although hearings are in public the deliberations of the judges are in secret. Secondly, a judge can be removed from office only by a unanimous vote of his or her colleagues to the effect that he or she is no longer capable of carrying out his or her functions.

1. These include a Budget Committee and a Special Committee on Agriculture. Coreper is itself divided into Coreper 1 and Coreper 2.

In order to speed up its process, the Court is divided into chambers. The decisions which the Court reaches are read out in the presence of the parties, usually some two to three months after the hearing. The Court produces its own reports containing the basic facts, the summing-up by an Advocate General and the judgement. This official is a stranger to English legal procedure. After the main hearing his or her tasks are to summarize the issues for, and to recommend a decision to, the Court. The Court is not bound by his or her views but great attention is paid to the arguments. The fact that the Court may not follow the Advocate General was well illustrated in 1973 in the *Continental Can* case when the Court took a fundamentally different line from that suggested by the Advocate General.

We have already given some indication of the kind of situations in which the Court is called upon to act. The Commission may call upon a member state to desist from some line of conduct which is contrary to the treaty, as for example the giving of state aid. If the member state does not desist, the Commission can take the state to the Court. If the state fails to come into line a fine can now be imposed. This new power was provided by the Maastricht Treaty. In the field of competition policy the Commission may by Decision forbid some action or impose fines. The enterprises concerned can appeal to the Court of Justice. Thus in one case several aniline dye producers appealed to the Court against the fines imposed upon them for an alleged concerted practice in relation to dye prices, and in another, Continental Can appealed to the Court against the Decision of the Commission forbidding its takeover of a Dutch can producer. The Parliament can take the Council of Ministers to the Court, as it did in 1983 in connection with the alleged failure of the Council to implement the Common Transport Policy. Equally the Council can take Parliament to the Court as it did in 1986 in connection with an alleged procedural breach in connection with the adoption of the Community budget. Individuals can of course sue their governments for breaches of Treaty rules in matters such as equal rights.

In addition to all these combinations of protagonists, mention should be made of the function of the Court in giving preliminary rulings for the benefit of national courts. Inevitably at national level issues arise which call for an interpretation of Community law, and this is a major task discharged by the Court. These preliminary rulings can be very important. We shall see later, when discussing State Monopolies, that such rulings, although relating to situations in one member state, have established precedents which have endowed the Commission with the authority to outlaw *generally* certain activities which have precluded the free flow of trade.

In conclusion we should note that the Single European Act provided for the Court of Justice to have attached to it another court which would have a right of appeal to it but only on points of law. In 1988 it was decided that this new Court of First Instance should be empowered to hear cases involving Community officials and actions against Community institutions in the context of competition policy. The Court is debarred from hearing actions brought by member states or by Community institutions or from hearing questions referred for a preliminary ruling.[1]

The Court of Auditors

The Court was established in 1975 and began operations in 1977. It has two main functions. First, it carries out value-for-money audits in respect of particular categories of Community financed expenditure. It is not empowered to decide whether or not the Community should introduce a particular kind of policy – e.g. support research in a particular area of technology – but it is required to report as to whether that chosen line of policy is being conducted in a cost effective way. Second, and more important, it is called upon to indicate whether previous expenditure under the Community budget was legally and properly incurred. This report is addressed to the Council of Ministers and to the European Parliament. The latter, as we shall see, has the final say in this area. The Court of Auditors has a staff of about 330.

The European Parliament

Until 1981 one third of the Parliamentary plenary sessions were held in Luxembourg – the remaining two thirds were held at Strasbourg in France in a building which belongs to the Council of

1. The two courts have a combined secretariat of 825 (1993).

Europe. In July 1981 Parliament decided not to hold any more of its plenary sessions in Luxembourg. This provoked the Government of Luxembourg to complain to the Court of Justice but in 1983 the Court rejected the Luxembourg plea.[1]

Originally, European parliamentarians were nominated by national parliaments by a process called indirect election. Each state adopted its own procedure of selection. But the Rome Treaty envisaged the possibility that in due course the members of the European Parliament would not be nominated by the national parliaments but would be elected by universal suffrage, a process referred to as direct election. For a considerable period no progress was made on this issue, but in 1974 there were signs that movement was possible. The European Parliament decided to press the matter of direct elections, and the Paris Summit communiqué of December 1974 indicated that the Heads of State and of Government awaited with interest these Parliamentary deliberations and envisaged the possibility that direct elections could take place in or after 1978. The UK, whilst not opposing the idea of direct elections, reserved its position on the ground that renegotiation was not complete. The Danish Government also chose to reserve its position. In January 1975 a new draft convention on direct elections was adopted by an overwhelming majority in the European Parliament, and at the European Council at Rome in December 1975 it was formally agreed that direct elections should be held in May or June 1978. During 1976 a good deal of effort was devoted to hammering out the direct election details. The Council of Ministers finally approved and signed the Decision and Act relating thereto in September 1976.

The first direct elections to the European Parliament were held in June 1979. The most recent occurred in June 1994. At that point in time the European Parliament had 567 seats. Germany had 99, Italy, France and the UK had 87 each, Spain had 64, the Netherlands had 31, Belgium, Greece and Portugal had 25 each, Denmark

---

1. This is greatly uneconomic since the secretariat is based in Luxembourg and committee meetings tend to be held in Brussels! Matters have now become even more complicated, which is putting it kindly, since Parliament has built itself a large building in Brussels. However, the French, no doubt for prestige reasons, have persuaded the other member states that plenary sessions will continue to be held in Strasbourg. The logical place for everything is Brussels. Parliament had a secretariat of 3790 in 1993.

had 16, Ireland 15 and Luxembourg 6. The Members of the European Parliament form political rather than national groups. Following the 1994 election the seats were divided among the parties as follows:

Left Unity Group	13
Green	22
Mainly regionalist Rainbow group	8
European Socialist Party	199
Independents and Non-attached	96
Liberal, Democratic and Reformist group	43
European People's Party	148
European Democratic Alliance	24
European Right	14

The powers of the European Parliament can best be viewed under three headings. First, powers to appoint and dismiss. Second, powers in relation to the legislative process. Third, powers to investigate.

We have already seen that, following Maastricht, Parliament plays a role in the appointment of the Commission. In addition, it can dismiss the Commission. For this to happen a motion of censure must be passed by a two-thirds majority of the votes cast, representing a majority of the members of the Assembly. This has never actually occurred but it was threatened at the end of 1972. The motion, which took the Commission to task for failing to introduce new proposals designed to increase Parliament's powers of control over the Community budget, was withdrawn before it was put to the vote.

A detailed discussion of Parliament's legislative powers in relation to the Community budget is best left until Chapter 3. At this point we need to note that when Parliament receives the Court of Auditors report on past budget spending, evidence of improper expenditure could lead Parliament not to grant a discharge of that budget. A possible consequence of that would be that the Commission, as executive, would have to resign.

We have already noted that whilst on some matters Parliament may still be merely consulted, over a wide range of issues its role is now a more active one. Apart from its enhanced Positive Assent powers, Parliament is now involved in the Cooperation procedure and the Negative Assent procedure. The Cooperation procedure modified the role of the Parliament, in relation to the Commission and Council of Ministers, in the legislative process. Under the old system the reader will recollect that the Commission proposed legislation. Parliament gave an opinion and might suggest amendments. Council finally adopted the legislation – possibly in amended form. Under the new Cooperation procedure the Commission continued to propose legislation but a first and second reading system emerged. At its first reading Parliament adopts an opinion by simple majority. The Council for its part adopts a 'common position' by qualified majority. Then comes the second reading when Parliament can approve, amend or reject the common position – an amendment or rejection could only be made by majority vote of those entitled to vote. If Parliament approved the common position then Council could go ahead and adopt the act in question. If, however, Parliament amended the common position then the Commission would review its proposal and might revise its proposals accordingly. In which case the Council could change the revised proposal by unanimity. Equally, if Parliament rejected the common position the Council could only agree to the common position by unanimity. Whilst the final decision continues to rest with the Council, the Parliament has the ability to send a powerful message to the Commission and Council telling them to think again. Thus if the Commission agreed with the Parliament they could collectively put considerable pressure on the Council since, as we have seen, Council could only change the revised proposal by obtaining a unanimous vote. In the case of the new Negative Assent procedure there is a stage of conciliation which, if it does not lead to a solution satisfactory to Parliament, can lead the latter to block the measure.

Finally, we have to note that Parliament's investigative powers were increased by the Maastricht Treaty. Under Article 138c of the amended Rome Treaty Parliament is permitted to set up temporary committees to investigate alleged contraventions or maladministration in the implementation of Community law. Following Maastricht, Parliament was also empowered to appoint a Community Ombudsman who would investigate complaints regarding maladministration by Community institutions. The Ombudsman reports his findings to the institution concerned and to Parliament.

The Economic and Social Committee

This body,[1] which operates in respect of EC and Euratom matters, and its ECSC counterpart, is purely consultative. The total membership of Ecosoc is 220 and is made up as follows:

France	24
Germany	24
Italy	24
UK	24
Spain	21
Belgium	12
Netherlands	12
Greece	12
Portugal	12
Sweden	11
Austria	11
Denmark	9
Ireland	9
Finland	9
Luxembourg	6

The membership is representative of the various categories of economic and social life and in particular includes representatives of producers, workers, farmers, merchants, the liberal professions, transport operators and the general interest. The members are selected by the Council from lists submitted by member states. A glance at the EC Treaty indicates that on a range of issues, before action is taken by the Council, Ecosoc must be consulted. Commentators do not, however, assign any great weight to its advisory role. The truth is that, as indicated earlier, the main power in the Community lies with the Council, the Commission and increasingly, the Parliament.

Foreign Policy and Defence

Whilst this book is primarily concerned with economic matters, we did note in Chapter 1 that the ultimate hope was that the process of

1. It has a secretariat of about 510.

integration would spill over from the economic to the political sphere. Given then that the fruits of integration were not conceived of as being purely economic, it is appropriate that we should give some consideration to the political impact of the European Community. Quite simply, a spillover has occurred – to an important degree – and more may follow.

Attempts at political integration are long-standing – as we have seen within the Six they go back to the European Defence Community and European Political Community era. Subsequently, a number of political initiatives were launched. For example, in 1960 the French President, General de Gaulle, following bilateral talks with the other Five, proposed the setting up of a supreme authority to formulate common foreign and defence policies. A summit of the Six was held in Paris in February 1961. This in turn led to the establishment of a committee to examine the problem of political cooperation, initially under the chairmanship of Christian Fouchet (of France). A second summit was held at Bad Godesberg near Bonn in July 1961. The Bonn Declaration issued at the end of the meeting contained three decisions. Political cooperation between the Six should be adopted on a regular basis leading in due course to a joint policy. Heads of State and of Government should meet regularly to concert policies. The summit members also instructed the Fouchet Committee to submit proposals 'on means and ways which would make it possible to give a statutory character to the unification of their peoples as soon as possible'. Later in 1961 the French Government put a 'Draft Treaty establishing a Union of States' to the Committee. The institutions proposed were as follows: (a) a Council of Heads of State and of Government and of foreign ministers whose unanimous decisions would be binding on members; (b) a European Parliament with power of interrogation and deliberation but having no decision-making role; (c) a European Political Commission, in Paris, to be staffed by senior officials of the foreign ministries of each participating state. The aim of this was to achieve common foreign and defence policies. There was to be a general review after three years which it seemed could lead to steps being taken to bring the European Communities within the union.

Disagreements between France and the Five soon became evident, although the Dutch had been distinctly nervous about the implications from the outset. The other Five were concerned because they saw the defence arrangements as being outside NATO and the ambit of the Atlantic Alliance. They also saw a threat to the existing communities – the supra-national elements of the Paris and Rome Treaties could be lost if they were subsumed within the new union which was clearly based on the unanimity principle. Although a later draft of the Fouchet plan went quite a way to allay fears, a third draft, drawn up by de Gaulle himself, went back on these accommodations and a reference to economic matters being within the competence of the union opened up all the old fears about a watering down of supra-nationality. The plan ultimately foundered on UK participation. Originally the Dutch and Belgians had indicated that their participation was contingent upon the British being involved in the discussions – it should be remembered that the UK was then negotiating for membership of the EC and its sister bodies. This the French refused to accept but a compromise was reached in December 1961. The UK was to be kept informed and membership of the union would be automatic for new members of the economic communities. However, ultimately the problem was raised again in April 1962 when the UK pressed its desire to take part in the discussions. This in turn precipitated a split within the Six. France, Germany, Italy and Luxembourg were willing to continue discussing the text of the treaty, to agree it, to communicate it to the UK and, if the latter did not have a major objection, to put it into effect. But Belgium and the Netherlands agreed only to examine the project and communicate it to the UK – they would not sign it until the UK had become a member of the economic communities. This was sufficient to provoke a termination of the formal negotiations.

Thereafter, despite other developments such as the de Gaulle–Adenauer[1] Franco-German treaty of friendship and cooperation, there was a distinct cooling on the political front. After the 1963 French rebuff to the British bid for membership of the three communities the other members showed their strong disapproval of de Gaulle's actions, temporarily bringing the Brussels machinery to a halt. By mid 1963 a formula for achieving progress on the

---

1. Konrad Adenauer was the West German Chancellor. He and de Gaulle had close personal links and successfully strove to establish good relations between their two countries.

economic plane was found and the EC began to gain ground. The disappearance of Adenauer from the stage and his replacement by Erhard was a blow to further progress on the Franco-German front. The supra-nationality crisis by 1965–6 did nothing to cement trust between the Six. The accession to the French Presidency of Georges Pompidou in 1969 did, however, open up a more cooperative era. The participants at the Hague Summit agreed to instruct their foreign ministers to study the best way to achieve progress in respect of political unification – a report was expected by July 1970. The foreign ministers duly reported in July 1970, and their 'Luxembourg Report', *The Problem of Political Unification* (EC, Council of Ministers, 1970), inaugurated the Davignon (named after the Belgian diplomat) or political cooperation procedure.

The political cooperation procedure was separate from the institutions of the European Community. Its membership was, however, identical with that of the Community. It did not compel the member states to agree on any issue. There was no majority voting. It was essentially an exercise in inter-governmental cooperation in which the member states endeavoured to work out common positions and to agree on common actions in foreign-policy matters. In the words of the Luxembourg Report:

The objectives of this cooperation are as follows:
– to ensure, through regular exchanges of information and consultations, a better mutual understanding on the great international problems;
– to strengthen their solidarity by promoting the harmonization of their views, the coordination of their positions, and, where it seems possible and desirable, common actions.

Not all foreign-affairs matters came within the purview of this system. Defence was excluded – for the most part that was a NATO function. However, after 1980 significant moves took place, encouraged by the UK, France and West Germany, to introduce discussion of security matters regardless of the sensitivities of some smaller states. Disarmament, on the other hand, was frequently discussed. The main focus was on foreign policy towards non-member countries, and so issues which divided members, such as Northern Ireland, were taboo. There were a number of other topics which were out of bounds, of which West Berlin prior to German reunification was one instance.

At the top of the political pyramid was the European Council. Under that title it did not exist when the mechanism of political cooperation first began to operate. As we saw earlier the Heads of State and of Government met three times a year, and foreign-policy matters as well as European Communities matters came within the ambit of their consideration. It will be recalled that the Paris Summit communiqué of 1974 also provided for them to meet as often as necessary in the context of political cooperation. In practice, the major burden of cooperation fell on the foreign ministers, and it should be noted that they were the original focus of activity when the system first began to operate in 1970. The Presidency of these foreign ministerial meetings rotated and ran for a term of six months, in parallel with the Presidency of the Council of Ministers. Theoretically such meetings were supposed to take place twice in each six-month Presidency, but in fact they occurred more often, frequently being held at the same time as the Council of Ministers' meetings in Brussels or Luxembourg.

The system worked with the minimum of bureaucracy. Originally there was no permanent secretariat. Meetings of ministers and officials were organized by the foreign ministry of the country which was providing the Presidency. In order to pave the way for such ministerial meetings, a steering body, called the Political Committee,[1] was established. It consisted of the senior foreign-policy civil servants of the Community countries. These political directors, as they were called, met once a month. In addition to preparing for the meetings of the foreign ministers, the Committee acted in a similar way for other meetings including the European Council and the UN General Assembly. There was indeed something of a parallel between the roles of Coreper and the Political Committee. A series of expert working groups was established to cover geographical areas and particular issues. They comprised national civil servants and operated under the jurisdiction of the Political Committee and reported to it.

The hammering out of common positions was very much in the hands of the foreign ministers and their senior civil servants in the Political Committee. The instruments of cooperation, however, were diverse. The cooperating partners kept in touch with each

1. The Political Committee was part of the original machinery established in 1970.

other via a special coded telex network known as COREU (after the French *correspondance européenne*). Although there were no common embassies abroad member state ambassadors of the foreign capitals often worked together. For example, during the siege of the American Embassy in Tehran in 1979, the ambassadors protested in unison to the Ayotollahs. At the United Nations in New York the ambassadors of the member states endeavoured to ensure that they all voted the same way.

Originally there was a lot of opposition to the involvement of the Commission in the European Political Cooperation (EPC) mechanism. However, it came to be realized that Community policy and political cooperation were capable of being at cross purposes, and so a liaison system came to be established. Apparently, after 1974, the position of the Commission was satisfactory – the President and members of the Commission were able to attend meetings of the foreign ministers without restriction.

The Single European Act 1986 was of considerable significance for political cooperation. In the first place the Act formally recognized EPC as one of the twin pillars of the Community, alongside the three economic communities. However, in the lead-up to the Maastricht negotiations a need was felt for a stronger and more forward looking arrangement. The result was the CFSP which is one of the two inter-governmental pillars of the Union Treaty. Security is now explicitly involved.

The objectives of the CFSP are:

(a) to safeguard the common values, fundamental interests and independence of the Union;
(b) to strengthen the security of the Union and its member states in all ways;
(c) to preserve peace and strengthen international security, in accordance with the principles of the United Nations Charter as well as the principles of the Helsinki Final Act and the objectives of the Paris Charter;
(d) to promote international cooperation;
(e) to develop and consolidate democracy and the rule of law, and respect for human rights and fundamental freedoms.

The policy will operate upon the following lines. The European Council will define the principles and draw up general guidelines for the policy. The actual implementation will be with the Council of Ministers. Here a distinction is made between defining a *common position* on an issue and adopting *joint action* in respect of it. When it comes to defining a common position any member state, or the Commission, may raise a question or submit a proposal. It will however be the Council of Ministers which actually defines the common position with respect to such questions or proposals. This is in contrast to the previous EPC system where member states were regarded as acting in political cooperation. Common positions defined by Council will be binding under *international* law. Member states are required to ensure that their national policies conform to them and that they uphold them in international conferences and organizations. The Council of Ministers will also decide (on the basis of general guidelines from the European Council) whether a matter should be the subject of a *joint action*. It will also decide the details of the joint action and these too will be legally binding on member states. In its proceedings, both in defining common positions and adopting joint actions, the Council of Ministers will act unanimously. The only exception to this is that the Council when adopting a joint action, and at any stage in its subsequent development, may define those matters where decisions can be made by qualified majority vote. The reader will recollect that in the run up to Maastricht considerable differences arose over the issue of whether political cooperation should be based on the Rome Treaty supra-national model or should be of an inter-governmental character. Quite clearly the inter-governmentalists won the main battle but the supra-nationalists made a limited gain.

The old Political Committee, consisting of political directors from member states, survives. Its task is to continuously monitor the international scene and to provide appropriate inputs into Coreper and the Council of Ministers. The small secretariat established under the Single Act has been quadrupled in size and fully incorporated into the Council of Ministers' secretariat.

The vexed question of the appropriate arrangements in relation to defence, in which France and Germany were ranged against Italy, the UK and the Netherlands, is resolved in Article J4. It requests WEU, which is declared to be an integral part of the development of the Union, to implement decisions and actions of the Union which have defence implications. Under Article J4 the policy of the Union must respect NATO obligations. We noted earlier that Maastricht looks ultimately to a Common Defence Policy and eventually a Common Defence.

The European Parliament's role in relation to all this is limited. It will be consulted, kept informed and may question the Foreign Affairs Council and make recommendations – but that is all.

Cooperation on Judicial and Home Affairs

The CJHA is the other inter-governmental pillar of the Maastricht Treaty. Established under Article K of that treaty, for the first time it places inter-governmental cooperation in these two fields on a formal treaty basis. We will however reserve the discussion of this process to Chapter 9 when we consider the provisions relating to the free movement of labour and persons.

3

THE COMMUNITY BUDGET AND BORROWING POWERS

The primary focus of this chapter is the Community budget. This relates to the taxing and spending of the Community. At the end of the chapter we consider the ability of the Community to borrow money.

If the EC had been merely a common market the financial transactions under the Community budget would have been small. The member states would have had merely to make provision for the raising of money to pay for an administrative and judicial machine designed to set and keep in motion the free flow of goods, services and factors of production. However, the Rome Treaty was less modest in its aims as it envisaged policies and institutions which involved spending on a scale that went well beyond the employment of Eurocrats and judges. In the first instance these policies and institutions included the CAP and the EAGGF, social policy and the ESF and overseas trade and aid policy and the European Development Fund (EDF). The EDF was the aid part of the trade and aid policy which the Six devised for their colonial and ex-colonial dependencies. Later the above three were joined by, amongst others, regional policy and the ERDF.

How the budget is financed – the original system

In the early days the Community budget was financed by direct contributions from member states, and percentage contributions were stipulated for each country. This arrangement was provided for under Article 200 of the Rome Treaty. The largest countries – France, West Germany and Italy – paid the biggest percentage contributions, Belgium and the Netherlands paid a good deal less, and not surprisingly Luxembourg paid very little indeed. The reader should, however, note that there were separate percentage contribution systems for different categories of spending such as the operational side of the budget, the EAGGF, the ESF and the EDF. The variation of particular member state contributions between the different types of spending was a reflection of two main factors – differences of ability to pay and differences of obligation and interest. Thus whilst Italy paid the same percentage contribution as West Germany and France in respect of the operational part of the budget, her weaker economic position was reflected in the fact that she paid proportionately less than the other two in connection with all other categories of spending. Differences of historical responsibility and of economic interest explain why the percentage contributions of France and West Germany to the EDF were comparatively high. In the case of France it was a reflection of economic obligations to her extensive overseas territories. In the case of West Germany it was recognized that since she would now enjoy trade access to these territories she should by way of *quid pro quo* bear a fair share of the associated aid burden.

Article 201 of the Rome Treaty envisaged that ultimately these national contributions might be replaced by a system of financing based on what were called the Community's *own resources*. In particular, Article 201 identified the proceeds of the common external tariff as one such resource. The idea of shifting to a more *communautaire* system in which the budget revenue was based on own resources was approved by the Heads of State and of Government at the Hague Summit of 1969. The member states formally agreed when in 1970 they took the enabling Decision. The Six in fact decided that own resources should include not only the proceeds of the common external tariff but also the income stemming from agricultural import levies together with a VAT component. All this requires further elaboration.

Prior to the introduction of the own resources system, the proceeds of both the common external tariff and agricultural import levies accrued to the national exchequers – the place to which they had gone in the days before the formation of the EC. These proceeds were in truth the Community's own resources and thus the member states were merely custodians pending the development of the own resources system. Under this new system the duties derived from applying the common external tariff were to be paid over to Brussels – member states were allowed to retain 10 per cent to cover their collection costs. The new system also required member states to pay over to Brussels the proceeds of levies imposed on agricultural imports coming into the Community from without. These were an integral part of the CAP and were designed to raise the price of imports and prevent the latter from undermining agricultural product prices within the Community. Again 10 per cent could be retained by the member states to cover collection costs. There was in fact another source of agricultural income, namely sugar storage levies. The VAT component is somewhat more complex, and it should be added that in budget theology it is not strictly a true own resource. In Chapter 5 we shall see that the Community decided to adopt the VAT as the common form of turnover tax. Under the 1977 Sixth VAT Directive the Six agreed on a common assessment base – a common collection of goods and services upon which VAT would be levied. The original own resources system required the member states to pay to Brussels the proceeds of up to a 1 percentage point VAT upon that common assessment base. This requirement was the subject of much misunderstanding. Some commentators appeared to believe that member states were required to pay 1 per cent of their national VAT revenue to Brussels. Were that to have been the case then member states could have reduced their contribution to the budget by lowering their national VAT rates – the latter are still determined by the member states since a harmonized rate level has not yet been agreed. It should be added that although the new own resources system was agreed in 1970 it did not become fully operational until 1980.

The relative importance of the various components of budget resources under the original system is shown in Figure 1. Quite clearly in 1982 VAT provided more than half the own resources revenue. It should also be mentioned that member states were originally only obliged to make *up to* a 1 percentage point VAT contribution. Any movement beyond the 1 point level would have had to be agreed by the member states and would have been likely to give rise to a renegotiation of the whole package. In the first half of the 1980s, budget expenditure rose faster than own resource revenue from customs duties and import levies, and as a result the VAT rate had to be raised to compensate. In 1980 it was 0.73, in 1982 it was raised to 0.92 and in 1984 it hit the ceiling of 1 point. Clearly if this trend had continued and member states had refused to make any accommodation the budget would have run out of resources. We shall return to this topic later.

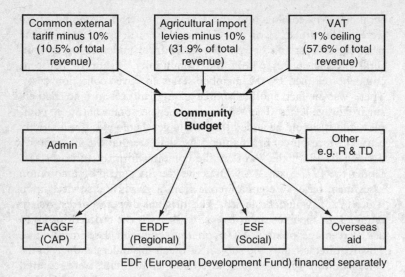

Figure 1. Community budget revenue – original sources. Revenue proportions in 1982. Main heads of expenditure

How budget monies are spent

The Community budget provides the finance necessary to administer the Community and to fund the various policies. The salaries and running costs of Brussels Eurocrats and their staff together with the running costs of bodies such as the Court of Justice and Parliament have to be met from the budget. However, the bulk of budget spending has always been concerned with the CAP. Therefore the majority of spending has always been channelled into the European Agricultural Guidance and Guarantee Fund. Under that general heading guarantee spending has dominated. It has been concerned with buying up and storing surpluses, selling surpluses abroad at a loss and, more recently, taking land out of cultivation and direct income support. Between 1973 and 1988 guarantee spending was never less than 63 per cent of total budget spending and on occasions swallowed up no less than 77 per cent. By contrast guidance spending devoted to improving farm structures and efficiency claimed only about 2 to 3 per cent of budget resources. In addition the budget has supported the ESF (training and mobility of workers) and the ERDF (regional development assistance) but these so-called structural funds[1] absorbed only about 11 to 14 per cent of the resources between them during the eighties. A multitude of other policies have also drawn support from the budget including R & TD programmes and aid for economic development. The latter has related to both member states and third countries. Examples of internal assistance are the Integrated Mediterranean Programmes and the Pedip programme. The first were designed to help regions adversely affected by the Iberian enlargement. The second was designed to modernize Portuguese industry.

The adoption of the budget

We have now explained what the Community budget consists of. We have not yet explained how the budget comes into existence. The initiating role is as usual vested in the Commission. It collates estimates of the various kinds of spending and embodies them in a *preliminary draft budget* which it submits to the Council of Ministers. The latter subjects the preliminary draft to a 'first reading'. Acting on a qualified majority voting basis the Council adopts[2] what is called the *draft budget*. Needless to say the budget which emerges from the Council of Ministers does not have to be the same as the one presented to it by the Commission. In practice it usually gets cut down in size. The draft budget is then dispatched to the European Parliament. There then occurs what euphemistically may be called a dialogue between the Parliament and the Council in which both sides can propose changes. At the end of the day the hope is that the European Parliament will be disposed to adopt the budget, thus bringing the process to a close. For the record it should be mentioned that the present budgetary powers of the Parliament derive originally from the Luxembourg Treaty of 1970 and the Brussels Treaty of 1975.

In order to understand the relationship which exists between the institutions in respect of the budget we have to look a little more closely at the powers which have been conferred upon them. To this

---

1. These include guidance monies.
2. The Rome Treaty actually speaks of the Council *establishing* the draft budget.

end we must first recognize that budget expenditure is divided into two broad categories – compulsory (sometimes called obligatory) and non-compulsory (non-obligatory). Compulsory is defined as expenditure resulting from the Treaty or acts in accordance therewith. The reader may find this definition confusing rather than enlightening. He or she may wonder how budget expenditure can result from anything other than the Treaty and acts in accordance therewith. The reader is, however, advised that no benefit would be derived from delving into the logic of this nomenclature. It is more fruitful to note that in practice compulsory expenditure has included EAGGF guarantee spending (e.g. buying surpluses), some EAGGF guidance spending (e.g. grants to improve farm structures and efficiency), some aid given to developing countries, some fisheries expenditure and part of staffing costs. Clearly this expenditure is dominated by EAGGF guarantee spending which of course also dominates the budget. The non-compulsory section has included the major part of guidance spending, most of the overseas aid, a minority of fisheries expenditure, virtually all R & D spending, most of the staffing costs and all the ESF and ERDF spending.

The exact division between these two categories was a matter of dispute between Council and Parliament. In rough terms compulsory expenditure in the late 1980s absorbed about three quarters of the budget appropriations – the remaining quarter was consumed by the non-compulsory section. Although there is a dialogue about both categories of expenditure, at the end of the day, by virtue of Article 203, Council has the last word on compulsory spending and the Parliament has the last word on the non-compulsory category. The reader will quickly realize that Council has in the past had the final say over the great bulk of the budget. However, as we shall see later, this situation is likely to change in the second half of the 1990s since CAP spending, which is largely compulsory, will tend to absorb a smaller proportion and structural spending, which is dominated by the ESF and ERDF, is set to become proportionately more important. The reader will note that the latter spending is non-compulsory and is controlled by Parliament.

In respect of the non-compulsory section, Parliament's final word means that it can increase or decrease the total of such spending and of course it can transfer expenditure between Heads. It must, however, be added that Parliament's power to increase such spending is not unconstrained. This arises from the fact that, while there is no limit to the degree to which compulsory expenditure can be increased (provided the Council and Parliament are so minded), the Commission is required to calculate and thus determine the maximum amount by which non-compulsory spending may be increased. This is called the maximum rate. The maximum rate is governed by three factors – the trends in the previous year in member states' (a) real Gross Domestic Product, (b) public spending and (c) cost of living. In, for example, the case of the 1988 budget those three factors produced an indicated maximum rate of increase of 8.52 per cent.

We noted earlier that it is the function and prerogative of the European Parliament finally to adopt the budget. This also carries with it the possibility that the Parliament may find the products of the dialogue unsatisfactory. If indeed the Parliament believes that there are 'important reasons' why the budget should not be adopted then it can reject it and ask for a new draft budget to be submitted to it. For this to happen the motion to reject must be supported by two thirds of the votes cast and those votes must represent a majority of the members of the Parliament.

Such a rejection has occurred. In Chapter 2 we discussed the first direct election of the European Parliament. That Parliament had not long been elected before it began to flex its muscles and the budget became the main source of contention. The contest originally centred on votes for additional spending in 1979 but finally focused on the Community budget for 1980.

The lines of battle became clear in November 1979. Parliament refused to make time available for consideration of a special vote to release extra funds to buy surplus farm products. Tension was heightened when later in the month the Council rejected a Parliamentary move designed to cut the amount of money available for buying up surplus dairy products. In December attention centred on the £10.8 billion Community budget for 1980. Parliament wanted a larger overall appropriation and a switch in emphasis away from agriculture to areas such as the ERDF. The Council of Budget Ministers considered Parliament's demands but replied with promises of possible agricultural curbs in the following spring and a number of small concessions. This did not satisfy the Parliament, and on 13 December it voted by 288 to 64, with 1 abstention, to throw out the budget. The Community remained without a budget until July 1980 – by that time the Commission had produced its preliminary draft budget for 1981! The reader will obviously wonder how the Community can carry on its activities if it has no budget. The answer is that if the budget remains unadopted it can spend per month one twelfth of what was spent in the previous year. Parliament has flexed its rejecting muscles more than once! In 1984 it did it again when, because the Community was running out of budget resources, the Council sent to Parliament a draft budget which did not cover the whole year in respect of certain items. Parliament rejected this as an unacceptable practice, and for several months the Community was once more back on the twelfths system. This latter experience was repeated for a short period in 1987 and again in 1988.

A brief mention must be made of the auditing of the Community budget. In earlier days external auditing was carried out by the Audit Board and the ECSC Auditor. As a result of the 1975 Treaty, which conferred the previously discussed budget adoption power upon the Parliament, a European Court of Auditors was created. It began work in 1977 and from November 1993 onwards, following the entry into force of the Maastricht Treaty, the Court of Auditors was raised to a status equal to that of the Court of Justice, European Commission, etc. The Court examines past budgetary spending and then renders a report to the Council of Ministers and to Parliament. The latter has the final say. It examines the report and decides whether to vote to discharge the budget. If Parliament decided not to grant a discharge it seems likely that the Commission would have to resign. A discharge implies that budgetary spending has been legally and properly incured. The actual act of discharge occurs in the April of the second year after the budget year in question. Thus if the budget year is designated as A, discharge occurs in the April of year A + 2. Incidentally, budget years are calendar years.

Budget problems and reform

It will be apparent from what has gone before and from Chapter 1 that the budget has been a controversial issue. Some of this controversy has been concerned with the division of powers between the

Parliament and the Council of Ministers and with the details of the budget-making process. We shall not concern ourselves further with such issues. Our task will be to examine the economic aspects and impact of the budget. This will require us to consider matters such as the equity, expenditure structure and distributional role of the budget as well as the need for additional resources. It should be added that these topics are highly interconnected.

The need for equity

Criticism was directed at the budget, which became fully operational from 1980, for its lack of equity. That in turn raises the question of what we mean by equity. In public finance theory a distinction is made between horizontal and vertical equity. Horizontal equity requires that equally situated individuals should be taxed equally. Thus in the context of personal income taxation, horizontal equity requires that two families with the same income should pay the same amount of tax. The phrase 'equally situated' would require that families of *equal size* and so forth should pay the same tax. The concept of vertical equity flows naturally from the horizontal concept. If equals are to be taxed equally then unequals should be taxed unequally. Usually vertical equity has been translated into the ability-to-pay principle, according to which those most able to pay should pay the highest taxes. Very often therefore the notion of vertical equity is taken to be synonymous with progressivity. If we look at Community budget revenue-raising it was difficult to see how the basic principles could satisfy either of these two equity criteria. Quite simply, equals did not inevitably pay the same tax. Thus two countries might have the same Gross National Product (GNP) and the same GNP *per capita* but if one country imported more food from third countries than the other then it would pay more into the budget. Equally, the common external tariff component could lead to one country paying in more than the other. This would arise if one country's foreign trade was more oriented towards third countries than the other. Indeed, it was pointed out that part of the UK's budget problem arose from its greater orientation towards the outside world. Fortunately this problem declined as trade with the Community became proportionately more important. It was also difficult to see how these two revenue sources accorded with the vertical equity principle. There was certainly no reason to expect that richer countries would pay proportionately more levies and duties *per capita* into the budget. It was also maintained that the VAT element was unsatisfactory. Daniel Strasser (Director of Budgets in the Commission) pointed out that the VAT component was actually regressive. There were a number of reasons for this, including the fact that consumption in poorer countries is a higher proportion of GNP and it attracts VAT whereas other components, such as investment, do not. This latter problem was finally addressed in 1988 and 1992 by capping down the VAT component (see below).

The UK budget problem

There is, of course, another concept of equity, namely the benefit principle. It emphasizes the obvious point that the impact of a budget on individuals arises from what they get out of it as well as what they pay into it. The benefit principle of taxation stresses the idea that those who reap the benefits of government expenditure should pay the taxes. This is a suitable concept with which to introduce the UK budget problem, the essence of which was that whilst the UK made a fair, indeed more than fair, contribution, her benefits were limited. We have already seen that the budget is dominated by CAP spending. Much of the money is devoted to buying up surpluses (i.e. guarantee spending). As the UK is a relatively small producer (farming in the UK in 1981 represented just over 2 per cent of Gross Domestic Product (GDP) whereas, for example, the figure for Ireland was close to 18 per cent) she got little back in the way of CAP guarantee spending. On the other hand, the UK was in a good position to benefit from the ERDF and the ESF, but since they commanded so little of the budget these return flows could not compensate for the smallness of her CAP benefits. This imbalance was expected to lead to the UK making a net contribution to the budget of £1.2 billion by 1980. The unfairness of this is heightened when it is recognized that while it would be a net contributor, and the biggest net contributor at that, it was in *per capita* terms one of the poorer countries in the Community – see Table 1.

The reader will recollect from Chapter 1 that one of the items

Table 1. Estimated net budget receipts 1980 and per capita national income 1979

	Estimated net budget receipts for 1980 (£m)	Per capita GDP 1979 relative to average	
		(a)	(b)
Belgium	} + 557	124	108
Luxembourg		125	111
Denmark	+ 188	138	116
France	+ 48	116	112
Germany	− 724	135	118
Ireland	+ 289	49	61
Italy	+ 491	62	77
Netherlands	+ 193	117	105
UK	− 1203	76	91
Community		100	100

Note: GDP (a) is based on a straight exchange rate conversion; GDP (b) is based on 1979 purchasing power parities.
Source: Budget: W. Godley, 'The United Kingdom and the Community Budget' in W. Wallace (ed.), *Britain in Europe*, Heinemann, 1980, p. 73.
Per capita GDP (b): ibid.
Per capita GDP (a): D. Strasser, *The Finances of Europe*, OOPEC, 1980, p. 346.

included in the 1974–5 renegotiation was the subject of the UK contribution to the Community budget. It will also be recollected that at the Dublin Summit in 1975 a Correction Mechanism was agreed which was designed to limit the UK contribution to the budget. Unfortunately, the provisions of the Correction Mechanism were such that it was never triggered, and it was thought to be unlikely that it would be triggered in 1980. It should also be pointed out that the Correction Mechanism applied to gross contributions whereas, as we have recognized, the inequality in UK eyes was the net impact. Equally there was a limit to the refund allowed. Even if triggered, the maximum refund was quite incapable of achieving the broad balance between payments and receipts which the Conservative Government aimed for. The British Prime Minister, Margaret Thatcher, therefore demanded a cut of £1 billion in the UK contribution, and this was discussed at the Dublin Summit which opened in November 1979. However, the Community was not prepared to make such a concession – the maximum reduction offered was

£350 million. The UK was not willing to accept this proposal but signified its willingness to compromise, and the matter was put off until a later summit. The Commission was asked to prepare more detailed proposals for extra spending to help the UK. The French for their part intimated that progress on the budget issue depended on the UK being willing to be more accommodating on other issues such as the fisheries policy and access to North Sea oil.

The budget debate was renewed at the European Council in Luxembourg in April 1980. Matters were complicated by the fact that the rest of the Community continued to couple agreement on the budget with other issues. Apart from the two previously mentioned, the UK was under pressure to accept an average 5 per cent farm price increase, although she wished to freeze the prices of products in surplus and to allow an increase of only 2.4 per cent on other products. The French also pressed for a Community-financed régime for sheep-meat. It will be recollected that France had defied the Court of Justice ruling that it should allow UK sheep-meat into the French market. The UK resisted the coupling of all these issues with that of the budget and took the view that these other topics should be dealt with separately on their merits. In the upshot the summit failed to resolve the budget issue. The rest of the Community advanced their Dublin offer – the UK net contribution was to be set at £325 million. The size of the reduction still did not meet Mrs Thatcher's target but an equally important factor was that of duration. The offer was guaranteed only for 1980 whereas the UK was looking to an agreed reduction applicable for several years. The summit broke up in some disarray with the UK indicating it would veto the farm price increase until a better budget settlement was offered.

However, subsequent discussions within the Council of Foreign Ministers in May 1980, under the distinguished presidency of Emilio Colombo, solved the immediate budget problem. The UK net contribution in 1980 was reduced to £370 million and in 1981 it was to be £430 million. There would also be a concession in 1982 if the Community had, by that date, failed to agree on a restructuring of Community finances. The UK, for its part, agreed to an average 5 per cent increase in farm prices. A community régime for sheep-meat was agreed. The agreement on fisheries was, however, relatively loosely worded and the details were left for subsequent hard bargaining. As things transpired, a restructuring had not been agreed by 1982, and therefore further *ad hoc* annual rebates were agreed in respect of the UK for the years 1982, 1983 and 1984.[1]

Closing the gap – the MacDougall Report

We must now move away from the problem of the UK although we shall return to the subject later. However, before we shift the focus of attention it is important to note that although the UK's espousal of the benefit principle was one which would bring her benefits, that approach has one severe drawback – it does not change the distribution of income. Under such a system all individuals get what they pay for. There is no question of poorer individuals getting more than they pay for in tax at the expense of richer individuals who therefore get fewer benefits than they pay for in tax. It is, however, possible to envisage a Community budget which could redistribute in this way.

Before we turn to consider that possibility it is important to establish where the Community budget stands in relation to such a notion. We could point to the preamble to the original Rome Treaty which refers to the desirability of 'reducing the differences existing between the various regions and the backwardness of the less favoured regions'[2] That is indeed what the contracting parties declared, but it would be wrong to conclude that as a consequence such a levelling out (or convergence of standards of living) was one of the functions of the Community budget. It had no such objective – its role was to finance whatever policies the Community decided to establish and finance. In any case, even if such a redistribution was an objective of the budget, its effectiveness was severely limited by its size – in 1984, for example, it represented only 0.9 per cent of Community GNP and only 2.7 per cent of national public spending.

1. These rebates were not always immediately forthcoming. In December 1982, Parliament blocked the 1982 rebate, not because it was opposed to it but partly because of accounting technicalities in connection with the rebate and partly because of its frustration at the delay in achieving a reform of the Community's financial system which would provide a long-term solution to the UK problem. However, Parliament lifted its veto in the following February, having been satisfied that measures of reform were shortly to be proposed. The rebate for 1983 was not agreed until the middle of 1984 when the budget system was finally reformed (see below).
2. We can interpret differences between regions to include differences between states.

To be able to exercise a significant levelling-out role the budget would have to be much bigger. The reader will, however, be aware that although the budget was not designed to even out, it does redistribute! The problem is that its redistributive effect can be haphazard. It can take from the relatively poor and give to, among others, the relatively rich – as the UK case illustrated.

Some consideration has been given to the question of whether a larger budget with a levelling-out role would be desirable. In 1974 the Commission invited a group of experts to examine the role of public finance in European integration. The resulting MacDougall Report (EC Commission, 1977b) was published in 1977.

The group noted that whereas public expenditure by the member states within the Community was about 45 per cent of the gross product of the area as a whole, expenditure by the Community institutions was less than 1 per cent. They also noted that in federal systems such as those in West Germany and the USA quite a high proportion of public spending was federal, as opposed to constituent state, spending. Indeed, federal spending tended to be in the region of 20–25 per cent of gross product. The group was particularly struck by the extent to which federal spending took the form of transfers from richer to poorer states within a union.

The group contemplated the possibility of increasing Community budget spending to federal levels. It was possible to conceive at a distant date of a European Federation, when the federal spending level of 20–25 per cent might be attained. An earlier stage of federation might involve a figure of 5–7 per cent, or 7.5–10 per cent if defence was included. However, they concentrated most attention on a much more modest prefederal stage where the level might be 2–2.5 per cent.

Consideration was given to the reasons why such an increase might be desirable – in so doing the group focused on economic considerations rather than merely on the point that such increased spending would be symbolic of European unity. There might, for example, be economies of scale in concentrating expenditure at the Community level – perhaps this might be accompanied by a compensating reduction at national level. However, the main motive for envisaging an increase was concerned with redistribution, since they placed emphasis on the growth of Community-financed structural, cyclical, unemployment and regional policies. The purpose of such measures would be to reduce inter-regional differences in capital endowment and productivity. In other words, the budget would seek to facilitate convergence. The group also noted that political cohesion was likely to be fostered if the less prosperous regions were able to share in the general advance of living standards. A larger reformed budget could also act as a built-in stabilizer.

Such a development would require greater Community revenue, and the group opted for a further tranche of VAT resources. Although the expenditure would itself be redistributive, they also recommended the injection of an element of progressivity into budget income.

The 1984 reform

The reader will already sense that as the 1980s progressed the budgetary system was coming under increasing strain. A major problem arose from the limitation on the own resources available for the budget. As we saw earlier, expenditure was rising faster than own resources from customs duties and levies, and therefore the VAT rate had to be progressively increased until, as we noted above, in 1984 it reached the 1 per cent ceiling. Quite simply the Community was in danger of running out of own resources. Indeed it did so in 1984. While in respect of their own domestic budgets member state governments have a more or less automatic right to cover any excess of expenditure by borrowing, the Community has no such automatic right. In principle the budget must balance. However, what the Community did in 1984 was to adopt a wholly *ad hoc* arrangement whereby member states were asked to make repayable advances in order to cover the budgetary shortfall. The same happened in 1985 except that on that occasion the advances were not repayable. Clearly the Community needed additional resources and the obvious answer was to raise the VAT rate above 1 per cent. Indeed the Commission produced a Green Paper in February 1983 – *The Future Financing of the Community* (EC Commission, 1983) – in which it envisaged such a solution. It also gave consideration to injecting an element of progressivity into the contribution so that those countries which were most able to pay on the basis of *per capita* income would be hit hardest. The Commission also considered the 1979 (Lange) Resolution of the European Parliament, which called for a system of equalization transfers between the member states. The Commission, however, pointed out that the smallness of the budget precluded any significant egalitarian effects. But it did accept that a limited programme of transfers to the least prosperous states would be a possibility.

Additional income for the budget was also necessary if the deadlock over Iberian membership was to be broken, as their entrance was almost certainly going to add more to expenditure than to income.

There was also a further problem, namely the excessive slice of the budget which was devoted to agriculture – i.e. to the storage and sale at a loss of surpluses. Steps needed to be taken to grapple with the surplus problem. At the same time as the Community devised its temporary settlement of the UK budget, the Commission was charged with the task of carrying out a review of the operation and funding of Community policies. This was called the mandate. The Commission duly reported in 1981 – *Report from the Commission of the European Communities to the Council pursuant to the Mandate of 30 May 1980* (EC Commission, 1981a). In the event, the report did not produce the basis for a quick solution to the budget problem – hence the behaviour of Parliament in December 1982.[1] The message the Commission appears to have wanted to get across was this. The budget should not continue to be dominated by the CAP. In the depressed industrial circumstances of the times there was a need to shift the emphasis of budget spending towards the ERDF and ESF. If CAP spending was to be reduced then the gap between Community and world agricultural product prices would have to be narrowed. This appeared to mean that CAP prices would have to fall so as to discourage surpluses, although the Commission also seemed to be interested in the idea that world prices ought to be increased. Obviously, even if only the latter occurred, such a change would reduce the size of the export subsidy burden which fell upon the EAGGF when surplus Community produce was unloaded on the world market. It should, however, be recognized that an improvement in world prices would not be likely to occur unless the Community itself ceased to dump surpluses on the world market. A radical reduction in the farm price level within

1. See footnote 1 on p. 89 above.

the Community or some other equally effective remedy therefore seemed inescapable. The Commission was also critical of other aspects of the CAP, including the degree to which the protection of farm incomes dominated price policy, and the open-ended nature of the guarantees accorded to products in structural surplus. More will be said on this subject in Chapter 8.

Finally there was the problem of the UK budgetary contribution, which needed to be settled on a permanent basis as opposed to a series of *ad hoc* annual settlements – the European Parliament held this view very strongly. (It should be added that the UK was not the only country which made a disproportionate contribution – West Germany could also legitimately claim some relief.) It is also important to note that the UK was determined not to support any move to increase own resources unless (a) its long-standing complaint about its excessive contribution was dealt with and (b) farm spending was brought under control. While the UK was committed to securing a rectification of its budgetary contribution it did ultimately accept that it should remain a net contributor.

The atmosphere began to improve in 1983 when the Stuttgart Summit adopted its Solemn Declaration on European Union and also agreed that there would have to be not only adequate budgetary resources but also budgetary fairness and budgetary discipline. The next step occurred in January 1984 when the Presidency of the Council of Ministers and the European Council passed into the skilled hands of France. The Council of Ministers made a breakthrough when it agreed (subject to an Irish reservation) to radical controls on milk production by means of quotas and agreed to other significant agricultural measures. At the Fontainebleau Summit in June 1984 the agricultural settlement was followed by an agreement to reform the budget. It was accepted that from 1986 the ceiling on VAT contributions would be raised to 1.4 per cent (the Commission had hoped for 2 per cent). The possibility of raising the ceiling to 1.6 per cent in 1988 was recognized, but this would require unanimity. The UK problem was dealt with by agreeing that from 1985 it would receive a rebate equal to 66 per cent of the difference between its share of VAT payments and its share of expenditure. The Summit also cleared the way for repayments to be made to the UK and West Germany in respect of 1983. It also reaffirmed the March 1984 Summit agreement on budgetary and financial discipline. This, among other things, required that net expenditure on agricultural markets should grow at a lower rate than the own resource base. In other words the CAP should progressively attract a smaller proportion of budget resources.

The 1988 reform

While these reforms were a considerable step forward, it soon became clear that they did not deal with the problem of own resource inadequacy. By 1986 the Community appeared to be heading for another budgetary crisis as agricultural spending was still excessive – thanks to the continued accumulation of surpluses. It is true that at the end of 1986 the Council of Agricultural Ministers did take some tough decisions, particularly in the milk sector – we will consider these further in Chapter 8. However, these measures were only likely to help in the medium term, and by 1987 a budgetary shortfall of about 6 billion ECUs was being forecast. Early in 1987 the President of the EC Commission, Jacques Delors, put forward a new plan for the financing of the Community budget. It suggested an own resource ceiling up to 1992 of 1.4 per cent of Community GNP. The funds raised within this limit would be derived from four sources. The first would be agricultural levies but with no deduction for collection costs. The second would be the proceeds of a common external tariff – again with no deduction for the costs of collection. The third would be the proceeds of a 1 per cent levy on the VAT base – including goods which were zero-rated. The fourth would be a levy on what was to be called the additional base, i.e. the difference between the collection of goods which make up the VAT base and GNP. The additional base levy would, for example, apply to items such as investment which are not included in the VAT base. The total GNP of each member state would therefore serve as a basis for financing the budget although the rates of the VAT base and the additional base would differ.

The Delors Plan was considered by the Heads of State and of Government at the Brussels Summit in July 1987. Unfortunately no agreement was forthcoming on the provision of additional long-term financing for the budget. Despite reference in the plan to the need for control of expenditure, as well as the need for greater revenues, the UK Prime Minister, Margaret Thatcher, rejected the package on the grounds that the provisions on controlling spending, particularly on agriculture, were inadequate. Work continued on the package and it was hoped that sufficient progress would be made for agreement to be reached at the Copenhagen Summit in December 1987, but this did not happen. The immediate problem of the budgetary shortfall in 1987 was dealt with by switching to paying farmers in arrears rather than in advance and by other savings.

Matters came to a head at the Brussels Summit in February 1988. Extremely tough negotiations ensued in which the UK and the Netherlands demanded strong curbs on agricultural overproduction. A last-minute compromise was finally worked out on the issue of agricultural curbs. The EAGGF would provide funds to persuade farmers to set aside land and in addition budget stabilizers were to be introduced. They would prescribe ceilings to the production of cereals, etc. and any tendency for production to over-shoot that level would lead to the automatic triggering of price cuts (see Chapter 8.).

The agricultural control issue having thus been disposed of, the way was then open for an agreement on a new budgetary regime. This is usually referred to as the Delors I budget. A ceiling on budgetary expenditure was agreed. As a proportion of Community GNP it should not exceed 1.2 per cent on a payments basis or 1.3 per cent on a commitments basis. It was also agreed that the growth of agricultural guarantee spending should not exceed 74 per cent of the growth rate of Community GNP. Structural spending (e.g. the spending of the ERDF and ESF) should by contrast grow relatively rapidly. It was decided that by 1993 structural spending would be increased by 100 per cent on the 1987 level. In addition, structural spending should be more concentrated on the poorest regions, and indeed spending on them should be doubled by 1992. All this was a clear gain for countries such as Spain, Portugal, Greece and Ireland.

A revenue-enhancing system was agreed. The three existing budget revenue sources – food import levies, the external tariff and the VAT – were retained. The VAT rate ceiling stayed at 1.4 per cent. Commission President Jacques Delors had suggested that the 10 per cent deduction which member states were allowed to cover collection costs should be dropped, but this was not agreed to. Most

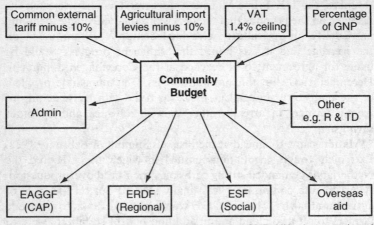

VAT base capped at 55% of GNP. UK rebate continued

Figure 2. Community budget revenue – 1988 Agreement

importantly, a fourth revenue source was added. This involved each member state paying a given percentage of its GNP. This was different from the Delors proposal which had envisaged that this levy should be applied to the difference between the VAT base and GNP. It should also be noted that in calculating a member state's VAT contribution it was assumed that the VAT base would not exceed 55 per cent of GNP.

The UK succeeded in renewing its budget rebate. In 1984 it was agreed that this rebate should be 66 per cent of the difference between the UK's VAT-related payment and its budget expenditure benefits. This system now applied to the difference between its VAT-and GNP-related payments and its benefits. The 1988 revenue base is shown in Figure 2.

The budget agreement was followed by an Interinstitutional Agreement between the Parliament, the Council of Ministers and the Commission which gave rise to improved budget procedures including the production of a five-year budget perspective.[1]

---

1. The perspective was motivated by two considerations. One was the desire of the European Council and Council of Ministers to place some restraints on Parliament's annual budgetary manoeuvres. The other was the desire of Spain to hold the Community to its commitments to shift resources to the poorer states.

The modern budget

Before we discuss the current agreement we need to give some consideration to the changing nature of the Community budget. Originally it did not have an egalitarian aim. That is to say it was not conceived as a mechanism by means of which resources would be transferred from the richer to the poorer states of the Community. This is a little surprising when we note that the preamble to the Rome Treaty did emphasize the desirability of reducing the differences in living standards as between the regions of the Community. It also contrasts with the role of budgets in federal arrangements – the redistributive role of such budgets was discussed earlier in connection with the MacDougall Report. However, with the passage of time the budget began to take on this kind of redistributive role, although its capacity is limited by its relatively small size in proportionate terms. The first development was the entry into operation of the ERDF in 1975. Then, in the negotiations leading up to the Single Act, countries such as Spain and Portugal pressed for a transfer of resources on the grounds that the poorer countries would find it hard to survive in the face of increased competition stemming from the completion of the single European market. This led to the formal incorporation of the Economic and Social Cohesion objective in the Treaty. As we have seen in the 1988 budget agreement the structural fund allocation was doubled and directed at the poorer regions.

Whilst some progress had been made, the poorer states – notably Spain – continued to voice some dissatisfaction. If we look at the way the budget impacted in 1989 in terms of net contributions or net benefits, we can see why. The evidence is based on an extremely penetrating study by Bowles and Jones (1992). They show (see Figure 3) that whilst the broad thrust was for the rich countries to be net contributors, and vice-versa, there were some anomalies. Thus Denmark, the richest per capita, was a net beneficiary per capita to almost the same extent as Portugal, the poorest. Some poorer countries, such as Ireland, had done well thanks to CAP spending on surpluses. On the other hand, Spain merely broke even.

In the lead-up to the Maastricht Treaty Spain demanded a reform of the budget. That it be structured so that contributions reflect the relative abilities to pay. Additionally, that a further transfer of resources be made to the poorer states. Also when the

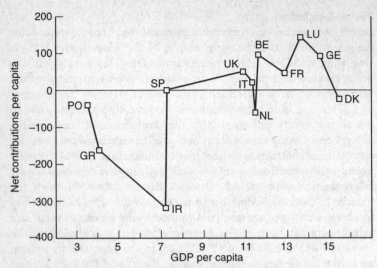

In ECUs at 1985 prices except GDP which is thousands of ECUs at 1985 prices.

Source: Bowles, R. and Jones, P. (1992), 'Equity and the EC Budget; A Pooled
Cross-Section Time Series Analysis', *Journal of European Social Policy*,
Vol. 2, No. 2. Copyright © *Longman Group UK Ltd*, 1992. reproduced by permission

Figure 3. Net contribution and net benefit positions in 1989

Community contributes to the cost of a project, the proportion provided by the recipient state ought to reflect its wealth. For example, if Denmark received a Community grant for regional development it might have to find three-quarters of the cost itself, whereas in the case of Portugal the proportions might be the other way round. These proportions are purely illustrative of the general idea.

In the event, the European Council did sanction, as part of the Maastricht settlement, a Cohesion Fund. It would be financed by the budget. The countries benefiting would be those with per capita incomes that were less than 90 per cent of the Community average. The grants would be for Trans-European Networks and environmental measures.

The Community budget was renegotiated in 1992. Commission President Jacques Delors wanted the European Council (which lays down broad financial guidelines) to raise the budgetary spending ceiling from 1.20 per cent to 1.37 per cent of Community GNP. But this was opposed by the UK, which was keen to keep public spending down, and Germany, which was saddled with the economic burden of the former East Germany.

In the end it was agreed that the ceiling would only rise to 1.27 per cent and over a seven-year period (see Table 2). It was agreed to cap the base upon which VAT is paid to the budget further down to 50 per cent of GNP. This would apply in 1995 in the case of poorer states but would occur in equal stages from 1995 for the richer ones. The VAT rate was also to be lowered back to the old 1 per cent rate. Both of these factors meant that VAT resources would be depleted and it follows that the GNP related source will become progressively more important. Indeed by 1999 the VAT share of budget revenue, which was 54 per cent in 1991, could fall to around 35 per cent, and the GNP related element could rise to about 50 per cent.

The European Council agreed to put a rising quantity of resources into the new Cohesion Fund. In addition, the bulk of the other structural spending was to be directed to Objective 1 regions. These are regions where the per capita income is less than 75 per cent of the Community average. Altogether the poorer states (e.g. Spain, Portugal, Greece and Ireland) did extremely well out of the negotiations. Incidentally, by 1993 Spain had become a major net beneficiary, but the Danes were still holding on to their net beneficiary position.

Whilst the CAP has been further reformed (see Chapter 8), it would be a great mistake to assume that agricultural spending in real terms will fall. Table 2 shows it to be on a rising trend but Table 3 also shows that as a proportion of budget spending it will fall whilst structural spending will rise.

The data in Tables 2 and 3 reflects the positions prior to the EFTA enlargement. Ex-EFTA states will be net contributors but, as we saw in Chapter 1, they gained a temporary delay in moving to that position.

Borrowing powers

So far the emphasis in revenue raising has been on taxing. Governments can raise revenue by borrowing, and so can the Community. A power to borrow has been enjoyed by the ECSC since its inception. Under Article 54 of the Paris Treaty the old High

Table 2. The Community Budget Delors II European Council Agreement December 1992 Financial Perspective Table

	Appropriations for commitments (ECU million 1992 prices)						
	1993	1994	1995	1996	1997	1998	1999
Agricultural Guideline	35,230	35,095	35,722	36,364	37,023	37,697	38,389
Structural actions	21,277	21,885	23,480	24,990	26,526	28,240	30,000
(a) Cohesion Fund	1,500	1,750	2,000	2,250	2,500	2,550	2,600
(b) Structural Funds & other Operations	19,777	20,135	21,480	22,740	24,026	25,690	27,400
—of which Objective 1 Regions*	12,328	13,220	14,300	15,330	16,396	17,820	19,280
Internal Policies	3,940	4,084	4,323	4,520	4,710	4,910	5,100
External Action	3,950	4,000	4,280	4,560	4,830	5,180	5,600
Administrative expenditure	3,280	3,380	3,580	3,690	3,800	3,850	3,900
Reserves	1,500	1,500	1,100	1,100	1,100	1,100	1,100
(a) Monetary Reserve	1,000	1,000	500	500	500	500	500
(b) External action							
—of which emergency aid	200	200	300	300	300	300	300
—loan guarantees	300	300	300	300	300	300	300
Total Commitment Approps.	69,177	69,944	72,485	75,224	77,989	80,977	84,089
Appropriations for Payments Required	65,908	67,036	69,150	71,290	74,491	77,249	80,114
Payment Approps. as a % of GNP	1.20	1.19	1.20	1.21	1.23	1.25	1.26
Margin for unforeseen expenditure (% GNP)	0.01	0.01	0.01	0.01	0.01	0.01	0.01
Own resources (% GNP)	1.20	1.20	1.21	1.22	1.24	1.26	1.27
Total external expenditure	4,450	4,500	4,880	5,160	5,430	5,780	6,200

The inflation rate applicable for the budget is 4.3%

Note: * Lagging behind.
Source: European Council, *Conclusions of the Presidency*, 11–12 December 1992 (Edinburgh).

Table 3. Allocation of Commitment Appropriations 1992 and 1999

	1992	1999
CAP	53.1	45.7
Structural	27.9	35.7
Internal (e.g. RT&D)	6.0	6.0
External Action (i.e. Aid)	5.5	6.7
Administration	6.0	4.6
Reserve	1.5	1.3
	100	100

Authority and now the Commission can borrow on the international capital market with a view to lending to coal and steel enterprises in connection with expansion and modernization programmes. Under Article 56 it can also lend to create new employment opportunities, in or outside the coal and steel industries, for redundant coal and steel workers. Although the Commission can make grants under the Paris Treaty, borrowed funds must not be used for that purpose (Article 51). Originally the EC Commission did not enjoy such a borrowing power. Nor, as we have seen, was there any question of automatically allowing budget expenditure to exceed tax revenue and financing the deficit by borrowing. The budget must balance. The EIB does, of course, enjoy substantial borrowing powers, and more will be said on that topic in Chapter 9. Subsequently, however, the EC acquired its own (non-budget) borrowing powers. The first power was taken in 1975 and was designed to raise money on the international capital market in order to lend on to member states in balance of payments difficulties. Loans to Italy and Ireland were authorized in 1976. More recently, loans were made to France (1983), Greece (1985) and Portugal (1986–91 – see Chapter 1 on Portuguese accession). The other EC power, which goes under the title of the New Community Instrument (the so-called Ortoli Facility), came into existence in 1978. On the basis of it the EC raises long-term loans on the international capital market and then passes the money over to the EIB which uses it to make loans for investment projects. Loans have been primarily provided for infrastructure investments connected with regional development; energy projects which have helped the Community to attain greater independence, security and diversification in its energy supplies;

promotion of innovation and new technologies (particularly in small and medium-sized firms); and reconstruction after earthquake disasters (Italy).

4

TARIFF BARRIERS AND THE CUSTOMS UNION

The immediate aim of the Rome Treaty was to promote the process of economic integration. Economic integration involves the removal of barriers to the free movement of goods, services, factors of production and possibly money, and the creation of a situation in which the national economies are increasingly interconnected and enmeshed. Such a state of integration could be achieved by a planning mechanism. Let us think purely of the trade in goods. Country 1 could be instructed to produce good A and country 2 could be commanded to produce good B and so forth. They could also be commanded to exchange their surpluses of A and B and a price could be prescribed – i.e. so much A for so much B. However, the predominant economic mode of operation in Western Europe did not admit of such an arrangement. The integration of economies had to arise through competitive trade interpenetration. In simplistic terms, if country 1 was indeed more efficient at producing good A, then removal of trade barriers would enable it to expand its sales of A to country 2 whose industry would contract. If country 2 was more efficient at producing good B, its B industry would expand if the barriers to trade were removed. It would sell B to country 1 whose industry would consequently contract. The two countries would become enmeshed in beneficial trade exchanges (we are assuming that in each country unemployed factors could shift from declining to expanding industries). Such free competition is indeed at the very heart of the Rome Treaty, and to that end Article 3(g) calls for the creation of conditions of undistorted competition.

The reader will recollect that the Rome Treaty envisages the creation of a common market. That is to say the participating parties agree to remove tariffs, quotas, etc., on trade flowing between them and also agree to apply a common level of tariff on goods entering the EC from without. The Rome Treaty refers to the latter as the common customs tariff but we will call it the common external tariff. In addition, the common market arrangement also envisages the free movement of factors of production such as labour, capital and enterprise. It is, however, important to note that some integration theorists have argued that even limited exercises in economic integration are capable of giving rise to spillover effects which may indeed lead to the process of economic integration proceeding further than was originally envisaged. The following is an example of a possible spillover effect. Assume that a group of countries has indeed embarked on a limited economic integration exercise which involves the free movement of goods, services and factors but excludes monetary matters. Because of the latter, exchange rates are free to rise and fall as market forces dictate. Subsequent experience may suggest that flexible exchange rates inhibit the flow of goods, services and factors. This arises from the uncertainties which are associated with exchange-rate volatility. It may therefore be argued that flexible exchange rates should be replaced by fixed rates. But exchange rates cannot remain fixed unless the monetary conditions in the member states are harmonized so as to give rise to uniform rates of inflation (or deflation). Such harmonization would require that national sovereignty over monetary matters would have to be given up in favour of Community monetary coordination or even one Community currency controlled by a Community authority. This is what is meant by a spillover effect. It implies that although the member states may embark on a limited integration exercise they may be remorselessly driven down the path to greater and greater economic integration. That at least was the expectation entertained by some theorists. Subsequent chapters will reveal to what extent that expectation has been fulfilled.

Having contemplated this longer-term possibility, we now return to the point that at least as far as the trade in goods was concerned the Rome Treaty's immediate requirement was for the creation of a customs union – i.e. internal free trade and a common external tariff. We shall begin by considering each of these two elements.

The removal of internal protection

It will be recalled that Article 3 of the Treaty sets down the basic objectives of the EC. Article 3(a) calls upon the member states to eliminate customs duties and quantitative restrictions (quotas, etc.)

on the import and export of goods in intra-Community trade, and it also requires the members to abolish all other charges and measures having the equivalent effect of customs duties and quantitative restrictions. Article 9 reiterates this specific requirement and Articles 10 to 17 and 30 to 37 contain associated implementing powers, provisions and exclusions. The exclusions of Article 36 are particularly important and we shall come back to them later.

The member states therefore imposed upon themselves four obligations. They agreed to remove (a) import (and export) duties; (b) charges having the equivalent effect of import (and export) duties; (c) quantitative restrictions; (d) measures having the equivalent effect of quantitative restrictions.

The reader will recall from Chapter 1 that at the time of the negotiation of the Rome Treaty the French, particularly, were anxious about the transition period to be allowed for tariff removal. In the event it was decided that the period should be twelve years so that all tariffs would have to be eliminated by 31 December 1969. Table 4 shows the progress in tariff reduction on industrial goods and indicates that the original Six accomplished their tariff disarmament ahead of schedule. When the UK, Ireland and Denmark joined the Community on 1 January 1973 they were allowed a five-year period within which to dismantle their various forms of protection. Greece, which became a full member on 1 January 1981, was given a similar period within which to adapt, while Spain and Portugal, which became full members on 1 January 1986, were given seven years.[1] The new EFTA members were of course already involved in a free trade system with the Community.

We noted above that member states accepted an obligation to eliminate charges which have the equivalent effect of import (and export) duties. The Italian Government, for example, was in the habit of applying what it called a statistical levy to imports and exports. The Commission pointed out that this was the equivalent of a customs duty and should be eliminated. When the Italian Government refused to comply, the matter was referred to the Court of Justice, which upheld the Commission's action.

In addition, member states were required to remove quantitative

1. During these transition periods all forms of protection – i.e. tariffs, quotas and equivalent charges and measures – had to be removed.

Table 4. Internal tariff reductions of the EEC (per cent)

	1.1.59	1.7.60	Acceleration of 1.1.61	1.1.62	Acceleration of 1.7.62	1.7.63	1.1.65	1.1.66	1.7.67	Acceleration of 1.7.68
Individual reductions made on 1 January 1957 level	10	10	10	10	10	10	10	10	5	15
Cumulative reduction	10	20	30	40	50	60	70	80	85	100

Source: EEC Commission, *Tenth General Report on the Activities of the Community*, OOPEC. 1067, p. 66.

restrictions on intra-Community trade. Clearly high on the list were quotas. Article 30 calls for the abolition of import quotas – they were to be eliminated by the original Six by the end of the transition period. Article 34 also required the abolition of the export variety – a shorter timespan was envisaged for their removal. In practice, quota disarmament gave rise to no great difficulty as by the time the Rome Treaty was signed such quantitative restrictions were no longer the hindrance to trade that they had been in the period immediately following the Second World War. The fact that quotas had ceased to be a major problem was due to measures of liberalization evolved within the framework of the IMF, the GATT and, above all, the OEEC.

Not only were quantitative restrictions to be eliminated but also measures having an equivalent effect were to be removed. What, it may be asked, are these equivalent measures? The answer is that there are many types and we shall content ourselves with one example which will serve to indicate the general nature of the problem. A particularly good instance was provided by the *Cassis de Dijon* case which we shall return to in Chapter 5. Cassis de Dijon is a French liqueur manufactured from blackcurrants. The German company Rewe-Zentral AG sought to import the French liqueur and requested an authorization from the West German Federal Monopoly Administration for Spirits. The latter informed Rewe that West German law forbade the sale of liqueurs with less than 32 per cent alcohol content although for liqueurs of the Cassis type a minimum of 25 per cent was allowed. This was no help to the Cassis importer as Cassis had an alcoholic content of only 15–20 per cent and thus it was illegal to import it. Rewe contested the ban in the German courts and the matter was referred to the Court of Justice for a preliminary ruling. The Court declared that the German law in question was in these specific circumstances an equivalent measure of the kind prohibited under Article 30 of the Rome Treaty. The minimum alcoholic content rule had in this particular case the effect of a zero import quota.

From all that had gone before it would appear that member states are obliged to eliminate *all* forms of protection. The obvious question which arises is – is this obligation absolute? Are there any escape clauses? There are in fact two possible major loopholes.

The first is provided by Article 109i. It is to be found in the section of the Rome Treaty devoted to macro-economic policy. Article 109i allows a member state to take protective measures when it experiences a sudden crisis in its balance of payments. No limit is placed on the protective measures which could be applied so that, in principle, tariffs, quotas, etc., could be reimposed. However, in practice this is not a realistic possibility for the following reasons. Article 109i requires that any protective measures must cause the least disturbance to the functioning of the Common Market and must not be wider in scope than is strictly necessary in order to remedy the sudden difficulty. Altogether more important is the point that a member state, having applied such protection, is not free to retain it. The Council of Ministers has the power, certain procedural requirements having been met, to amend or indeed to abolish protective measures. In practice, if a member state experienced balance of payments problems it would be expected to pursue courses other than protectionism and facilities exist to enable it to do so. In the first place credit arrangements exist within the Community under the EMS (for as long as it exists) and the 1975 loan arrangement, as well as externally via the IMF, which would enable the member state to finance the deficit whilst other policy measures were being introduced which would eventually rectify the problem. In addition Article 109h empowers the Council of Ministers to grant mutual assistance to a state in balance of payments difficulties. The state could deflate demand, thus reducing imports and forcing goods into the export market, and in the longer term deflation might be expected to restore international price competitiveness. Even membership of the EMS super-snake has not in practice precluded devaluations of the exchange rate, and this would be another possible avenue to a restoration of competitiveness. Domestic interest rates could also be raised and this could encourage a helpful inflow of foreign currencies. All this freedom of action would of course disappear under conditions of full EMU. Under the original Rome Treaty if a balance of payments deficit was at least in part associated with capital movements and if those capital movements disturbed the working of the capital market in the member state, then protective measures, but only relating to capital movements, could be introduced under old Article 73. But following Maastricht all this has changed. In the run up to EMU, new Article 73b lays down that all restrictions on the movement of capital shall

be abolished although in some cases this can be put off until the
end of 1995. The upshot of all this is that while restoration of tariff
and other protection is possible *de jure, de facto* it is not normally a
serious option.

The other loophole is to be found in Article 36. It declares that
member states may, under certain circumstances, continue to apply
quantitative restrictions and measures having equivalent effect. It
does not, however, allow member states to retain tariffs. Restrictions
on imports or exports can be maintained when they are:

justified on grounds of public morality, public policy or public security; the
protection of health and life of humans, animals or plants; the protection of
national treasures possessing artistic, historic or archaeological value; or the
protection of industrial or commercial property.

The concepts of public morality, policy and security are not easy
to define and differences of national interpretation are likely; indeed
the Court of Justice is prepared to allow a margin for national
discretion. The protection of public morality has been invoked as
grounds for a ban on imports of pornographic material. The second
clause obviously allows member states to prevent the importation
of dangerous drugs, foodstuffs containing dangerous additives, and
animals and plants which may spread diseases and so forth. Bans
may also be placed on the export of national treasures.[1] Finally, it
would appear that the safeguarding of patents, trademarks and
copyrights may also justify the application of protection.

Article 36 does, however, throw up some knotty problems. We
know that member states do seek to protect their citizens by laying
down standards in respect of drugs, foodstuffs, etc. Such standards
may differ between states, and to that extent trade is prevented. On
the face of it, Article 36 legitimizes the laying down of such
protective standards. Were that the end of the matter then trade
could be severely impeded. In order to circumvent that problem
Article 100 provides for the possibility of standards being harmonized. Such standards can continue to protect citizens but by being
uniform they allow goods to cross frontiers. We shall return to this
point in Chapter 5. The provision relating to commercial and
industrial property also poses a difficulty. On the one hand Article

1. Provided they are outside the area of commercial exploitation.

36 seems to permit the restriction of imports on the grounds of the need to protect such property, but this conflicts with the concept of goods being free to move between markets, and the latter is central to the idea of a common market. Which principle, we may ask, should prevail? We shall return to this topic in Chapter 5.

Two final points remain to be made. We have seen that, subject to certain very limited exceptions, the free movement of goods is a cardinal principle of the Rome Treaty. The other cardinal principle of the treaty is that there must be no discrimination on grounds of nationality. This principle is set out in Article 7, and it provides a reinforcing general authority for the attack on a wide range of barriers to trade. The other point relates to dumping. The prevention of dumping normally provides grounds on which a state may take protective action. Anti-dumping powers do not, however, exist in respect of intra-Community trade. It is of course possible that a cartel or a dominant firm might finance loss-making export sales out of monopoly profits made in the home market. If such was the case then the appropriate remedial action would have to be based on Articles 85 and 86. (The nature of these anti-trust powers is discussed in Chapter 5.) Alternatively, such loss-making sales might be financed by the state, in which case remedial action would have to be based on Articles 92 to 94 which relate to state aids. (We also discuss these powers in Chapter 5.)

The common external tariff and related issues

The customs union element of the Community arrangement requires the member states to establish a common external tariff (CET). Article 9 reiterates this specific requirement and Articles 10 to 11 and 18 to 29 contain associated implementing powers and provisions. We should also note that Article 3(b) calls for the creation of a common commercial policy towards third countries.

In accordance with Article 18, the original common external tariff was calculated on the basis of an unweighted average of the import duties of the four customs territories (Germany, France, Italy and the Benelux Customs Union) on 1 January 1957. There was, however, a series of lists of commodities in respect of which rates of duty other than those based on the simple averaging rule were to apply. Taking the structure of imports into the Community

Table 5. The creation of the common external tariff (per cent)

	Acceler-ation of 1.1.61	1.1.62	Acceler-ation of 1.7.63	1.1.66	1.7.68
Industrial products adjustment	30		30		40
cumulative adjustment	30		60		100
Agricultural products adjustment		30		30	40
cumulative adjustment		30		60	100

Source: EEC Commission, *Tenth General Report on the Activities of the Community*, OOPEC, 1967, p. 66.

in 1958 as a base, it appears that the unweighted average incidence of the original common external tariff was 7.6 per cent whilst the weighted average was 9.1 per cent. However, these figures conceal considerable variations. Whereas the average incidence for raw materials was 0.1 per cent, that for capital goods was 12.5 per cent and in the case of industrial products 17.3 per cent.

The Community subsequently took part in international tariff negotiations within the GATT which reduced the level of the external tariff. The Dillon Round (1960–61) led to a cut of 7–8 per cent while the Kennedy Round (1964–7) resulted in the further fall of 35–40 per cent. Subsequently the EC was involved in the some-what protracted Tokyo Round (1973–9). This was planned to lead to a reduction of about a third over an eight-year period which began in 1980.[1] The Community was satisfied that this cut would still preserve a reasonable degree of protection for its producers. A further cut in the external tariff has emerged from the more recent Uruguay Round of tariff negotiations. These came after bitter disputes concerning the EC's farm policy and its tendency to pro-duce surpluses – see the discussion of the CAP in Chapter 8.

Although Article 23 merely envisaged that the Six would align their import tariffs on the common level by not later than the end of the transitional period, in fact the alignment was completed by 1 July 1968 – see Table 5. Under the terms of the accession treaties,

1. In fact the Community decided to speed up the process. The final cut was brought forward from 1 January 1987 to 1 January 1986.

new members were given five- or seven-year periods within which to bring their tariffs into line although, with limited exceptions, the new ex-EFTA members were required to conform immediately

We turn now to the common commercial policy referred to in Article 3(b). The key provisions are to be found in Articles 110, 112, 113 and 115. According to Article 113 such a policy will be based:

on uniform principles, particularly in regard to changes in tariff rates, the conclusion of tariff and trade agreements, the achievement of uniformity in measures of liberalization, export policy and measures to protect trade such as those to be taken in case of dumping or subsidies.

One of the most important aspects of the common commercial policy particularly after the single market is that member states cease to be free unilaterally to determine the level of tariff and quota protection *vis-à-vis* third countries. Thus if changes in the level of the common external tariff are to be negotiated (as for example in the Tokyo and Uruguay rounds) or if quotas are to be negotiated in respect of imports (as is the case in the Multi-Fibre agreements[1]) then Article 113 implies that the Council of Ministers will lay down the guidelines and the Commission will do the bargaining. When the negotiations are finalized they will be adopted by the Council of Ministers (according to the Treaty this will be done on a qualified majority basis) and are then binding on the individual member states.

Protective action against dumping *by third countries* is possible. But it is important to note that individual member states are not empowered to initiate protection. This (other than on an interim basis) is the prerogative of the Council of Ministers acting on a proposal of the Commission. Moreover, such a protective response is permitted only when the dumping threatens to cause, or actually causes, material injury to a *Community* industry. Normally, damage suffered by a national segment of a Community industry will not provide sufficient grounds to launch an action.

However, we should not conclude that injury suffered by a national industry as a result of imports from third countries can never justify protective action. Regulations have been introduced

1. See Chapter 10.

which enable *quotas* to be applied to imports from third countries or state trading nations where the increase of such imports threatens a national industry. A member state may take such protective action on an emergency basis but that action can be revoked by the Commission. In the absence of a revocation other member states can appeal to the Council of Ministers to terminate the protection. Once again we see that member states are not normally free to impose unilateral protection permanently.

In 1984 a new development occurred when the Community adopted what has come to be called the New Commercial Policy Instrument. Unlike the above two measures, it can be invoked against illicit practices which affect Community exports to the rest of the world as well as Community imports. When such illicit practices are proved to exist, various retaliatory actions can be introduced by the Council of Ministers, including increasing the level of import duties and the application of quotas.

The growth of trade interdependence

It would hardly be surprising if the removal of internal protection and its retention *vis-à-vis* the rest of the world led to the Community becoming more interdependent in terms of trade. This indeed happened. Intra-Community exports as a proportion of total exports and as a proportion of Gross Domestic Product increased quite markedly – see Table 6.

The basic theory of a customs union

We have now seen how the Treaty has required the member states to construct a customs union, and we have seen something of its effects. It is now appropriate to consider what economic theory has to say about customs unions. Present understanding of the theoretical implications of such arrangements is based on the pioneer study of the subject by Professor Jacob Viner. The issues involved were subsequently developed by Professor James Meade and others. What follows is an elementary analysis based on Meade's basic theoretical formulation. This is designed for readers who do not have any knowledge, or only a limited knowledge, of economic analysis. Those who have some knowledge may prefer the partial

Table 6. Intra-Community exports

	% of Total Exports		% of GDP		
	1958	1980	1958	1973	1980
Benelux	35	71	15.0	35	38
Denmark	58	50	14.0	10	13
Germany	35	48	5.4	9	11
France	28	51	2.5	8	9
Ireland	83	74	19.0	25	36
Italy	32	48	2.7	7	9
Netherlands	57	73	19.0	29	34
United Kingdom	20	42	2.8	6	9
The Nine	34	53	4.9	10	13

Source: EC Commission, *The Economy of the European Community*, OOPEC 1982, p. 24.

equilibrium approach which follows the elementary analysis and should regard the exposition immediately below merely as an introduction to the problem.

Elementary analysis

An important point which emerges is that the advantages of trade liberalization within the framework of such a union need to be kept in perspective. Customs unions *per se* are not so unambiguously beneficial as is universal free trade. Classical economists, such as David Ricardo, were able to demonstrate theoretically that the universal elimination of protection, particularly if it was at a high level, would lead to a great increase in world welfare.[1] Each country would specialize in the production of those goods for which it was best fitted – in economists' language, countries would specialize in producing those goods in respect of which they had a comparative advantage. Taking the world as a whole, greater production would result than if countries insisted on protecting their industries and producing all or most of the goods which they needed. The division of the increase of production would, of course, depend on the terms

1. We ignore special arguments for protection, for example that relating to infant industries.

of trade – i.e. the rate at which one country's specialism(s) exchanges for other countries' specialisms. But we cannot conclude that because a customs union involves an element of freeing of trade it likewise is unambiguously beneficial. Quite evidently a customs union is not a case of universal free trade – it represents free trade within a bloc and discrimination against the rest of the world. Thus in appraising the results of a customs union, two effects have to be distinguished. One is trade creation, which represents an improvement in resource utilization, and the other is trade diversion, which narrowly defined[1] represents a deterioration. These two effects are illustrated in Table 7. We assume the following:

1. The world consists of two countries, I and II, which wish to form a customs union, and a third outside country which we term country III.
2. Only three commodities are produced – A, B and C.
3. Prior to the customs union, country I applied a 50 per cent *ad valorem* tariff to all imports, but after the formation of the union the tariff applies only to imports from country III.
4. Transport costs can be ignored.

Taking good A first, the lowest-cost producer is country III, which lies outside the proposed union. Before the union, good A produced by country III (with duty applied) undersells A produced by country I, or A produced by country II (with duty applied). But after the union is created, A produced in country II no longer has duty applied to it and as a result undersells A produced in country III (bearing duty) and A produced in country I. This is called trade diversion. In the case of good B the lowest-cost producer is country II. But even prior to the union B produced in country II does not enter country I. This arises because the customs duty renders B produced in country II uncompetitive with B produced in country I. But after the union is created B produced in country II no longer has a customs duty applied and it enters country I and undersells B produced in country I. Here we have trade creation. In the case of good C, the lowest-cost producer is country I. It produces the good before and after the union. As a result neither trade diversion nor trade creation occurs.

1. The meaning of the phrase 'narrowly defined' will become apparent later in this chapter.

It follows that in assessing the effects of a customs union we have to take into account that it can shift production away from the lowest-cost producer to a higher-cost member of the union. Such trade diversion is a departure from a previously more rational pattern of resource allocation. On the other hand, the creation of the union can shift production away from a less efficient to a more efficient member of the union and such trade creation represents a shift towards a more efficient pattern of resource allocation. As a first approximation, therefore, we can conclude that whether or not a customs union is beneficial depends on the balance of these two effects.

How can the balancing be carried out? In the case of good A in Table 7, suppose that country I imports one million units first from country III and then from country II. The original cost was therefore £12 million but is now £14 million.[1] The cost of trade diversion – the extra cost incurred by virtue of obtaining supplies from the higher-cost source – is therefore £2 million. In the case of good B, suppose country I consumes half a million units; then the saving of trade creation is £2.5 million. On balance therefore, taking account of production effects only, the customs union is beneficial.[2]

This analysis, like all simplifying devices, has its strengths and its weaknesses. Its strength is that it does enable us to see how the customs union can lead to both improvements and deteriorations in resource allocation. It does so via the production effects – a shift to a more efficient source of supply (as in good B) leads to a production gain whilst a shift to a less efficient source of supply (as in good A) leads to a production loss. Its main weakness is that it is based on a number of simplifying assumptions. Not the least of these is the point that demand for the goods in question is totally price inelastic. That is to say when price falls, because of the change in the tariff level, the quantity consumed does not change. This assumption rules out consumption effects. We shall be able to take consumption

1. This cost is calculated exclusive of tariff, the point being that although consumers in country I pay the tariff, the proceeds of the tariff accrue to the government of country I which we will assume provides its consumers with an equivalent and thus compensating quantity of free goods. The cost to consumers of the tariff is therefore not material to the argument. The material point is the cost *net of tariff* of obtaining supplies of good A (and good B) from alternative sources.
2. We can ignore good C since there was no change from pre- to post-union.

Table 7. Trade creation and trade diversion (£)

Good	Cost or cost plus duty per unit	Country III exporting to country I	Flow of trade	Goods produced by country I	Flow of trade	Country II exporting to country I	Results
A	Cost	12		20		14	Trade diversion
	Cost plus duty prior to customs union	18	↑	20	No trade	21	
	Cost plus duty after customs union	18	No trade	20	↓	14	
B	Cost	14	No trade: country I produces B	17	No trade: country I produces B	12	Trade creation
	Cost plus duty prior to customs union	21		17		18	
	Cost plus duty after customs union	21	No trade	17	↓	12	
C	Cost	16	No trade	10	↓	12	Neither trade creation nor trade diversion. Country I is the lowest-cost producer and provides C before and after the union
	Cost plus duty prior to customs union	24	No trade	10	No trade	18	
	Cost plus duty after customs union	24	No trade	10	No trade	12	

effects into account when we adopt the partial equilibrium approach to which we now turn.

The partial equilibrium approach

Before we endeavour to apply partial equilibrium analysis to a customs union we need to acquaint ourselves with the welfare effects of tariffs. It will perhaps be helpful if we begin by considering the situation where a country which has applied a tariff then decides to remove it. This will throw up some of the relevant effects which also arise when a country decides to participate in a customs union and is therefore required to lower some of its tariffs. When we have acquainted ourselves with the relevant effects of removing a tariff we can move on to apply these ideas to customs union situations.

In Figure 4 we show country I's domestic demand curve dd, and country I's domestic supply curve ss, for good A. The supply curve ss has the normal positive slope – it indicates that the industry within country I supplying good A will be disposed to supply more per unit of time the higher the price of the good. The dd demand curve has the normal negative slope – it indicates that consumers in country I will be disposed to demand more per unit of time the lower the price of the good.

Since we are dealing with tariffs and trade we now have to recognize that there is a competing source of supply of good A in the form of imports from the rest of the world. This is represented by the supply curve SS(W)1. This is drawn as a perfectly elastic supply curve. The assumption here is that the imports of country I represent only a very small part of the demand for the good in question in the world market. Country I is therefore a price taker – it must take the price of imports of good A as being determined in the world market by world supply and demand. Whether it imports a little or a lot of A it will not drive the price down or up by so doing. We are in fact assuming that there is no terms of trade effect arising from country I importing good A.[1]

If we assume that there are no tariffs then we can say that the

---

1. We shall assume throughout the chapter that the supply curves of countries other than country I are perfectly elastic.

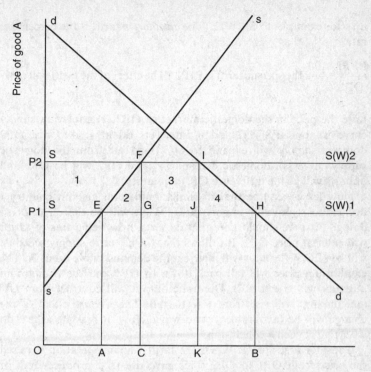

Figure 4. Welfare effects of a tariff

price in the domestic market of country I will be OP1. This follows from the intersection of the supply curve sES(W)1 with the demand curve dd at H. The equilibrium price is OP1 (the price at which imports enter the domestic market). Domestic demand is OB, and domestic supply is OA (read off from the domestic supply curve ss), and imports will be the difference, i.e. AB in quantity.

Let us first assume that country I decides unilaterally to adopt a protective stance by applying an import tariff. Whether the tariff be *ad valorem* (i.e. a certain percentage on the import price) or specific (i.e. a certain absolute sum imposed on the import price) the effect on the supply curve of imports SS(W)1 will be to cause it to shift up – for example, to SS(W)2. (The *ad valorem* tariff is the percentage rate

$$\frac{P1\ P2}{OP1} \cdot \frac{100}{1}; \text{the specific tariff is P1P2.)}$$ The effect of the tariff will be to

raise the price in the domestic market to OP2. The relevant supply curve is now sFS(W)2 and it intersects dd at I. At price OP2 domestic supply will expand to OC (read off from the domestic supply curve ss), domestic demand at price OP2 will be OK, and imports will be the difference CK in quantity.

Now let us assume that in similar unilateral fashion country I decides to remove its import tariff. What will be the effect of so doing? First we should note that imports, now being free of tariff, will enter at price OP1. It follows that the effective supply schedule will be sES(W)1 and it will intersect the demand curve dd at H. The equilibrium price will fall back down to OP1 and the equilibrium quantity will rise to OB. Domestic output will contract from OC and imports will rise from CK to AB. The *welfare* effect of the change will be favourable in two ways. How, it may be asked, do we arrive at such a conclusion?

Consider first area 1. When the tariff was in operation it raised the price from OP1 to OP2. This gave rise to a producer rent or surplus equal to the area sP2F – i.e. the cost of production was only OsFC (the area under the supply curve) but producers actually received OP2FC. When the tariff was removed and the price fell, producer rent declined by the amount of area 1. Taking country I as a whole, no gain or loss arises. Producers lose area 1 but consumers enjoy a counterbalancing benefit in that they pay that much less. There is a straight transfer of benefit, and if we attach no welfare significance to the redistribution then we can say that area 1 is neutral in its effect on welfare.

Consider now area 2 – this does represent a positive welfare gain. More precisely we can say that a production effect arises which takes the form of a production gain. When country I originally applied the import tariff the effect was to cause its output of A to rise from OA to OC. As a result it sustained a production loss since quantity AC was originally imported at cost AEGC whereas the cost of producing AC domestically is AEFC – a production loss of

EFG therefore arose. However, when country I reduces its tariff domestic output falls from OC to OA – i.e. by AC. This generates a production gain since by reversing the previous logic we know that AC obtained by importation costs only AEGC whereas AC when domestically produced costs AEFC. It is important to note that this net gain does presume that the resources previously used to produce AC can be transferred to alternative uses. Indeed their value in alternative uses will be AEFC so there is no doubt that country I has gained by being able to import AC at a lower cost than that which it would incur if it produced it itself.

Now let us focus on area 3. When the tariff was operating, this area represented the tariff revenue which accrued to the government. Let us assume that as a result the government supplied its citizens with free goods such as schools and parks. When the tariff was removed the government would no longer have the revenue to supply these free goods but, on the other hand, consumers would be paying a reduced amount for imports and that reduction would be equal to area 3. The fact that consumers pay less for good A offsets the fact that they no longer receive free goods. Again we shall attach no welfare significance to any redistribution of income which might result.[1]

Finally there is area 4 – here too there is a positive welfare gain. More precisely we can say that there is a consumption effect which takes the form of a consumption gain. This is new to our analysis – it arises because the abolition of the tariff causes the price to fall and demand or consumption to extend. Our earlier elementary analysis of customs unions precluded this possibility because we assumed that demand was totally price inelastic.

The origin of this consumer gain is connected with the concept of consumer surplus, which is illustrated in Figure 5. When the import tariff is not operating, the price of good A will be OP1. Consumers will purchase OB and pay OP1 per unit, so their total expenditure will be OP1 HB. However, the welfare they derive from consuming OB is greater than this. For example, there are some consumers who value the good so highly that they will be prepared to pay as

---

1. Quite clearly redistribution can occur. If good A was luxury yachts then rich citizens would gain by lower prices and this would then help to offset their loss of free goods. On the other hand poor citizens, who presumably do not purchase luxury yachts, would have nothing to offset their loss of free goods.

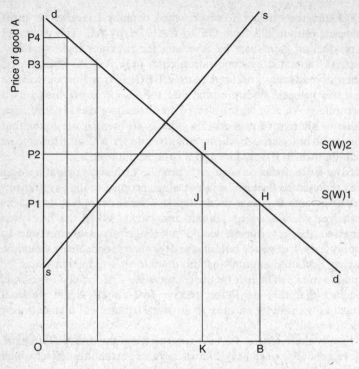

Figure 5. Consumer surplus and consumer gain

much as price OP4 and there are others who will be prepared to pay somewhat less, i.e. OP3, and so on. We shall assume that the price they are willing to pay is a measure of the utility or welfare they derive, or expect to derive, from consuming the good. In practice they all pay OP1, but if we take the price consumers are *willing* to pay as an indicator of the welfare they derive, then in total the latter is equal to the area under the demand curve, i.e. OdHB. The excess of the area under the demand curve over the amount they actually pay – P1dH – is called consumer surplus. The application of the tariff reduces consumption from OB to OK, i.e. by KB. The welfare loss in respect of good A is therefore the area under the demand curve, i.e. KIHB. However, expenditure equal to

KJHB can be transferred to other goods and, following the equimarginal principle, the utility or welfare per unit of expenditure on the other goods will not be greater than that which is enjoyed on the OBth unit of good A. Therefore when the expenditure is transferred to those other goods the welfare they produce will not be greater than KJHB. Therefore there is a net loss of welfare – a consumption loss – equal to JIH. It also follows that if the tariff is removed consumption of good A will increase by KB. Consumption spending will be transferred from those other goods to good A. The welfare lost on the other goods will be KJHB but the welfare derived from the extra KB of good A will be KIHB and so there will be a net gain of welfare – equal to JIH.

By way of recapitulation we can say that of the four areas only areas 2 and 4 constitute welfare changes. Indeed these areas, often called Marshallian triangles, respectively represent the production and consumption gains which country I derives from unilaterally abolishing its tariff.[1]

We can now proceed to apply this type of analysis to a customs union. We shall identify two cases. The first gives rise to trade creation, the second to trade diversion together with an element of trade creation.

In Figure 6 we show the usual domestic demand and supply curves dd and ss for country I. We now have to introduce supply curves of imports from country II, who will be the customs union partner, and country III, who will remain outside the union. The relative position of the supply curves of these two latter countries is important. In other words it is important whether the more efficient of the two is inside or outside the union.

In Figure 6, SS(CII)1 is the supply curve of country II and SS(CIII)1, the supply curve of country III, in both cases before tariff. Prior to the union, country I applies a non-discriminatory tariff – that is to say it applies the same tariff to imports irrespective of where they come from. The tariff of course raises the supply curve of both outside countries but because country II is the more efficient, its supply curve with tariff – SS(CII)2 – lies below the

---

1. The welfare benefit is easily measured. We know the former tariff was P1 P2 and that the increase in imports was AB minus CK. The product of these multiplied by one half approximates areas 2 + 4.

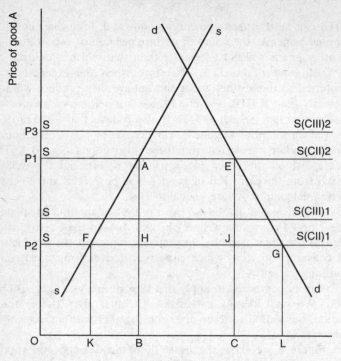

Figure 6. Pure trade creation

supply curve with tariff of country III, i.e. SS(CIII)2. It follows that the effective supply curve prior to the union is sAS(CII)2 and it intersects dd at E. It follows that the equilibrium price prior to the union is OP1. Domestic production is OB, domestic consumption is OC and imports are BC. Note that since country II is the lowest cost and therefore most competitive outside supplier it is the source of the imports BC.

Now let us assume that a customs union is formed between countries I and II while country III is discriminated against by having to face the old tariff. (We are in fact assuming in this case and the next one that the common external tariff which countries I and II agree to apply is country I's old non-discriminatory tariff.) Country II can now supply at price OP2 since its supply no longer bears the tariff, whilst country III will only be able to supply at price OP3. The effective supply curve is therefore sFC(II)1. Equilibrium is now at point G where sFC(II)1 and dd intersect. The price falls from OP1 to OP2. Domestic output contracts from OB to OK. Domestic demand expands from OC to OL and imports rise from BC to KL.

In this case we have trade creation. Additional trade is created equal to KB plus CL. This increased trade is also directed towards a more efficient source, i.e. country II. The fall in price causes a shift in production – country I produces less and extra imports KB come from more efficient country II. This gives rise to a production gain FAH. But the fall in price also causes an extension of demand and this is also met by extra imports CL which also come from country II. This gives rise to a consumption gain JEG. Incidentally, we can ignore the areas represented by reduced producer surplus and lost tariff revenue for reasons which were explained in connection with the analysis of the welfare effects of a tariff.[1] One thing is clear – the customs union gives rise to welfare gains and no losses. This result stems from the fact that the most efficient of the two previously outside suppliers is now within the union.

Now we come to our second case, and here we shall observe the existence of a welfare loss of the kind identified by Viner. This second case is illustrated in Figure 7. On this occasion the most efficient source of supply is country III. SS(CIII)1 is the supply curve before tariff of imports from country III, and SS(CII)1 is the supply curve before tariff of imports from country II. Once again we start with a situation where a non-discriminatory tariff is applied to all imports. This causes both supply curves to shift up, but because country III is the more efficient its supply curve with tariff, i.e. SS(CIII)2, lies below that of country II, i.e. SSC(II)2. The effective supply curve is sAS(CIII)2. Equilibrium will be at E, the equilibrium price will be OP1, domestic production will be OB, domestic consumption will be OL and imports will be BL. As country III is the most competitive outside supplier it supplies the imports BL.

Now let us assume that once more countries I and II form a union, while country III is left facing the external tariff. Country II

1. In the second case discussed below the tariff revenue element is, however, relevant.

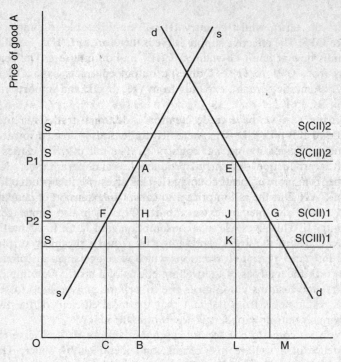

Figure 7. Trade diversion and trade creation

can now supply at price OP2 but country III, although more efficient, can only supply at price OP1 because it has to continue to bear the tariff. The effective supply curve is now sFS(CII)1. Equilibrium point will be at G. The price will fall from OP1 to OP2. Domestic output falls to OC, domestic demand expands to OM and imports rise to CM. *Most significantly, those imports, which used to come from country III, now come from country II.*[1]

How do we assess the welfare effects in this case? Firstly there is a welfare loss in the sense that trade is diverted from a more

---

1. Country III will, however, be no worse off, because the resources originally used to produce good A supplied to country I will now be transferred to other uses where their value productivity will be just as high.

efficient source (country III) to a less efficient source (country II). This as we know arises because the less efficient source is within the union but escapes the tariff, whereas the more efficient source is outside the union and therefore has to go on bearing the tariff. This trade diversion is represented by the rectangle IHJK. This requires a little more explanation. The pre-union level of imports BL used to come from country III and cost BIKL exclusive of tariff. Those imports now come from country II and cost BHJL (they bear no tariff). The extra cost (ignoring tariff) is therefore IHJK. Another way of looking at this development is as follows. Prior to the union country I collected revenue equal to IAEK. The amount consumers paid for imports was consequently inflated by exactly that amount. By way of compensation the revenue was used to provide free goods. After the union there is no tariff revenue and therefore the supply of free goods declines by IAEK but, on the other hand, the amount which consumers pay for imports only declines by the smaller amount HAEJ and the difference – IHJK – is a pure social loss.

However, the new situation is not purely one of welfare loss. The price of good A has fallen, and because of that country I experiences a decline of production and an increase in consumption, and respectively they give rise to a production gain FAH and a consumption gain JEG.

The reader will note the contrast between the two cases. In the first case there is an increase in the original level of trade – which gives rise to welfare gains. In the second case there is a diversion of the original level of trade – which gives rise to a welfare loss – but there is also an increase in the original level of trade which gives rise to welfare gains. The situation is a little less clear-cut than our elementary analysis would suggest – it envisaged nothing but gain in the trade creation situation and nothing but loss in the trade diversion situation.

We can now appreciate the full import of the observation by Viner that customs unions are not unambiguously beneficial. They can give rise to welfare gains but they can also give rise to welfare losses. Thus, in the second case if the Marshallian triangles of production and consumption gain are greater than the rectangle of trade diversion then the customs union leads on balance to a better allocation of resources and greater welfare than the previous protected situation. But if the rectangle is greater than the sum of the triangles then the customs union leads to an inferior allocation of resources and a lower level of welfare than previously.

Economists have also pondered about why groups of countries decide to involve themselves in customs union arrangements. The dilemma has centred on the point that even if in respect of all goods the customs union gave rise to benefits similar to our first case, it would not be superior to a policy of unilateral tariff reduction of the kind which we considered when analysing the welfare effects of a tariff. One solution, which has much to commend it, is that there are other benefits which arise from clubbing together that would not be available if countries merely adopted an independent policy of unilateral tariff reduction. One obvious benefit is the political cohesion which is expected to spill over from economic integration. This manifests itself in terms of greater harmony between the member states, but it also promises to provide them with greater political influence on the world stage than they could hope to enjoy in isolation. On the economic plane the participating states can also enjoy the fruits arising from collective bargaining in the context of international trade and monetary negotiations.

General conclusions

One thing is clear: the static analysis of customs unions does not of itself provide a basis for categorically commending or rejecting them. Whether they are good or bad depends upon the particular circumstances. However, some generalizations do emerge, although it must be admitted that there is no substitute for measurement in deciding the actual results of a union. First, a customs union is more likely to be advantageous on balance if the economies of the partners are actually very competitive but are potentially complementary. If they produce similar products but efficiencies differ, they will each contract their relatively inefficient industries and expand their efficient ones. There will be a beneficial increase in mutual trade without much diversion of imports or exports from other markets. If, on the other hand, their economies are already complementary, the prospects of gains on the production side would be correspondingly small. Secondly, a customs union is more likely to increase economic welfare the higher the initial duties on imports from partners. High duties imply high levels of inefficiency which are being protected. Thus the higher the inefficiencies, the greater the gains from trade after such protection is removed. Thirdly, the production effects of a customs union will be the more advantageous the lower its tariff against the outside world. Fourthly, the greater the proportion of world production, consumption, and trade covered by a union, the more likely it is to raise welfare. The larger the union becomes, the greater the probability that trade creation will outweigh trade diversion, until, in the case of a union embracing the world, trade diversion ceases to exist.

Empirical findings on static effects

There is now an extensive literature on the static effects of customs unions. These studies have attempted to estimate to what extent trade flows have been created and diverted as a result of the EC customs union. Michael Davenport surveyed the various findings. The studies have usually produced a number of alternative estimates, and Table 8 presents the results preferred by those carrying out the studies, or the ones which Davenport felt were based on the most defensible assumptions. There is a fair degree of consensus that trade creating flows have outweighed trade diverting flows. The majority cluster in the range from $7½ billion to $11½ billion for the former and $½ billion to $1 billion for the latter. Davenport points out that if we take trade created as $10 billion and trade diverted as $1 billion then the net 'gain' would be some 10 per cent of the combined imports of goods of the EC at the time, or nearly 2 per cent of Community GDP. This is non-negligible. However, these estimates relate to changes in trade *flows*, which is not the same thing as the welfare effects with which the Marshallian triangles are concerned. Estimates of such static gains suggest that they were less than 1 per cent of the members' combined GNP.

Why is the beneficial effect so limited? One answer is that a rather small part of total production is traded internationally. Thus services, building and much of the purchases of the public sector have not entered into international trade and the net gain from customs unions can only arise in connection with that part of production which is traded. Secondly, as has been pointed out by Nils Lundgren (1969, p. 52), if the removal of protection is to be significant it must have been costly to maintain. However, examples of really costly protection are rare since there is no great political support for such protection. For example, raw materials are normally duty free, largely because the production of them at home would involve astronomic costs. Much the same is true of more specialized commodities such as ships and aircraft. It is important to stress that we are not implying that the gains from international trade are small. On the contrary, because of the uneven geographical distribution of natural resources and so forth, they are enormous. But the fact is that these gains are already being substantially reaped since no one can afford not to reap them, and the existence of a substantial volume of international trade is a proof of this fact. As a consequence further gains from customs unions are bound to be limited.

Dynamic analysis

We may therefore legitimately ask why so much emphasis is placed on the creation of customs unions. The answer is, as we noted earlier, partly political in that the process of economic integration prepares the ground for political unification. But the other reason is that the trade creation/trade diversion analysis of customs unions ignores many of the other advantages which can accrue to the participants. First, a larger market gives rise to opportunities for the fuller exploitation of economies of large-scale production. National markets may not be big enough to enable firms to expand sufficiently to achieve the minimum optimal scale, and such a scale of plant or firm may require the sales area of the much larger Community market. (However, whether this is strictly a dynamic effect as opposed to the once-and-for-all nature of the trade creation/trade diversion static analysis is doubtful. It can be argued that once the economies of scale have been reaped the effect is exhausted and thus it is really static in character.) The much bigger Community market may also enable firms to expand and thus mount the research and development efforts which are necessary if European firms are to compete successfully with their American and Japanese rivals. Secondly, there are some reasons for believing that the intensity of competition may increase as a result of the formation of a union. For example, industrial structures undergo a

Table 8. Estimates of trade creating and trade diverting flows in the EEC[1]

Study	Date	Coverage	Trade Creation ($ billion)	Trade Diversion ($ billion)
Truman	1968	Manufactures	9.2	1.0
Balassa	1970	Manufactures	11.4	0.1
Balassa	1970	All goods	11.3	0.3
Verdoorn and Schwartz	1969	Manufactures	11.1	1.1
Aitken	1967	All goods	9.2	0.6[2]
Kreinin	1969–70	Manufactures	7.3	2.4
Truman	1968	Manufactures and raw materials	1.8	3.0

Notes: 1. Original Six only; 2. Diversion from EFTA only.
Source: M. Davenport, 'The Economic Impact of the EEC' in A. Boltho (ed.), The European Economy Growth and Crisis, Oxford University Press, 1982, Table 8.1, p. 227.

change. National monopolies become Community oligopolies and the situation in established oligopolies becomes more fluid, with a reduction of oligopolistic collusion and mutual awareness. Then again there is a possibility of a psychological change. Thus it has been argued that prior to the formation of the EEC, relations between competitors in the relatively small national market were personal and friendly. Competition manifests itself in the attempts of producers to expand at each other's expense. This was unlikely to happen under such circumstances. However, when trade liberalization occurred firms in one national market could seek to grow not at each other's expense but at the expense of producers in other national markets with whom relations are impersonal. Not only that but producers in those other markets would tend to behave likewise. As a result, every firm would become aware of the fact that its own national market share could no longer be regarded as secure. Because of this they would tend to look less favourably on the preservation of less efficient compatriots. (The competition effect can only be said to be dynamic if it leads to a *sustained* higher rate of investment and/or technological improvement.) Of course, the much more aggressive business behaviour which now exists in the Community is due not only to the opening up of markets, but also to the infiltration of US and Japanese investment which has brought with it more aggressive business strategies and better management techniques. But this infiltration was undoubtedly to a considerable degree the result of the bigger market, or the prospect thereof, which the Rome Treaty opened up, and is in effect another advantage of the customs union from the point of view of the members. The point about foreign influence also emphasizes the fact that access to the enlarged market may not only stimulate a greater level of investment by Community firms but may also attract direct investment from outside Europe.

5

NON-TARIFF BARRIERS IN THE CUSTOMS UNION

Although the EC was able to complete its internal tariff disarmament by the middle of 1968, the task of creating a truly unified market in which goods could move freely was not thereby achieved. There still remained other significant non-tariff barriers (NTBs) which could continue to prevent totally, or in some degree to restrict, or in some way to distort, the flow of intra-Community trade. Some of these factors pose considerably greater difficulties than mere tariffs. We shall discuss the nature of these NTBs, what the Rome Treaty says about them, and what specific actions have been taken by the Commission, Council of Ministers and Court of Justice. It is perhaps worth adding that in dealing with NTBs the focus will be on industrial goods – agricultural goods are of course subject to a separate régime.

Before we turn to a discussion of the various NTBs, it is necessary to point out that by the beginning of the 1980s it was becoming increasingly obvious that although the Community had been in existence for more than twenty years, the creation of a true internal market for goods (and services) had not been achieved. This was of great concern to the Commission, which noted that in the recession which afflicted the Community from the middle of the 1970s onwards, member states had become more protectionist – barriers tended to rise rather than fall. Subsequently the mood changed, and in a series of summits (Copenhagen 1982, Fontainebleau and Dublin 1984, Brussels 1985) the European Council called for the completion of the internal market. However, the creation of an internal market depends upon deeds and not just words. In 1985 the Commission said just that in the White Paper *Completing the Internal Market* (EC Commission, 1985a) presented to the Milan Summit. This was the famous Cockfield White Paper which identified some 300 measures that had to be introduced before the single European market could be said to be completed. This proposal was adopted by the Council of Ministers. The concept of completing the internal market was also incorporated in the IGC discussions held later that year. As a result the SEA of 1986 amended the Rome Treaty to require the progressive establishment of the internal market by the end of 1992. As we saw earlier, it also made procedural alterations to help achieve that aim.

The Cockfield White Paper did not estimate the benefits of completing the single market. Instead, the Community acted first and carried out the calculations later. One of the most publicized studies was the so-called Cecchini Report, whose detailed evidence ran to sixteen volumes (EC Commission, 1988b). Cecchini approached the problem from both micro and macro angles. The microeconomic analysis focused, sector by sector, on the benefits to be derived from the removal of trade barriers (customs formalities and related delays), the removal of barriers to production (barriers to the play of competition such as those connected with standards and public procurement – see below), the greater enjoyment of economies of scale, and the reduction of costs caused by increased competitive pressures. On various assumptions these benefits ranged from 4.3 to 6.4 per cent of Community GDP. *It should be emphasized that these were once-and-for-all gains like the gains from customs union creation discussed in Chapter 4.*

Looking at it from a macroeconomic angle, when the full range of interactive effects could be allowed for, the estimated gain amounted to 4.5 per cent of Community GDP. However, it was argued that these beneficial effects helped to reduce the constraint on macroeconomic management. That being so, a variety of more favourable scenarios were envisaged, the most plausible of which was declared to be a medium-term increase in Community GDP of 7 per cent and the creation of 5 million jobs. These estimates were regarded by some commentators as being on the high side. It should be noted that while these gains were largely derived from finally getting rid of the NTBs which we discuss below, they also derived in part from such things as greater freedom to supply services and factors – matters which are discussed in Chapter 6.

Cartels and concentrations

These were an obvious device which could frustrate the process of integration through trade. There was plenty of evidence that before the dismantling of tariffs and quotas various forms of business arrangement, sometimes international in membership, existed which restricted trade flows and allocated and partitioned markets. It was recognized that where such devices did not exist initially, businesses might resort to various practices as the tariff barriers went down in order to offset the effects of the removal of protection.

The anti-trust problem can be divided into two main compartments – (a) restrictive arrangements between otherwise independent firms, and (b) the practices of dominant (or even monopoly) firms coupled with phenomena such as mergers, which can create conditions of dominance or monopoly.

Instances of the former abound in Community case law. For example, there are price agreements whereby firms in one member state, when selling to another, agree on the prices which they will charge for exports. Sometimes indeed such firms may create a separate company which will conduct the export sales of all the participants – this is known as a common selling syndicate. These arrangements have been common in fertilizers: we can cite Cobelaz (Belgium – ammonium sulphate), CFA (France – ammonium nitrogenous fertilizers), Seifa (Italy – simple nitrogenous, phosphatic, potassic and compound fertilizers) and Supexie (France – phosphatic fertilizers) as instances of this practice. Parallel price behaviour may indeed be international in character. Thus in the *Aniline Dye* case the Commission and Court of Justice had to deal with a situation in which equal and simultaneous price movements were made by ten firms – six were from Common Market countries but three were Swiss and one was British. As a result of international agreements, each home market may be reserved for home producers. Quota agreements may be entered into whereby home and foreign firms agree not to overstock the home market. Firms supplying a home market may enter into reciprocal exclusive dealing arrangements whereby signatory suppliers will only supply signatory dealers, and signatory dealers will only buy from signatory suppliers. If most of the dealers in a member state are locked in the arrangement, non-signatory suppliers, perhaps located in another member state, may have difficulty in penetrating the market. Firms in a member state may operate an aggregated rebate system in which domestic purchasers enjoy a progressive scale of rebate dependent on the (usually annual) volume of purchases from the signatory firms as a totality. The effect of this is to induce domestic purchasers to buy from the domestic firms rather than to import.

In respect of the concentration problem, it is not difficult to see how a dominant firm would, for example, be in a powerful position to induce domestic dealers to deal exclusively with it, and as a result importation would be reduced or even eliminated. Mergers and take-overs can have similar effects on the flow of trade. Thus in the now famous *Continental Can* case the burden of the Commission's case was that Continental Can, already dominant in the German market, had taken over one of its few remaining competitors in the shape of Thomassen & Drijver-Verblifa of the Netherlands.

Cartels

The key provisions are to be found in Rome Treaty Articles 3(g) and 85. Article 3 lays down the prime objectives of the EC, and among these is a call for 'the institution of a system ensuring that competition in the Common Market is not distorted'. It is, however, in Article 85 that we find the substantive law. This is best viewed in three parts. Article 85(1) prohibits a range of practices – agreements, decisions of associations of enterprises and concerted practices in the supply of services as well as goods. The first would include not only enforceable agreements (i.e. those that have some documentary base) but also gentlemen's agreements that are not intended to be enforced in the courts. Decisions of associations of enterprises cover the possibility that a firm being part of an association might conveniently claim that it did not agree with this or that association policy. Being a member of the association, it will be assumed to be bound by the decisions thereof. Decisions of associations of enterprises also cover the situation where a trade association makes a recommendation to its members even when there is no obligation to comply. A concerted practice is more difficult to define. It may be invoked where there is a parallelism of action but where straightforward collusion may not be admitted nor indeed exist. Mere parallelism of action would not, however, be sufficient proof. This concept was first used in the *Aniline Dye* case where on three occasions the most important suppliers of dyes in the EC introduced equiproportionate price increases within a few days of each other. Although agreement was not admitted by the parties, the Commission did point to circumstantial evidence of collusion and the firms were found guilty of being involved in a concerted practice and were fined. In the appeal case before the Court of Justice the Commission pressed the matter further when it observed that:

In order that there should be a concerting, it is not necessary that the parties should draw up a plan in common with a view to adopting a certain behaviour. It suffices that they should mutually inform each other in advance of the attitudes they intend to adopt, in such a way that each can regulate its action in reliance on its competitors behaving in a parallel manner.

The Court of Justice upheld the Commission's Decision, observing that a concerted practice was:

... a form of coordination between undertakings which, without going so far as to amount to an agreement properly so called, knowingly substitutes a practical cooperation between them for the risks of competition.

It added that parallelism of action was not to be identified with a concerted practice although it constituted a strong indication of such a practice, particularly when it led to prices above the equilibrium level expected from competition. The concept of a concerted practice also arose in the *Sugar* cases. On that occasion the Court amplified the concept, saying:

Although it is correct to say that this requirement of independence does not deprive economic operators of the right to adapt themselves intelligently to the existing and anticipated conduct of their competitors, it does, however, strictly preclude any direct or indirect contact between such operators. The object or effect thereof is either to influence the conduct on the market of an actual or potential competitor or to disclose to such a competitor the course of conduct which they themselves have decided to adopt or contemplate adopting.

In short, the Court lays emphasis on conscious efforts to evoke matching responses from competitors – as we have just noted mere parallelism of prices is not sufficient to carry the day.

The second feature of Article 85(1) is that the object or effect of the forms of conduct discussed above must be to prevent, restrict or distort competition *in the Common Market*. This provision does not mean that Community law only applies to Community firms. Firms belonging to states outside the EC can be subject to the anti-trust rules. Thus in the *Aniline Dye* case to which we have just referred, British and Swiss firms were fined by the Commission for their involvement with Community firms in activities leading to parallel price movements within the Common Market, and this was prior to UK membership of the Community. In other words, the Commission and Court of Justice have claimed an extra-territorial jurisdiction in their application of Article 85. The Article provides some examples of preventions, restrictions and distortions such as direct or indirect fixing of selling or purchasing prices and terms, limits on production, market allocation, etc. These are not exhaustive but merely illustrative.

Thirdly, a prevention, restriction or distortion of competition in the EC must be one which 'may affect trade between member states'. The word 'may' implies that this provision covers both agreements, etc., which actually do affect such trade and also those which have the potential to do so and may actually have that effect in the future even if not at present. The effect may be direct or it may be indirect. It would be direct if a group of firms in one member state agreed the prices which they charged for exports to other member states. It would be equally direct if various national groups decided to keep out of each other's national markets. It would be somewhat more indirect if producers and dealers in one member state agreed to deal exclusively with each other. Such an arrangement would not directly regulate inter-state trade but it would have the effect of inhibiting or even totally preventing the entry of third party supplies from without.

It would be easy to interpret the inter-state clause as meaning that the offence is to reduce the level of such trade below that which would obtain if the competitive restriction did not exist. However, this is not true. An effect upon trade between member states also arises when a restrictive arrangement artificially stimulates it. In the *Cimbel* case Belgian cement producers operated a price equalization scheme between the home and other member state markets. The practical effect was to subsidize sales in the latter and thus to stimulate them. The Commission observed that the arrangement 'artificially distorts trade between the member states because exports which, if the agreement did not exist, would not take place or would be made to a country situated at a more favourable distance, are deflected from their natural channels'. In short, trade must not be distorted one way or the other.

Article 85(2) declares prohibited agreements to be automatically void. It is, however, in Article 85(3) that we encounter the exemption aspect. It holds out the possibility that the Article 85(1) prohibition may not apply if an agreement, etc., 'contributes to improving the production or distribution of goods or to promoting technical progress'. There are, however, a number of caveats. (a) Any agreement, etc., which contributes to such an improvement must allow consumers a fair share of the resulting benefit. (b) The agreement in achieving the improvement and the fair sharing must not impose restrictions which are not indispensable to the attainment of those objectives. In other words, if an agreement is to get through it must impose no more restrictions than are absolutely essential. (c) The agreement must not allow the parties to eliminate competition in respect of a substantial part of the products in question. All these conditions are cumulative.

It should be added that for Article 85(1) to apply there has to be an appreciable restraint of competition. In 1970 the Commission issued a Notice on agreements of minor importance[1] – thus establishing a *de minimis* rule. Currently, if the firms participating in an agreement have a market share of not more than 5 per cent in a substantial part of the Common Market and their aggregate turnover does not exceed 50 million ECU, then a significant restriction of competition does not exist.

The application of Article 85 lies primarily with the Commission although its formal Decisions to prohibit, etc., are subject to appeal to the Court of Justice. To aid it the Commission established a system of notification. Notification is clearly of assistance to the Commission in locating violations. There is also a strong incentive for companies to notify since if they do not do so there can be no

1. However, a Notice is merely for information and ultimately has no legal status. The Commission earlier (1968) issued a Notice indicating the various kinds of cooperation which did not in its view violate Article 85 – they cover such things as joint market research, joint advertising, joint selling where the parties do not compete, joint collection of debts, etc. The Notice stated that the Commission welcomed cooperation among small and medium-sized enterprises where such cooperation enabled them to work more rationally and increase their productivity and competitiveness in the larger market. It went on to add that cooperation among large enterprises could also be economically desirable and might not raise difficulties from the competition standpoint.

question of their agreement being exempted. For example in the *Quinine* case the parties were advised to notify but decided not to do so. Subsequently they were caught by the Commission and not having notified they were denied the possibility of an exemption hearing and were indeed heavily fined. If on the other hand the agreement is duly notified it enjoys a provisional or temporary validity, until the Commission renders a formal Decision to the effect that it falls within Article 85(1).[1] But once the Commission issues a Decision to the effect that the agreement is prohibited (exemption not being possible) then it would be an offence to continue it, and financial sanctions could be applied. Apart from formal prohibitions and exemptions, mention should be made of the Negative Clearance. This is granted when the Commission finds that the contents of an agreement are not such as to render it subject to Article 85 – in short the Commission finds no reason to intervene. It should be emphasized that prior to the granting of a Negative Clearance or an Exemption the parties may have had to modify the agreement, stripping it of offending matter. However, even with some stripping the agreement may not be capable of being made innocuous or acceptable, and a formal prohibition may be on the cards, in which case the parties may choose to abandon rather than press the matter to the stage where a formal prohibitory Decision has to be issued.

It should be emphasized that this description of the enforcement process tended to change over time. The length of time taken to issue a formal Negative Clearance or Exemption might be two or three years and this was unacceptable to businessmen. To circumvent this the Commission decided to resort to the issuing of what are called 'comfort letters' which in a more informal way indicate that the practice in question is acceptable.

The Commission in locating violations does not rely solely on notifications. It also keeps its eyes and ears open, receives complaints from injured parties (for which there is a formal mechanism)

1. When a group of companies introduces a new agreement, etc., they are well advised to notify immediately. If, for example, they introduce the agreement first and then notify it at a later date, the act of notifying does not put an end to a pre-existing state of infringement. That is to say if, when the Commission comes to investigate the agreement, it decides to prohibit it then fines can be imposed for the period between entry into operation and the date of notification – see *Pittsburgh–Corning* case.

and can carry out sectoral investigations where the flow of trade between states is suspiciously small or in some way distorted. The Commission is endowed with powers to obtain from governments, competent state authorities, trade associations and undertakings information necessary for the prosecution of a case. Associations and undertakings which fail or refuse to render information, or give false information, can be fined.

We turn now to the record of the Commission in applying Article 85 to horizontal cartels concerned with price fixing, output restriction, market sharing, etc. The record is extremely impressive – virtually no cartel with significant market power has been exempted.

Price agreements have been consistently attacked. We have already referred to the *Aniline Dye* case, where exemption was precluded by virtue of the fact that the concerted practice had not been notified. Heavy fines were ultimately imposed upon the participating firms. In the *Glass Container* case the major manufacturers of bottles, jars and flasks in five member states had entered into a fair trade practice rules agreement which was operated by the International Fair Trade Practice Rules Administration (IFTRA), registered in Liechtenstein. Ostensibly the agreement was designed to eliminate unfair practices. Parties were precluded from selling below cost in order to drive out competitors, it was unfair to discriminate and to operate tie-ins, etc. However, the true purpose of the agreement was to ensure that a manufacturer making deliveries outside his normal business territory did not undercut the prices of a party to the agreement who was the national (or local) price leader. In order to achieve this, price-lists and terms were circulated so that it was possible to check on quotations made by other suppliers. Equally crucial to the system was the obligation not to deviate secretly from the listed prices. In order to strengthen group solidarity, the IFTRA partners had devised a common method of calculating costs and had agreed to adopt a delivered price system. The Commission saw the fair trading rules and the system of aligning on a national price leader's offer as offending under Article 85(1) but not being capable of exemption, not least because it seemed to offer no benefit to consumers. Quite the contrary – the consumer lost the benefit which import competition would have provided had such alignment not been required. The other parts of the agreement (information, costing and delivered price arrangements) had not been notified and could not be exempted. The whole arrangement was formally prohibited. More recently, in July 1994, the Commission imposed a record fine of 132.15 million ECUs on a group of nineteen carton-board producers who were alleged to have formed Europe's 'most pernicious' price fixing cartel. Exercising strict discipline and making virtually no written notes, the firms carefully orchestrated price increases every six months. The parties involved included Swedish and Norwegian firms.

Common sales syndicates are best treated as a form of price agreement and in so doing we should note that the Commission has taken a consistently hostile attitude where significant market power has been apparent. Syndicates of this kind have usually been encountered in markets where products are homogeneous and price-cutting activity could be intense – i.e. fertilizers, cement, sulphuric acid, etc. Several early cases concerned fertilizers. In, for example, the *CFA* and *Cobelaz* cases the arrangements covered both home and export sales. Modifications therefore had to be made so that sales to other EC countries were carried out independently by individual manufacturers. This change having been carried out, the Commission was able to grant a Negative Clearance. Interestingly, three leading French producers of fertilizers which were involved in the CFA arrangement also set up an export sales syndicate during the year in which the CFA Decision was handed down. This was called Floral Gmbh and handled their compound fertilizer sales in West Germany. In 1979 the Commission banned this arrangement. In doing so it pointed out that the legal position of common selling syndicates had been made abundantly clear to the firms in the 1968 CFA Decision. However, because Floral handled only a small proportion of their fertilizer sales the fine imposed was a modest one. Where a common selling syndicate controls only a small proportion of the relevant market and thus has no appreciable market power, the arrangement may be granted a Negative Clearance as it stands.

Competition may also be restricted by the application of quotas to output or sales. This is often resorted to when price agreements alone will not suffice. Three interesting cases recently brought to light by the Commission involved leading chemical producers in Western Europe. Systems of floor or target prices had been supplemented by agreements to allocate participants output quotas, which by reducing supply helped to strengthen the control over the market. One case involved cartel practices by fifteen companies between 1977 and 1983 concerning bulk thermoplastic polypropylene, the other two cases related to various arrangements operated by twenty-five companies between 1980 and 1984 in respect of the supply of PVC and Low Density Polyethylene. In the first case a collective fine of 57.85 million ECUs was imposed in 1986. In the latter two cases the total fine imposed in 1988 amounted to 60.5 million ECUs. However the Commission suffered a reverse in respect of the PVC cartel. It was appealed against to the Court of Justice in 1994; it threw out the case, not because it felt the firms were innocent but because it found discrepancies between the various language texts of the Commissioner's Decision. This illustrates the difficulties which arise when the Commission had to operate in up to nine different languages. The Commission indicated that it would re-commence the case.

Territorial market sharing is an obviously offensive practice and one which has been consistently opposed. In 1984 the Commission revealed that it had been investigating major producers of hydrogen peroxide and its derivatives for a period of twenty years. These included Solvay, Laporte Industries, Air Liquide, Degussa and Produits Chimiques Ugine Kuhlmann. The firms had operated an arrangement whereby they restricted their sales to a certain national market or markets. In addition, a national market where more than one producer was selling was shared in agreed percentages. Because of the gravity of the offences fines totalling 9 million ECUs were imposed.

The Commission has also attacked exclusionary practices which have sealed off a part of the Common Market. This was so in its recommendation to the Belgian Pottery Convention, which was concerned with reciprocal exclusive dealing arrangements affecting the Belgian market, and in the *German Wall and Floor Tile* case, where a group of German producers had instituted an aggregated rebate arrangement. The rebate was payable only on purchases from German manufacturers which had obvious implications for inter-state trade. The Commission objected that rebates should relate to purchases from individual producers in which case they had the possibility of reflecting actual savings. Moreover if the aim of the arrangement was to favour tiles relative to substitute products, purchases of foreign tiles ought to be taken into account.

The Commission has also encountered a number of important cases of information exchange and has not hesitated to insist on the termination of offensive elements. It did so in 1977 in connection with an informational arrangement operated by enterprises in the UK, France and West Germany who were engaged in supplying metal and plastic paper machine wire. In its original form the agreement required the parties to supply to the Secretariat-General of the International Association of Paper Machine Wire Manufacturers (a) price-lists and terms within two to three weeks of their becoming effective and (b) copies of all invoices for deliveries (except to the US) within ten days – the invoice to specify the name of the customer, the type of wire, the price and any other relevant terms. The Secretariat-General was authorized upon request to communicate the price paid by any particular customer to any national association or member firm, the object being to prevent customers playing one supplier off against another. The Commission saw this interchange as being inconsistent with a competitive relationship. Following the Commission's intervention, the parties agreed to cease the exchange of price-lists, to supply copies of invoices without identifying the customer and to use the latter purely for the purpose of preparing statistics.

Quite early on, the Commission showed itself to be concerned with (vertical) sole or exclusive distribution agreements. The key case – the first occasion on which a prohibition was handed down – was *Grundig-Consten*. The West German firm Grundig had appointed the Paris firm Consten as sole dealer of its products at its particular stage of the distributive chain (i.e. importer/wholesaler). Grundig had banned its sole dealers in other states from delivering goods into the French distributive network and undermining Consten – this is known as territorial protection, whilst lawyers like to refer to it as the no-poaching rule. The position of Consten was reinforced by the assignment to it of the trademark GINT (Grundig International). The Commission prohibited the agreement, but on appeal to the Court of Justice the sole distribution element was upheld, the offending element being the territorial protection. The latter buttresses the sole dealer's monopoly in the chain of distribution and by compartmentalizing the Common Market gives rise to differences in prices for the same goods in the different member states. Goods which have entered into trade must be allowed to move freely across frontiers in the hope that inter-state price differences will be ironed out. Sole dealers are allowed to poach. The sole dealing element does constitute a restrictive agreement within the meaning of Article 85(1), but because it gives rise to advantageous effects in aiding the penetration of markets it is capable of being exempted. A number of pure sole dealing agreements were subsequently exempted and this was followed by Regulation 19 of 1965, and Regulation 67 of 1967, under which bilateral sole dealing agreements (between enterprises in two states) unencumbered by devices such as territorial protection were accorded block exemption status. This concern with the need to allow parallel imports has with only minor exceptions characterized the Commission's general stance in approaching all forms of distribution agreement. Under Regulation 83 of 1983, Regulation 67 of 1967 was modified. The structure and essential contents of the earlier Regulation were retained, but changes were made in the interest of facilitating intra-Community trade.

Those firms that seek to prevent parallel imports within their European distribution systems run the risk of severe penalties. In 1979 in the *Pioneer* case, Pioneer Electronics Europe, a subsidiary of a Japanese multinational ranking among the world's leading suppliers of hi-fi equipment, was, together with its sole distributors in France, Germany and the UK, fined 6.95 million EUA for operating what were in effect export bans.

Restrictions of competition may arise in connection with industrial and commercial property – i.e. trademarks, patents and copyrights. Recognizing that these are supposed to confer a monopoly position on the owner (or licensee) of the property right in question, it seems possible that, particularly in the light of Article 36 (see Chapter 4), they could legitimately be invoked to prevent imports, thus compartmentalizing the Common Market. However, this is not so, thanks to Article 85 which has been successfully applied in such situations. It should be added that Article 30 *et seq.*, relating to the free circulation of goods, has also been applicable. This is a complex area of Community law and we shall not attempt to present an exhaustive account of relevant cases. Rather we shall confine ourselves to outlining a couple of instances in which the

Rome Treaty Articles have been employed to prevent the partitioning of the Common Market.

A good example is provided by the *Sirena-Eda* case. It concerned trademarks. In this particular instance an American company, Mark Allen, had assigned its trademark Prep, registered in Italy, to an Italian company Sirena. Mark Allen had also allowed a German company to use the mark. There was no problem while the two companies confined their sales of Prep toiletries to their own national markets. However, an import-export company, Novimpex SRL, obtained supplies of the German product and sold them in Italy and this provoked Sirena to ask the appropriate Italian court to forbid these imports. They were undermining Sirena's trademark monopoly. The matter was referred to the Court of Justice for a preliminary ruling. The case was considered under Article 85 because an agreement existed in connection with the assignment of the trademark. The Court decided:

Article 85 therefore applies where, by virtue of trademark rights, imports of products originating in other member states, bearing the same trademark because their owners have acquired the trademark itself or the right to use it through agreements with one other or with third parties, are prevented.

The Court was therefore prepared to allow goods bearing a particular trademark to flow across frontiers and offer competition to domestically produced supplies bearing that same trademark. In the *Centrafarm v. Sterling Drug* case the matter at issue was patents and patent licensing. Sterling Drug possessed parallel drug patents in several member states including the Netherlands, UK and West Germany. It licensed its subsidiaries in the various member states to produce and market the drug. The case arose because the Dutch firm Centrafarm obtained supplies of the drug in West Germany and shipped them into the Netherlands. This provoked an appeal by Sterling on the grounds that its Dutch patent was being infringed. This was referred to the Court of Justice for a preliminary ruling. The Court did not consider the case under Article 85 because no agreement arises between a parent and a subsidiary. The Court instead based its judgement on Article 30 *et seq*. It maintained that an attempt by the owner of a patent to prevent the import of a product, protected by that patent, which had been marketed in another member state by the patent owner, was incompatible with the concept of the free movement of goods. The Sterling subsidiaries exhausted their rights in the first marketing of the goods. If a party who acquired them sought to sell them in another territory where a parallel patent existed, that was perfectly compatible with the idea of a common market.

Thus far the Commission has been cast in a prohibitory role. But not all agreements have fallen foul of Article 85. Following the 1968 Notice on Cooperation, the Commission has been anxious to encourage certain forms of cooperation where efficiency gains are in prospect. The 1968 Notice referred primarily to forms of cooperation which were not likely to give rise to restrictions of competition, but in the Notice the Commission indicated its intention to address itself to situations where there was some restrictive effect but where counterbalancing gains might none the less accrue. There followed a number of Decisions concerning specialization and joint research and development. The former can be fairly obvious candidates for exemption. The arrangement is restrictive in that it reduces the number of competitors, etc. On the other hand, the longer production runs reduce costs. Provided the parties have only a small share of the market, competition will probably ensure that some of the efficiency gains are passed on to the consumer. The Commission will clearly require that the agreement contains no extraneous restrictions, and the small share of the market will ensure that the last element of Article 85(3) is satisfied. These conditions were amply fulfilled in the *Jaz-Peter* and *Clima Chappée-Buderus* cases, but in others such as *Fine Papers* structural conditions were different. *Fine Papers* involved the principal French producers of cigarette paper, who had a market share of 80 per cent in France and 70 per cent in Benelux. However, the Commission found effective competition from West German and Italian producers, potential competition from third country producers, countervailing power in the shape of the French and Italian tobacco monopolies as well as other larger producers, and noted that the agreement was not irreversible.

The Decisions on cooperation cases paved the way for a block exemption of specialization and joint research and development agreements. These have however required that the firms involved represented only a small share of the market. However, in the case of research and developments agreements, if the firms were not previously competitors, the market share condition did not apply.

Before leaving the subject of cartel practices, it is necessary to point out that there are also block exemption arrangements for exclusive purchasing agreements, patent licensing agreements and motor vehicle distribution and servicing agreements.

Dominant firms and mergers

The Rome Treaty provisions concerned with concentration situations are to be found in Article 86, which provides that:

Any abuse by one or more undertakings of a dominant position within the Common Market or a substantial part of it shall be prohibited as being incompatible with the Common Market in so far as it may affect trade between member states.

There are three important elements. (a) There must be a dominant position. (b) But dominance is not the sin, it is the abuse thereof. (c) There must be the possibility of an effect on trade between the member states – this is typical of the Rome Treaty approach. The first two call for further comment.

The dominant position has a geographical element since it may relate to the whole of the Common Market or it may be in a substantial part thereof. The Treaty offers no definition of what substantial means, but the territory of one member state, West Germany, was deemed to be large enough in the *GEMA* and *Continental Can* cases, and that of Belgium when the Court of Justice dealt with a copyright dispute. In the *Sugar* cases the Commission treated Holland on its own, and Belgium and Luxembourg combined, as substantial parts of the Common Market.

The concept of dominance also implies that the company (or companies) involved must enjoy some market power, and this requires that the relevant market and the degree of control thereof must be identified. The *Continental Can* case provides a particularly good example of the approach which is adopted. *Continental Can* concerned the activities of the Continental Can Company Inc., a large American multinational manufacturing metal containers, other packaging materials and machines for the manufacture and use of containers. It acquired a majority shareholding in a large West

German producer of light metal containers – Schmalbach-Lubeca-Werke AG of Brunswick. Continental Can then transferred its holdings in Schmalbach to a holding company, the Europemballage Corporation. It also agreed to make an offer for the shares of the large Dutch can producer Thomassen & Drijver–Verblifa NV of Deventer – actually the offer was made by Europemballage. This was accomplished and thus control of both Schmalbach and Thomassen came to be vested in the one holding company created by Continental. The Commission then intervened. It saw the acquisition of Thomassen as being a violation of Article 86. This was a controversial interpretation of Article 86 since it was being applied to a merger. Essentially the Commission was arguing that Schmalbach had a dominant position in the West German market for light containers for preserved meat and fish and metal caps for preserve jars. (Proof of the existence of a dominant position is stage number one in the successful prosecution of a case under Article 86.) The Commission also argued that the extinguishing of Thomassen's competition, via the acquisition, was an abuse within the meaning of Article 86. An effect on inter-state trade was likely in that Thomassen would not now sell competitively in the West German market, and for that matter Schmalbach would not now do likewise in the Benelux market. The case is instructive because much turned on the question of whether Schmalbach really had a dominant position in West Germany. The Court in fact found against the Commission. In doing so it did not invoke any particular market share as being critical but pointed to the existence of other sources of ongoing or potential competition such as containers made of plastic or glass, suppliers of metal containers for other goods who could turn their attention to the meat and fish container market and the fact that food packers could manufacture their own containers. Although Schmalbach did not dominate the West German market it might appear that the merger did suppress one source of independent competition. However, it appeared that there had been little competition from Thomassen. Apparently the Commission had been investigating the possibility that there was an agreement at the time of the merger but had not completed its investigation. In the circumstances the Commission ultimately had to rely on the notion that the merger would suppress *potential* competition.

Whilst *Continental Can* was instructive in indicating the kind of considerations which are important in defining the relevant market, that case did not, as we have just seen, indicate what *proportion* of the market has to be controlled if a firm is to be declared dominant. A number of subsequent cases did throw light on this issue.

Obviously a 100 per cent share must be one of dominance – this was so in the *GEMA* case. In the *Sugar* cases, Raffinerie Tirlemontoise had an 85 per cent share of the Belgium–Luxembourg market and it too was declared to be dominating. However, the proportion can sink much lower. In the *Hoffman-La-Roche* case 47 per cent of the market for vitamin A was deemed to be dominant. In that case however the fact that the two largest competitors only possessed 45 per cent of the market between them was important. In the *Chiquita* case, concerning the market in bananas (see below), United Brands possessed only a 40 per cent share. But there were good structural reasons for accepting such a low figure. First, the competitors of United Brands were very small. Secondly, there were substantial barriers to new entrants. In the subsequent *IBM* case, IBM had 40 per cent of the computer market (mainframe and mini) and only 39 per cent of the data processing market. But again, IBM was in sales terms seven times larger than its nearest rival.

The second aspect of Article 86 is the abuse of the dominant position by a firm or firms. A number of examples are given but these are merely illustrative. They are: directly or indirectly imposing unfair purchasing or selling prices or other unfair trading conditions; limiting production, markets or technical development to the prejudice of consumers; applying dissimilar conditions to equivalent transactions with other trading parties, thereby placing them at a competitive disadvantage – this obviously refers to price discrimination; making the conclusion of contracts subject to acceptance by other parties of supplementary obligations which, by their nature or according to commercial usage, have no connection with the subject of such contracts – clearly this refers to tie-ins.

In actual cases one of the main forms of abuse encountered has been the granting of fidelity rebates. In the *Sugar* cases two large West German sugar producers had in concert offered rebates which were conditional upon buyers taking all their supplies from them. In *Hoffman-La-Roche* the Commission dealt with a similar practice in respect of supplies of vitamins for bulk use in medicines, foods and feeding stuffs. The Commission observed: 'Whether to compensate for the exclusivity or to encourage a preferential link, the contracts provided for fidelity rebates based not on differences in costs related to the quantities supplied by Roche but on the proportion of the customer's requirements covered.' Moreover, Roche was able to extend its power to products where it was not dominant, as the rebates were not calculated separately for each particular group of vitamins but were aggregated across all purchases. A fine was imposed.

The Commission has also attacked the practice of refusal to supply. This arose in the *Commercial Solvents* case. Commercial Solvents, a monopolist of raw material needed to produce a particular drug, decided (through its subsidiary) not to supply the raw material to an existing producer of the drug. The Court of Justice stated that an undertaking which is in a dominant position in the supply of a raw material, and is thus in a position to control the supply to producers of products manufactured from that material, cannot refuse to supply such a customer with the effect of eliminating all competition therefrom.

In the *GEMA* case the Commission objected to the activities of a performing rights society which in fact enjoyed a monopoly of the German market. GEMA was established to protect the rights of member composers, authors and publishers. Rights were assigned to it and it exploited them in return for royalties. GEMA had imposed unduly restrictive terms on its members – they had to assign to it all existing and future rights in all respects and in all countries, for a minimum period of six years. The Commission objected to the universality of the assignment required of members. It felt that they should be free to assign only a part of their rights and be able to retain the other part for individual exploitation. The Commission also singled out for criticism the exclusion of non-residents – a provision which was apparently designed to consolidate the market power of other national societies.

In the *Chiquita* case the Commission attacked the practice of charging different prices in different parts of the Common Market for the same product. On appeal the Court took the view that prices should be related to costs and should not be set at the various levels that the different national markets would bear.

In the *IBM* case the allegations, which led to a negotiated settlement, concerned matters such as the failure of IBM to produce advance technical information about its equipment, failure to offer equipment without items which other suppliers could offer to attach and failure to exclude software from the price of the hardware. The latter two are referred to as bundling – i.e. different pieces of equipment, or equipment and software, are bundled together in the total price. The effect of these devices was to delay competitors producing equipment which could be plugged into IBM products (i.e. equipment which was plug-compatible) and in the case of bundling to eliminate the possibility of other firms supplying hardware and software which could be used in conjunction with IBM hardware. In the more recent *AKZO* case another abuse has been identified, namely predatory pricing, whereby a firm sells below cost in order to drive out a competitor, thereafter being able to hoist prices to more profitable levels.

We have already touched on EC merger policy when discussing the *Continental Can* case. Our discussion in that instance was concerned with the light that *Continental Can* threw on the meaning of Article 86. In that case the ECC attempted to prohibit a merger but failed to provide the proof of dominance necessary to convince the Court of Justice that the ban on the takeover of Thomassen & Drijver-Verblifa ought to be upheld. But there was also the important question at stake of whether Article 86 could actually be said to apply to mergers. There were some who said it did not. They argued that Article 86 does not proscribe a dominant position – it attacks the abuse thereof. Therefore if a dominant firm took over another and became more dominant no offence arose. An offence would only arise if the now more dominant firm misbehaved. However, the Commission, at least as far back as 1965, maintained that the Rome Treaty was seriously deficient without a power to control mergers. It considered a number of possible remedies, one of which was that Article 86 could be applied to acquisitions. In its memorandum on *Concentration by Firms in the Common Market* (EEC Commission, 1965) it declared that if a dominant firm took over another and so established a monopoly, that was an abuse within the meaning of Article 86.

The real importance of the *Continental Can* case was that it considered these opposing views and came out in favour of the Commission. The Court of Justice did so because it adopted a pragmatic approach. It noted that Article 3(f) of the Treaty called for the establishment of conditions of undistorted competition. It also saw that if firms were debarred from colluding by virtue of the effect of Article 85(1) they could still acquire their control of the market by merging. There was a serious loophole and this dictated that Article 86 be given the more generous interpretation. The Commission maintained that in *Continental Can* an undertaking in a dominant position had strengthened its position by means of a merger so that actual or potential competition in the Common Market (or a substantial part of it) was almost eliminated. The Court concurred that such an elimination, and it need not be total, was an abuse of Article 86. The important point to prove was that 'competition was so substantially impaired that the remaining competitors could not constitute an adequate counterweight'.

Unfortunately, Article 86 is not a perfect merger instrument. It requires a firm to be in a dominant position before it can be invoked. It may in fact be desirable to prevent that dominance arising in the first place – otherwise it is a case of locking the stable door after the horse has bolted. In fact, such was the weakness of Article 86 as a merger-controlling device that it was never employed in any *formal* Decision although apparently it was invoked in a number of informal settlements. The Commission first put forward a proposal for a separate merger regulation in 1973. However, it was not until 1987 that the Council of Ministers indicated broad approval although some countries continued to express considerable misgivings. The Council was in part provoked into acceptance by the *Philip Morris* case in which the Court of Justice indicated that certain kinds of merger could also be attacked under Article 85. This encouraged the Commission to take a more active stance. The *Philip Morris* judgement also raised all kinds of procedural uncertainties and it became increasingly obvious that a regulation was necessary to restore some degree of certainty. It should be added that while the merger regulation of 1989 was not one of the measures specified in the Cockfield White Paper, the Council of Ministers indicated that effective merger control was essential to the completion of the internal market.

The 1989 regulation does not refer to mergers but to concentrations with a European dimension. A concentration applies to two situations: (a) where previously independent enterprises merge, and (b) where by acquisition of securities, assets, etc., one enterprise obtains control over another. For a concentration to have a Community dimension the aggregate worldwide turnover of all the undertakings must be more than 5,000 million ECU and the aggregate Community-wide turnover of each (of at least two) undertakings must be more than 250 million ECU. Also each (of at least two) undertakings must achieve less than two-thirds of its turnover in one and the same state. Concentrations will be judged according to whether they create or strengthen a dominant position and as a result significantly impede effective competition in the Common Market or a substantial part of it. While other criteria are referred to, according to former Competition Commissioner Sir Leon Brittan the effect on competition will be the sole criterion. Concentrations have to be notified in advance and delayed until the Commission has decided whether to act. The Commission can forbid concentrations and break up illegal ones.

The Commission has applied its merger controlling powers. A celebrated case being the proposed Aerospatiale-Alenia/de Havilland merger. The French and Italian companies jointly owned a company called Avions de Transport Régional (ATR). De Havilland was a division of Boeing. The two EC companies had combined their regional turbo-prop aircraft production in ATR and intended by the acquisition to take over Boeing's turbo-prop production capacity at de Havilland. The Commission forbade the merger on the grounds that the resulting concentration of production capacity would lead to a dominant position and that competition in the relevant market would be significantly impaired.

Fiscal factors

The need for action in the field of taxation was recognized in the Rome Treaty – Articles 95 to 99 are the relevant ones. It should, however, be noted that although Article 99 refers to harmonization of taxation it is only in respect of *indirect* taxes that specific action is contemplated. Article 99 requires that the Commission

Shall consider how to further the interests of the common market by harmonizing the legislation of the various member states concerning turnover taxes, excise duties and other forms of indirect taxation . . . [and] shall submit proposals to the Council.

The actual process of harmonization is provided for in Article 100. We will concentrate primarily on the turnover tax issue – this will be followed by some brief observations concerning excise duties.

It is not immediately obvious why indirect taxes of the turnover variety should give rise to a NTB problem. The full import of that remark must, however, wait upon a discussion of two other issues. The first is the nature of turnover taxes as they existed in the Community at the time when the Rome Treaty was being drafted. The second is the traditional treatment of indirect taxes on goods entering into international trade.

Within the general category of turnover tax the Community operated two main kinds – the cascade and the value added systems. (The latter was of course adopted by the UK in place of purchase tax and selective employment tax in anticipation of British membership of the Community.) The French had opted for the TVA (*Taxe sur valeur ajoutée*, i.e. VAT) but the rest of the Community applied cascade systems.

The cascade tax was a multi-stage tax in that it was levied at each stage of the productive process. In practice it covered a broad range of products. It was therefore unlike the British purchase tax, which was a single-stage tax levied at the wholesaler stage, covering a relatively narrow range of goods. Cascade taxes were levied on the gross value of output at each stage in the chain of production. The important point to note is the cumulative nature of the system: tax is applied at each stage upon the whole selling value including tax. If the product is used in further production the selling price of the resulting product upon which tax is charged will be inflated by tax paid at the previous stage. Under the cascade system the cost of producing a given item excluding tax (that is, the value added) may be the same whether produced by a vertically integrated firm or by a vertical series of independent enterprises, but the tax paid on the product of the latter will be greater than that levied on the former.

The basic feature of VAT is that it is paid at each stage in the process of production upon the value added at each point in the productive chain. The final price of the product, in the absence of turnover tax, is equal to the sum of the values added at each point. Because of this fact it makes no difference whether the tax is collected at several points or as a single payment on the final product. The tax collected will be the same in either case – the tax is therefore neutral as between production which is carried out in a vertically integrated firm and production which is carried out by several separate firms with tax levied at the intermediate stages.

We turn now to the treatment of indirect taxes in international trade. (In practice we will assume that the trade takes place between members of a customs union.) Here we have to distinguish between the origin and destination principles. The origin principle can be explained as follows. Let us suppose that good X is manufactured in Country I and Country I applies a general turnover tax which amounts to 10 per cent on the cost of producing a good. If good X is exported to Country II it retains the 10 per cent and is thus delivered to consumers in Country II with the tax applied. Suppose that Country II applies a 20 per cent tax to good X which it produces itself then, other things being equal, good X coming from Country I has an artificial competitive advantage. Indeed if producers of X in Countries I and II are equally efficient then producers in Country II will find their sales falling as they are undersold in both countries by Country I producers.

In the case of the destination principle, however, good X produced in Country I will, when exported, have the 10 per cent tax remitted. It would thus be exported to Country II free of the tax and Country II would apply its own tax at the 20 per cent rate. In other words the exported good bears the tax of the country of destination and not of origin.

The importance of the remark made earlier is now clear. In the case of the destination principle, *and this is the principle normally applied in international trade*, good X produced in Country I and good X produced in Country II are treated equally, in terms of the tax levied on them, when sold in Country I and Country II. *Differences in tax rates do not therefore lead to distortions of competition between the two countries.* Then why be concerned with the need to harmonize the tax *systems* and *rates* of the countries in the customs union?

In part the answer lies in a consideration of the problems encountered in remitting turnover taxes on exports when a cascade system is operating. Specifically, the problem is that it is extremely difficult to know with any accuracy just how much tax is incorporated in the price of the good and therefore how much should be remitted. Too little could be remitted, in which case exports are artificially disadvantaged. But too much may deliberately be remitted in which case an artificial export aid, and probably a concealed one at that, will operate. In this case we have an NTB which *distorts* trade and production.

There were, however, a number of other points which also compelled action. From what has gone before it is evident that the cascade system gives an artificial incentive to vertical integration. This has several disadvantageous effects. First, it may be more efficient to specialize in one stage of a productive process, but the tax discourages this. There may, of course, be no advantage between vertically integrated and non-vertically integrated firms from the point of view of productive efficiency. But the vertically integrated firm enjoys an artificial competitive advantage. Secondly, although from the view of maintaining competition it is usual to regard horizontal concentrations as a main problem, there are reasons for fearing the vertical variety. A firm which is integrated backwards can control supplies of raw material and semi-finished products to competitors and force them out of business or force them to conform to its wishes. However, this problem only arises if firms at an earlier stage in the production process are concentrated horizontally, and this is not inevitable since the tax does not bias industrial structures in this way. But it could be argued that by integrating vertically an enterprise could acquire financial resources which would enable it to concentrate horizontally. Such resources would enable it to endure the price wars which might be necessary to discipline non-vertically integrated firms. Thirdly, there are reasons for believing that vertical integration in industry tends to impede cross-frontier competition. This argument is based on the proposition that in the absence of such integration, firms at any stage of production have the alternative of buying the products of the previous stage either from domestic enterprises or from foreign firms. In effect an import gap exists. With vertical integration this possibility does not exist.

By deciding in 1967 to adopt the VAT system the Community dealt with these kinds of problem. For example, the Commission claimed that with VAT it was easier to police tax remissions on export and also there was no artificial incentive to vertical integration. Why then, given that the destination system deals with the problem of competitive distortions which would otherwise arise

Table 9. VAT rates in EC at 1 April 1989 (%)

	Lower	Standard	Higher
Belgium	1 and 6	19	25 and 33
Denmark		22	
France	2.1, 4, 5.5 and 7	18.6	28
Germany	7	14	
Greece	6	18	36
Ireland	0, 2.4	10	25
Italy	2 and 9	18	38
Luxembourg	3 and 6	12	
Netherlands	6	20	
Portugal	8	16	30
Spain	6	12	33
United Kingdom	0	15	

Source: EC Commission, *Europe without frontiers: Completing the internal market*, OOPEC, 1989, p. 52.

from differing national rates, did the Cockfield 1985 White Paper still look for further change?

The answer lies in the continuing need for border controls when national rates differ as indeed they do – see Table 9. The reader will recollect that the SEA looks forward to a single market 'without internal frontiers'. A number of reasons have been put forward as to why such controls are necessary. One is to guarantee that goods which are zero-rated for export are indeed exported and are not fraudulently and unfairly sold domestically. Another is that in the absence of controls consumers will cross frontiers and buy where rates are lower – to the disadvantage of suppliers in the higher-rate state.

The proposed solution is that national rates of VAT should be harmonized and going along with that the Community should move over to the origin system.[1] With respect to rates the Commission has suggested that identical rates are not necessary. All that is needed is that they be brought closer together so as to prevent any significant distortion of trade and competition. In other words rate

---

1. This will affect national tax revenues – possible ways of dealing with this problem are being considered.

approximation will suffice. In July 1987 the Commission proposed a standard band of 14–20 per cent together with a lower band of 4–9 per cent. The Commission showed flexibility by being prepared to accept, at least temporarily, zero-rating for some goods – a matter which has concerned the UK and Ireland. The ending of zero rating would raise considerable opposition in the UK, which has insisted on continuing to apply it to commodities such as food.

This proposal has, however, been subjected to various conditions and subsequent refinements. First, the Commission asked member states not to do anything to make the differences between national rates any greater and that any nationally decided changes should move standard rates in the direction of the 14–20 per cent bracket. Second, the shift to the origin system may not happen until as late as 1996. Third, the Commission later proposed that there was no need to add an upper bracket since any state charging above 20 per cent would lose out through competition from other members. In other words, the Commission is relying in some degree on market forces to bring rates into line. Fourth, in June 1991 ministers of finance agreed that the *normal* minimum VAT rate should indeed be 15 per cent. This was, however, a political agreement – the UK refused to be bound by a directive. The reader will recollect that under the SEA fiscal matters are not subject to majority voting. This latter fact explains the relatively slow progress on the fiscal front. Finally, in June 1991 the Commission indicated its acceptance of zero rating for a limited range of goods provided there is no risk of competition being distorted. It also identified the goods and services to which the lower rate band would apply.

In the past excise duties have given rise to a number of disputes. These have arisen in connection with Article 95, which requires states not to impose internal taxation on the products of other member states that affords indirect protection to *other goods*. What, it may be asked, is that particular provision trying to prevent? The answer is that it refers to situations where two products may compete (i.e. are substitutes) and a member state applies a higher excise duty on one than on the other. The most obvious temptation is to apply a high excise duty on a mainly imported good and a lower one on the domestic substitute. For example, the UK was accused by the Commission of applying a higher excise burden on wine (largely imported) than on beer (largely home-produced). That was the issue in a case before the Court of Justice – *Commission v. UK* – and ultimately the UK lost. In a similar case – *Commission v. Denmark* – the Danes were accused of applying a lower excise on schnapps (largely home-produced) compared with other spirits (largely imported). The Commission claimed that the behaviour of the Danish Government was an offence under Article 95 and the Court concurred. Problems of this kind would probably disappear if, as the Commission has indicated, excise duties were themselves harmonized. This will involve deciding what goods are to be subject to excise duties, what common rate structures should be adopted and what the common excise rates will be. The Commission has proposed that excises should be confined to mineral oils, beer, wines, spirits and tobacco products. Relatively little progress has been made on the excise front. Until recently the only notable step had been a series of directives on tobacco products which envisaged the ultimate harmonization of rates. The concrete element of these directives was concerned with the tax structure for cigarettes. The Community system was to be part specific and part *ad valorem*. More recently progress has been made on rates. Minimum levels of excise were agreed in June 1991 despite a dispute between France, who wished to retain excise on wine, and certain southern countries, who wished to retain zero rating.

State aids

It is not difficult to see that aids given to enterprises by states may distort competition between union members by giving some an artificial competitive advantage. Articles 92 to 94 of the Treaty are designed to deal with this problem.

Article 92(1) enunciates the basic principle. State aids which distort (or threaten to distort) competition by favouring certain enterprises, or the production of certain goods, are *in so far as trade between member states is affected* incompatible with the Common Market. Obviously aids with purely local effects are excluded – there is a parallel here with the law on cartels and dominant positions. With this as its general posture, the Treaty then explicitly recognizes two categories of exception. One consists of a series of aids which are *definitely* excepted from the general ban (Article

92(2)). The other consists of a series of examples of aids which *may* be excepted (Article 92(3)).

The definitely excepted category consists of aids of a social character granted to individuals. Aid granted to children in the form of free school milk would presumably fall into this class. The aid has, however, to be given without reference to where the goods come from. Discriminatory treatment whereby British milk was subsidized but other EC milk was not would not normally be acceptable. Aids could also be given in connection with natural disasters and to areas in West Germany bordering on the German Democratic Republic which, prior to unification, were disadvantaged by that geographical division.

We come now to the second category. Clearly, although there was no separate title in the Treaty relating to regional policy, those who drafted it were aware of pronounced differences in standards of living within the EC and of the existence of regional problems which could only be dealt with if policies of (possibly intensified) regional aid were pursued. There is in effect a recognition of all this in the Preamble and in Article 2 which calls for the promoting '. . . throughout the Community [of] an harmonious development of economic activities, a continuous and balanced expansion . . .' It was therefore inevitable that Article 92 would have to provide for the possibility of regional aids being deemed compatible with the Common Market. This is indeed the posture – they may be, but are not automatically, compatible. Clearly a blanket exception could not be given since regional aids might be excessive and thus become not a means of offsetting or overcoming certain locational disadvantages but a source of unfair competitive advantage. The theory that aids may be compatible applies not only to regional aids but also to assistance for the development of certain economic activities (i.e. industries). We have therefore the possibility of sectoral as well as regional aids. Aids may also be compatible if designed to promote an important project of common European importance or to remedy a serious disturbance in the economy of a member state. The Maastricht Treaty has added aids to conserve the heritage and environment to this list.

Article 93 imposes on the Commission the task of keeping state aids under constant review. Member states are required to inform the Commission of plans to grant aids or to alter them. Member states must also abide by the Commission's recommendations in connection therewith. If the Commission finds that an aid is not compatible with the Treaty it can issue a Decision requiring the aid to be terminated or modified. If member states do not comply, the Commission can initiate an enforcement action under Article 169. This carries with it the ultimate possibility that failure to comply could involve the Commission in taking the offending state to the Court of Justice for a final determination and fines.

Before we turn to a discussion of the approach of the Commission to the different forms of state aid, it is important to note a trend. State aids have always posed a problem for the Commission, but from the middle of the 1970s, and particularly in the early 1980s, states increasingly sought to give aids in order to cope with the generally depressed conditions and the problems encountered by specific industries. The Commission for its part was involved in an increasing number of actions which informally or formally led to modifications or abandonments of aid-giving plans.

Regional aid schemes have indeed posed a very considerable control problem for the Commission. The basic difficulty was that the various regions of the Community began to compete with each other to attract footloose investment capital. Regional aid schemes became more costly as a result of competitive outbidding and this process of bidding up did not appreciably increase the flow of investment. Rather it tended to give rise to reciprocal neutralization with unjustified profits for the beneficiary enterprise. Also aids tended no longer to correspond to the relative seriousness of the situation and in some cases the aid schemes were such that it was difficult to estimate just how generous they were. In 1971 the Commission decided to take action to control this process of aid escalation. Proposals were elaborated governing the scale of aid-giving in different regions. These were further elaborated in 1975, 1979 and 1988. The current arrangements specify the most generous aid ceilings for those regions which *by comparison with the Community average* suffer from abnormally low standards of living or where there is serious underemployment. Greece, Portugal and Ireland fall into this category, as do, for example, Southern Italy and Northern Ireland. Lower and differentiated aid ceilings are also allowed in other regions which, while not suffering abnormal and serious problems, nevertheless can be regarded as candidates for further development. To qualify, a region must be a prescribed amount below its *national* average in terms of prosperity although the generosity of the aid ceiling will depend on where the national average lies in relation to the Community average. In other words a UK region which is 15 per cent below the UK average will enjoy a higher ceiling than a German region which is 15 per cent below the German average.

It is important to emphasize that these arrangements relate to aid *ceilings*. It does not automatically follow that because a region has, for example, an aid ceiling of 23 per cent, the state can subsidize investments to the extent of 23 per cent of the cost. Rather the Commission will appraise the socioeconomic conditions in that region and determine what degree of aid (up to 23 per cent) is appropriate.

Before we leave the subject of regional aids, it needs to be recognized that the Commission has sought to regulate not only the level of aid given, but also the kinds of aid instrument employed. The UK has been particularly influenced here since the regional employment premium – a continuing labour subsidy – was not acceptable to the Commission. It was never banned and eventually the UK abandoned its use except in Northern Ireland. The UK regional development grant has also been attacked. The Commission favours once-and-for-all aid that should render a project sufficiently profitable for the enterprise to replace the capital in due course. In the case of the UK regional development grant, aid was not only granted initially but also made available when the capital was depreciated and was being renewed. Moreover, the second dose of aid was also granted even though no new employment was being created. The Commission forced the UK Government to modify the grant system accordingly.

Another main area of the Commission's supervisory activity is sectoral aid. As already indicated, aids to specific industries can be compatible with the Common Market, but the Commission has laid down certain criteria which must be respected. These (as spelled out in its *First Report on Competition Policy*, EC Commission, 1972a, p. 130) are as follows:

(a) Aids must be selective and must only be granted to enterprises the development or reorganization of which justify the presumption that they will be competitive in the long run having regard to the expected developments in the industrial sector concerned.

(b) Arising out of (a) is the condition that aids must be degressive. Aid must eventually be phased out and the enterprises must then be able to manage without further assistance. Aids must therefore not allow indefinitely a continuance of a situation of less than optimum allocation of resources. Aids may, however, be envisaged as going on indefinitely if at the Community level it is decided to continue them in order to compensate for competitive distortions emanating from outside the Community.

(c) Aids must be as transparent as possible so that they can be evaluated by, among others, Community institutions.

(d) Aids must obviously be well adapted to the objectives in view and if there is a choice of method, then the method adopted should be that which has the least effect on intra-Community competition and the common interest.

Subsequently, the economic position within the Community changed. From the end of 1974 onwards the Community economy was depressed, and added to that was the problem of intense competition from Japan and the Newly Industrializing Countries (NICs). State aids had a role to play here in keeping firms afloat whilst they introduced rationalization programmes. These take time to implement, and given the rising unemployment it was increasingly difficult for displaced workers to find new jobs elsewhere. The problems of industries in distress had been highlighted at the Copenhagen Summit of 1978 and this was followed by a dialogue between the Council of Ministers and the Commission, after which the latter issued new aid guidelines. Whilst these reiterated some of the ideas of 1972 there was a noticeable softening of tone, particularly in respect of the need for a breathing space which would allow longer-term restructuring solutions to be worked out. Aids could be used as an interim measure to avoid sudden and severe social and economic shocks. The new guidelines also explicitly recognized the valuable role that state aids could play in (a) speeding up the response of the private enterprise system to new investment and technological opportunities and (b) the adaptation of industries which needed to contract and redeploy resources.

The Commission has not defined its attitude to aid in every specific industrial sector. Only in the case of industries which have been encountering structural problems across the Community has the Commission felt the need to take a specific stance. This has been the case in textiles, clothing, man-made fibres and shipbuilding. We shall not discuss these approaches at this point but reserve discussion until Chapter 10 when we consider Community Industrial Policy and notably its policy stance towards problem industries.

Four further developments are of particular note. First, following the post-Copenhagen guidelines, the Commission became more sympathetic towards aids designed to stimulate research and development (R&D). This was undoubtedly a reflection of the growing appreciation of the need for the Community to match the technological might of the US and Japan. However, because assistance was increasingly taking the form of aid to R&D, the Commission in 1986 laid down a Community framework. The basic rules are as follows: (a) such aids must be notified like any others; (b) the level of aid for *basic* research should not exceed 50 per cent of the research programme or project, and the nearer the research is to the market place (i.e. applied as opposed to basic) the lower the aid level must be; (c) the possibility that such aid will distort competition and affect inter-state trade has to be taken into account.

The second point is that there has been a growing tendency for sectoral aid to take the form of state participation in the capital of *private* undertakings. The Commission maintains, and has been supported by the Court of Justice, that this constitutes an aid if the capital is injected at less than commercial terms. The Court made this clear in the 1984 *Intermills* case when it said that loans advanced on more favourable terms than are available in the market and equity capital advanced when private investors would not do so are just as much aids as is a straight capital grant.

The third point is an extension of the second. The Rome Treaty does not preclude nationalization. However, Article 90, subject to one qualification,[1] does declare that the rules on competition (Articles 85 and 86 *et seq.*) and on state aids (Article 92 *et seq.*) do apply to public enterprises. In respect of state aids, the Commission has been concerned about the financial relationship between govern-

---

1. Article 90 declares that although public utilities and state monopolies of a commercial character (see below) are subject to the competition rules, the application of those rules must not obstruct the performance of tasks assigned to such enterprises.

ments and their public corporations. Obviously the concern of the Commission is that capital could be provided at favourable rates and that this would give the corporations an artificial competitive edge when competing with firms in the same industry in other member states who operate on a private basis. In order to more effectively regulate the activities of member states in relation to their public enterprises, the Commission in 1980 took the controversial step of adopting a directive requiring states to provide data on the financial relationships between themselves and their public corporations. This provoked strong opposition from some member state governments. They challenged the Commission's action in the Court of Justice – in the event the Court supported the Commission.

The fourth point to note is that the tendency for governments to want to grant aids to support unsuccessful, loss-making enterprises shows no signs of abating. In the 1990s the Commission had to face attempts by several member states to support loss-making airlines who were struggling in the new more competitive, deregulated climate (see Chapter 8). France, Portugal, Ireland and Greece were among those who in 1994 secured approvals for aided reconstructions. The subsidy to Air France, personally pressed for at the Commission by the French prime minister, was particularly controversial. It was opposed by privatized British Airways which was making profits. The British carrier indicated that it would challenge the aid at the Court of Justice. France was also involved in another controversy when, having in 1992 secured Commission approval for aid to assist the Bull computer group's research programme, it then in 1993 proceeded to grant further bail-outs.

There is also a third category of aid, which in the past has caused the Commission some trouble. This is the general aid which, as its title suggests, has no designated specific objective and can be applied on an individual, sectoral or regional basis as the national need arises. The attitude of the Commission has been that, as they stand, such aids are incompatible with the Rome Treaty and ought to be made specific – i.e. they ought to be transformed into sectoral or regional aids which address themselves to particular kinds of problem. The Commission also indicated that it should be kept informed about such general aids. (Its attitude was well summarized in *Second Report on Competition Policy* (EC Commission, 1973, pp. 101–6.) However, as we noted earlier, the economic situation subsequently worsened. During the second half of 1974 the Community economy began to enter its worst postwar recession. Unemployment began to rise and the economic downturn began to aggravate the situation in industries which had structural problems dating from the energy crisis and earlier. Even in sectors not suffering from such problems, some enterprises found themselves in financial difficulties. The upshot of all this was an intensification of general aid schemes and the implementation of various general recovery measures. Although the Commission could have raised objections, it seems to have recognized that the exceptional economic and social situation confronting the member states justified the adoption of these exceptional measures. In so doing it drew attention, prudently perhaps, to Article 92(3)(b) which allows aids to be granted which are designed 'to remedy a serious disturbance in the economy of a member state'.

Next we must note the other important form of state assistance – the export aid. The Commission has taken a very categorical stance on this topic. Such aid cannot benefit from any exception whatsoever and the Commission has constantly been on the attack. For example, in 1976 it took the Italian Government to task because the Istituto Nazionale per il Commercio Estero (ICE) was making grants to cover approximately two thirds of the promotional cost of toy sales in the French market. Subsequently, it was discovered that ICE was also making grants in respect of the sales promotion of footwear, textiles and clothing in other member state markets. The Commission therefore initiated a procedure which finally led to the issuing of a Decision formally instructing the Italian Government to desist.

For completeness we should note that at various times the Commission has produced other guidelines on aid giving. Following the tendency for states to insist on higher environmental standards the Commission in 1974 advised governments on the principles which ought to govern the bearing of the cost. Central to this was the 'polluter pays' principle. In 1989 the Commission also issued guidance on aid giving to the motor industry.

The Cockfield White Paper on completing the internal market did not call for any new legislative measures. Instead the emphasis has been on more vigorous enforcement of existing treaty powers. The White Paper did, however, require the Commission to produce an inventory of state aids and to report on their implications for policy. Three reports were subsequently published (EC Commission, 1989, 1990a and E Commission, 1992).

The Commission's more vigorous stance has three main elements. First, it is seeking to give more publicity to the aid issue so that governments and enterprises know what is acceptable and what is not. Second, the Commission is moving to a position where states that grant aid but do not follow proper *procedures* will find that the aid is declared to be illegal. Third, with increased vigour it is demanding the actual repayment of illegal aid. A celebrated instance of this was the 1990 *Renault* case. The Commission forced the repayment of FF 6 billion of aid to Renault on the grounds that promises concerning restructuring and company status, made when the aid was approved, were not kept.

Official and technical standards

Member state governments interfere on a very considerable scale in establishing official and technical standards. These are laid down for a variety of reasons but mainly to protect the public against physical harm and deception. As an example of the first we can cite the case of drugs and proprietary medicines. The need for government surveillance and control is all too obvious – experience with thalidomide leaves no doubt on that score. Then in the case of foods, standards have to be established in respect of flavouring, colouring and other additives; we can cite the ban on cyclamates as a case in point. But there are many others – electrical equipment and the emission of pollutants by road vehicles are two examples taken at random. Where consumers are not likely to be harmed they may be deceived. For this reason there are rules on labelling designed to indicate to consumers what certain designations, for example of textiles, really mean.

The desirability of such standards is not in question, but to the extent that they differ significantly between states they do undoubtedly constitute a form of NTB. Either they mean that goods cannot be exported, with a consequent loss of competition across frontiers, or if they are exported they have to be adapted to the rules of each national market. Either way the economies of large-scale production, in the form of long runs of a standardized product, are in some degree sacrificed. The obvious answer is to harmonize standards, and the E Commission has pointed out that such harmonization can raise the quality of life in matters such as safety and the environment, since the Community standard can be based on the best national practice available. Consumer choice is also increased. The notion that harmonization leads to less variety is erroneous. Rather, the existence of NTBs reduces national choice. Although products may be standardized in certain essential respects, they can still exhibit wide variations of styling and performance. Thus the car in the EC has been subject to considerable harmonization but the range of choice is still vast.

The original approach

The need to harmonize standards was recognized by those who drafted the Rome Treaty, the relevant provisions being Articles 100 to 102 on the approximation of laws. Article 100 provides for the Council, on a proposal by the Commission, to issue unifying directives when laws, regulations or administrative actions of member states directly affect the setting up or operation of the common market.

Harmonization measures fell into either the 'total' or 'optional' category. Total harmonization required that all products covered by a directive had to conform to the standards set out in the directive. In such a case national standards had to be abolished and the Community standard substituted. Such total harmonization was usually adopted when consumer safety was involved (e.g. cosmetics), although this approach was also adopted in the case of textile labelling which was purely informational. Optional harmonization permitted the parallel existence of Community and national rules. Manufacturers who produced in accordance with the Community standard acquired access to all national markets, whilst those who continued to apply only national standards had access to only their home market.

Up to 1985 the Council of Ministers had adopted approximately 180 directives relating to industrial products as well as a number concerned with foodstuffs. The industrial products included motor vehicles, metrology (i.e. measuring instruments), cosmetics, solvents (and other dangerous substances) and electrical equipment. In the case of foodstuffs, directives governed their labelling (durability, additives used, etc.), packaging (restriction on the use of PVC), presentation, advertising and composition. Additives were subject to provisions specifying maximum levels. Much had therefore been achieved but there was still a long way to go. Moreover, the harmonization process is very time consuming. Not only that, but technological progress rendered existing standards obsolescent, and therefore effort had to be diverted into bringing them up to date. The Community was in fact forced to adopt a speedier process in respect of amendments to standards.

The new approach

In Chapter 4 we said we would return to the *Cassis de Dijon* case. We do so because it and related cases have implications for harmonization. It will be remembered that that case involved the application of a standard which in practice precluded the importation of the liqueur in question. The standard therefore had the effect of a zero import quota and was an offence under Articles 30 *et seq*. In the process of delivering its judgement the Court of Justice also made the point that any product legally made and sold in one member state must in principle be admitted to the markets of the others. National rules and standards can only create barriers where they are necessary to satisfy 'mandatory' requirements such as public health, consumer protection, etc. Moreover, and this is the key point, any rule must be the 'essential guarantee' of the interest, the protection of which is regarded as being justified. It will be remembered that in the *Cassis* case the German Government defended its minimum alcoholic content rule on grounds of consumer protection. But the Court noted that that objective could have been achieved by merely requiring the label to show the actual alcoholic content. The rule was not essential to guarantee the protection of the consumer. It did not follow that in the light of *Cassis* the need to harmonize no longer existed. There would be some situations where the need to have rules was inescapable, and goods not conforming to them would be excluded. In such cases the only way forward was to harmonize. But there would be many cases where the standards involved relatively trivial issues. In such cases harmonization would no longer be required.

What was needed was a new more streamlined approach (building on the *Cassis de Dijon* case) to the problem. In the Cockfield White Paper of 1985 the Commission noted that in 1984 the Council of Ministers had recognized the essential equivalence of the objectives of national legislation. That being so, freer trading conditions could at least in part be achieved by making use of the principle of mutual recognition. Thus, the fact that countries had different views about the appropriate ingredients for making ice cream could hardly be invoked as a defensive argument for not importing from each other – no harm was likely to ensue to consumers. It was true that if the Community wished to take full advantage of the scale economies available in a continental sized market then standardization had its virtues. But to proceed exclusively down that path would be over-regulatory. There would, however, be some situations where, as we have indicated, the need to have particular rules was inescapable and goods not conforming to them could be excluded. In such cases the only way forward was to harmonize. Several changes were therefore made. First, and as we have already noted, thanks to the Single Act such harmonization activity would only require a qualified majority vote. Second, the Council would not get bogged down in the detail but would merely seek in its directives to identify the objectives to be attained – e.g. the essential safety requirements with which products would have to comply in order to qualify for free movement. Third, the detailed process of standard setting would be off-loaded on to special European standards bodies. Fourth, governments would be obliged to presume that if a good was manufactured according to such standards then it complied with the fundamental objectives stipulated in the directive and had to be granted free access. Fifth, in the absence of European standards, conformity to national standards carried the same benefit.

It is perhaps worth mentioning that the SEA has stipulated that in the process of following this new procedure, proposals concerning health, safety, environmental protection and consumer protection 'will take as a base a high level of protection'. In respect of food the Commission has totally rejected the idea that it shall be subject to standardization. Rather the culinary riches of Europe must remain. Therefore instead of producing a host of recipe laws, consumers will be protected by being advised as to what they eat by means of labelling. Of course where there are dangers to health – e.g. additives and packaging – some harmonization of standards will still be needed. By 1990 much of this aspect of food harmonization, as part of the single market programme, had already been accomplished.

Product liability

Since at least 1972 the EC has been developing a policy on consumer protection. Apart from the harmonization, to which we have just referred, the Commission has tabled draft directives on matters such as unit pricing, doorstep selling and product liability. Except for the latter, these are not matters of central concern in this chapter and will be reserved for discussion in Chapter 10.

Product liability refers to the liability of a producer towards a consumer who is injured or killed when using, or in some way consuming, his product. National laws on this matter have varied. Some, as for example those of the UK, required the injured party to prove negligence on the part of the manufacturer. On the other hand, some laws adopted a 'strict liability' approach, whereby a producer was automatically liable for goods which lead to death or material injury. No proof of fault or negligence was necessary. These laws may also make manufacturers bear the development risk. In other words the producer is still liable even if at the time the good was produced it was from a scientific point of view regarded as harmless – i.e. the subsequent harm was unknowable. Thus if a strict liability approach, with the development risk falling on the producer, had been operative in the UK when the thalidomide tragedy occurred, there would have been an automatic case for compensation even though at the time when it was marketed the drug was, in the light of the existing scientific knowledge, thought to be harmless.

Manufacturers can insure against claims, but obviously the cost of the insurance will vary according to the posture of the law. Laws such as those of the UK made it difficult to establish a claim, because proving negligence was extremely difficult. Insurance costs in such circumstances will be modest, whereas they will be heavier when strict liability prevails. The Commission, noting that the laws of the member states varied, drew the conclusion that insurance costs would also vary and that this distorted competition. It also argued that the decision whether or not to sell in a market might be influenced by the kind of claims which might arise there. The Commission therefore proposed that national laws be harmonized. It also sought to kill two birds with one stone by espousing a measure which would improve the position of many consumers. To these ends it proposed in 1976 that national laws should be modified so as to provide for strict liability with the development risk falling on producers. In 1985 the Council of Ministers adopted a directive which went some way down the track to a strict liability approach. The directive required member states to incorporate the new approach in their national laws within three years. Under the new approach producers are liable for injury caused by their products, but certain defences are provided for including the so-called development risk or state of the art argument – i.e. that at the time it was marketed scientific knowledge was such that the risk of injury from the product was not knowable. The UK incorporated this approach in Part I of the Consumer Protection Act of 1987. The directive did allow member states to opt for a tougher regime which ruled out the state of the art defence but the UK chose not to do so.

Public purchasing

The public sector – that is to say central and local government and nationalized bodies – is a major spender in the economic systems of western economies. Such public spending does not always take place in a non-discriminatory way. Rather than accepting the cheapest and/or best offers, the institutions of the public sector often adopt 'buy national' attitudes. The motives are various, but include balance of payments considerations, the desire to build up particular industries (for example computers), prevention of unemployment and sheer prestige.

This kind of discriminatory and restrictive behaviour is contrary to the Rome Treaty – specifically Articles 7, 30 and 59. The latter relates to the freedom to supply services. It should also be said that the Council of Ministers adopted a directive in 1970 to give effect to the ban on discriminatory practices. That directive prohibits measures, imposed by law, regulation or administrative practice, which prevent the supply of imported goods from other member states, which grant domestic products a preference or which make the supply of imported goods more difficult or costly than domestic products.

The Commission seems to have recognized that a general directive would not suffice and that there was a need to produce specific directives relating to particular kinds of public purchasing. The initial focus was public works contracting. In 1971 the Council adopted two directives. The first swept away all obstacles to the freedom to supply services. The second drew up common rules for the awarding of contracts. By a separate Decision it established an advisory committee on the subject of public works contracting. The second directive related to contracts of one million ECUs and more but left those relating to energy and water for separate treatment. As a result of this directive, contractors throughout the Community were promised free and effective competition on all major public works contracts offered by member states. Contractors were informed of pending contracts through the Community's Official Journal. Competent authorities were obliged to accept tenders from all qualified contractors in the Community and were required to award contracts on purely economic and non-discriminatory grounds. All discrimination of a purely technical nature was to be eliminated. A complaints procedure was established. In 1976 the Council followed up with a directive on public procurement – it was officially described as a directive co-ordinating procedures for the award of public supply contracts. As a result, central, regional and local authorities seeking to award public supply contracts in excess of 144,000 ECUs[1] had to publish a notice in the Official Journal, giving potential tenderers all the information needed to make an offer. In considering tenders the contract-awarding authority had to treat all offers equally – i.e. there had to be no discrimination as between home and foreign bids.

The settlement of complaints was dealt with by the body which discharged that role in respect of public works contracts – it was given the title of Advisory Committee for Public Contracts.

All this legislative activity did not prove sufficient to persuade member states to behave in a non-discriminatory way. There was

---

1. This related to central and federal authorities. The figure for regional and local authorities was 200,000 ECUs.

ample evidence that the Community law was flouted. For example, in 1981 the Commission had to institute cases against France and Ireland. Both were accused of encouraging and promoting the purchase of domestic goods in preference to imported ones – a clear breach of Article 30 of the Rome Treaty and of the obligations set out in the 1970 directive.

Not only that, but member states employed all their ingenuity to avoid being subjected to the directives. Various loopholes were exploited. Thus whilst directives might distinguish between open contracts (i.e. anybody could bid), restricted contracts (a limited list could bid) and negotiated contracts (i.e. only one firm would be approached), there was an unwarranted tendency to prefer the latter two and often the last – i.e. the man down the road. Contracts were divided to bring them below the threshold levels covered by directives. Contract values were underestimated with the same end in view. Emergency procedures were employed which, by having shorter notice periods, made life difficult for foreign suppliers. The Cockfield White Paper recognizing these and other problems therefore made four proposals.

(a) The directives should be tightened up to eliminate these loopholes.
(b) The purchasing of public authorities in water, transport, energy and telecommunications had been exempt from the public supply contract directive. It was desirable that they should be covered. This was also desirable in respect of areas exempt under the public works directive.
(c) The public purchasing of services – e.g. data processing – should also be governed by specific public purchasing rules.
(d) Quick-acting methods of redress should be established at national level.

In 1988 the public supply and in 1989 the public works directives were therefore tightened up. Thus the 1988 directive made open contracts the rule: the use of other procedures had to be justified to the Commission. In 1990 purchasing rules for public utilities were also agreed. The rules were also extended to services in 1992. In 1989 each member state was required to establish a system of legal redress so that where a contract was going to be let, or had been let, in ways which breached Community rules, the disadvantaged parties could either halt the letting of the contract or seek damages if it had been let. The emphasis was on quick-acting on-the-spot remedies although the Commission can also intervene. This was part of the single market programme.

State monopolies

In a number of member states – France, Italy and Germany – the Commission has encountered problems raised by what the Rome Treaty calls State Monopolies of a Commercial Character – a phenomenon singled out for attention in Article 37. The reader should note that these are not what are usually thought of as nationalized industries or public utilities. Indeed case law has indicated that nationalized industries engaged in transport, gas, electricity, water and broadcasting are not relevant. Rather, these monopolies are concerned with products such as alcohol and manufactured tobacco. The main reason for such monopolies is fiscal – the monopoly revenues of the sales organizations accrue to the state as part of its fiscal revenues. Additional motives for the foundation of these monopolies have been the protection of national production and the assurance of supplies. From the point of view of the Common Market the main drawback of these organizations is that they have a discriminatory effect on the conditions of supply and marketing of goods emanating from other member states. These have consisted of the following: (a) refusal to import; (b) quantitative restrictions on imports; (c) the application of relatively more onerous marketing conditions on imported goods compared with home-produced goods; (d) discriminations against the advertising of foreign goods. These monopolies have also enjoyed exclusive exporting rights and, among other things, this has led to discrimination in the terms offered between home and foreign buyers.

Article 37 did not require the abolition of these monopolies. Instead, it required that during the transition period they should be adjusted so as to eliminate discrimination regarding the conditions under which goods are procured and marketed between nationals of the member states. The Commission has waged a long war of attrition on them with a view to securing changes in their behaviour which would bring them into conformity with Article 37. Fortunately, the task of the Commission was considerably eased by virtue of the fact that some monopolies were abolished and others were reformed in various ways. However, a hard core of problems remained – alcohol, manufactured tobacco and petroleum in France, alcohol in West Germany and manufactured tobacco and matches in Italy.

It was extremely important to eliminate the monopoly control over imports – this would then open up the national markets to supplies from other states. In 1970 the Commission was able to secure the compliance of Italy and France in the removal by 1976 of such restrictions in respect of imports of manufactured tobacco. Then in 1975, in the *Pubblico Ministero v. Manghera* case, the Court of Justice declared against exclusive rights to import. As a result, the Commission was endowed with authority to attack such rights not only in the tobacco trade but also in other areas. Having secured what appeared to be a victory, the Commission then found that the state monopolies were indulging in other activities which were designed to prevent free importation. Taxes were being manipulated and subsidies employed to keep imports out. Thanks however to a series of preliminary rulings by the Court of Justice these various loopholes were plugged. Considerable progress has therefore been made in this area of policy. But the battle is not over. Indeed the battle never will be over, since state monopolies will presumably from time to time attempt to behave in ways which are contrary to the Rome Treaty. In addition the Commission had to deal with the further problems of enlargement – i.e. Greek and Iberian monopolies. The new ex-EFTA members agreed to reform their import and wholesale monopolies by the time of accession – this was part of the 1994 accession agreement. However, no Court of Justice rulings existed in respect of retail monopolies and these were allowed to remain, at least temporarily, provided they did not discriminate against products from other member states.

6

FACTOR MOVEMENTS AND THE COMMON MARKET

Introduction

As we indicated earlier, the original EC was based on the concept of a common market rather than just simply a customs union. That meant there should be free movement of factors of production such as capital, labour (and the professions) and enterprise as well as goods. Not only that, but there should be freedom to supply services across frontiers as well as goods. The free movement of labour was provided for in Articles 48 to 51; the free movement of capital was covered in the original Rome Treaty by Articles 67 to 73, 106 and 109 while the free movement of enterprise (known as the right of establishment) was dealt with in Articles 52 to 58. The free movement of services was governed by Articles 59 to 66.

The distinction between the right of establishment and the freedom to supply services requires elaboration. If a UK insurance company located in London wishes to insure a risk in Germany it has a choice. It could establish a subsidiary in Germany and insure from there, or it could insure directly from London. The first arrangement would involve invoking the right of establishment. The second is an example of the freedom to supply services.

Before the SEA only limited progress was made in realizing these rights and freedoms. The residual obstacles were connected with the continued existence of domestic regulation systems and state intervention which were concerned with consumer protection, the guaranteeing of professional competence, domestic taxation, macroeconomic management and industrial stability. The Cockfield Report identified the nature of the continuing obstacles and for the most part called for their elimination by the end of 1992. In this discussion we shall therefore continue to deal with aspects of the single market programme. Measures concerned with labour, the professions, capital and financial services will be dealt with in this chapter. Those concerned with transport, and notably air passenger transport, are discussed in Chapter 8.

The free movement of labour, professionals and persons

It is convenient to treat this subject under three headings. First, there is the free movement of labour (workers). Second, there is the free movement of professionals. Third, there is the general issue of the free movement of persons across frontiers. The latter is important because, as we noted in the last chapter, the SEA called for the creation of an internal market 'without frontiers'. In addition the Maastricht Treaty confers citizenship rights, which involve free movement, and has introduced the Cooperation on Justice and Home Affairs system.

In keeping with the concept of a common market, the Rome Treaty provides for the free movement of labour.[1] (There is a provision that freedom of movement can be limited on grounds of public safety, public security and public health.) Article 48 required that free movement be achieved before the end of the transition period. In fact, in this sphere of operations the Six registered a distinct success in that complete freedom of movement was achieved in July 1968, one-and-a-half years ahead of schedule. Article 48 complements the principle of free movement with a ban on discrimination based on nationality in regard to employment, remuneration and other conditions of work.

The Six approached the establishment of free movement of labour in stages. The first, which was provided for in Council Regulation 15 of 1961, operated between September 1961 and May 1964. During this period the movement of labour into another member state required the issue of a permit by the state of destination. Workers were permitted to renew the permit for the same occupation after one year of regular employment. After three years they were able to renew their permit for any other occupation for which they were qualified and after four years for any kind of paid work. In effect after four years discrimination ceased. During this first period a preference was given to national workers in that any

---

1. It should be noted that free movement does not apply to employment in public administration.

vacancies in the national labour market were compulsorily notified for three weeks in the job centres of the home country, but after this period offers of employment were transmitted to other member states. But if, for example, an employer asked for a worker by name, the temporary preference for home market supply could be waived. During this stage a Community preference also existed, in that Community workers were to have priority over workers from third countries in filling job vacancies.

During the second stage, which extended from May 1964 to June 1968, progressive freedom under the permit system was speeded up, in that after two years of regular employment a migrant worker could move to any job on the same terms as nationals. The national preference was abolished, but a safeguard clause was inserted which enabled a member state to restore it for fifteen days when a surplus of manpower existed in certain areas or trades. If a member state operated the safeguard clause it had to be justified adequately. The priority of Community workers over non-Community workers was preserved.

In July 1968 complete freedom of movement became a reality. The principle of national priority was abandoned and so Community workers could then have the same access to jobs as nationals. Work permits were abolished, and as a result Common Market migrant workers could take up employment without having to comply with any formalities other than those for residence permits. The latter are issued for a period of five years and are renewable automatically. The priority of Community workers over non-Community workers was, however, retained. New members have had to conform to these requirements. Those who entered in the 1970s were given five-year transition periods within which to adjust. Greece (from 1981) and the two Iberian members (from 1986) were given a seven-year adjustment period.

It hardly needs saying that complete freedom of movement could not have become a reality unless a lot of other problems had been dealt with. To take just two examples, workers need to be informed of job opportunities in other member states and social security rights need to be transferable. In order to deal with the first, the Commission in 1972 adopted its *Système européen de diffusion des offres et demandes d'emploi et de compensation internationale* (SEDOC). This was conceived as a uniform system for codifying jobs and their remuneration so that data on job availability might be transmitted between member states. A European Coordination Office to facilitate this process was established, and the system began to operate in 1973.

A generous level of social security benefits would be a considerable deterrent to labour mobility if migrant workers had to sacrifice them on moving to another member state. Having made contributions to the social security system in one member state, workers are less likely to migrate if their rights are not transferable. At a relatively early date the Community therefore addressed itself to this problem. An ECSC Convention on Social Security for Migrant Workers had been signed in 1957, ensuring that all social security contributions, in whatever member state they were paid, counted for benefit eligibility. The EC Treaty contained a similar requirement, and in 1959 the provisions of the ECSC Convention were extended to *all* workers. As a result the following principles apply. Migrant workers from all the member states are eligible for the same social security benefits as national workers. Periods of employment and insurance completed in several member states are aggregated for the purpose of calculating benefits. At any time a beneficiary may request the transfer of benefits from one member state to another. In 1970 the Council of Ministers extended these principles to self-employed insured persons.

The upshot of all this was that Community nationals came to have equal rights in applying for vacant jobs in any member state. They enjoyed equal treatment compared with the citizens of the state to which they have moved in respect of social security and taxation. They were eligible for election to trade unions and works councils. They were entitled to equal access to property ownership and housing. Migrant workers could bring their family and dependants with them – this however, required the availability of suitable accommodation. Rights of this kind were progressively improved as the regulation of 1961 gave place to the 1964 regulation, which in turn was supplanted by that of 1968. For example, eligibility to vote for candidates for works councils was followed by the right to be a candidate. Originally, on moving the worker could only bring his wife and minor children, but this was modified later – the definition of the family being expanded to include not only the wife and minors but all children, parents and grandparents dependent on the worker. Although some of these issues seem to be relatively innocuous they were in fact the subject of keen bargaining and debate between the member states (see Dahlberg, 1968). The 1968 regulation did not see the end of progressive improvement. For example, in 1975 the Council adopted a regulation extending equality of treatment in the exercise of trade union rights to cover admission to the leading positions in trade union organizations.

It could also be argued that the free movement of labour would be distorted if levels of personal income tax varied from state to state. Labour would shift to low tax states. In practice this has not been felt to be a problem. When the Neumark Committee (EEC Commission, 1962a) reported on various aspects of tax harmonization, it pointed out that labour was less mobile than capital and therefore the problem of disparities in personal income tax did not pose a major problem. It has, however, been proposed that workers crossing frontiers daily should be taxed according to their country of residence and that a husband and wife should be taxed separately. In 1985 the Commission indicated that the former should have a high priority in the programme for completing the internal market by 1992. However in the longer term a progressive tendency to harmonize income tax rates and structures may arise. Here we have to take account of the fact that Maastricht Treaty granted various Union citizenship rights to the nationals of the member states. As time passes individuals may take greater and greater advantage of the right to move to, and to take up residence in, other states of the European Union. Such movement may in part be motivated by differences in national tax regimes. Governments may respond to this by bringing their tax systems into line with those of their neighbours. Here we are identifying an important property of economic integration namely that harmonization may arise as a result of market forces rather than from legal requirements.

In the professions the issues have been the need to provide for the right of establishment and the freedom to supply services. At the outset we must take account of two important cases which were heard before the Court of Justice in 1974 – the *Reyners* case and the *Van Binsbergen* case. The upshot of these was that from the end of the transition period, the right of establishment and the freedom to supply services could be invoked in the courts, and all discrimination *on grounds of nationality* was automatically prohibited. The implication of all this will perhaps be clearer when we note that as early as 1961 the Council of Ministers adopted two general programmes, one for the abolition of restrictions affecting the right of establishment, and one on the removal of restrictions on the freedom to supply services. In these it established priorities for action and thereafter patiently started to produce separate directives for many areas of trade and industry and for some professions. As a result, a significant amount of liberalizing legislation was enacted. However, it would appear that some of this activity was really redundant since in the light of *Reyners* and *Van Binsbergen* this basic right and this basic freedom are automatically enjoyed.

Nevertheless it would not be true to say that there was no need for legislative activity of any kind on the part of the Community. Take, for example, the position of many of the professions in earlier years. Despite what the Rome Treaty might say and how the Court might interpret it, the right and the freedom would not have been sufficient to enable a professional person to supply a service to another state or to set up in business in another state and proceed to practise his or her profession. The reason for this was that member states had laid down the qualifications which various professional persons had to possess before they could practise. Unfortunately, the qualifications possessed by a professional person might not be recognized in another member state. Moreover, the cases which we have discussed recognized the right of states to enact such protective legislation: what those cases outlawed was discrimination on grounds of nationality. In order for professional persons to be able to practise anywhere in the Community, legislative activity was needed which led to a recognition by states of each other's professional qualifications, provided for training to be harmonized, etc. The original approach of the Community to the problem of professional mobility was a *sectoral* one. It later developed a *general* one. The sectoral approach consisted of agreeing directives for particular professions. The general one consisted of an across the board mechanism for recognizing professional qualifications. We will treat them in that order.

One of the earlier professions to be approached on a *sectoral* basis was that of doctors. But because of the poor progress Commissioner Ralf Dahrendorf, before he left Brussels, decided to hold a unique Common Market meeting. This occurred in 1973 when the

Commission invited ninety-nine doctors to a public hearing to discuss the central problem of the mutual recognition of medical qualifications and the training which lies behind them. The doctors who attended were members of the Standing Committee of Doctors of the Common Market, and of Universities, and there were observers present from other professional bodies and from governments. Draft directives had been published in 1969 indicating the solution envisaged by the Commission but much criticism had been levelled at them. The public hearing was judged to have been a success and certainly substantial progress was subsequently made in 1975 when two directives and two Decisions were adopted by the Council. The object of the directives was to make the right of establishment and the freedom to provide services a reality in the case of doctors. One directive provided for the mutual recognition of diplomas, certificates and other evidence of formal qualifications in medicine. The specific diplomas, etc., were listed in the directive. Provisions were also laid down which are designed to meet the requirements of a host state when proof of good character or good repute is called for. Clearly, requirements such as compulsory registration with a professional organization (e.g. the General Medical Council in the UK) could be an obstacle to the freedom to supply services. The directive therefore exempted nationals from other member states from that requirement but subjected them to the domestic rules of professional conduct in the state where the service was being supplied. The second directive in effect recognized that some greater degree of harmonization in the length and content of medical training – in terms of what is a minimum acceptable standard – was desirable. It therefore laid down such requirements and provided for their subsequent introduction. One of the Decisions established an Advisory Committee on Medical Training to assist in the introduction of comparably demanding standards of medical training as between the member states. The other Decision set up a Committee of Senior Officials in Public Health whose job it was to assist in dealing with difficulties arising in the implemention of the two directives.

The *sectoral* approach was also employed in respect of other professions – veterinarians and dentists are two instances. However, it was a slow and tedious business. Nowhere was this more obvious than in the case of architects. It took seventeen years to achieve agreement in respect of the architectural profession – the directive was adopted in 1985 with 1987 as the date for implementation. The agreement allows architects who are nationals of any member state to practise in other member states provided they possess an approved qualification. A system of mutual recognition of qualifications has been agreed. The approved qualification may or may not include a period of practical training. Once registered in a member state, an architect must abide by the regulations governing that country's profession. For example, some countries require compulsory indemnity insurance.

In 1988 the Council of Ministers took a step forward when it adopted a directive which established a *general* approach to the professions. It applies to all those professions in which access is restricted by the state and require at least three years' university training or its equivalent – such as lawyers, accountants, engineers, teachers and surveyors. It enables a qualified professional in one member state to become a member of the equivalent profession in another member state without having to requalify. If the length of training is shorter than that in the country receiving a professional, then the receiving country can demand evidence of an additional period of professional experience. If the content of the training is deficient, examinations or supervised practice may also be required.

As we noted earlier, the SEA called for an internal market without frontiers. This would give rise to completely free personal mobility – a matter about which there has been, and no doubt will continue to be, considerable controversy. Mrs Thatcher was forthright on this subject. In her famous – to some infamous – speech at Bruges in 1988 she declared: 'It is a matter of plain common sense that we cannot totally abolish frontier controls if we are also to protect our citizens from crime and stop the movement of drugs, or terrorists, and of illegal immigrants.' The UK argued that while it envisaged easier passage for the nationals of member states, it did not intend this to apply to the nationals of third countries. Therefore it could maintain border controls to control third country nationals. This may have been a convenient piece of logic chopping. Nevertheless there is no doubt that the SEA did provide support for UK resistance as one of the declarations at the end of the Act guaranteed that nothing in it should prevent states taking such measures as they considered necessary to control third country immigration, terrorism, crime, drug trafficking and illicit trade in art and antiques.

There is indeed a serious problem here, because before they remove border controls member states do need to be assured that adequate alternative safeguards exist. These require developments such as adequate policing at the common external frontier by all the other member states and arrangements which guarantee that the ability to apprehend criminals, terrorists and drug traffickers is not undermined. From the mid-1980s two approaches were followed. First, some countries – initially France, Germany, Belgium, Netherlands and Luxembourg – sought to develop a comprehensive treaty abolishing all frontier controls on the movement of people between them. The now-famous Schengen Treaty, signed in June 1990, began life in 1984 as a Franco-German endeavour but the Benelux countries joined in in 1985. Eventually all the Community countries became signatories except Denmark, Ireland and the UK. Secondly, and in the light of the Adonnino Committee's aspirations, Ministers of Justice and Internal Affairs sought agreement on a piecemeal basis on subjects such as the right of asylum. An important agreement on the latter subject was arrived at in Dublin in June 1990. The result was that asylum-seekers were guaranteed that at least one state would process such an application and situations where individuals were shuffled from state to state would not arise.

Under the Schengen agreement the partners agreed to shift controls away from their internal borders to their external frontier. To this end they agreed on a common list of countries whose citizens required visas to enter the zone, a common right of asylum policy, to pool their crime data in a giant computer, to let their police forces pursue criminals on each other's territories and to narrow differences in narcotics policies. There would be no border controls of people travelling between the participating states, and passport controls on flights between the Schengen partners would be scrapped.

As a result of the Maastricht Treaty these developments were followed by CJHA which as we noted earlier is one of the three main pillars of the Union Treaty. CJHA is covered by Maastricht Treaty Article K – for the first time it places inter-governmental cooperation in these fields on a formal treaty basis. In the interests of achieving the objectives of the Union, and in particular the free movement of persons, the Member States have agreed that the following topics are to be regarded as matters of common interest:

(a) asylum policy;
(b) rules governing the crossing by persons of the external borders of Member States;
(c) immigration policy;
(d) the combating of drug addiction;
(e) the combating of fraud on an international scale;
(f) judicial cooperation in civil matters;
(g) judicial cooperation in criminal matters;
(h) customs cooperation;
(i) police cooperation for the purposes of preventing terrorism, drug trafficking and serious forms of international crime, combined with an information exchange system (to be centred on a still controversial European Police Office or Europol).

There is specific commitment to deal with these matters in compliance with the European Convention on Human Rights and the Convention Relating to the Status of Refugees. All Member States are in fact already parties to these undertakings.

The emphasis is on the coordination of national actions in the fields referred to above. The focus of decision making is once again the Council of Ministers, and there is now a single Council of Interior and Justice Ministers to replace the previously more diverse arrangements. This Council adopts both joint positions and joint actions. Joint positions, like common positions under the CFSP, are binding under international law. Proposals, which may lead to joint positions or joint actions, will come from the member states and the Commission except that the latter is debarred from making proposals relating to (g), (h) and (i) above. In addition a Coordinating Committee of Senior Officials has been set up to prepare Council work and the Commission is fully associated with that activity. This is, of course, an inter-governmental arrangement outside the normal Rome Treaty decision-making system. The general rule is that Council decisions will be based on unanimity. However, Council may decide that the implementation of joint actions may be decided on a qualified majority basis.

Whilst the kind of matters covered by the CJHA arrangement usually fall outside the Rome Treaty decision-making system, there is one issue which the Maastricht Treaty did decide to treat as a normal Community competence. This relates to the issue of visas to third country nationals crossing the external borders of Member States. Following Maastricht it was decided that the Council of Ministers, acting unanimously on a proposal from the Commission and in consultation with Parliament, would decide which third country nationals would have to possess a visa. After 1996 the process would shift to qualified majority voting.

A common market for financial services

Our discussion of the right of establishment and freedom to supply services conveniently leads us to the subject of financial services such as insurance and banking. As we shall see, some progress had been made in this area before the SEA but, as the Cockfield Report noted, a good deal remained to be done before it could be claimed that a common market had been fully realized in financial services. Since this is an extremely complex subject, we will not attempt to discuss all the measures which have been proposed and adopted. Rather we will indicate the broad lines of policy by reference to two cases – non-life insurance and banking.

An early success was achieved in the field of non-life insurance. In 1973 the Council of Ministers adopted a directive on the right of establishment. It required the abolition of restrictions which prevented companies from establishing themselves in a host country under the same conditions and with the same rights as those enjoyed by the nationals of that country. For example, Ireland had previously required that in the case of insurance companies two thirds of the shares had to be owned by Irish citizens, and that the majority of the directors (other than the full-time managing director) had to be of Irish nationality. In the light of *Reyners*, national discriminations of this kind were clearly contrary to the Treaty. Not surprisingly, a number of draft directives which were addressed to this kind of problem in other areas were subsequently dropped.

Much more important was the directive on the coordination of laws relating to taking up and pursuing the business of non-life insurance. This was necessary because in order to protect their citizens the member states require insurance companies to be licensed, and a condition of holding a licence was that companies met certain standards in terms of reserves, solvency margins and so forth. These differed between states and therefore the possibility existed that a company wishing to set up a branch in another member state could be debarred from doing so if the conditions demanded by the host government were more stringent than those demanded by the government of the country in which the company had its headquarters. The directive requires that the taking up of the business of non-life insurance should be subject to official authorization by each member state. This applies to an undertaking which has its head office in a member state and also to branches of enterprises which have head offices in other member states. Most important of all, uniform standards are specified in respect of reserves and margins of solvency.

Although the 1973 directives dealt satisfactorily with the right of establishment, they did not tackle the problem of freedom to supply services. In other words, obstacles still existed when, for example, an insurance company *located in the UK* wished to insure a risk in Germany. The problem here is that member states with consumer protection in mind tend to intervene in the matter of the terms and conditions of insurance contracts. Clearly, were a UK company's branch in Germany to insure the German risk then the German authorities would be able to exercise control, as German law would apply. However, in a situation where the insurance was carried out by the UK company direct then it is possible to envisage that the contract might be governed by UK law, German law or indeed the law of a third country. Such a choice was indeed suggested by the Commission in its original draft directive. This was criticized in the European Parliament and the draft was subsequently amended to require contracts to be governed by the law of the country in which the risk was situated. However, in respect of certain risks the amended draft allowed for an important exception whereby the parties could choose the law which should apply. The effect of this was that in the case of large commercial risks, where those insured could be expected to be able to take care of themselves, the choice of law principle was to operate. In respect of the insurance of those risks where the insured were likely to be less expert, the domestic law requirement was to operate.

Unfortunately this amended proposal did not find favour. Much of this was due to German opposition. The Germans subjected insurance contracts to relatively close legal control and were aware that countries such as the UK leave these matters more to self-regulation by the insurance companies. The Germans were opposed to allowing some insurance business to be conducted under what they would no doubt regard as laxer systems. The UK, on the other hand, took the position that the amended draft dealt adequately with the need for consumer protection. For example, airlines are quite capable in a choice of law situation of insisting that the necessary protective terms be included in contracts. Those who are more vulnerable would continue to be protected by domestic provisions.

The Commission indicated that a resolution of this problem was essential as part of the programme for completing the internal market. Support for the idea that the insurance of *large* risks should not require establishment and local authorization came from a Court of Justice judgement in 1986. This arose from a case in which the Commission attacked France, Germany, Ireland and Denmark for refusing to implement properly an earlier directive on co-insurance. The latter refers to collaboration between insurance companies when insuring large risks. The Court attacked the practice of requiring establishment and local authorization in such instances. Happily, agreement to introduce freedom to supply services in non-life insurance was achieved late in 1987. The directive followed the line laid down in the judgement of the Court by applying different supervisory treatment for large risks as opposed to mass risks involving smaller policy holders. Supervision of large risks occurs in the home country – the country where the head office of the insurer is located. Mass risks, on the other hand, are broadly regulated by the host country in which the risk is situated.

In the case of banking a somewhat similar series of events occurred. A directive was adopted in 1973 abolishing restrictions on the right of establishment and providing for the freedom to supply services. While this was a welcome move, it did not provide for a free Community market in banking as member states continued to apply supervisory rules which could have the effect of excluding banks from other member states. A major step was taken in 1977 with the adoption of what is referred to as the First Banking Directive. It established the principle of home country control – the overall supervision of a bank operating in several member states would be discharged by the competent authority in the state in which the bank had its head office. While further progress was made in 1983, the Cockfield Report had to recognize that a number of other actions were still necessary including the adoption of a Second Banking Directive which would lay down *common* rules of banking supervision. This occurred in 1989. The common rules do not apply to all aspects of a bank's activities but only to those matters which are of central concern, e.g. the size of a bank's own funds which underpin its operations. Of extreme importance is the single banking licence. It is based on the principle that if a bank is authorized to pursue activities in its home country it is also entitled to conduct similar operations in other member states without further authorization.

The free movement of capital

There are two main strands in Community policy in respect of the capital market. First, as in the case of labour, the Rome Treaty calls for mobility of capital between the member state economies. The Treaty explicitly provided for the abolition of controls on capital movements and restrictions on payments. Secondly, there were a whole series of other factors which could affect the free flow of capital, including some which could quite obviously give rise to serious distortions in the allocation of capital between member states. It was therefore desirable that such factors should be eliminated or harmonized as appropriate.

The Original Rome Treaty Rules on Capital Movements

These as we noted earlier were provided by Articles 67 to 73 and 106 and 109. Broadly speaking they were concerned with exchange controls, emergency measures and factors distorting capital movements.

Exchange Controls and Emergency Measures

The treaty required member states to liberalize payments in connection with *current* transactions. In other words exchange controls, whereby member states refused to grant foreign exchange to an importer of goods or services which were coming from another member state, had to be lifted. Had this not been so the effect of creating the custom union could have been nullified since even if tariffs, quotas and NTBs had been removed, goods could not flow across borders because importers would not have been able to obtain the foreign exchange necessary to purchase them. In respect of *capital* transactions a progressive removal of exchange controls was also envisaged. In 1960 and 1962 directives were introduced which led to a limited degree of liberalization. The capital transactions involved were divided into four lists – A, B, C and D. Transactions in Lists A and B were *unconditionally* freed. Broadly speaking, the implication was that member states were obliged to make foreign currency available to enable these transactions to take place. However, it is important to remember that member states could seek to resort to protective measures. Items under List C were only *conditionally* freed. In this case the implication was that the liberalization which had been achieved by 1960 (or, in the case of new members, that which had been achieved by the accession date) should not be reversed. Again, exceptional circumstances could lead to protective measures which could override the conditional requirement. In the case of List D there was no obligation to liberalize.

In 1985 and 1986 further liberalization measures were agreed. Broadly, the effect of these was to shift items which were only conditionally freed to the unconditional category. Examples were the admission of securities to the capital market; the buying and selling of unit and investment trust securities and securities not dealt with on the Stock Exchange (i.e. unlisted securities); and long-term commercial credits.

These acts of liberalization were really minimum requirements. In addition, some member states unilaterally liberalized exchange controls and went a good deal further than the directives required. The UK is an example. Following its accession to power in 1979 the Thatcher administration proceeded more or less immediately to sweep away all exchange controls. The Cockfield Report quite clearly saw such radical liberalizing as essential in the medium term. In fact the Community acted quite decisively when in 1988 it introduced a directive which was designed to remove all remaining

Table 10. Exchange liberalization rules 1960–85

Current Transactions	Member states had to supply foreign currency for such transactions (Articles 67 and 106)
Capital Movements	
List A	
Direct investments	Unconditional
Investments in real estate	liberalization
Personal capital movements	
Short- and medium-term commercial credits	
Transfers relating to life and credit insurance	
Transfers related to supply of services	
List B	
Buying and selling of securities dealt with on stock exchanges (listed securities)	Unconditional liberalization
List C	
Admission of securities on the capital market	Conditional
Buying and selling of unit and investment trust securities	liberalization
Buying and selling of securities not dealt with on stock exchanges (unlisted securities)	
Long-term commercial credits	
Medium- and long-term financial credits	
List D	No Community
Monetary Transactions:	obligation to liberalize
Acquisition of short-term securities	
Short-term financial credits	
Opening of deposit accounts	

Source: EC Commission, *Bulletin of the European Communities*, OOPEC, no. 5/86, p. 15.

exchange controls by mid 1990. Greece, Ireland, Portugal and Spain, however, were given until the end of 1992 to comply. There were also safeguard clauses which allowed member states to take protective measures against short-term movements where these were disruptive.

Apart from the protective measures to which we have just referred, we also need to recollect (see Chapter 4) that the old Article 73 provided for protective actions involving capital movements to be introduced if free capital mobility disturbed domestic capital markets. Additionally, under Article 109, balance of payments difficulties provided another ground for emergency measures.

The New Maastricht Treaty Rules

The rules concerning capital movements had to be reconsidered in the light of the decision to move progressively towards EMU. As a result old Articles 67 to 73 were scrapped. In addition Articles 106 and 109 were replaced by new articles relating to the conduct of a monetary policy leading to EMU. The new provisions relating to capital movements are now contained in Article 73a to 73h.

These rules are quite categorical. Restrictions of the movement of capital between member states and restrictions of payments between member states are prohibited. The safeguard clauses which characterized the 1988 directive on capital movements have been removed. Restrictions on capital movements and payments between member states and *third* countries are likewise prohibited. Some derogations were however allowed until the end of 1995. The only significant escape clause is contained in Article 73f which declares that if movements of capital to or from *third* countries cause difficulties, the Council of Ministers can authorize safeguard measures.

Factors distorting capital movements

Not only has the Community had to deal with factors which have inhibited capital movements, such as exchange controls, it has also had to consider the problem that some factors could possibly distort the allocation of capital among the several states of the Community. In other words, capital might not be invested where it obtained the best return. Distorting influences might cause capital to be invested in country A rather than country B even though it produced a poorer return in A than in B. A major possible source of such distortion could arise not only from differences in national *rates* of corporation tax but also from the detailed operation of the various national corporation tax *systems*.

The Rome Treaty, both before and after Maastricht makes no

explicit reference to the need for the harmonization of *direct* taxation. But Articles 100 to 102, dealing with the approximation of laws, provide the basis for a solution where discrepancies in the rate of tax and its method of operation produce distortions in the free movement of capital. Let us first consider differences in rates. Such discrepancies can give rise to problems. Suppose member state A levies a tax of 50 per cent while member state B is content with 25 per cent. Other things being equal, capital will flow from A to B until the accumulation of capital in B leads to an equalization in the rates of return net of tax in both countries (in respect of investments of equal risk). But if the rates of return net of tax are equal then it follows that the returns *before tax* must be unequal. This in turn implies that the distribution of capital is distorted. Theoretically, it could be argued that there would, from a Community point of view, be a gain if capital was shifted from the member state where its return before tax was low to one where its return was high. (It should be emphasized that such an approach ignores a number of problems, and also assumes that businessmen seek to maximize returns net of tax.) A harmonization of rates would help to solve the problem. But, as we indicated above, further difficulties also arise as a result of the way in which national corporation tax systems operate. The problem is essentially concerned with the double taxation of dividends. The latter arises when distributed dividends have corporation tax deducted from them and then that taxed income is also liable for personal income tax. In the classic system a single rate of corporation tax is applied to both distributed and retained profits. This, it is argued, discriminates unfairly against the shareholder, who is subject to this double taxation. It is said that it also distorts the system towards ploughing back profits when it might be desirable to distribute them in order that they can be reinvested in other companies needing to grow. Some, on the other hand, argue in favour of the system in that it encourages retention of profits and therefore investment, whereas dividends may be spent on consumer goods.

Some Community countries attempted to compensate for this double taxation effect. This took the form of the tax credit or imputation system, which grants the shareholder a credit to set against his or her personal tax liability. But although the tax credit system has much to commend it, the Commission, in examining national systems, encountered some major drawbacks. For example, the Belgian and French systems allowed tax credits only for residents and only for companies registered in their own states. The latter restriction induced French or Belgian investors to invest in French or Belgian companies rather than companies elsewhere in the Community. The former meant that residents in other Community countries who invested in Belgian or French companies were discriminated against.

In respect of the harmonization of corporation tax rates and systems, we must also record that no directive has yet been adopted by the Council. The Commission did in November 1975 submit to the Council a draft directive designed to harmonize national systems of company taxation, and withholding taxes, on dividends. The Council's Resolution of March 1971 had agreed that such harmonization was an essential ingredient in the creation of an Economic and Monetary Union. Quite clearly, free and undistorted movement of capital is an essential feature of such an arrangement, and its attainment would require not only the sweeping away of the distorting factors we are now discussing as well as the elimination of the remaining exchange controls to which we referred a little earlier. The Commission's 1975 proposal would have required the member states to adopt a common imputation system of corporation tax and a common system of withholding tax[1] on dividends. The proposal would also have led to similar but not necessarily identical rates of corporation tax and tax credit and to an identical rate of withholding tax. Member states would in fact have had to apply the same rate of corporation tax to profits whether distributed or undistributed. The normal rate would not have been higher than 55 per cent or lower than 45 per cent. Each state would also have

---

1. Withholding taxes are designed to prevent tax fraud – i.e. the concealment of dividend income from the tax authorities. They take the form of a percentage deduction from distributed dividends. In a sense a tax credit is an incentive to declaration of dividend income, as it can be set off against the shareholder's personal income tax liability. For shareholders with small incomes this may suffice, but for those with large incomes it may be beneficial for them to conceal their dividends rather than declare them with a view to claiming the tax credit. This is where the withholding tax comes in – it too can be reclaimed and would make declaration worthwhile whereas the tax credit alone might not. The draft directive provided that, where a withholding tax collected by one member state was set off or repaid in another member state, the state collecting the withholding tax would refund it to the other member state.

granted tax credits which would, to quote the draft directive, have been 'neither lower than 45 per cent nor higher than 55 per cent of the amount of corporation tax at the normal rate of a sum representing the distributed dividend increased by such tax'. Such tax credits would have accrued not only to nationals but also to recipients of dividends who were resident in other member states.[1] This approximation of corporation and tax credit rates would clearly have gone a long way to eliminating the distorting effects referred to earlier, and of course an important aspect of this attack upon distortion was the fact that tax credits would have accrued to residents in other member states.

We have just indicated that no action has yet been taken in respect of the corporation tax problem. It is notable that the Cockfield Report did not single out this problem for treatment. Nevertheless the Commission did subsequently indicate that it intended to take action. Progress has however been difficult and in 1990 the Commission announced that it had set up a study group (the Ruing Committee) to assess the severity of the problem and consider what action was appropriate.

The Committee reported in 1992 in favour of harmonizing the corporation tax base together with uniform maximum and minimum rates of 40 and 30 per cent respectively. In response the Commission did not welcome the idea of a maximum rate and felt that the minimum rate could be too high.

There are two features of the legal position in regard to corporation tax discrepancies which need to be mentioned. The first is that whilst, as we saw earlier in the book, under the SEA Article 100 harmonization was shifted to a majority voting basis, this does not apply to fiscal matters. This will make corporation tax harmonization more difficult to achieve, particularly in the light of UK hostility to interference from Brussels. The second is that the treaty position in respect of differences in treatment of tax payers (i.e. according to where they reside or invest) has changed. Old Article 67 envisaged that discriminations of any kind should be progressively

---

1. In the case of the cross-border tax credit the state where the dividend receiver lived would pay out the tax credit, but the draft directive observed that in principle the budgetary cost of the tax credit should be borne in the state where the profits, from which the dividends had been derived, had been subjected to corporation tax. Nevertheless, the directive saw no objection to the states agreeing bilaterally to share the cost.

abolished. But new Article 73d arising from Maastricht allows member states to perpetuate such fiscal distinctions. It would of course, always be open to member states to agree to give up such a right.

7

ECONOMIC AND MONETARY UNION

Introduction

It is clear from what has gone before that the Rome Treaty provided quite explicitly for the creation not merely of a customs union but indeed a common market. We can be equally categorical in saying that it did *not* call *explicitly* for the development of an economic union. Nevertheless, as we noted at the beginning of Chapter 4, we have to recognize the possibility that having embarked upon the process of economic integration, it might prove difficult to stop short of economic union. In other words, having developed the kind of Community envisaged by the Treaty, the member states might find themselves forced to proceed yet further in order to make secure, and to benefit more fully from, the free movement of goods, services and factors and from the various common policies such as the CAP. Economic union might therefore prove to be an inescapable ultimate destination.[1] Moreover, by virtue of its self-expanding property, the Rome Treaty would not stand in the way of such an evolution. However, if in 1969 the member states had concluded that for the foreseeable future the original Rome Treaty blueprint was viably the end of the line then this chapter would be largely a speculative exercise. In practice we know that in the early 1970s the Community did decide to embark on EMU – the nature of the motivations which lay behind that decision will be discussed in due course. Although the venture did ultimately run into the ground, EMU continued to be a long-term possibility and in 1979 the member states, in launching the EMS, took a *limited* step[2] in

1. Not all economists would accept that economic union is inevitable. Some would argue that it is possible to halt at any point along the way.
2. Although the EMS was much more limited in scope than the earlier EMU proposal, it has to be said that the fixed exchange rate aspect of EMU was not a radical departure, since it was an essential feature of the Bretton Woods system. By contrast, the fixed exchange rate aspect of the EMS was a significant change, since by then floating exchange rates were very much the order of the day.

that direction. Then in 1992 the Twelve signed the Maastricht Treaty on European Union which once more launched the Community on the path to EMU. These three ventures are discussed below.

Definition and motivations

Before we turn to the details, it is necessary to deal with one problem of terminology. We have been talking rather loosely about economic union and EMU. Are they the same?

We must begin by admitting that the literature on this subject exhibits a degree of imprecision and ambiguity. Economic union is an established term in economics and refers to the ultimate state of economic integration in which member states become merely regions of the union. The important word here is region. The trouble with this definition is that it tells us little about the process of attaining such a state or indeed about the nature of the state itself. The phrase economic and monetary union is in some ways more helpful, although it is not an established term in economic theory but is one which has gained currency by virtue of its use in connection with EC aspirations. In Figure 8 we endeavour to identify the main components of an EMU. It should be emphasized that there is no unique set of arrangements which constitute an EMU. Rather alternative scenarios are possible. The 'economic' component can be said to consist of the free movement of goods, services and factors of production within the confines of a common external tariff. In other words the economic component consists of a Common Market. This, incidentally, will involve a significant degree of fiscal harmonization if the cross-frontier flow of goods, services and factors is to be undistorted. Figure 8 indicates that there is a choice in respect of the monetary aspect, and it should be emphasized that we are at this point defining the word 'monetary' in a rather narrow sense. The parties to the union could agree to fix their exchange rates irrevocably and combine that with full convertibility of their currencies. The latter refers to a situation where individuals, companies, etc. can change one member state currency into another in whatever quantity they wish whenever they wish. In other words exchange controls are eliminated. The continued existence of fixed exchange rates would also require a coordination of

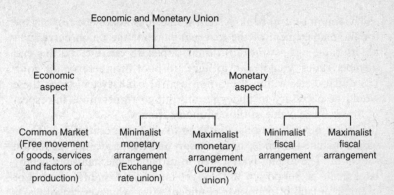

Figure 8. The components of EMU

national monetary policies. This is a *minimalist* approach to the monetary aspect. The *maximalist* approach can be viewed as a logical progression from the minimalist. If a fixed quantity of one currency can always be exchanged for a fixed quantity of another then one is to all intents and purposes a substitute for the other and it could then be argued that for convenience and economy it would be logical to take the further but *considerable* step of replacing the separate currencies by a *common* currency.

If the latter path was followed then there would be a need to create a central organ (a union central bank system) to control the supply of the common currency and to determine the union interest rate (more precisely the union interest rate *structure* of long-, medium- and short-term rates). An identification of the ingredients of monetary union does not suggest that there is any unique formula governing the organization, political relationship or objectives of a union central bank system. It could be monolithic or it could be based on a federal arrangement in which the union central bank was linked to the old national central banks. The union central bank system could be independent of political influence (as in the case of the Deutsche Bundesbank) or it could take instructions from the political authorities (as in the past has been the case with the Bank of England). Its aims could be price stability, the maintenance of a high level of employment, economic development or any combination of such objectives.

The union central bank system would presumably be responsible for the management of the external value of the union currency – i.e. its value against the US dollar, Japanese yen, etc. To this end member states would have to agree to pool their reserves of gold, US dollars, etc. within the union central bank system since these would be necessary to underpin any support operations in respect of the exchange value of the common currency.

Certain other functions would be likely to be centralized. These would include the lender of last resort and the prudential regulation functions. The former is designed to provide a mechanism whereby banks can be supported if they get into liquidity difficulties. For example, a lack of depositor confidence (for whatever reason) in a bank could lead to a drastic withdrawal of cash which, working as they do on a fractional reserve basis, individual banks cannot cope with. The resulting individual bank failure could be contagious leading to a widespread banking collapse. A central bank therefore has to support the commercial banks in such circumstances. The second function relates to the setting down and enforcement of rules which are designed to prevent imprudence in the day to day conduct of banking operations. This helps to prevent systemic failure and also protects the interests of depositors.

All this is concerned with monetary matters – i.e. the supply of the common currency, its rate of interest and its exchange rate. Monetary union would also impinge on national *fiscal* policies. Indeed here too it is possible to identify minimalist and maximalist models. However, before we discuss that, we need to establish the point that member states would no longer be able to run budget deficits of any magnitude they chose since the larger the deficits (assuming these to be financed by borrowing) the more they would be likely to drive up interest rates. Moreover, since there would no longer be separate national monetary systems, the effect of driving up interest rates would be felt *by the union as a whole*. Indeed the effect upon interest rates would probably be contrary to that desired by the union central bank system *in the interests of the whole of the union*. A control over the level of national budget deficits would therefore be a feature of a monetary union.

What we are specifying here is a minimalist fiscal condition in which taxing and public spending formally remain in the hands of the member states of the union but taxes are harmonized to avoid competitive distortions in the Common Market (see discussion in Chapters 5 and 6) and the size of national budget deficits is controlled. However, it is also possible to envisage a maximalist model where the levying of taxes and public spending, together with the consequent level of what would be a *union* budget deficit or surplus, are all *centralized* in some union body. As a modification of such a centralizing arrangement, it is possible to envisage the injection of a federal element by means of which some of the centralized budget income would be transferred back to the constituent states for locally determined allocation. The reader will readily discern that we are outlining a system of the kind which exists in the USA. It is important to note though, that some limited fiscal autonomy is enjoyed by the individual states of the American union.

Even on a minimalist view of the kind discussed above it is generally argued that EMU would require the existence of a union budgetary system which would be capable of giving rise to a substantial transfer of resources to the less successful states (regions) with below average per capita income levels and above average unemployment. It could be argued that states would be reluctant to give up their economic sovereignty (e.g. the power to devalue the currency) unless they could be assured of some resource transfer if their economies were to under perform. This would be all the more necessary if individual member states, whose economies were uncompetitive, did not believe that automatic corrective mechanisms such as wage/price flexibility or emigration would come to their rescue.

It can be argued that EMU would require a degree of political unification. Even on a minimalist view of the budgetary process, the scale of the redistribution of income would require a strong central decision-making system. *A fortiori* a high degree of political centralization of the budgetary process would not make sense unless there had already been a parallel agreement to shift major activities such as defence to the centre. Moreover, such a wholesale centralization of the budgetary process would require a parallel centralization of the system of political and democratic oversight – no taxation without representation! In such circumstances the member states do indeed become mere regions of the union.

When we come to analyse the two EMU plans that the Community has sought to introduce, we shall see that it has never aspired to develop an EMU which simultaneously embraced both a maximum monetary and a maximum fiscal stance. We shall also see that the relatively visionary Maastricht plan involves a maximum monetary arrangement i.e. single currency together with minimal (i.e. relatively decentralized) fiscal arrangements.

We turn now to the general motivating advantages.

(a) Most commentators refer to the benefits of fixed exchange rates. Businessmen thereby enjoy a greater degree of certainty and it is said that this stimulates cross-frontier trade in goods and services. As a result, consumers benefit to an even greater extent from intensified competition, the possibility of greater economies of scale and so forth. In other words the benefits of a customs union are *more fully* enjoyed.

(b) It is also argued that there is a beneficial effect on the allocation of factors of production. Notably, the optimum allocation of capital, associated with the equalization of rates of return at the margin discussed in the previous chapter, is more likely to be achieved under a fixed exchange rate régime. In other words the benefits of the free movement of factors within the common market are *more fully* enjoyed.

(c) If EMU gives rise to one currency then there is also an economy of resources associated with the elimination of the transaction costs incurred when one participating currency is exchanged for another.

(d) EMU could, by eliminating the risk premium associated with unstable exchange rates, lead to lower interest rates, which could lead to greater investment and therefore faster economic growth.

(e) A single currency also gives rise to greater transparency in international economic transactions as compared with a situation where economic calculations are complicated by the need to use exchange rates. This leads to an economy of effort and is likely to enhance both trade and cross-frontier factor-flow.

(f) If the union currency becomes an international reserve asset then the participating states enjoy further benefits. One is seigniorage. The states can allow imports to exceed exports, the balance being financed by the willingness of the rest of the world to hold the union currency. There is therefore a transfer of resources from the rest of the world to the union. The benefits of seigniorage should not be exaggerated. The rest of the world will presumably enjoy interest on its union currency balances which gives rise to a reverse flow. It is also important not to underestimate the risks and problems of running a reserve currency. It is significant that while some European circles pointed to the advantages arising from the international status of the US dollar in the Bretton Woods era, European countries, notably Germany, have shown a marked reluctance to assume a reserve currency role. The advantage of reserve currency status can also be viewed in terms of the reduction in the external constraints on internal demand management. Internal imbalance leading to a trade deficit is compensated by the willingness of foreigners to accumulate the reserve currency.

(g) If there is a pooling of international reserves then there will also be a saving of them. That is to say, the reserves needed to be held by the union would be less than the sum of the reserves needed to be held if the states acted independently. This economy of scale in international reserves arises from the law of large numbers whereby external shocks tend to cancel each other out. The participants in the EMU could, as a result, enjoy a once-and-for-all real resource advantage by allowing imports (real resources acquired) to exceed exports (real resources sacrificed) and thus running the reserves down to the new economized level. Pooling would also enable participating states to run higher temporary trade deficits than would be the case if they were to remain independent. In other words, the correction of trade imbalances could be postponed for a longer period.

(h) Whilst it may be argued that EMU leads to a loss of economic sovereignty, it can also be argued that collectively it may enable the group to exert a powerful influence in international monetary negotiations and fora. Small countries in particular may have little to lose and much to gain by being part of a larger monetary entity.

The original Rome Treaty system

Whilst it is true that the Rome Treaty, in its original form, did not call for the creation of an EMU, it did nevertheless contain rules regarding the conduct of macro-economic policy. We now turn to a brief consideration of them. The rules were to be found in Articles 103 to 109. Article 103 related to conjunctural policy which may be best defined as policy concerned with cyclical problems or short-term trends. The remaining Articles 104 to 109 were concerned with policy towards the balance of payments.

Article 103 declared that member states should regard their conjunctural policies as a matter of common concern and should consult each other and the Commission on measures to be taken. Article 104 placed the onus on member states to pursue the economic policies needed to ensure equilibrium in their balance of payments whilst simultaneously maintaining confidence in their currencies and maintaining a high level of employment and stability of prices – all of which sounds very worthy though not without its difficulties. In order to facilitate the achievement of these objectives Article 105 called for coordination of economic policies. As we noted in the previous chapter, Article 106 required the member states to remove exchange controls in connection with those transactions in goods, services and factors which are liberalized under the common market arrangement. Article 107 declared that each member state should treat its policy with regard to rates of exchange as a matter of common concern but the rest of the Article clearly recognized that member states were free to alter their rates. Article 108 provided that when a member state was in balance of payments difficulties the Commission should recommend appropriate remedial measures. If action taken by the state and measures proposed by the Commission did not prove sufficient to overcome the difficulties, the Council of Ministers could grant mutual assistance. If mutual assistance was not given, or if measures taken and mutual assistance granted did not rectify the problem, then the Commission could authorize the member state to institute protection. The Council could, however, overturn the latter. Article 109 allowed member states to apply protection in the case of a sudden crisis but again the Council could call for the suspension of such an action.

The conclusion we can draw is that the EC did not envisage a centralized control over macro-economic management. In broad terms the conduct of such affairs was left in the hands of member states. They were also free to alter exchange rates. They could even apply protection, although this could be revoked by the Council. However, it was clearly recognized that economic integration gave rise to increased economic interdependence, and to that end the Treaty emphasized the need for *consultation* and *coordination*.

Commentators have pointed out that the Community made no real significant progress, in moving beyond a Common Market, in the time up to the end of the transition period. Why was this? The answers are not difficult to find. First, the Six were preoccupied with the problems of creating the kind of Community envisaged by the Rome Treaty, a preoccupation which was made no easier by internal dissension over matters such as majority voting and the continuing French rebuff to the UK's membership aspirations. By 1969, however, the basic structure of the common market had been created, and political change in France had removed a major impediment to progress – the Community could then afford to look expansively to the future. Bloomfield (1973, p. 7) ascribes the failure to make appreciable advances in the field of monetary integration to the continuing payments surpluses and mounting reserves of the member states. There is some truth in that observation but a key factor was undoubtedly what Tsoukalis has called the agricultural mythology (1977, pp. 59–60). Under the CAP, the price of agricultural products was fixed in terms of a unit of account, and those prices were then translated into national currency terms. If a member state devalued, the price of agricultural products in national currency terms was automatically raised. Farm incomes would rise and output also. If a state revalued its currency, a contrary course of events would ensue. Clearly, changes in parities would lead to prices, incomes and outputs other than those which were intended when the unit of account farm prices were originally fixed. It was therefore regarded as essential for the proper working of the CAP that exchange rates should not be altered. It was indeed assumed that the successful operation of the CAP was so important to the member states that they would be forced to pursue the necessary monetary discipline which would enable exchange rates to stay put. This somewhat naïve view was to prove unfounded. In 1969, following the political events of 1968 and the inflationary impetus to which they gave rise, France devalued and shortly afterwards Germany revalued. 1969 was also the year in which the Heads of State and of Government decided at The Hague that the Community should work together to create an EMU. The two events were, of course, not unconnected.

The first EMU experiment

Motivations

What motivations lay behind this bold decision? It is possible to identify three sets of reasons. First, and notably in the mind of the Commission, was the desire to make secure the achievements of the EC. Whilst pinning some faith on what we have called the agricultural mythology, the Commission could clearly see that as far as the CAP and the free movement of farm products were concerned, EMU would make exchange rate assurance doubly sure. As for the industrial common market, the Commission was all too well aware that if a member state got into balance of payments difficulties it might be forced to take protective measures, thus jeopardizing the free movement of goods, services and indeed factors such as capital. This was very much the thinking behind the first Barre Plan (EC Commission, 1969a). Raymond Barre was the member of the Commission responsible for economic and financial affairs – we shall return to the first Barre Plan later.

Secondly, there were national interests which, while they varied from state to state, all had one thing in common – they were best served by EMU. France in particular had much to gain from the CAP, and therefore an EMU with its immutable exchange rates was an attractive prospect. The smaller states were interested in EMU because the openness of their economies rendered them extremely vulnerable to events occurring in other member states. EMU offered them an opportunity to exercise an influence on those events. Some member states also entertained the idea that EMU would enable the EC to develop a distinct monetary personality – this would help to redress the balance *vis-à-vis* the US dollar, which was regarded by some as enjoying an unfairly privileged position in the Bretton Woods system. Undoubtedly a major motivating factor was the desire to avoid having to devalue and revalue currencies. It should be explained that the Bretton Woods system involved fixed exchange rates, and parity adjustments were infrequent and tended to be preceded by fairly lengthy periods of trauma during which member states vainly tried to resist the inevitable. The French and German adjustments of 1969 were no exception. Parity changes were unpleasant for various reasons. Devaluation tended to be regarded as indicating that a particular economic strategy had failed – political credibility was therefore undermined. Devaluations were also usually accompanied by painful deflationary medicine. Even revaluations had unpleasant consequences, notably for export industries. In saying that EMU was seen as a way of escaping these traumas, we are not implying that the member states were naïvely assuming that, Canute-like, it was only necessary to declare that exchange rates were immutable in order for the problem of parity changes to go away. Clearly the necessary monetary discipline would have to be applied. Whether the immutability would compel the application of discipline or whether a disciplined condition should be attained first was a matter yet to be decided.

The third motivating factor was undoubtedly political. EMU would be symbolic of the growing unity of the member states. While it would not be a backstairs route to political unification, it would be a step in the direction of the ultimate unity envisaged by the founding fathers.

The first development following the Hague Summit was the decision by the Council of Finance and Economics Ministers to establish a machinery for prior consultation on short-term policy measures. This had been called for in the first Barre Plan. Barre had called for a system of compulsory consultation before the taking of any national decision, relating to the trend of prices, incomes and employment, overall budgetary policy and tax policy, which affected the economies of the other member states. More forward-looking was the decision to authorize formally the Central Banks to establish a short-term monetary support scheme. This would provide automatic and unconditional short-term credits for three months, renewable for a further three months. It amounted to $1000 million made up of the following contributions – $300 million each from France and Germany, $200 million from Italy, $100 million from Belgium–Luxembourg and $100 million from the Netherlands. In addition, a further $1,000 million of conditional short-term aid could be made available. This aid was obviously designed to tide over member states in balance of payments difficulties, thus reducing the possibility of parity changes or the imposition of protection.

Economists versus monetarists

Meanwhile the 'great debate' on monetary integration and economic union had begun, and it soon became evident that pronounced differences of view existed. Two schools, curiously called the economists and monetarists,[1] emerged. Insofar as countries can be said to belong to schools of thought, it can be said that the Germans and Dutch were economists whilst the French, Luxembourgers, Belgians (and the Commission) were monetarists. These two schools differed not in terms of the ultimate objective to be achieved but over the path that should be followed in order to achieve the objective. Boiled down to its essence, the monetarist position emphasized early action on locking exchange rates, on the assumption that the requisite monetary discipline would therefore be imposed upon member states. By contrast, the economists saw the need for a convergence of economic performance on matters such as the price level before proceeding to immutable parities.

The champion of the economist school was Dr Schiller, the West German Economics and Finance Minister. His 1970 plan for Monetary, Economic and Financial Cooperation envisaged a progression through four stages. Stage one would be mainly concerned with setting up a firm base for coordination of economic policies. Counter-cyclical weapons of control should be developed in each member state as required. The second stage would be concerned with securing a more evenly balanced economic development between the various states. This would be achieved by central recommendations on budgetary policy and more cooperation through the various monetary and banking committees. A system of medium-term monetary aid would be set up. The third stage would witness the introduction of a supra-national element with majority decisions at Community level on such matters as national budgets and so forth. A federal reserve system on the US model would be introduced. The margin of exchange-rate fluctuation around basic parities would be reduced. At this stage the basic parity could still be modified, but an intensified degree of Community control would be applied in this area. A European Reserve Fund would be set up and

---

1. They are not to be confused with those who hold views similar to Professor Milton Friedman.

a part of national reserves would be transferred to it. In the fourth and final stage power over economic, financial and monetary matters would be centralized under a system of supra-national control. Exchange rates would be totally fixed and irrevocable. A single unit of European currency would make its entry. The existing Committee of Central Bank Governors would become a European Central Council of Banks.

Economists will recognize this as being a sensible way of proceeding to the goal of economic and monetary union. In particular, until a very effective mechanism for coordinating the macro-economic policies of member states is established, any move to adopt irrevocably fixed exchange rates is exceedingly dangerous. Different national macro-economic policies can lead to differential rates of inflation, and exchange rates may begin right but end up being wrong. If a country inflates faster than its competitors, but is precluded from devaluing, then it is likely to experience an adverse balance of payments, and the only (or most likely) way to deal with this would be to deflate. The possible early adoption of irrevocably fixed exchange rates was at one stage regarded by many UK economists as being one of the most serious arguments against joining the EC. Such critics had in mind the propensity of the UK to inflate relatively rapidly.

The monetarist school was really personified by Barre, who produced what is now called the second Barre Plan. It would be tedious to list all the various aspects of this proposal. Like the Schiller Plan, it envisaged a phased progression towards the ultimate goal. But it contrasted with the Schiller Plan in two respects. The first related to the role of exchange rates. Peter Coffey and John Presley in their study of this topic put the matter thus:

... the idea of allowing fluctuating exchange rates is categorically rejected as a matter of principle ... Whilst changes in exchange rates might be considered in cases of exceptional necessity, it would be preferable to *irrevocably* fix the exchange rates as soon as possible. A satisfactory move would be the immediate reduction of the margin of parity between the national currencies from 1.5 per cent to 1.0 per cent. The demand for fixed exchange rates could hardly have been stated in a more emphatic fashion! (Coffey and Presley, 1970, p. 12)

Secondly, Barre also laid considerable stress on the role of the Community in the international monetary sphere.

The Werner Committee

The response of the Council of Ministers to this diversity of view was to set up a Committee to examine the problems involved. This Committee was led by Pierre Werner, the Prime Minister of Luxembourg. The Werner Committee presented an interim report in June 1970 and a second and final report in October of that year (EC Commission, 1970). The Committee proposed the achievement by 1980 of an EMU. In particular, the nature of the final union was delineated. Community currencies would be freely convertible against each other and their parities irrevocably fixed. It would be preferable if they could be replaced by a Community currency. Monetary and credit policy would be centralized. There would be a Community monetary policy *vis-à-vis* the rest of the world. Member states would unify their policies on capital markets. The main components of budget policy would be decided at Community level. The Committee also recognized that significant institutional changes would be needed. There would have to be a central decision-making body which would influence such matters as national budgets, and the parity of the single currency (or the interlocked Community currencies). There would also need to be a Community central banking system to determine monetary conditions over the Community as a whole.

In explaining how the Community would achieve the union, the Committee was only really specific about the first stage – 1971 to 1973 inclusive. Its proposals for this stage involved an element of compromise between the monetarist and economist schools. It proposed that action should be taken on both fronts – exchange rates and policy coordination. This has been called the strategy of parallelism. The Committee did not follow the monetarists who were anxious to lock the exchange rates at the outset. Rather (thanks to the Central Bank Governors) it proposed a scheme in the shape of a reduction of the margin of fluctuation around the central parities when one Community currency was exchanged for another. This band of fluctuation was to be narrower than that operating in respect of exchanges of Community currencies for the dollar. This was the famous snake in the tunnel mechanism. The snake was the narrower band of fluctuation allowed in respect of intra-Community exchanges whilst the tunnel was the wider band allowed in respect of exchanges against the dollar. Emphasis was also placed on the need to achieve greater harmonization of national economic policies – a central plank of the economist position.

The first stage – eventually

The Werner Committee having duly reported, the ball was now back in the political court. A vigorous debate ensued which revealed the existence of substantial differences of opinion and hesitations. Nevertheless, in March 1971, the broad substance of the Werner blueprint for the first stage was formally adopted by the Council. From June, intra-Community exchange margins were to be narrowed – an initial reduction would be made from 0.75 per cent[1] on either side of parity to 0.60 per cent. Procedures were authorized for strengthening central bank cooperation and the coordination of economic policies. Indeed, the Council of Ministers was to meet three times a year to establish guidelines for the short-term economic policies to be followed by the member states. A medium-term (two to five years) financial assistance mechanism was to be added to the existing short-term scheme. It would be endowed with $2 billion. Assistance would be conditional on the recipient member state taking effective steps to tackle the causes of its payments deficit. No rallonge[2] would be allowed.

However, before the system could be introduced a series of international currency crises obtruded. It should be explained that during the 1960s the US balance of payments steadily deteriorated, notably as a result of the combination of the Vietnam War and large-scale investment by US companies abroad. In the second half of 1970 and in 1971 the US balance of payments recorded deficits of unprecedented size. Increasingly the view was taken that the dollar would have to be devalued. In May 1971 a large movement of hot money occurred as dollars sought refuge from devaluation, and currencies, including the dollar, sought the benefit of a possible upward revaluation of the D-mark and the Dutch guilder. The former, particularly, was thought ripe for revaluation. The

1. Under the European Monetary Agreement contracting states were only allowed a 0.75 per cent fluctuation either side of parity whereas under the Bretton Woods system the margin was 1 per cent either side.
2. Extension beyond the permitted limit.

Community showed little capacity to formulate a common stance in the face of this onslaught. While the US sought to press the Six to contribute to the adjustment of the American balance of payments by revaluing their currencies, France in particular was opposed. It took the view that it was up to the US to correct its deficit by applying controls on capital movements and by devaluing the dollar. The Commission was against revaluation and proposed that the Six should take concerted action to curb inflows. This was supported by France but was opposed by Germany, which suggested a joint float with each member state currency remaining fixed against each other within narrow margins. No agreement could be reached, so member states acted independently – the D-mark and the Dutch guilder were floated and Belgium ceased to intervene in the section of the market concerned with capital movements. In late July and in August the speculative flight from the dollar resumed – this time the main target was France and Belgium, since Germany and the Netherlands were effectively protected from inflows by virtue of their floating rates. On this occasion the US itself took action – it applied a 10 per cent import surcharge and suspended the convertibility of the dollar into gold. Once again the Community was unable to agree on a common stance. Germany once more advocated a joint float and once more France refused to accept the idea. The idea of floating did, however, collect more adherents in the shape of Italy and the Belgium–Luxembourg Customs Union. Later in the year the Community was able to hammer out a common position in preparation for an internationally negotiated solution to what was essentially a US balance of payments and dollar problem. The Six would press for an end to the surcharge and a restoration of convertibility. They would accept appreciation of their currencies against the dollar but would require a formal devaluation of the dollar against gold. Agreement was reached at the Smithsonian Institute in Washington in December 1971. The Smithsonian Accords involved a return to fixed exchange rates, although the margins of fluctuation around what were now called the central rates were increased to 2.25 per cent on either side. The dollar was devalued in terms of gold by 7.9 per cent, the Italian lira declined by 1 per cent, the French franc and the pound remained unchanged, while the Belgian franc, the D-mark and the Dutch guilder all appreciated. In terms of the dollar, all the European currencies appreciated. The United States abolished the import surcharge. It was hoped that convertibility would be restored in due course.[1]

The way was now clear to set in motion the EMU experiment. This was agreed in March 1982. The snake and the tunnel were, however, wider than previously conceived. Following the Smithsonian Accords the margin of fluctuation on either side of the central rate in relation to the dollar was 2.25 per cent, giving a maximum band of 4.5 per cent. This was the tunnel. However, the Council decided that this condition could not apply to intra-Community currencies since if, simultaneously, one currency rose from the bottom to the top of the band while another fell from the top to the bottom, then their relative fluctuation would be 9 per cent. This would have an unacceptable effect on the CAP pricing system. The Council, therefore, decided to restrict the intra-EC rate band – the snake – to 2.25 per cent. It was, of course, necessary to intervene in the foreign exchange market in order to keep currencies within the prescribed limits. For example, if a currency was weak, what was called a debtor intervention involved the intervening country borrowing from its partner the strong currency needed to purchase its own weak one. A very short-term credit facility had, therefore, to be created in order to make such interventions possible. In a creditor intervention, the intervening country would buy the weak currency with its own strong currency which of course it would itself be able to supply. At the end of the month settlement was required. The creditor would wish to exchange the weak currencies which it accumulated for a more acceptable asset. Equally it would require repayment of the credits it had extended to the debtor country. In anticipation of their accession to the Community, the UK, Ireland, Denmark and Norway also joined the scheme.

The snake in the tunnel scheme enjoyed only a very limited success, although, as we shall see, the snake did outlive the EMU exercise. Quite quickly it was placed under considerable strain when in June 1972 the pound encountered heavy speculative pressure, and the support burden was such that the UK authorities decided to allow the pound to float out of the snake and the tunnel. Ireland and Denmark followed suit. The UK and Ireland stayed out

1. This did not transpire.

permanently but Denmark rejoined and stayed inside. In February 1973 Italy floated out and stayed out. France left in January 1974, rejoined in July 1975 and finally left in March 1976. Thus by the end of 1977, although the Community consisted of ten members, only half – Germany, Belgium, the Netherlands, Luxembourg and Denmark – had stayed the course. The arrangement also lost its Community character as a result of the adherence of Norway, which had rejected EC membership, and Sweden, which joined in March 1973 but left in August 1977.[1] The system also departed from the original plan when, in March 1973, Germany, France, Belgium, the Netherlands, Luxembourg and Denmark decided to float collectively while maintaining the reduced level of fluctuation amongst themselves. More important perhaps was the fact that the latter aspect proved impossible in practice, and individual members of the snake were from time to time forced to resort to central rate changes.

It will be recalled that the other major objective of the first stage was the coordination of national economic policies. How did the Community respond? Here we can quote from John Presley, who carried out a review of Community endeavours in this field.

The Council of Ministers does meet three times each year to examine the economic climate in the Community, and it does put forward very general policy objective guidelines; but there is no detailed attempt to formulate economic policy, as the Werner Report envisaged, to achieve these objectives. Coordination Committees have been set up, their main function being to monitor the national policies, and to examine them in relation to the common guidelines laid down by the Council. Even the European Commission, however, admits that little progress has been made in coordination: 'few concrete measures have been adopted beyond recommendations of a very general nature'. (Presley, 1974, p. 153)

Kruse puts the matter quite bluntly when he observes:

. . . the member states continued to make decisions principally on the basis of national interest rather than according to the dictates of economic and monetary unification. (Kruse, 1980, p. 193)

We have so far been concerned with the main tasks of the first stage – the setting up of the exchange rate scheme and the coordina-

1. Switzerland and Austria were also associated with the snake.

tion of national policies. As the Community progressed through the first stage, consideration began to be given to the second. A number of conditions were laid down which had to be satisfied if that progression was to occur. One related to regional policy. The Werner Committee recognized that, in an EMU, regional policy would have an important role to play, but it did not develop the theme. In March 1971, when the original decision to enter upon stage one was made, the importance of regional measures was highlighted as a means of reducing tensions which would otherwise impede progress to EMU. Kruse (1980, p. 177) takes this to imply a transfer of resources. At the Paris Summit of 1972 consideration was given to a series of developments which were preparatory to stage two. Included in these was the creation of the ERDF. In practice, differences of opinion over the size of the fund delayed its creation until 1974, when the issue was settled at the Paris Summit in the December of that year. The Paris Summit also decided to set up a European Monetary Cooperation Fund – this was to be achieved by April 1973. It was also required that in 1973 reports should be submitted on the adjustment of the short-term monetary support scheme and on the progressive pooling of reserves. The latter was no new idea – it had been identified as a topic for study at The Hague in 1969. The European Monetary Cooperation Fund was duly created. It was responsible for the running of the snake and for the associated very short-term credit facility, and in addition it was in charge of the short-term monetary support scheme. During 1973 the pooling of reserves was considered but rejected – the funds available under the short-term monetary support scheme were substantially increased.

In due course a vigorous debate ensued over the question of formally proceeding to the second stage. In the light of what had not been achieved this was more than a little absurd. In the end it was agreed that the Community could, from the beginning of 1974, proceed to 'a' second stage of EMU. The word 'the' was deliberately omitted. By 1974 it was increasingly realized that EMU was not going to materialize. At the Paris Summit in December 1974 the EMU scheme was to all intents and purposes shelved. The Heads of State and of Government noted the difficulties which in 1973 and 1974 had prevented the hoped-for progress being made. They reaffirmed that their will to achieve the union was not weakened, but they attached no date to its achievement. The 1972 Paris Summit aspiration that the grand design would be achieved by not later than 1980 was not reasserted. The mini-snake continued to exist, but of course it was very different in character from the original concept. In short, EMU was a 'dead duck'.

Post-mortem

Why did EMU fail to materialize? Two main reasons can be adduced. First, it was launched at an unfortunate time. As we have seen, the international monetary system was very unsettled and the oil crisis, which began in October 1973, only served to aggravate matters. Lack of confidence in the dollar threw great strain on the snake in the tunnel arrangement – the Smithsonian Accords did not bring that strain to an end and neither did the dollar devaluation of February 1973. The second factor has already been noted, namely the failure of the member states to take seriously the need to coordinate their policies. In the absence of a convergence of economic performance on matters such as the price level, exchange rates were bound to need adjustment. Indeed, as Dennis has shown (see Table 11), differential inflation was very much the order of the day.

It is of course tempting to ascribe some of the failure of the EMU to the oil crisis. However, it should be pointed out that the first oil price increase did not occur until October 1973 and took time to feed into the system. By then EMU was well on the way to failure. In any case all the member states were affected by the oil price rise although not to exactly the same degree. Kruse emphasizes that the oil crisis was not the main underlying factor. The main factor was the failure to coordinate, and that gave rise to divergent trends. As Kruse so penetratingly points out:

It must be stressed that these differences in national economic policies and trends antedated the events of October: the oil crisis did not produce them but merely intensified and highlighted them. (Kruse, 1980, p. 154).

Although EMU was to all intents and purposes dead for the time being, there were some who would not let it lie down. We have already noted the Tindemans Report in Chapter 1 with its suggestion for a two-tier Community. In 1975 a study group set up by the Commission under the chairmanship of Robert Marjolin also pro-

Table 11. Annual inflation rates in the EEC 1971–5 (%)

	Belgium	Denmark	France	Germany	Ireland	Italy	Netherlands	UK
1971	4.3	5.8	5.5	5.3	8.9	4.8	7.5	9.4
1972	5.4	6.6	5.8	5.5	8.7	5.7	7.8	7.1
1973	7.0	9.3	7.3	6.9	11.3	10.4	8.0	8.1
1974	12.6	15.0	13.6	6.9	16.9	19.4	9.5	16.0
1975	12.7	11.0	11.6	5.9	20.8	17.1	10.2	24.1
1971–1975	49.5	57.4	52.2	34.7	86.4	71.3	51.2	82.5

Source: G. E. J. Dennis, 'European Monetary Union: in the "Snake-Pit"', The Banker, October 1976, p. 1109.

duced a report (EC Commission, 1975b). Its verdict on the initial attempts at EMU was quite pessimistic – if there had been any movement it was backwards! But it would not be fair to lump Marjolin with Tindemans. The Marjolin report did not advocate any grandiose plans. It did not regard EMU as feasible in the then near future and concentrated its attention on some concrete short-term measures rather than another long-term plan. Mention should also be made of the 1975 All Saints' Day Manifesto on EMU. This was a proposal by nine prominent economists and contained at least one very interesting idea. It suggested that instead of regarding the Europa (a new Euro money) as a reserve currency it should at least initially be used as a private asset. In a sense it could be created as a kind of parallel currency which pragmatically could be left to sink or swim. If it proved popular then national currencies could be gradually phased out.

The EMS

Jenkins and Schmidt

When in 1977 the then President of the EC Commission, Roy Jenkins, made a strong plea for the Community to take up the idea of monetary union again, many felt that the timing was particularly inopportune. His initial plan envisaged a big leap forward with a single European currency and monetary authority. However, the idea did not fall on stony ground. At the Copenhagen and Bremen Summits of 1978 Chancellor Schmidt took up the initiative. On this occasion the plan which emerged was much less ambitious than the former EMU. There was no question of immutable exchange rates or a common currency. The emphasis was more modestly placed on the need to create a zone of monetary stability in Europe. It came to be called the European Monetary System. We shall turn to the details later. The immediate question is: what were the motivations lying behind this new proposal?

Motivations

Jacques van Ypersele, who was intimately involved in the EMS negotiations, draws attention to three factors. First, there was a general dissatisfaction with the floating exchange rate system which came to replace the fixed rates of the Bretton Woods system. Secondly, fixed rates had a beneficial effect upon business conducted across frontiers. In his words:

Greater monetary stability would encourage business confidence and investment. In talks with European business executives one often hears complaints that they are unable to give their companies a full European dimension because of the ever-present exchange risks and uncertainty about exchange rates. It has been difficult to forecast correctly the cost in national currency of inputs from abroad or the revenue in national currency from exports. These uncertainties contribute to the fact that businesses are not harvesting the potential benefits of a market as large as Europe. (van Ypersele, 1979, p. 7)

Thirdly, exchange rates had been subject to over-shooting. The latter requires a little more explanation.

There can be no doubt that the main reason for the creation of the EMS was the destabilizing effect of foreign currency movements, particularly those of the dollar. *The motivation behind the EMS was therefore significantly different from that which inspired the EMU.* When people moved out of, say, the dollar, because of a lack of confidence in it, they did not tend to move equally into all European currencies. Rather they tended to rush towards one currency – the D-mark. This distorted the relationship between European currencies (and with other currencies). It caused the D-mark to move up and, since the D-mark was scarce, other Community currencies would command fewer D-marks – in other words they depreciated relative to the D-mark. These movements of both the D-mark and other Community currencies, caused by what may be termed international portfolio adjustments, tended to overshoot the levels justified by the relative price levels of goods and services in their respective economies. Van Ypersele maintains that overshooting, both upwards and downwards, was perceived as having a depressing effect on national economies. Excessive appreciation tended to depress profits and activity in export industries. Excessive depreciation tended to lead to inflationary pressures and made governments reluctant to revive economies for fear of adding yet more fuel to inflation.

The lead given by the German Government can be explained in terms of a desire to take the pressure of speculative inflows off the D-mark. If a really effective fixed exchange rate system could be established as between the member states then the pressure would be shared. An ex-dollar holder would be as happy to hold the French franc as the D-mark, since the former could always be turned into the latter without loss.

The ECU and the exchange rate mechanism

One of the central features of the EMS was the European Currency Unit (ECU). When the Community was first set up it needed some denominator of value. While one of the member state currencies could have served that purpose, there were reasons which militated against such a solution. First, there was the possibility that that particular currency might prove to be unstable. Secondly, national rivalries and prestige precluded selecting any one country's currency as the Community currency. Instead, the Six initially adopted the Unit of Account (UA), which had a gold content equal to that of the US dollar. Later, on the recommendation of the Monetary Committee, this was followed by the European Unit of Account (EUA), which was a composite currency – see below for the meaning of that term. In terms of construction, the EUA was a direct precursor of what came next, namely the ECU. The latter was introduced in 1979 in connection with the EMS.

The ECU played three main roles – two were official and one was unofficial.

(a) The ECU acted as the denominator of Community transactions. Thus the Community budget was specified in terms of ECUs. When firms were fined, the penalty was fixed in terms of ECUs and so on.

(b) The ECU was also the central feature of the EMS, and it is this aspect which concerns us at this point. Briefly, in the EMS the ECU was the denominator of the exchange rate mechanism; it provided a basis for the divergence indicator; it acted as a denominator for operations in the intervention and credit mechanisms; and it acted as a means of settlement between monetary authorities. We shall say more about these below.

(c) Unofficially, the ECU was also being increasingly used in connection with *private* transactions, both within and indeed outside the Community.

Table 12. Currency weightings in the EMS basket (21 September 1989)

	Number of units of national currencies making up ECU	Percentage weightings
D-mark	0.6242	30.1
French franc	1.332	19.0
UK pound	0.08784	13.0
Italian lira	151.8	10.15
Dutch guilder	0.2198	9.4
Belgian franc	3.301	7.6
Luxembourg franc	0.130	0.3
Danish krone	0.1976	2.45
Greek drachma	1.440	0.8
Irish punt	0.008552	1.1
Spanish peseta	6.885	5.3
Portuguese escudo	1.393	0.8
		100.0

Source: EC Commission, *Bulletin of the European Communities*, Nos. 6 and 9, 1989.

We now turn to the exchange rate mechanism. At its centre was the ECU. This was a composite currency – we may in fact describe it as a currency cocktail. That is to say it was made up of specified amounts of all the member state currencies. A basic question which had to be resolved was: what weight should be attached to each of the currencies in the basket? The criteria which had been used in the EUA were threefold – a country's share of collective GNP, its share of collective trade (exports) and its size (the latter criterion was employed in the short-term monetary support scheme which gave countries quotas according to whether they were 'large', 'medium' or 'small'). These criteria were also adopted in respect of the ECU. The weights were recalculated at five-yearly intervals – e.g. 1984 and 1989, when the peseta and escudo were included. For example, the 1989 weights are shown in Table 12 and reflected relative economic strengths.

The next point to appreciate is that at any time each member state's currency had a specified value in relation to 1 ECU. Moreover, these values, once fixed collectively, had to persist until a

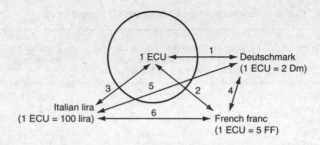

Figure 9. Hypothetical example of EMS bilateral grid (based on three states)

decision was made by the participating states to alter them. In Figure 9 we provide a purely hypothetical three-country example. The relationships between each national currency and 1 ECU are labelled 1, 2 and 3. If each national currency has a definite relationship to 1 ECU it inevitably follows that we can derive the implied relationship (i.e. cross rate) between each national currency and all the other national currencies. Thus in Figure 9, Dm 1 must be worth FF 2.5 (see 4) and Dm 1 must be worth L 50 (see 5). Equally FF 1 must be worth Dm 0.4 (4 in reverse) and FF 1 must be worth L 20 (see 6). These are the bilateral central rates. A key obligation of each of the countries participating in the exchange rate mechanism was that they should not allow the exchange rate of their currency against the other currencies to fluctuate by more than a given percentage above and below these central rates.

We now need to specify the exact conditions. When the scheme was set up the general principle was that participants undertook not to allow their currencies to fluctuate by more than 2.25 per cent above and below the central rate. Germany, France, Belgium, the Netherlands, Luxembourg, Denmark and Ireland chose the 2.25 per cent margin. Italy, the UK and Ireland were in fact offered the possibility of a wider band of 6 per cent either way. Italy initially adopted this arrangement but finally shifted to the 2.25 per cent margin in January 1989. Ireland, as we have seen, chose the 2.25 per cent margin while the UK opted to remain outside the system. However, in 1990 the UK finally decided to join the ERM arrangement with a 6 per cent margin. Spain joined the ERM, also on a 6 per cent basis, in July 1989. Thus by the time the Maastricht Treaty was agreed in 1991 only Greece and Portugal remained outside the ERM. Absence from the ERM did not however mean that countries were totally uninvolved in the EMS arrangement – the UK participated in other aspects (see below) prior to ERM membership.

The prescribing of such limits would not of itself keep actual exchange rates within those limits. For this to happen, interventions might be required. Once a currency reached its bilateral limit against another currency, the two central banks concerned had to intervene in order to prevent yet further departure from the central rate. If, for example, the French franc fell to its 2.25 per cent floor against the D-mark the Bank of France had to sell D-marks while the German Bundesbank had to buy French francs. If the Bank of France needed to borrow D-marks from the Bundesbank to finance its defensive intervention, its debt would be denominated in ECUs and would be repaid in them. Not all interventions were carried out in terms of Community currencies. In some instances the US dollar acted as the intervention currency. This appeared to be the case when interventions took place at a time when a currency had not reached the fluctuation limit. Thus the French authorities could pull up the value of the French franc by purchasing the latter with US dollars.

The exchange rate mechanism also incorporated a divergence indicator. Once a country's currency had diverged by three quarters of its permissible margin above or below its central rate *against the ECU*, a divergence indicator warning light in effect began to flash. There was then *a presumption* that a government would take remedial action. In the case of a weak currency, a rise in interest rates, a tightening of fiscal policy and support operations using a diversity of currencies would all be appropriate, and *vice versa* for a strong currency. Apparently there was some difference of opinion as to whether, when a currency had moved three quarters of the way to its permitted limit,[1] intervention was mandatory or whether all that was required was the initiation of consultations. The phrase 'a presumption' was a compromise.

The exchange rate mechanism was a fairly flexible arrangement.

1. This point was called its divergence threshold.

Apart from the relatively wide margins allowed for the UK and Spain, the system quite explicitly incorporated the possibility that currencies might be devalued or revalued against the ECU or that countries might temporarily depart from the system. However, devaluations and revaluations were not unilateral acts but were subjects for negotiation among the exchange rate partners. Member states might not always secure the degree of adjustment they desired. For example, as David Llewellyn (1983, p. 254) has pointed out, in February 1982 Belgium wished to devalue by 12 per cent but had to settle for only 8.5 per cent. Adjustments might also involve an element of sharing. In March 1983 France was able to persuade countries with stronger currencies, e.g. Germany, to revalue at the same time as she, and others, devalued. The fact that the system was so flexible meant that it could exhibit significant fluctuation and change without being declared a failure – in practice the emphasis was on relative stability rather than immutability.

In establishing the system the member states were aware of the need for convergence of economic performance and recognized that this would be a particular burden on the less prosperous countries – Ireland, Italy and the UK being the economies in question. The EMS agreement therefore provided for a limited transfer of resources. Over five years the New Community Instrument (see Chapter 3), in collaboration with the EIB, would make available loans totalling 1000 million EUA per annum. Interest rate subsidies of 3 per cent would be available on these loans. This assistance would only be available to member states which fully participated in the exchange rate mechanism. Since the UK chose not to do so it did not benefit from that provision.

This conveniently brings us to the subject of the UK's relationship with the EMS. The original decision to stay outside represented a continuation of the Labour Party's attitude to European monetary experiments (see Chapter 1). Given the UK's inflationary proclivity, an inability to devalue would force the British Government to deflate, thus creating unemployment. When the Thatcher Government came to power the argument against membership was very different. When the pound was strong and rising it was argued that, were it a member, the UK would be required to adopt an expansionary monetary policy in order to prevent the pound from rising above its upper limit. Such an expansionary monetary policy would be at odds with the monetarist stance which had been adopted. The Medium-Term Financial Strategy was indeed incompatible with the EMS, since strict adherence to it implied no exchange rate target. David Llewellyn (1983, p. 265) pointed out that subsequent UK monetary strategy switched from sole reliance on the money supply as the target and began to take account of interest rates and the exchange rate. This suggested that the stance of UK policy was becoming more compatible with EMS membership. Nevertheless, the latter was still regarded as posing problems, and the UK Government merely indicated that it might join eventually. This hesitancy was probably a reflection of the views expressed in the 1985 report of the Treasury and Civil Service Select Committee of the House of Commons. It expressed reservations about membership of the exchange rate mechanism. It drew attention to the loss of autonomy – that is an old point. It expressed concern about the exchange rate relative to the D-mark. At that time sterling was felt to be overvalued, and it was anticipated that there would be resistance to inserting it into the exchange rate mechanism at an appropriately adjusted rate.

British resistance to full membership persisted under Mrs Thatcher, whose reluctance to give up sovereignty was reinforced by her adviser Sir Alan Walters, who considered the EMS to be 'half-baked'. This caused some tension in the Conservative Party leadership as the Chancellor of the Exchequer, Nigel Lawson, was clearly favourable to ERM participation and later resigned because of disagreements over policy. Equally the Foreign Secretary, Sir Geoffrey Howe, took a more favourable view and seems to have persuaded Mrs Thatcher to take a more conciliatory approach at the Madrid Summit in 1989. The reader will recollect from Chapter 1 that at Madrid the Heads of State and of Government committed themselves to setting up EMU. Moreover they agreed to embark on stage one which involved membership of the ERM. On this occasion, while not accepting such a commitment, Mrs Thatcher moved her position from one of joining when the conditions were right to one of joining when certain specific conditions were fulfilled. These included completion of the internal market, the abolition of exchange controls by other states and the reduction in the UK's inflation rate. In fact the UK joined the ERM in October 1990. Strictly speaking none of the Madrid conditions had been fulfilled –

the inflation rate had not fallen (although it was expected to), the internal market was not then complete and not all exchange controls had been abandoned.

Financing the EMS

As we have seen, operations to support currencies require financing. The EMS incorporated and expanded three previously existing EC credit mechanisms – the very short-term financing and the short-term monetary support (STMS). Both of these were the responsibility of Central Banks. In addition there was the medium-term financial assistance (MTFA) which was granted by the Council of Ministers. It was ultimately envisaged that a European Monetary Fund (EMF) would be created. In the interim, the old European Monetary Cooperation Fund (EMCF) continued to exist as the precursor to the new institution. The EMCF was empowered to receive monetary reserves from the appropriate authorities of the member states and to issue ECUs in exchange. The latter could be used to settle debts between member states and in transactions with the EMCF. The ECU was thus an asset and not just a denominator for expressing debts and claims. Although the UK did not initially join the supersnake, it did participate in the work of the EMCF by depositing with it 20 per cent of its reserves of gold and foreign exchange in return for ECUs.

Convergence

When the member states agreed to set up the EMS, they recognized that it was important to coordinate their national macro-economic policies. In Community parlance this is referred to as policy convergence – the objective of which is to achieve a convergence of economic performance. In other words rates of inflation (or deflation), etc., should come into line. Without such a convergence, exchange rates cannot long remain unchanged. Thus those who inflate relatively rapidly will lose competitiveness and will be forced to devalue in order to restore it. It is of course possible for those who inflate too rapidly to seek to persuade their more successful partners to bear some of the adjustment burden by revaluing. This would make the latter less competitive and the excessive-inflation countries correspondingly more competitive. Convergence of policy sounds fine, but it does involve a giving up of national sovereignty – as we have seen, the UK was less than enthusiastic about the prospect. In the context of policy convergence, it is important to note the relevance of the SEA. The reader may have wondered why we referred earlier to the *original* Rome Treaty rules on macro-economic policy. The reason is partly that although the rules remained intact, the SEA added Article 102A. It came under a new section headed 'Cooperation in economic and monetary policy (Economic and Monetary Union)'. The new article went on to call for measures to ensure the convergence of economic and monetary policy, and in that connection it required the member states to take account of experience in the EMS and in developing the ECU. Thus, while the SEA did not compel full membership of the EMS the Rome Treaty now explicitly took account of it.

Assessment and Lessons for the Future

It is all too apparent that the EMS did not render currency realignments a thing of the past. Table 13 indicates that between the inception of the EMS in March 1979 and the Maastricht Treaty negotiations there were twelve occasions when one or more of the participating currencies was realigned. On the other hand there is evidence that as compared with currencies such as the Japanese yen and US dollar the scheme had the effect of reducing day-to-day fluctuations between member state currencies.

If we ask why realignments were necessary, the answer is partly that rates of inflation varied between member states. As we anticipated above, member states with unduly rapid rates of inflation had lost competitiveness and had been forced to devalue, while the successful ones bore part of the adjustment burden and had to revalue. This point is brought out in Table 14, from which it is apparent that, broadly speaking, in the period 1979–91 those with the lowest rates of inflation tended to revalue, whilst those with the highest rates tended to devalue.

Another factor which affected the stability of the EMS was external in origin – i.e. the state of the US dollar. When the US dollar was quiescent there was a better prospect of quiescence in the EMS. But when the US dollar fell, or was expected to fall, there

Table 13. EMS exchange rate realignments 1979–91

23 September 1979	D-mark revalued by 2%, Danish krone devalued by 3%, each against all other EMS currencies
19 November 1979	Danish krone devalued by 5%
22 March 1981	Italian lira devalued by 6%
4 October 1981	D-mark and Dutch guilder revalued by 5.5%, French franc and Italian lira devalued by 3%
21 February 1982	Belgian and Luxembourg franc devalued by 8.5% and Danish krone by 3%
12 June 1982	D-mark and Dutch guilder revalued by 4.25%, French franc devalued by 5.75% and Italian lira devalued by 2.75%
21 March 1983	D-mark revalued by 5.5%, Dutch guilder revalued by 3.35%, Danish krone revalued by 2.5%, Belgian and Luxembourg franc revalued by 1.5%, Italian lira devalued by 2.5%, Irish punt devalued by 3.5%
20 July 1985	Italian lira devalued by 6%, all others revalued by 2%
6 April 1986	D-mark and Dutch guilder revalued by 3%, Belgian and Luxembourg franc and Danish krone revalued by 1%, French franc devalued by 3%
2 August 1986	Irish punt devalued by 8%
1 January 1987	D-mark and Dutch guilder revalued by 3%, Belgian and Luxembourg franc revalued by 2%
5 January 1990	Italian lira devalued by 3.11%, band widened to 6%

Source: EC Commission, *General Report* and *Bulletin,* various dates.

Table 14. Inflation 1979–89 and EMS realignments 1979–91

	Inflation league table	Devaluations	Revaluations
Dutch guilder	32·1	0	6
D-mark	32·9	0	7
Belgian franc	51·2	1	4
Luxembourg franc	60·2	1	4
Danish krone	78·3	3	3
French franc	83·7	3	1
Irish punt	103·8	2	1
Italian lira	126·5	4	1

was a flight out of it into safer havens. The safest haven in the EMS was the strongest currency – i.e. the one most likely to appreciate rather than depreciate. That tended to be the D-mark.

There are several lessons to be derived from the Community's monetary experimentation. The first is that, in the post-Maastricht era, it is important to recognize that there is nothing new about EMU – it has all been tried before and, unfortunately, it failed. Why did it fail? Part of the answer in the case of the 1970s episode must be ascribed to a lack of convergence coupled with disturbances from abroad. Lack of convergence was due to an unwillingness to cede sovereignty over monetary matters. Member states would not formally surrender their autonomy and agree to formulate their domestic policies in common. This unwillingness was apparent not only under EMU but also under the subsequent EMS. Kruse put it as follows: 'The member states were not prepared to cede their authority in 1971 and they were not prepared to do so in 1980.' (Kruse, 1980, p. 259). We may therefore legitimately speculate as to whether at the end of the day member states will, under the current Maastricht plan, be prepared to change their tack. If the French prime minister is prepared to personally intervene in Brussels over the fate of one French firm (the Air France subsidy in 1994), what prospect is there that he will be willing to hand over the whole of the French economy to outside management?

Having noted an unwillingness to formally hand over sovereignty, we have had to acknowledge that under the EMS there was in the late eighties and early nineties a noticeable tendency for the economies to converge and for the number of realignments in the ERM to decrease – see Table 13. In effect the EMS came increasingly, but mistakenly and dangerously, to be regarded as a fixed exchange rate regime. This convergence was however not because member states had changed their ways and had formally given up their policy-making autonomy. It was instead a reflection of the dominance of the German economy. The Bundesbank's firm control of inflation meant that if other member states wished to compete and avoid realignments then they had to accommodate themselves to the German rate of inflation and the German monetary stance.

It is also worth noting that federal systems, involving as they do a single currency, usually incorporate a budgetary system which is of such a nature that a substantial shift of resources to the less successful regions of the union is possible. The Community has however failed to expand Community budget resources to a comparable level (see Chapter 3). The fact that a substantial transfer of resources might be needed in an EMU context was indicated by the experience of the two Germanies following their reunion and adoption of a common currency.

The idea that the EMS had progressively changed into a fixed exchange rate system was conclusively undermined in the period which followed the signing of the Maastricht Treaty in February 1992. From that relatively euphoric point onwards expectations quite quickly began to go downhill. A series of events took place which sent shock waves through the European currency markets. The Danish 'No' vote on Maastricht on 2nd June 1992 was probably a critical event undermining confidence in a smooth monetary transition to EMU. Not only did it reinforce the view that the Danes would require special treatment but it launched an anti-monetary union atmosphere across Europe. In Germany an opinion poll revealed that a majority of Germans were not favourably disposed towards giving up the stable Deutsche Mark in favour of a single currency. The 'Yes' vote in the French referendum in September 1992 did something to restore confidence in the likelihood that a single currency would transpire but the closeness of the vote gave rise to concern.

The speculative pressures and episodes experienced by the ERM will not be discussed in any great detail. Suffice it to say that currency after currency was tested. The lira was devalued in September 1992. Subsequently sterling came under intense pressure and on 16th September (referred to as 'Black Wednesday') massive intervention by the Bank of England failed to prevent the pound from breaching its lower limit against the D-mark. The lira too came under renewed pressure and both currencies were floated out of the ERM whilst the peseta was also devalued. Both Spain and Ireland reimposed exchange controls in order to protect their currencies. In November 1992 further speculative attacks focused on the peseta and escudo and led to a third round of devaluations and in January 1993 the punt went the same way. In May the escudo and peseta were devalued yet again. These references to the pound, peseta, escudo, lira and punt should not disguise the fact that at various times other currencies were in difficulties, plummeting to the bottom of the ERM bands. Notable among these were the French franc, the Belgium franc and the Danish krone. The French policy of refusing to devalue (the *Franc Fort* policy) inevitably implied high domestic interest rates that ran counter to the needs of its domestic economy which was moving sharply into recession. Friday 30th July 1993 ('Black Friday') was the most frenetic in the history of the ERM. On Monday 2nd August the world woke up to the news that the finance ministers had reformed the ERM. The fluctuation bands had been widened to ± 15 per cent for all currencies except the D-mark and the Dutch guilder.[1]

This year of turmoil highlighted three potential causes of ERM instability. The first was that the single market programme itself, reinforced by the commitment contained in the Maastricht Treaty, had required the removal of controls on capital movements. Vast amounts of footloose money were sitting in the various financial centres of the Community and were consequently absolutely free to move. Moreover the quantity was dauntingly large, sufficient indeed to overwhelm even the most determined central bank. Added to that was the fact that the ERM constituted what might be termed as a speculator's charter. Under a floating-rate system, speculative movements out of a currency could cause the rate to weaken, thus undermining the expected profit to be made on repurchase of the currency. Under the ERM, member states were obliged to support the rate – certainly not letting it drop below the lower band level. Speculators were therefore supported on their way out and thus could make a healthy profit, if the currency was devalued, when they repurchased. The third problem was associated with the possible consequences of asymmetric shocks – i.e. economic shocks which affect only one member state and dictate a policy response on its behalf which is not appropriate to other member states who are not directly affected by the shock. The asymmetric shock which undermined the system was German reunification. Its inflationary effects dictated a need for relatively high German interest rates. Other member states in the interests of supporting their exchange rates were forced to follow the German interest rate policy although their domestic recessionary conditions demanded lower rates. Attempts to persuade Germany to cut its interest rate, as in June 1993 when the French Economics Minister openly criticized the restrictive German policy and pressured the Bundesbank to ease its rates, fell

1. In March 1995 further ERM devaluations occurred – the peseta was devalued by 7 per cent and the escudo by 3.5 per cent.

on deaf ears. The Bundesbank's first, and really only, obligation was to preserve the stability of its own currency and not to solve Europe's unemployment problem. Inevitably some countries, the UK was an early example, decided to break ranks. Devaluing or leaving the system enabled domestic interest rates to be lowered.

The conclusion drawn by commentators on the ERM was that a policy of staying put was unsustainable. There had to be either a movement backwards or forwards. One possible backwards movement was to generally reinstate exchange controls. Spain and Ireland had introduced temporary controls in 1992 but this was by virtue of a special transitional arrangement allowed in the capital movements directive. The possibility of a general imposition was reported to have been advocated by Commission President Jacques Delors in an address to the European Parliament in September 1993 but the Commission quickly mounted a damage limitation exercise, claiming that the President had been misinterpreted. An alternative idea, essentially a backwards movement, was canvassed by Eichengreen and Wyplosz (Eichengreen and Wyplosz, 1993). This involved the imposition of a tax on speculators by, for example, requiring institutions who took an open position in currencies to make a non-interest bearing deposit with their central bank. They argued that for long-term capital movements of beyond a year the cost would be negligible but for short-term round trips, which were characteristic of pure speculation, the costs would be high. However, Foley pointed out that such a tax would only be effective if applied in all countries where ERM currencies are traded. Much of the speculative pressure emulated from outside the EC and it was unlikely that the authorities in Japan or the US would cooperate in such a scheme (Foley, 1993, p. 2). Wyplosz also argued that the most effective approach would be in fact to move forwards (Wyplosz, 1994, p. 4) to a quick monetary union. In short he appeared to be arguing in favour of the old Monetarist approach – i.e. fix the exchange rates irrevocably and force members to converge. However he regretted that this was not an available option, being ruled out by Bundesbank. Here he was obviously referring to the German preference for convergence first and the single currency second – the old Economist stance.

In the event, and as we have seen, the solution chosen was to move backwards by widening the ERM bands for most but not all states. Some commentators felt that this threatened to undermine the process of achieving greater convergence since national rates of inflation could differ significantly before exchange rates fell or rose to the floor or ceiling. On the other hand the wider band was a deterrent to the speculator. Wyplosz argued that the wider bands ought to be declared normal since the defence of realistic parities was less hopeless than was the case with narrow bands. Goodhart was of the view that the perceived benefit of the ERM in forcing convergence had obviously taken a knock. Instead he favoured relatively wider bands or bands with soft edges. In parallel domestic economic policies should be directed towards the achievement of convergence. In tandem with this, political developments should focus on underpinning the mandate of federal institutions. When convergence had been achieved there should be a quick move to a single currency, thus avoiding a potential unstable period of pegged exchange rates (Goodhart, 1994).

EMU – The Maastricht Plan

Motivations

As we indicated in Chapter 1, it was decided in 1990 that an IGC on EMU should in fact commence in Rome in December 1990 in parallel with the IGC on political union. The IGC on EMU followed in the wake of the Delors Committee report on EMU which had been commissioned in 1988 by the European Council and had been delivered in 1989. It explored the nature of the final state of EMU and how it might be achieved. The subsequent Maastricht Treaty on European Union broadly followed the path outlined by Delors but not in every particular. In terms of the scheme laid out in Figure 8 above, Maastricht embodied a maximalist monetary goal (a single currency) and a minimalist fiscal goal (tax harmonization as part of the Common Market together with Community control of national budget deficits and debt levels).

What forces gave rise to this second attempt at EMU? The first was a spill-over effect or motivation. Those who had planned the SEA did not, like Mrs Thatcher, assume that the Single Act was the end of the road. It was merely a staging post on the road to a closer union. It was logical to first complete the single market. But that in turn would support the argument that the single market would be even more effective if the costs and inconveniences of separate national currencies could be removed. It also has to be noted that whilst Mrs Thatcher was, at least by implication, opposed to EMU, she did in signing up to the SEA actually agree to a document whose preamble recollected that the Community had set itself the goal of EMU way back in 1972. That goal had never been jettisoned and in 1988, in commissioning the Delors Report, the European Council took the first step to re-activating the whole idea. In this connection we can say that the SEA contained a delayed action device which in due course would explode into life!

But these were background influences. In addition we have to take account of the motivations of two of the leading actors – Germany and France. Three factors were disposing Germany in favour of EMU. The first was that German industry had benefited from the Common Market and thus a development which under-pinned it had to be regarded favourably. Second, and of crucial importance, was the reunion of the two Germanys. West Germany was anxious to secure the approval of the Community for this development. In order to reassure the Community that this would not lead to Germany deserting the European fold, Germany was as an earnest of good intent willing to immerse itself monetarily in the Community. The Community for its part was anxious to bind Germany into the Community. Thirdly, the German political élite was concerned about the effect of German economic strength. This was likely to give rise to a growing antagonism – i.e. member states would resent having to dance to the Bundesbank's tune. The German élite feared the growth of such antagonism and sought to prevent it. One solution was to merge Germany monetarily in a larger entity. Having said that, it has to be recognized that any such monetary arrangement would have to embody a commitment to price stability and embody an independent central bank – i.e. to be the Bundesbank system writ large!

France was a keen supporter of EMU because it recoiled against a situation in which monetary policy in France was subservient to the monetary policy adopted by the Bundesbank. France could not hope to influence the Bundesbank to adopt a policy more attuned to French interests. However, a European central bank might be more amenable to pressure.

Background

The Maastricht Treaty contains a number of new policy competences of which by far and away the most important is associated with the commitment to turn the Common Market into an EMU. To this end old Articles 103 to 109, which we discussed earlier, were dropped. In their place are new Articles 102a and 103 to 109 together with associated protocols. Before we turn to the stages which lead up to EMU we need to review the background conditions which derive from these new articles. Four aspects are worthy of note. They are the coordination and convergence requirements, the excessive deficit procedure, the 'no bail-out' clause and the free movement of capital obligation.

Under new Article 102a, Member States are required to conduct their economic policies with a view to achieving the objectives of the Community as laid down in Article 2. Article 2 includes the need for economic convergence and the establishment of an EMU. In respect of coordination, new Article 103a declares that it will be under the direction of the Council of Ministers. The latter will draw up broad guidelines on member state economic policy and these will be discussed by the European Council. On the basis of the conclusions drawn by the Heads of State and Government, the Council of Ministers will adopt recommendations setting out these broad guidelines. To facilitate coordination a Monetary Committee was set up with immediate effect. Its role was to be purely advisory.

This call for coordination highlights the important role which has to be played by convergence. The reader will recollect that in the 1970s the Community took on board the aspiration of achieving EMU by 1980. It failed but we shall not dwell on that fact. What is relevant are the different views which were then advanced about how best to proceed to the ultimate objective. As we noted earlier, during the 1970s debate two alternative views were put forward – the Monetarist and Economist positions. The Monetarists believed in locking the exchange rates at the outset. This, it was felt, would force member states to apply the appropriate monetary discipline and converge their economic performances. The Economists on the other hand called for convergence first and the locking of exchange rates and a common currency second. The Maastricht programme clearly adopts the latter approach since it envisages a stage by stage transition to the final goal and emphasizes the need to achieve convergence before the final monetary act is accomplished.

The Maastricht Treaty also inserted into the Rome Treaty a requirement (Article 104c) that governments should avoid excessive deficits. A protocol was attached to the Maastricht Treaty which stipulated that budget deficits as a ratio to GDP should not exceed 3 per cent and that government debt in relation to GDP should not exceed 60 per cent. Member states that breached these guidelines would find themselves on the receiving end of Council recommendations requiring them to bring the excessive deficit, etc., to an end. Failure to come into line would be followed by an order to do so which could be backed up by financial sanctions. These include invitations to the EIB to reconsider its lending to the errant state, a requirement for the state in question to make a non-interest bearing deposit with the Community or the imposition of a fine. The excessive deficit procedure of course points up the fact that monetary union has a fiscal dimension and this fiscal dimension is designed to be a continuing feature of the EMU plan. Later we shall see that macroeconomic management is a divided responsibility since the Union central bank system will be primarily responsible for handling monetary (narrowly defined) matters whilst the Council of Ministers will be responsible for the appropriate fiscal (government borrowing) discipline.

New Article 104b also imposes a no 'bail-out' condition on member states. In the Maastricht negotiations Germany in particular was concerned to impose this restriction. The problem here is that a government, for example Italy, might continue to run budget deficits and consequently pile up an ever-growing burden of debt. Eventually this could lead to a situation where the capital markets came to doubt the ability of Italy to service and repay its debt. Whilst in the monetary union that debt would be Italian, it would nevertheless be denominated in the Union currency. The fear of that consequence could lead other debtor countries to bail the Italian government out and indeed the Italian government might be tempted to rely on this, and to that extent would not be constrained in its borrowing. What Article 104b does is to declare that this kind of bribery would not work. The Italian government would be responsible for its debts and moreover would, as we have just seen, be subject to excessive deficit control.

The final background condition is imposed by new Article 73b which states that all restrictions on the movement of capital between member states and between the member states and third countries are prohibited. The reader will of course recollect that as part of the single market programme, a capital liberalization directive had been adopted in 1988.

The Stages

As we noted the Maastricht Treaty envisaged a stage by stage movement to EMU. The second and final stages are detailed in new Articles 109e to 109m of the Rome Treaty. In stage one the main condition was that all member states should be members of the ERM of the EMS which, it will be recollected, centred on a limited normal margin of fluctuation of ± 2.25 per cent around the central parities against the ECU.

Stage two opened on 1st January 1994. The avoidance of excessive budget deficits (see above) continued and by the beginning of 1994 the Council of Ministers was required to have introduced detailed rules for the operation of the excessive deficit mechanism. On the monetary side the significant development was the creation of the European Monetary Institute (EMI). This body was to have a legal personality and be managed by a Council consisting of a President and the Governors of the national central banks. Alexandre Lamfalussy, a former General Manager of the Bank for International Settlements, was the first President and Maurice F. Doyle, a former Governor of the Central Bank of Ireland, was appointed Vice-President.

The Institute (located in Frankfurt) had three main tasks to perform. The first was to facilitate convergence by strengthening the coordination of national monetary policies. In effect it was to manage a process of transition from a condition of coordinated national monetary policies to a single Union monetary policy. It would seek coordination through the issuing of recommendations to member states on the conduct of their monetary policies. Second, it was to be responsible for overseeing the operation of the ERM. In this connection the European Monetary Cooperation Fund was to be dissolved and its tasks were to be discharged by the Institute. Third, it was to prepare all the procedures, mechanisms of control and so forth, which would be necessary when the final stage monetary union came into existence. For example, an appropriate quantity of paper currency would have to be ready for use. Apparently the physical task of printing all the notes that would be put into circulation when the single currency made its appearance was bound to take several years.

During the second stage the member states were also required to take steps to render their central banks independent. The Statute of the European System of Central Banks (ESCB) and the European Central Bank (ECB) defines such independence as a situation where neither a central bank nor any member of its decision-making bodies seeks or takes instructions from a government or any other body. The reason for this move was, of course, that in the final state of monetary union the Union central banking authority was to be independent and the Maastricht Treaty envisaged a collaborative arrangement involving the national central banks.

Preparations for the entry into final stage three were required to begin not later than the end of 1996. According to new Article 109j, during 1996 the European Commission and the EMI would report to the Council of Ministers on the degree to which member states had achieved a convergence of economic performance. Each member state's performance would be judged against five criteria which were fully set out in a protocol attached to the Maastricht Treaty. Those criteria are shown in Table 15 opposite. The assessment would also take account of 'the development of the ECU, the results of the integration of the markets, the situation and development of the balances of payments on current account and . . . of the development of unit labour costs and other price indices.' On the basis of these reports the Council of Ministers, acting by qualified majority, would assess which member states fulfilled the conditions necessary for the introduction of a single currency. The Council of Ministers 'meeting in the composition of Heads of State or of Government' would then by qualified majority make three final decisions. First, whether a majority of states fulfilled the necessary conditions. Second, whether it was appropriate to enter the third and final stage. Third, assuming it was appropriate, when the third stage should start.

Whilst it is therefore possible that the third stage could commence in 1997, it is also possible for one reason or another that the

Table 15. Maastricht Treaty on European Union EMU convergence criteria

---

1. In the year prior to examination an inflation rate no more than 1.5 percentage points above the average of the three EC states with the lowest price rises.
2. In the year prior to examination a long-term rate of interest within two percentage points of the average of the three members with the lowest rates of inflation.
3. A national budget deficit less than 3 per cent of GDP.
4. A public debt ratio which does not exceed 60 per cent of GDP.
5. A currency for two years in the normal band of the ERM of the EMS which has not been devalued.

---

member states might choose not to. If by the end of 1997 a date has not been set for the beginning of the third stage, then indeed Article 109j declares that the third stage will start on the 1st January 1999. Before 1 July 1998 the convergence assessment procedure will once more be carried out. On this occasion the majority requirement will be dropped. As long as at least two countries satisfy the criteria they will proceed to form a monetary union as from 1 January 1999. In the lead-up to the Maastricht Treaty the German Chancellor was keen to see an irreversible process set on foot and the 1999 provision seems to meet his requirement (but see below).

The Final Stage

The third and final stage is characterized by the emergence of a single currency, in the form of the ECU, the supply of which is controlled by the ESCB – this institution is discussed below. The reader will recollect that the Delors Report had proposed that the ECB should appear at the second stage. But this was resisted notably by Germany. At the outset of the final stage Article 109(i) requires the Council of Ministers to decide the irrevocably fixed conversion rates between the national currencies and the ECU. Having done that the single currency has to be rapidly introduced. It will, however, only be introduced amongst those countries that are qualified to participate by virtue of having satisfied the convergence criteria. The Maastricht Treaty explicitly recognizes that some countries may not qualify – they are referred to as 'member states with a derogation'. Thus a 'two-tier Europe' is a potentiality under Maastricht. Countries may also opt out – indeed the UK and Denmark obtained such a concession.

According to Article 105 the ESCB is assigned the task of defining and implementing the monetary policy of the Community. Thus control of the supply of the single currency (the ECU) and interest rates falls under its aegis. Equally, the ESCB is charged with the task of conducting foreign exchange operations – in other words, it will carry out support operations in respect of the exchange value of the ECU against the US dollar, yen, etc. In this connection the foreign exchange reserves of the member states are to be centralized in the ESCB. The ESCB involvement in foreign exchange management is, however, a qualified one – i.e. day-to-day management. The ESCB is also called upon to promote the smooth operation of the payments system. Oddly the Maastricht Treaty does not specifically refer to the ESCB acting as lender of last resort. Perhaps references to its role in contributing to the smooth operation of the system and to the achievement of financial stability imply such a responsibility. It is also possible that its role in conducting open market operations may be stretched to include rescue operations. Hopefully the EMI will, during the second stage, flesh out the details of this vital central bank function. Alongside these monetary (narrowly defined) elements, the final stage also continues the system of fiscal discipline associated with the excessive deficit procedure. This, of course, is in the hands of the Council of Ministers and not the ESCB.

This brings us to institutional structure. In the final stage the EMI disappears and is replaced by the ESCB. The ESCB is a collaborative structure involving two operating arms, namely the National Central Banks (NCBs) – each with separate legal personalities – and the newly created ECB, which is also envisaged as having a separate legal personality. The use of the world 'collaborative' should not however disguise the fact that the decision-making centre is the ECB. Thus in the Protocol setting out the Statute of the ESCB and ECB, Article 8 enunciates the general principle that 'The ESCB shall be governed by the decision-making bodies of the ECB' and Article 14(3) further reinforces the centrality of the ECB when it declares that 'The national central banks are a integral part of the ESCB and shall act in accordance with the guidelines and instructions of the ECB.' The ECB Governing Council is made up of the Executive Board of the ECB together with the Governors of the NCBs. The Executive Board is itself composed of a President, a Vice-President and four other members.

In passing we should also note that the acts and omissions of the ECB are open to review or interpretation before the European Court of Justice. Also, the ECB may itself institute proceedings before the Court. Incidentally this latter possibility includes bringing actions against individual NCBs where the latter have failed to fulfil an obligation under the Statute governing the activities of the ESCB and ECB.

We have already identified the central tasks of the ESCB in broad terms – defining and implementing Community monetary policy, etc. But the main text of the Maastricht Treaty and the Protocol on the Statute assign specific *functions*. The ECB has the exclusive right to *authorize* the issue of notes and a non-exclusive right to *issue* notes. Such notes shall be the only notes to have the status of legal tender. The member states may issue coins but subject to control as to volume by the ECB. The ECB will (alongside the NCBs) be empowered to engage in open market operations. It will be able to impose minimum reserve requirements on credit institutions and employ any other method of monetary control which it deems appropriate. The ECB (alongside the NCBs) will be empowered to carry out support operations in the foreign exchange market. By contrast its role in the prudential control of credit institutions is the more limited one of contributing to the smooth operation of the system. However, the Council of Ministers has the power to confer specific control tasks on the ECB – insurance undertakings being explicitly excluded from the remit of the ECB.

The specific functions of the NCBs can be deduced from the above. Against the general background that they will act in accordance with the guidelines and instructions of the ECB, the NCBs can in particular issue notes and conduct open market and foreign exchange operations.

In the final stage the Monetary Committee is dissolved. It is replaced by an Economic and Financial Committee. Its task is to keep the economic and financial situation of the member states and the Community under review. It is required to report regularly on this issue and may deliver opinions to the Commission and Council on its own initiative or at their request. The scrutiny of the Committee is particularly directed towards the state of affairs in respect of the freedom of payments and the movement of capital.

The Maastricht Treaty opts for central bank independence. Article 107 stipulates, and the Protocol on the Statute reiterates, that neither the ECB, nor any NCB, nor any member of their decision-making bodies shall seek or take instructions from Community institutions, member state governments or any other body. The Statute obliges Community institutions and governments to respect this principle.

The Statute also states that the primary objective of the ESCB in the conduct of monetary policy must be the maintenance of price stability. Without prejudice to that objective it must also support the general economic policies of the Community.

Will it ever happen?

It seems difficult to resist the view that ultimately a group of countries trading intensively and with each other, as in the case of the European Union, will find it convenient to adopt a common currency. European business circles tend to favour monetary union although it is not always obvious whether this refers to the desirability of stable exchange rates or of a common currency. Public opinion however, notably in Germany, is not enthusiastic. The 1996/97 date for full EMU seems extremely unlikely – not least because in the mid-nineties debt levels were running well above convergence criteria levels which, incidentally, the German Constitutional Court has declared to be sacrosanct. The President of the EMI stated in November 1994 that although he expected a European central bank to emerge, it might only be in four, five or even ten years' time. He also envisaged the possibility that a single currency might come at a late stage and that there could be a substantial interim period in which member states adopted a system of irrevocably fixed exchange rates. This is a new slant on the EMU process since it has usually been assumed that irrevocably fixed exchange rates would be quickly followed by a single currency. We cannot of course rule out the possibility that a small group of countries might decide to go it alone. Germany, France, Austria and the Benelux countries are usually viewed as the most likely members of such a venture.

8

AGRICULTURE, TRANSPORT AND ENERGY

The common agricultural policy

The logic of inclusion

First we must ask why such a policy was required at all. The Six could have adopted the approach of EFTA and left agriculture out of the arrangement. However, a programme of economic integration within the Six which excluded agriculture stood no chance of success. It is important to appreciate that the Rome Treaty was a delicate balance of the national interests of the contracting parties. Let us consider Germany and France in terms of trade outlets. In the case of Germany the prospect of free trade in industrial goods, and free access to the French market in particular, was extremely inviting. In the case of France, the relative efficiency of her agriculture (particularly her grain producers) compared with Germany held out the prospect that in a free Community agricultural market she would make substantial inroads into the German market. This was obviously likely to result if the common price level of grain, for example, was set well below the German level but at or above the French level. Agriculture had therefore to be included.

These factors do not, however, explain the emergence of a common policy. Agriculture could have been brought within the ambit of the Treaty without resort to common support systems and common price levels. Each member state could have operated its own agricultural support programme, with protection at the frontier and so forth in order to achieve predetermined price levels. Trade could have been fitted into such a system through the agency of bilateral agreements between members, whereby they could have agreed to absorb certain quantities of each other's agricultural output. In practice the Six chose to go further than this since they agreed to free inter-state agricultural trade of all obstacles. This in turn implied uniform prices over the whole Community market. It also gave rise to the establishment of a centralized system for deciding what the common price levels should be and Community machinery for manipulating markets in order to bring them about. A Community system for financing the support policy was also clearly called for. The decision to establish free movement of agricultural goods within the Community was probably the result of two factors. First, anything less than free trade in agriculture would have struck the French as discriminatory when compared with the treatment proposed for industrial goods. Secondly, if trade was not free, and national price levels could differ, then countries with low price levels would enjoy a competitive advantage in so far as low food prices give rise to low industrial wages.

In explaining the inclusion of agriculture within the Rome Treaty, some account should also be taken of the sheer size of the agricultural sector in 1958. At that time farming occupied fifteen million persons – about 20 per cent of the working population of the Community. A process of economic unification, leading to eventual political integration, could hardly succeed if it failed to address itself to the problems faced by such a large proportion of the population. Within the Six, agriculture was an occupation in which the problem of relatively low incomes was particularly acute. In any case the agricultural vote was so important that agriculture could hardly be ignored. This kind of consideration was extremely important in the case of France. French farmers were highly dissatisfied with the kind of support provided by the French Government and looked to the EC as a means of improving their lot. To them the exclusion of agriculture was unthinkable, and French politicians were fully aware of that point.

Policy objectives

The provisions relating to the CAP are found in Articles 38 to 47. The Rome Treaty did not specify the forms of price support which would be adopted for each product. Instead, Article 43 indicated that the Commission should convene a conference to thrash out the matter, after which it would make appropriate proposals for adoption by the Council of Ministers. The various methods of market organization which were finally adopted are discussed below. While the Treaty did not commit itself on the form of market organization, it did specify the objectives of the CAP – these are to be found in Article 39. The policy should:

(a) increase agricultural productivity;
(b) ensure a fair standard of living for the agricultural community;
(c) stabilize markets;
(d) provide certainty of supplies;
(e) ensure supplies to consumers at reasonable prices.

We should also take cognizance of Article 110 relating to the creation of a common commercial policy. It indicates that the member states should aim to contribute to the harmonious development of world trade.

The reader will recognize that there is plenty of scope for conflict here. The improvement of farm incomes might require significant price increases, but this would conflict with the interests of consumers. It must be admitted that no indication is given as to what is a fair income level or what is a reasonable level of prices. Certainty of supplies could be taken to justify a greater degree of self-sufficiency, but that would reduce the access of third countries to the Community food market which in turn would jeopardize the achievement of the objective of Article 110.

The original system of price support

The basic problem was that if the Community market was open to free importation many farmers would go to the wall since world market prices were low and the price required by most of the farmers of the Six (many of whom were relatively inefficient small-scale producers) was high. The solutions devised to deal with this problem varied from product to product but, typically for northern temperate products (e.g. cereals), the general thrust of the price (and thus income) support mechanism was as portrayed in Figure 10.

In the diagram SS is the supply curve of EC producers and DD is the demand curve of EC consumers. P1S(World) is the supply curve of imports from the world market. If free importation had been allowed the internal price would have ridden down to the world market price level P1 with equilibrium between supply and demand occurring at J. Only the most efficient EC farmers would

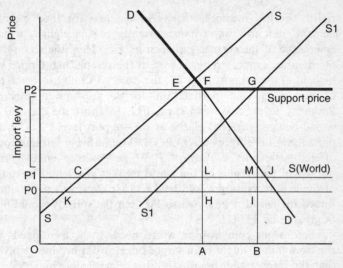

Storage cost AFGB
Export subsidy HFGI

Figure 10. Support under the CAP

have survived – i.e. those on the supply curve below C. In order to protect the less efficient farmers a levy was introduced which raised the price of the imported product, i.e. it caused a parallel upward shift of P1S(World). A levy of P1P2 per unit would in fact lead to equilibrium at F.

More EC farmers would now be protected, i.e. those below E on the supply curve. Imports would fall from CJ to EF. However, the Community would not be self-sufficient. But we now have to introduce a further factor, namely technological change. Better breeds of animal, improved strains of crop, more fertilizers, more pesticides, etc., tended to lead to greater yields per cow, per acre, etc. This tended to cause the supply curve to shift to the right, e.g. to S1S1. The combined effect of increased prices and increasing yields was the emergence of surpluses, i.e. at price P2 the surplus is FG. It should be noted that whilst supply increased (shifted to the right), the low income elasticity of demand for food meant that demand did not shift commensurately to the right – hence the emergence of the surplus gap such as FG. Here the second aspect of the price support system came to the rescue. If the price was to be held at the support level P2, the excess FG had to be taken out of the market. One approach was for the appropriate intervention authority to purchase and store FG. In short the demand curve would become perfectly elastic at the support level P2. The cost of purchasing the surplus was AFGB. Alternatively farmers could be offered an export subsidy of P1P2 per unit to enable them to dispose of the surplus on the world market at a loss. The total cost of the export subsidy would be LFGM. However, if the dumping forced the world price down to P0 then the subsidy would have to be greater, i.e. HFGI.

There is one complication which needs to be mentioned. Whilst the Community might set a target price, it did not inevitably mean that the intervention board would automatically enter the market and initiate price support operations once the price fell below the target level. Indeed cereals prices could fall 23 to 30 per cent below the target level before they hit the intervention level where support operations were required to start.

In order to finance these kinds of operation, the Community established the EAGGF which was fed from the Budget. Guarantee money was devoted to price support operations. Guidance money (a very small proportion of total farm spending) was for structural improvements in the farming industry. The Community also introduced *common price support mechanisms* for all the major agricultural products. Internal trade barriers were also removed with the *aim* of leading to *common prices* for those products.

The expenditure problems of the CAP were exacerbated by the *open-ended* nature of the support mechanism depicted in Figure 10. That is to say, in order to support prices, whatever surplus farmers produced had to be taken out of the market. Because of the tendency for the increase of supply to outstrip the increase of demand (i.e. the effect of the low income elasticity of demand) the size of the gap FG tended to become greater and greater over time. Unless support prices fell and/or world prices rose, this implied a growing guarantee spending burden which inevitably fell upon the Community budget.

There are a number of observations which need to be made in relation to the above account. First, we must emphasize that the above description of the EC mechanism merely describes the general thrust of support policy, which covered about 70 per cent of output.

Secondly, within the 70 per cent category there were quite marked variations from product to product. The reader is invited to contrast the variable levy and automatic intervention buying at the target price minus 23 to 30 per cent for most cereals with the arrangement for fruit and vegetables. In the latter case the external protection was limited to an *ad valorem* import duty or to a duty on top of a minimum import price. Internally, prices were able to fall a long way before intervention buying had occurred. The internal régime involved the calculation of basic prices – these were derived by averaging EC domestic prices over the previous three years. However, these basic prices were not guaranteed. Indeed *national intervention agencies* were not allowed to step in until market prices had fallen to the buying-in level – i.e. 40 to 70 per cent (depending on the product) of the basic price level. In practice this device was little used. Instead, a system of withdrawal prices was determined, and when market prices fell to the withdrawal level *producer organizations* were allowed to step in and buy up surplus produce. This produce was used for animal feed, industrial purposes or was destroyed. Such withdrawal operations were financed by the Community. Withdrawal prices were set at the buying-in level plus 10 per cent. The withdrawal price could therefore be as low as 50 per cent of the basic price (e.g. 40 per cent of the buying-in price plus 10 per cent).[1]

Thirdly, our general description of the régime in respect of 70 per cent of output is actually a description of a system which existed until 1984. In 1984 it began to change when quotas were introduced for milk. This was followed by budget stabilizers and set-aside in 1988 and by the McSharry reforms in 1992. We will say more about these topics later.

Fourthly, as we implied above, a significant minority of output was subjected to different forms of assistance. *Broadly speaking*, in the case of about 25 per cent of output support was concentrated

---

1. The pricing system was further complicated by factors which adjusted for quality, size and variety.

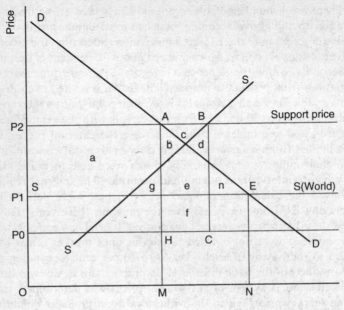

Figure 11. The welfare effects of the Common Agricultural Policy

mainly on measures of external protection as opposed to a balanced combination of external protection and internal manipulation.

Finally, in a very small minority of cases the price of imports could not be raised because duties at nil or low levels had been agreed in various international accords. When the price of imports could not be raised to Community levels, Community prices were brought down to match world levels by the granting of various forms of aid. Olive oil, oil seeds and tobacco were cases in point.

A Critique

The CAP has over the years come in for much criticism. The cost of the CAP can be portrayed in terms of its adverse effects on economic welfare. Its deficiencies can also be identified in a less abstract way. We will approach it in that order.

In Figure 11 the support price (i.e. import price from the world market plus import levy) is set at OP2 whereas the import price from the world market is OP1. EC supply exceeds EC demand by the amount AB. If however there was free importation, EC demand would intersect with supply at E. It follows that we need to contrast free importation equilibrium quantity and price (ON and OP1) with CAP equilibrium-price OP2 and a demand of P2A and a supply of P2B. It follows that consumers lose consumer surplus equal to a + b + e + g + n. On the other hand the rise in price means that producer surplus increases by a + b + c which helps to cancel out some of the consumer surplus loss. Then we have to add in the financial cost (i.e. loss) incurred by selling the surplus AB at a loss on the world market. The loss from AB sales would be e + b + c + d. However if the dumping of the surplus AB pushes the world price down to OP0, the financial cost of dumping the surplus would rise to e + b + c + d + f. If we net all this out, the final welfare cost of the CAP is 2e + b + d + f + g + n.

In a less abstract way the criticisms levelled at the CAP were as follows. It was supposed to increase agricultural productivity. Productivity did increase but it did not, in the period up to the price support reforms, exceed the increase of agricultural productivity outside the Community.

It was supposed to provide a fair standard of living for the agricultural community. Again in the period up to the support reforms the evidence is that agricultural incomes did increase but broadly they only kept in line with incomes in activities outside agriculture. Of extreme importance was the point that the price support system tended to favour the larger producers – the more a farmer produced the more he gained from the resources poured into support.

The CAP was supposed to stabilize markets and provide security of supplies. Here we record a distinct success. The evidence did suggest that thanks to the support mechanism agricultural prices in the EC were more stable than in the USA or on the world market. Security of supplies was certainly achieved since the Community tended to progressively become self-sufficient and indeed more than self-sufficient over a wide range of products. But this self-sufficiency, and more than self-sufficiency, became an embarrassment for reasons which are set out below.

The main criticisms levelled at the CAP really focused on five aspects. The first related to the effect on consumers when prices were set well above world levels – the reader will recollect that the policy was supposed to ensure supplies to consumers at reasonable prices. It could indeed be argued that the CAP was regressive in its effect on consumers since poor people spend a bigger proportion of their incomes on food than do relatively well-off individuals.

The second criticism related to the burden imposed on the Community budget by the growing surpluses of food. We saw in Chapter 3 that in 1984 and again in 1988 the budget was running out of resources because of the impact of the surplus problem.

The third criticism related to the fact that the CAP gave rise to international tensions. Because of self-sufficiency, the Community offered reduced market opportunities for outside producers and outside producers were also aggravated by the fact that prices in export markets in the rest of the world were undermined by Community surplus dumping. In due course these tensions were to surface in a major way in the Uruguay Round (see below).

Fourthly, the CAP tended to encourage farmers to try to produce more and more from the land and this had an adverse effect on the environment.

The final problem arose in connection with exchange rates. As originally conceived, the aim of the CAP was quite literally to provide for common prices. To this end prices were specified not in terms of national currencies but in terms of the Community's unit of account (UA), which had a gold content equal to that of the US dollar. In the pre-Smithsonian era, the US dollar was equal to 0.88867088 grammes of gold, and this was also the value of the UA. An assumption of the CAP, which early commentaries tended to overlook, was that the rates of exchange of individual Community currencies against the dollar and against each other would not be changed. If, however, a member state devalued this would have the effect of causing its farm prices in national currency terms to rise. The contrary would occur if it revalued.

In fact the common system of pricing had hardly begun to operate before it was subjected to the first of what was to prove to be a series of currency upsets. In August 1969 the French Government decided to devalue the franc by 11.11 per cent. This immediately created a minor crisis, since the common price arrangements were disturbed and there was a danger that French farmers would enjoy an increase in prices while farmers in other member states would not experience any improvement. More important, a rise in French prices would stimulate production and aggravate the already existing surplus problem. A Council meeting was therefore hastily summoned on 11 August. One possibility was that the UA could be devalued. However, although this could have offset the effect of devaluation on French producer prices and left them unchanged, it would have automatically worsened the prices received by producers in other member states. The policy was therefore rejected. Instead, a more complicated arrangement was adopted. During the marketing year 1969–70 the buying-in prices paid in respect of interventions in the French domestic market were to be reduced by 11.11 per cent, with the intention of preventing a rise in prices. The devaluation would also give French food exports a competitive edge, whilst imports into France would be disadvantaged. It was therefore decided that France should grant subsidies to imports from member states and levy compensatory duties on French exports in order not to distort the free movement of agricultural produce. In the 1970–71 period it was intended that intervention prices should be reduced by 5.5 per cent. Thereafter French agriculture was to be reintegrated into the CAP. In fact the reintegration took place in late 1972.

The decision to float the German mark, and then to revalue it at a new fixed rate which was 9.29 per cent above the old parity, also promised to upset the working of the common policy. The result, if not counterbalanced, would have immediately reduced the price paid to German farmers in terms of the domestic currency. This the German Government was not willing to accept. Instead, Germany was allowed to reduce her farm prices gradually, and in the meantime aid was given to German farmers on a diminishing scale – some of it being provided by the EAGGF. In the West German case the revaluation had the potential effect of cheapening imports and making exports dearer – the reverse of the French case. In order to offset this it was empowered to apply levies on imports and subsidies on exports – the reverse of the French case.

These levies and subsidies were in fact the precursors of the monetary compensating amounts (MCAs), which formally came into existence in May 1971. As events were to transpire they were not to be a transitory phenomenon. As a result of the Smithsonian

Accord of 1971 and after, the currencies began to float or were adjusted from time to time, and the Community found itself with two exchange rates. One was the Green Rate, which was the rate employed to convert UA (and later ECU) farm prices into national prices, and the other was the actual market rate of exchange. MCAs, variable in amount, which might be positive or negative, were employed to bridge the gap. It also follows that prices in national currency terms could change for two reasons. First, the ECU price might change. Secondly, the ECU price might not change but the Green Rate could change. The latter could be selectively applied to certain countries.[1] The important point about MCAs was that they meant that common prices, a supposedly crucial feature of the CAP, ceased to exist. National prices for particular products exhibited substantial variations. When the European Monetary System was introduced, an attempt was made to eliminate MCAs. This gave rise to a dispute which delayed the inception of the system. In the end it was agreed to dismantle existing MCAs gradually within the context of annual price determinations and to eliminate within two years any new MCAs arising from subsequent currency adjustments. In practice, MCAs continued to exist.

All this suggested that the CAP needed to be reformed. Initially reform of the CAP under the Mansholt Plan focused on farm structures. This failed because it was too controversial. Thereafter for quite a considerable period nothing much happened by way of reform although it was increasingly recognized that the system of price and income support would itself have to be rethought. This only bore fruit in the 1980s, specifically 1984 and 1988, and was followed up in 1992 by the McSharry reforms which were clearly partly prompted by the hostility to the CAP experienced in the Uruguay Round of tariff negotiations. To all this we now turn.

Reform – farm structure

The CAP had scarcely got off the ground before the surplus problem began to loom large. A movement towards self-sufficiency or more than self-sufficiency leads on the one hand to a reduction

1. A country might have different Green Rates applied to different commodities.

of revenue from levies and on the other to an increased expenditure on refunds. A reform of what was proving to be an economically and financially burdensome system was therefore called for. It should, however, be emphasized that proposals for reform during the late sixties were centred on the farm structure rather than the pricing system.

The Mansholt Plan of 1968 came as a considerable shock. The CAP had barely been established when farmers were confronted with the unpalatable news that many of them were redundant! Not surprisingly Dr Mansholt was given the title of 'the peasant killer'. Clearly the Plan was a political hot potato – so much so that the Council of Ministers gave it the cold shoulder. The need for structural reform was, however, accepted, although change on the scale envisaged by Mansholt was not thought feasible. Instead, a series of limited measures was introduced in 1972. EAGGF finance was available partially to finance three schemes. One was designed to modernize farms. Another offered farmers lump sums or annuities in return for leaving the land. The land so released would first be offered to those farms which were being modernized as above. The third was designed to train and thus raise the income-earning potential of farmers. In 1975 another measure was introduced to assist farmers in mountainous and remote areas in order to prevent depopulation. In 1977 measures were introduced to facilitate structural improvements at the processing and marketing, as opposed to production, stages. Later on, and notably in the light of Greek membership, measures were introduced to facilitate structural improvements in the Mediterranean region.

In 1983 the Commission, noting that the 1972 socio-structural measures were due to expire, and that modifications were needed to the 1977 regulation, submitted new proposals. At the same time it also proposed that Integrated Mediterranean Programmes should be introduced for the benefit of Greece, Italy and France. We mentioned this point in Chapter 1 when we discussed the problems likely to stem from the accession of Spain and Portugal. The Mediterranean areas of the three former countries rely heavily on agriculture and suffer from relatively high unemployment and relatively low incomes. Assistance needed to be channelled in their direction because they would suffer from Iberian competition. We will reserve further discussion of this policy measure for Chapter 9 when we consider regional policy.

In 1983 a revised regulation concerning processing and marketing was agreed, and in 1984 a measure was approved in place of the 1972 socio-structural regulations. The 1984 regulation was introduced against a background of some disappointment with the 1972 socio-structural programme. The new structural policy had the following features. Assistance for structural improvement would be aimed in particular at farmers in the lower income brackets. It would seek to improve incomes by cost reductions rather than output increases. Indeed, aid would not be given where output would be increased and the product was in surplus. Assistance would be given to enable younger farmers to establish themselves. It would also be designed to create alternative employment in tourism and craft activities and to turn land over to forestry. Payments would also be made in order to compensate farmers who adopted methods which were compatible with conservation.

The price support reforms of 1984

The year 1984 marks the beginning of a serious reform process. It began in the milk sector where the surplus problem had proved to be particularly intractable and costly. The Community decided to impose quotas on Community milk output – these quotas would operate for five years. The Community total would be broken down among the member states and in turn the states would allocate quotas to their producers or purchasers. In order to discourage deliveries in excess of quota, a swingeing super-levy was to be imposed of 75 to 100 per cent of the target price for milk. In short, the Community was prepared to pay the guaranteed price only on the stipulated quantity – production in excess was to be penalized out of existence. The original total appears to have been designed broadly to stabilize deliveries. However, in April 1986 the Council of Ministers decided to introduce a 3 per cent cut – 2 per cent in 1987/88 and 1 per cent in 1988/89. Then in December 1986 it returned to the subject in a more decisive way – it agreed to bring about a 9.5 per cent cut by 1988/89. This was hailed as a major breakthrough.

It should be added that following the 1984 agreement member states introduced their own 'outgoers' schemes to ease farmers out of milk production. These compensation schemes were financed by member states. In the UK the quotas so released to the government were reallocated to other producers to enable them to attain a more economic size. It should be added that the individual quotas have been attached to land. This raised some conflict between landowners and their milk-producing tenants, i.e. on cessation of production the compensation went to the former. Subsequently in 1986 the UK Government introduced legislation which granted tenants some compensation. Also in 1986, in consequence of the quota cuts, the Community introduced its own 'outgoers' scheme. The Community provided finance but also took over and destroyed the quotas so released.

The milk reforms were followed by a more determined attack in other sectors. Thus in 1985 the Council agreed on a general price package for 1985/86 which meant that agricultural prices in national currency terms increased by only 1.8 per cent as compared with 1984/85, while the rate of inflation in the Community in 1985 was running at 5.8 per cent. Real prices were therefore set to fall. In 1986 the prices package represented a 2.2 per cent increase in national currency terms (among the Ten) against an inflation rate of about 2.5 per cent. On this occasion the Community was just about holding the line in real terms. Significantly, it decided to apply a co-responsibility levy to cereals. Even more significantly, in December 1986 it decided to modify beef support arrangements. In the past the intervention price had acted as a floor. But on this occasion the Council decided that support buying would occur only when (a) the average market price in the Community was 90 per cent of the intervention price and (b) the price in the country where the intervention was to take place was 87 per cent of the intervention price. This implied a 13 per cent drop in price, although it was modified by some national Green Rate changes. The 1987 prices package was not agreed until July of that year. In general terms it provided for a price freeze together with cuts for cereals and vegetables. However, national Green Rate changes meant that some of the edge was taken off these measures. In the general context of reform, mention should also be made of the fact that the Commission had been increasingly introducing tougher quality controls – this meant that the policy became less open-ended.

While milk quotas represented a real step forward in reform, they by no means solved the problem. Basically the problem was to be found in the *open-ended* nature of much of Community farm support. The system was open-ended in the sense that the Community authorities concerned with the support of farm prices were obliged either to buy up and store or to finance the sale abroad of all surplus produce. Farmers were not really responsible for finding a market for their output – all they had to do was to produce! They could leave it to the Community to pick up the bill for disposing of any output that Community consumers did not wish to purchase. As we have seen, milk quotas marked the beginning of the end to this open-ended system as the Community was responsible for supporting only a limited quantity of output and not all the milk that the farmers could produce.

The price support reforms of 1988

It was in 1986 that the seeds of further reform were sown. As we indicated in Chapter 3, despite the 1984 increase in Community budget resources Commission President Jacques Delors was forced to announce in 1986 that the budget was once more running out of funds. Additional sources of finance were therefore needed. This provoked a vigorous debate during which the UK and the Netherlands demanded strong curbs on agricultural overproduction. The UK in particular indicated that it would not agree to more funds for the budget until the agricultural overproduction issue had been properly and thoroughly addressed.

Extremely tough negotiations ensued. In this connection two particular issues gave rise to controversy. First, what kind of device should be used to control output? Germany favoured set-aside measures – i.e. farmers should be compensated for taking land out of surplus production. The UK, however, favoured stabilizers. Under such an arrangement an output threshold would be agreed, and if output exceeded that limit then price cuts would be introduced as a deterrent. Secondly, if stabilizers were introduced then the level of the output threshold was absolutely crucial. The British argued for a low threshold, but this was opposed by France and Germany. Measures had already been introduced in respect of the milk and beef surpluses and these seemed to be having the desired effect. A major residual problem was the surplus of cereals. The UK therefore proposed an annual cereal threshold of 155 million tonnes – Germany and France wanted 160 million tonnes.

The February 1988 Brussels summit meeting at which these matters were finally addressed at one stage seemed to be heading for complete collapse, but fortunately a last-minute compromise was arrived at on the issue of agricultural curbs. It was agreed that the main emphasis in agricultural control should be placed on stabilizers, although set-aside measures would also be provided for and the Community would contribute to the cost thereof. It was agreed that for the agricultural seasons 1988–89 to 1991–92 a cereals threshold of 160 million tonnes would be employed. If output went beyond this level, price cuts of 3 per cent would be applied. If output consistently overshot the target, the price cuts would cumulate. A somewhat similar penalty system was agreed for oil-seeds. In endorsing the Community budget package the UK and the Netherlands indicated that their agreement was contingent upon similar stabilizer arrangements being applied to a range of other farm products.

The Uruguay Round

In 1985 it was agreed to launch a new round of GATT trade negotiations (see also Chapter 11) and it was also agreed that agricultural support measures should be included in the discussions. Following the reforms of 1984 and 1988 it was possible to hope that the CAP would be given a less hostile reception than previously. However, as things transpired this was not so. Agriculture became a major sticking point in the talks and threatened to torpedo the whole of the negotiations. Major food producers such as Australia, Argentina, Canada and New Zealand formed the Cairns pressure group and in 1990 in alliance with the US demanded a 90 per cent cut in EC farm export subsidies and a 75 per cent cut in other agricultural supports. These demands the Community flatly opposed. Eventually, after seven meetings of the Council of Agriculture Ministers at which considerable differences emerged, the Community agreed to table a greatly reduced offer. This consisted of a willingness to reduce farm support by 30 per cent over an extended period. This in turn was regarded as wildly inadequate by the other major food producers.

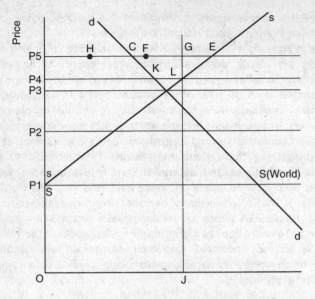

Figure 12. The EC surplus problem

How do we explain this conflict? A number of possible explana-
tions can be advanced. Let us consider them by reference to Figure
12 in which the demand and supply curves are the same as those in
Figure 11. First consider the quota as a feature of supposed CAP
reform. If the target price is P5 then it might be argued that the
desirable quota is quantity P5C. This would then be divided up
among the member states and they in turn would divide up their
share of the quota among their farmers. The open-ended guarantee
is replaced by a limited guarantee. However, the actual quota might
for political reasons (farmers' votes) be P5F. The Community
would still be applying a limit but would in this case be producing
more than it needed. CF might have to be dumped on the world
market to the intense annoyance of the US and the Cairns group.
The US and the Cairns group might argue that from their angle
even a quota equal to P5C is not ideal. It ought to be a smaller
quantity such as P5H. This would create an import gap HC.
Outside producers would now once more be able to sell to the

Community, thus reversing the self-sufficiency of recent years.

Let us now consider budget stabilizers. Suppose the stabilizer ceiling is set at OJ and the target price is initially P5. Quite clearly there is likely to be overproduction of the amount GE. If price cuts were triggered in subsequent seasons and the price fell to P4, the Community output would fall to the ceiling quantity OJ. However, this still leads to production in excess of demand and therefore to dumping abroad of KL. If the target price was reduced to P3 dumping would stop. But if the US and the Cairns group were to find outlets in the Community market, the price needed to be cut further, possibly to P2. Even price P2 was above the world price. They could therefore have demanded a further cut to price P1. However, that would have encountered some resistance as the EC industry would have been wiped out!

Once the aim of the US and the Cairns group becomes not just an end to dumping but also renewed access to the Community market, the reason for the demand for substantial quantity or price cuts becomes clear. We should also recognize that price cuts may not have the effect of cutting output. If productivity is increasing and costs are therefore falling, price cuts may indeed be offset by cost cuts. Farmers will therefore continue to overproduce.

The price support reforms of 1992

It was no doubt this continuing tendency to overproduce and the need to find an accommodation in the GATT talks which helps to explain why early in 1991 Agriculture Commissioner McSharry proceeded to put forward radical reform proposals. These met with substantial opposition from Community Ministers of Agriculture. Mr McSharry was being assailed from both sides! Later in 1991 McSharry returned to the attack with further radical proposals designed to deal with the problem of surpluses. As a result in June 1992, the Council of Ministers adopted a set of proposals which embodied what was claimed to be a fundamental reform of the CAP. As we have indicated, the 1988 budget stabilizer experiment had not been a great success. The growth of Community production was checked but not permanently stopped by the introduction of stabilizers. After an initial decline, both production and intervention stocks had continued their upward trends. What was needed was a system which would break the linkage between the reward to farmers and their production. This is precisely what the third phase of agricultural reform, the McSharry proposals, aimed to do.

Rather than reviewing every sector of the new policy, we will concentrate on cereals (including oilseeds and pulses) and livestock since the approach to them exhibits the core of the new philosophy. Over three years, starting in 1993/94, the price of cereals would be reduced by 29 per cent, bringing them close to world levels. Larger arable farmers would be required to take 15 per cent of their land out of production if they were to receive compensation for the price cut. This set-aside would itself help to reduce production. In addition the compensation for the price cuts would relate to *historic* yields per acre. Thus, to that extent, if a farmer increased his yield per acre he would receive no more per acre since compensation would be based on *what he used to produce* per acre. This together with the price cut would reduce the incentive to increase output. Hopefully the balance of farm remuneration expenditure would tend to shift from export subsidies to direct income compensation. Lower cereal prices would feed through as lower input costs (and therefore output prices) for those using cereals in cattle, pig and poultry rearing. A less intensive, more environmentally friendly farming system would emerge. In the case of livestock a similar approach has been adopted. Farmers are being encouraged to reduce their stocking levels, i.e. number of cattle per acre. Again, they will be directly compensated for adopting this less intensive and more environmentally friendly method of production.

In all this it is apparent that environmental considerations are becoming a more important aspect of the CAP. This 'greening' of the CAP is in line with more recent environmental action programmes, notably the fifth, and with new Article 130r, inserted by virtue of the Maastricht Treaty. They have emphasized the importance of integration; that environmental considerations must not just be peripheral but must be a central consideration in the formulation of all policies.

The common transport policy

There are a number of reasons why a common transport policy was called for under the arrangements envisaged by the Rome Treaty. The first is that transport costs are an important factor influencing trade. Since the Community was seeking to build up inter-state trade activity it was therefore desirable that there should be a cheap and well-coordinated Community transport system. Another way of putting the above point would be to say that if the common transport policy led to more efficient methods of transporting goods between states, benefits would be derived which were similar to those derived from the trade creation arising from internal tariff cuts. Secondly, it is necessary to recognize that transport on the Continent was subjected to considerable state intervention. Since these interventions were not coordinated between states, considerable distortions could arise. But more important was the fact that transport had been manipulated so as artificially to aid exports and inhibit imports. Experience in the early days of the ECSC indicated that this would also be a problem in a general common market. But there was a third factor. As was indicated earlier in discussing agriculture, the Rome Treaty involved a delicate balance of national interests. In the case of the Netherlands it was clearly anticipated that since transport, particularly that along the Rhine, was a very important contributor to the Dutch GNP, a growth of intra-Community trade would be very advantageous to the Netherlands. It was therefore very obvious from the Dutch point of view that transport should be brought within the ambit of the Treaty and that, in so far as this could be accomplished, member states should be prevented from hiving off transport activity as a sphere where national interests would predominate. This desire to take advantage of the transport opportunities opened up by the Rome Treaty was reflected in Article 75. Whilst the treaty was remarkably silent on the detailed nature of the common transport policy, it did definitely require the Community to devise common rules applicable to international transport going from one member state to another or passing across the territory of a member state. It is also called for rules to be laid down whereby a non-resident carrier could operate transport services in another member state. In practice, the Council of Ministers neglected these requirements to such an extent that in 1983 the European Parliament took it to the Court of Justice because of failure to act. In its 1985 judgement the Court supported Parliament and instructed the Council to remedy the deficiency.

The Commission's original blueprint

The Rome Treaty itself is, as we have indicated, remarkably uninstructive on the nature of the common policy. It was left to the Brussels Commission to provide a basis for such a policy. In 1961 the Commission produced a memorandum which laid down what it thought should be the general principles of the common transport policy – this was known as the Schaus Memorandum (EEC Commission, 1961) after Lambert Schaus, who was the Commissioner responsible for transport affairs. Then in 1962 the Commission produced its Action Programme (EEC Commission, 1962b) which reviewed the measures which the Commission proposed should be implemented. The memorandum outlined three main objectives which the transport policy should achieve. One was to remove obstacles which transport could put in the way of a general common market. Another was that the policy should not merely negatively aim to sweep away factors which delayed the creation of a common market, but should be a positive and powerful stimulant to the growth of trade and the opening up of national markets. Both these were generally acceptable. The third was much more controversial. The Commission suggested that the Community should 'endeavour to create healthy competition of the widest scope'. In the light of the highly regulated nature of transport within the Community this was bound to be a controversial proposition, all the more so as the Commission proposed that the common transport policy should apply to national as well as international transport activity. The Commission has continued to press for a policy which gives greater scope to undistorted competition and the forces of the market. As time has passed, this decision has been revealed to have been a wise one, as in various parts of the world, and notably in the US, opinion has moved in favour of deregulation. This has been particularly true in the case of road haulage (trucking) and air passenger transport.

Before we turn to discuss the Commission's approach, it is important to recognize that in the first instance the common transport policy only applied to three modes – road, rail and inland waterway. Air and maritime transport were excluded, although the Council of Ministers, on the basis of unanimity, could make provisions for these two latter modes. In fact the Council has in recent years been involved in policy-making in these two areas, and later we will focus on one of them – air transport. It is also important to appreciate the relative contribution of the various modes. Table 16 clearly shows that the dominant mode for the transport of goods within the Community is road haulage.

In working towards a basically competitive solution, the Commission had to deal with the fact that national authorities in varying degrees exerted two general kinds of control over transport. One was a control over rates – in some cases transport rates were fixed by government agencies as opposed to being freely determined by competitive market forces. The Commission wished to see much more price flexibility. The other related to control over entry into the market. In the case of road haulage, which will dominate our discussion, control over entry was applied through the agency of licences and quotas. Licences may of course be qualitative – e.g. a haulier must be technically competent, financially sound and so forth. If these standards are relatively undemanding then such a system may not effectively restrict the number of enterprises in the market. Altogether more important is the quantitative variety – i.e. the actual quantity of licences may be deliberately restricted. In connection with quantitative licensing, the Commission identified two problems. First, licensing by member states governing access to their own national markets had been too restrictive. The Commission did not propose to abolish national quantitative licensing but (a) to harmonize licensing practices and (b) to make the system more flexible. Secondly, the Commission saw the need for substantial changes in respect of international road transport. Here we have to make a distinction between own account operations, when producers carry their own goods, and hire and reward, when professional hauliers carry other people's goods. In respect of own account transport the Commission took the view that there should be complete liberalization. This would imply that producers could carry their own products in their own vehicles anywhere in the Community and that no member state should be able to set a limit to the number of such foreign vehicles that could be admitted to its territory. In respect of hire and reward vehicles, however, the Commission's original proposals were more complicated. This form of transport has been governed by agreements between the administrative authorities of member states. They were typically bilateral in

Table 16. Domestic transport of freight – modal split within the Twelve in 1990 in tonne/kilometres

	%
Road	73
Rail	17
Inland Waterway	10

Source: EC Commission, *Transport White Paper*, COM (92) 494, 1992

character, in that each state laid down the number and load capacity of vehicles from the other state which it would allow on its territory at any one time. Broadly speaking, the Commission concluded that the quotas had not been expanded to the extent corresponding to the growth of trade between the member states concerned. The Commission therefore proposed, first, that bilateral quotas should be enlarged in conformity with the growth of inter-state trade. Secondly, it was proposed that the bilateral licences should be progressively phased out. As the bilateral licences disappeared, Community licences would come into existence at a rate sufficient (a) to compensate for the disappearance of the bilateral licences and (b) to cope with the growth of intra-Community trade. The new body of licences was to be termed the Community Quota.

In all this the Commission was being quite controversial. At that point in time there still existed a body of opinion which regarded transport, particularly road transport, as being inherently unstable. If unfettered competition was allowed to operate there would be bouts of intensive price-cutting which would lead to a neglect of safety standards. Moreover, cut-throat competition would lead to firms being driven out of business and to the emergence of monopoly conditions. It should also be said that states were fearful of competition because it might lead to their railway systems being driven out of business by road hauliers.

A competitive solution also required a whole range of other changes. Inter-enterprise competition had to exist. Competition also had to be fair and undistorted as between enterprises in different states and as between different modes. Furthermore, transport rates should not be subject to discrimination; nor should they be manipulated so as to subsidize particular producers or industries. It was also desirable that the transport infrastructure of the various member states should be integrated, and that the Community should contribute financially and in other ways to the creation of a Community transport network.

Policy achievements

In respect of pricing, the Commission originally proposed what was in effect a compromise between the rigid fixed rate system which had been operated in Germany and the relatively free rate system which was desired by the Dutch. This consisted of a rate bracket system which would apply to all transport modes – national and international. Under the system the relevant authorities would specify maximum and minimum rates for particular types of traffic on the various routes. Consignors and carriers would be able to negotiate rates within the spread. The apparent logic of this arrangement was that the upper limit was designed to prevent monopolistic exploitation, while the lower limit was intended to prevent the detrimental effects of excessive competition. In practice, the proposal was greatly whittled down. From 1968 tariff brackets applied only to international road transport. The authorities were to publish fixed upper and lower brackets with a maximum spread of 23 per cent below the ceiling level. Under certain circumstances tariffs could be agreed outside these levels. In 1977 the Community decided to provide a choice. A pair of states could continue with the obligatory bracket system or they could choose a reference rate system, in which the published price was purely a recommendation. In 1983 this was replaced by a system in which reference rates were to be the norm, but a pair of states could employ rate brackets. It seems not unreasonable to say that the Commission has achieved some loosening up in respect of pricing. First, on many routes the system now in operation is based on the reference rate system. Secondly, the spread between brackets is about 45 per cent. The latter is so great that it seems reasonable to conclude that market forces rather than brackets are now determining the actual rates.

On the licensing and quota front, the picture is mixed. It is true that in 1974 the Community agreed to introduce qualitative criteria in respect of national road-haulage licences. The relevant directive laid down uniform requirements in terms of the professional competence, good repute and financial capacity of prospective operators. There is of course nothing to prevent a member state from operating these standards in parallel with a quantitative licensing system. In other words a haulier might satisfy the qualitative conditions but not be able to get a licence if the quantitative ceiling has been reached. It should be emphasized that the Community has not agreed to harmonize and loosen up national quantity licensing systems. Nevertheless, some countries have abandoned quantitative limits – the UK did so prior to membership.

On the international front, we have to note that after some delay the Community did in 1968 agree to introduce a Community Quota. But the member states did not undertake to phase out the bilateral licences. The actual number of licences under the Community Quota (they were shared out among the states) remained miserably small. About 95 per cent of traffic continued to be carried under bilateral agreements. However, the 1985 Court judgement had a powerful effect. In the same year the Council of Ministers agreed, as an interim measure, to accelerate the growth of the Community Quota (whilst keeping but expanding the bilateral system). Then, as part of the single market programme, they were eventually persuaded to drop the bilateral licence system. They also agreed to drop the quantitative limit and replace it by a qualitative licensing system. Haulers of good repute, financial standing and professional competence could automatically qualify. There still remained the question of the Article 75 requirement concerning freedom of non-resident transport operators to carry out transport operations in a member state. Here we need to make a distinction. Road hauliers have a right to establish themselves in another member state and supply road haulage services therein. The Community has agreed on a mutual recognition of qualifications in order to make this Right of Establishment a reality. The hauliers still have to satisfy national (but harmonized) qualitative conditions and any national quantitative conditions. The alternative possibility is that the hauliers do not establish themselves but seek to avail themselves of the freedom to supply services. Thus they might make a journey from Paris to Rome and on the return journey might make a backhaul from Rome to Florence and another backhaul from Florence to Milan. The intra-Italy journeys are examples of cabotage. The 1985 judgement quite clearly required the Council of Ministers to address itself to this possibility and the 1985 single European market programme reiterated the need for cabotage to be introduced. In 1993 remaining problems concerning cabotage were overcome and an agreement was reached which means that unrestricted cabotage will come into operation in 1998. A liberalization of international licences and cabotage was also agreed in respect of international coach and bus operations.

We now come to the issue of competition, distortion and discrimination. The following are some of the more important measures which have been agreed. In order to maintain inter-enterprise competition, the Council agreed in 1968 that, with modifications, transport should be subject to the Article 85 and Article 86 competition rules. With regard to inter-country competition within modes, the Council has agreed the following measures which are designed to achieve equal conditions of competition. In 1968 it provided for social harmonization in the road haulage industry. This relates to uniform driving hours and rest periods – the most recent rules were decided in 1985. It also agreed in 1970 to the use of the tachograph (the so-called 'spy in the cab') to police these rules. In 1984 the Council also agreed on uniform weights and dimensions for lorries – the UK and Ireland were granted some temporary exemptions. The Commission is aware that differences in national excise rates on fuel and in national vehicle taxes also distort competition. It proposes to harmonize both. In practice the latter have a bigger impact on the cost of operation. In order to create fairer conditions of competition between modes, the Commission a long time ago recognized that it was important to ascertain the costs of infrastructure – i.e. track costs – and to allocate them among beneficiaries. For example, it would be inequitable and uneconomic if railways had to pay for their rail-bed, etc., while road hauliers did not make their due contribution to the cost of building and repairing the road system. As yet no final agreement has been reached on this issue. The Community has also introduced measures which grant the railways greater commercial freedom and require them to be compensated when they are obliged to discharge social or historical obligations. Article 7 of the Rome Treaty requires that there should be no discrimination on grounds of nationality. Article 79 reiterates this in the case of transport. Article 80 concerns the activity of using transport rates to help certain firms or industries. Such rates are referred to as support rates and are banned.

There are two final points we need to note. One is that as far back as 1966 the Community agreed to coordinate national transport infrastructure investments. In 1978 a more comprehensive system was agreed, and in 1982 the Council declared that Community budget monies could be used to aid priority projects which would help to build up the Community network. The other point relates to border formalities. These are a major problem for international transport and have given rise to considerable costs. The Commission therefore set itself the task of achieving a radical simplification as part of the single European market programme. As a result a directive simplifying border checks was adopted in 1986.

Air transport

As we observed earlier, this form of transport did not automatically fall within the common transport policy. Nevertheless, the Council of Ministers could introduce appropriate measures. Until recently, little progress had been made. More recently a breakthrough occurred – see below. What were the problems?

The fundamental problem was that air passenger transport was subject to inter-government agreement and to international cartel price fixing. Access to routes between pairs of states was governed by inter-governmental air services agreements. In Europe these bilaterals tightly controlled entry – perhaps restricting entry to one designated airline from each state. Typically the traffic between the two states was shared on a 50/50 basis. The revenue on any route was pooled and the proceeds divided in proportion to the capacity supplied by each national airline. In the past air fares were agreed by airlines in the traffic conferences organized by the International Air Transport Association. Governments subsequently approved these agreed rates. This was the position in respect of scheduled services; charter operations were relatively free of restraint.

The result was that scheduled air fares in Europe were high and much play was made of the lower fares in the US – distance for distance – under a deregulated, i.e. competitive, régime. The reader may therefore wonder why the Rome Treaty competition rules, and specifically Article 85, were not invoked against this restrictive activity. The answer is twofold. In the first place it was not clear to what extent air transport was subject to the competition rules. However, in 1974 this point was resolved in the *French Merchant Seamen* case before the Court of Justice. The competition rules did apply. However, a second problem then arose. Article 85 is fully applicable only if the Council of Ministers approves the necessary implementing regulation. In the first instance they neglected to do this. In the absence of such a regulation, the enforcement of Article 85 lay largely with the member states – the villains of the piece – although the Commission could play a limited role.

The position was not wholly without hope, as three avenues of attack were still available. First, deregulation on a piecemeal basis was possible provided the parties to bilateral agreements were of a like mind. This happened notably in the case of the UK–Netherlands bilateral in 1984. Effectively, air traffic was deregulated, as the agreement provided for the free entry of new carriers, eliminated capacity controls and allowed the country from which the traffic originated to determine fares. Other agreements, although not as liberal, followed.

Secondly, the member states might be induced to accept at least a limited amount of liberalization. The Commission had been striving to achieve such an end since at least 1972, and memoranda on the subject were addressed to the Council of Ministers in 1979 and 1984. In 1986 a package of measures was under consideration by virtue of which the airlines would be exempted from attack under Article 85 provided agreement could be secured on some degree of liberalization. These measures involved reducing the share of traffic allocated to the designated national airlines, allowing more than one airline from a given country to fly the same route and permitting certain forms of price-cutting. At the November 1986 meeting, when the UK was holding the presidency of the Council of Ministers, the Community failed to achieve agreement on what was regarded as a fairly weak package of such measures. Thus, whereas the Commission would have liked to see each national airline's share being reduced from 50 per cent to 25 per cent, the UK opted to push a proposal which only required a reduction to 40 per cent over three years. Critics tended to see the UK position as reflecting anxiety about the effect which more radical measures would have on the privatization value of British Airways. In July 1987 the Council of Ministers returned to the reform proposals but agreement again failed to materialize.

The third approach was for individuals, companies or governments to seek to invoke Article 85 against airline agreements. Lord Bethell attempted to do this but failed. However, in 1986 a breakthrough occurred in the *Nouvelles Frontières* case. This concerned a French budget travel company which had sold air tickets at lower prices than those sanctioned by the French authorities. The case was first heard by a French court which decided to refer the matter to the European Court of Justice for a preliminary ruling. The important feature of the Court's verdict was the additional light it threw on the position which arises when an implementing regulation does not exist. This new light suggested that the Commission's hands were not entirely tied – there was a way forward. Thus the Commission could investigate the various agreements entered into in the airline industry and might then decide to prohibit them. In which case national courts would have to take cognizance of the fact that the agreements in question were null and void. This would then open the door to lawsuits against airlines. Such cases would of course require that those bringing the suits had the required legal standing and that the Commission had made the correct decision in the first place. Up to June 1986 the Commission stayed its hand, hoping that the Council of Ministers would agree to a liberalization package of the kind discussed above. When that failed to materialize the Commission decided to commence proceedings. These proceedings were obviously likely to provoke the ministers of transport into achieving an agreement, as it was always possible that the cases instigated by the Commission would outlaw the restrictions in their entirety, whereas the Council of Ministers was willing to contemplate only a limited degree of competition. This move seems to have done the trick as the ministers ultimately agreed to introduce a liberalizing package. The ministers having acquiesced to the introduction of competition, the Commission then agreed to withdraw the cases!

The liberalizing process has proceeded in stages. The first liberalizing package was introduced in December 1987 and, it should be noted, was foreshadowed in Commissioner Cockfield's single European market programme of 1985. Under the provisions of the first stage Articles 85 and 86 were made directly applicable to air passenger transport activities. The Commission therefore now has the power to itself apply those competition rules and no longer needs to rely on member states for implementation. Some temporary block exemptions were provided for – these are best regarded as a bribe by the Commission designed to reassure member states reluctant to accept the idea of competition in air travel. They were a kind of temporary safety net. In addition greater scope for air fare competition was provided for. The economy fare was treated as a benchmark and zones of rate freedom below that level were prescribed which allowed airlines to introduce cut-price fares. The member states at either end of a route continued to approve fares but they lost the power of veto. Thus if British Airways put in a low but otherwise reasonable fare bid on the London–Paris route, and this was approved by the British regulators, then the French regulators could not veto it. In particular the French could not veto it merely because it undercut the Air France fare. Rather British Airways could go to arbitration and the arbitrators might find in its favour. The 1987 package also required the old 50/50 traffic split to be dropped. Competition should be allowed to change the share of traffic to 55/45 and eventually to 60/40. The new arrangement also allowed each bilateral state to allow more than one of their airlines to enter the bilateral market. Previously single designation had been the norm – i.e. one from each state. Now multiple designation was to be allowed. It should also be mentioned that progress was also made in allowing airlines from states other than the bilateral partners to enter the market previously reserved for the airlines of the bilateral partners.

In 1989 the Council of Transport Ministers pressed the process of deregulation yet further. First they agreed to greater rate freedom. Only if *both* states which were party to a bilateral agreement refused to sanction a fare application would an airline be precluded from offering it to its customers. Secondly, the limits on the division of traffic were to totally disappear.

This deregulatory programme is one of the main achievements of the 1992 single market programme. However, to be successful competition will have to be maintained. This means that the Commission will have to be ready to use the new merger-controlling power (see Chapter 5) and it implies a willingness to apply Articles 85 and 86 to agreements which restrict competition and to attempts to abuse dominant positions. It will also require the Commission to be vigilant in policing the giving of state aids. A number of airlines have in recent years been bailed out by government subsidies, notably Air France in 1994, whilst privatized British Airways has been making profits. Such subsidies distort competition and clearly run counter to the whole philosophy behind the single market deregulatory programme. Really effective competition will be possible only if aircraft parking slots are available to new entrants. In the past they have been dominated by the incumbent major airlines. Deregulation will stimulate competition and thus keep fares down. This will contribute to a growth of air travel. This is turn emphasizes the need for more air traffic control facilities and more airport capacity. Both are likely to be in short supply. All these points indicate that if the 1992 programme is to succeed it will be necessary to back up the liberalizing measures with a host of supporting policies.

The common energy policy

We must begin by considering why a common energy policy has been thought to be necessary. Originally two kinds of justification could be advanced and they both sprang from the effects of differential government intervention in the energy market.

First, distortions of competition can arise from differing national energy policies. If, for example, third-country energy sources undercut domestic supplies, different national approaches may be devised. It would be possible to adopt a low price policy, allowing imports to enter without protection and subsidizing competing domestic supplies in order to enable them to survive. Alternatively, a member state could impose protection, by applying either import duties or indirect taxes, thus driving the price of imported energy up to equality with that of domestic sources. The problem which arises from such a difference of approach is that energy-intensive industries under the latter policy would be at a marked competitive disadvantage compared with their counterparts situated in states adopting a low price policy.

Secondly, left to themselves member states might adopt different approaches to the problem of dependency on third-country supplies of energy. Prudent countries would hold stocks in case of international crises affecting supplies and would seek to develop indigenous sources. All this would involve a substantial commitment of resources. Imprudent countries would allow themselves to become dangerously dependent and would avoid the resource cost of ensuring regular supplies. While it is true that if an interruption of third-country supplies occurred the prudent would fare better than the imprudent, it is also true that the exports of the prudent to the imprudent would be depressed while the exports of the imprudent to the prudent would tend to hold up. In other words, and putting it metaphorically, as all the member states are in the same boat it is important that they adopt similar policies towards dependency and bear an equitable share of the burden involved in reducing vulnerability.

Progress in the field of energy policy has been limited. There are four reasons for this. First, the responsibility for energy matters has been a divided one. The Paris Treaty placed responsibility for coal fairly and squarely on the shoulders of the ECSC. The Rome Treaty established that oil, natural gas, hydro-power and electric current were the province of the EC. The task of dealing with nuclear power was assigned to Euratom. Secondly, none of the three Treaties contained a word about a common energy policy or even laid down a timetable for its elaboration. In some degree this fact is a reflection of the circumstances of the time when the Treaties were drafted. They all belong to the period when coal was the major source of energy in the Six. (In 1950 it met almost 75 per cent of the primary energy needs of the Community.) The main problem then was guaranteeing that the supply of coal was available, first on non-discriminatory terms to all Community purchasers, and secondly at reasonable prices. The latter meant the Six had to address themselves to the problems of the coal cartels, in particular the Ruhr cartels of which Georg was the most notorious. The decline of coal, the emergence of associated regional difficulties, together with the growing dependence on imported sources of energy, were problems of the future and were not then foreseen.

The third reason for lack of progress was the involved nature of the problem. Governments, even in liberal economies, tend to get caught up in regulating the energy market. The Six were no exception – the regional problem, state monopolies, nationalized undertakings and fiscal policy are just a few of the complicating elements. The fourth reason has also been connected with governments. Their pursuit of national self-interest has made it difficult to achieve a common policy. This concern to defend national interests has been evident from the beginning, but it became even more marked in the oil crisis of 1973 and after, which we shall turn to later.

Before we discuss the specific factors which have given rise to the need for a common policy, it is important to note that the motivating factors have varied over time. In the period 1956–73 the problem was that imported oil fell in price, as did imported coal. As a result the Community became increasingly dependent on imported energy – the Commission was of the view that the Community was *dangerously* dependent. As we shall see, not a great deal was achieved by way of response. Politicians tend to be concerned with pressing problems and there were no overwhelmingly pressing problems during this period. Indeed, energy was becoming cheaper by the day and interruptions of supply were purely speculative. The compulsion to act was lacking. After 1973 the problem was quite different. Imported energy rapidly became expensive. It was also uncertain in supply because most oil came from the Middle East, and the latter was much more obviously politically unstable.

The need for a common policy – 1956–73

As has already been indicated, during this period the main factor dictating the need for a common policy was the increased competition which coal encountered, particularly from oil. This threw up a series of issues including unemployment and regional decline, the problem of the security and stability of energy supplies as the Community became steadily more dependent on imported sources, and the likely long-term evolution of the price of imported energy sources.

An appreciation of this set of interrelated issues requires that we go back in time to the first half of the 1950s. In this period there was a coal shortage, which in turn prompted users to do two things.

They sought to economize in the use of coal; for example, the steel industry succeeded in developing techniques which curtailed heat losses. They also began to turn to substitutes – in practice this usually meant oil. However, this tendency to take decisions against coal was masked by the rapid economic growth of the period. Indeed, when in 1956 the OEEC produced the Hartley Report (OEEC, 1956), the essential message was that there was a danger of a possible shortage of energy in Europe. Stress was also laid on the balance of payments problems inherent in dependence on imported energy. The Suez crisis appeared to vindicate this view as the immediate effect was rising prices stemming from high ocean freight rates for imported oil and coal. But the picture soon changed. The major oil companies, in order to cope with the growing demand, embarked on a programme of expanded production. They also began to diversify the areas in which they were prospecting and in so doing discovered substantial new reserves. In addition, the majors were joined by new companies who sought to carve out a place for themselves in the world market by offering low prices. The US Government also played a part. In order to protect the home market it applied import quotas and as a result the bulk of the increased supplies flowed to markets such as Western Europe. Moreover, the Soviet Government decided during this period to resume selling Russian oil on the world market. Then again, imported oil gained the advantage of lower freight rates arising from major economies in transportation as a result of the use of bigger and faster ships.

The result of all this was that coal's competitive position deteriorated drastically. After 1956 the price of oil fell and thereafter stayed low, whereas the price of domestically produced coal (despite a great increase in mechanization and in output per manshift) climbed steadily upwards. The position in 1956 and 1965 is shown in Table 17.

The effect of oil (and natural gas) on coal's position was dramatic. As we have indicated, coal was responsible for almost three quarters of the Community's primary energy supplies in 1950, and petroleum contributed 10 per cent. By 1966 coal had fallen to 38 per cent and petroleum had risen to 45 per cent. The rapid rise in the energy requirements of the Community was met by oil, whereas between 1957 and 1966 coal production fell by 12 per cent, the mining

Table 17. Comparative price movements of imported coal and oil and community coal ($ per ton)

	Community coal[1]	Imported US coal[2]	Imported crude oil[3]
1956	12.53	21.60	20.30
1965	16.68	14.20	16.40

Notes: 1. Ruhr bituminous (schedule ex-mine).
2. American coking fines c.i.f. Amsterdam/Rotterdam/Antwerp.
3. Kuwait crude c.i.f. Naples.
Source: ECSC High Authority, *Fifteenth General Report*, Luxembourg, 1967, pp. 27–8.

labour force below ground fell by 24 per cent and the number of pits in operation by 42 per cent.

This gave rise to three problems. First, there were the pockets of unemployment caused by the decline of the coal industry. Second, there was the security problem. The Community, unlike the USA and USSR, was dependent on imported energy (oil) and it was to become steadily more dependent on import. A political upheaval in an area from which the Community drew its oil could be disastrous. Third, there was the question of the long-term development of the world energy market. The coal producers of Western Europe argued that the cheap energy was but a passing phase – in the longer term it would become expensive. Therefore it made good sense to keep the pits in production by means of subsidies.

This is indeed what happened. In 1964 the Council of Ministers adopted a protocol on energy policy. This paved the way for a coordinated system of coal subsidies. These were financed by the individual member states. Later in 1966 a Community contribution was granted in the form of subsidies for coking coal.

This, however, was all that emerged by way of response. Later, in 1968, the Commission produced a memorandum on energy policy which it addressed to the Council of Ministers.

In November 1969 the Council of Ministers approved the basic outlines of the 1968 memorandum and asked the Commission to submit the most pressing proposals as soon as possible. In practice not a great deal emerged. In December 1968 the Council adopted two directives requiring member states to hold oil stocks equal to 65 days' consumption. (The Commission proposed that this should be increased to 90 days as from 1 January 1975.) National governments, and not the Commission, can commandeer these stocks if a crisis arises. In January 1972, as a result of the pressure of oil-producing countries for substantially higher prices, the Council adopted two regulations under which member states were required to notify the Commission of investment plans for oil, natural gas and electricity, and of import programmes for oil and gas. The Commission sought direct notification but in practice, other than in periods of crisis, the process takes place through the member states. These two regulations did not give the Commission any power of action in the energy field but they were designed to provide the necessary information on which a common policy could be built – given the goodwill of the member states. These were the main fruits of the 1968 initiative.

The oil shocks of 1973 and 1979

Even before the crisis of 1973 there were signs that a new energy situation was about to emerge. This was apparent from the activities of the oil producers organized in the Organization of Petroleum Exporting Countries (OPEC) who, it should be noted, were pressing for a higher price for oil. This posed a danger to the Community as it had become increasingly dependent on imported oil. By 1971 the Six derived only 20 per cent of their energy from coal and 60.8 per cent from oil. (The position of the Nine at the time of the first enlargement was very similar, the figures being 24.8 per cent and 58.4 per cent respectively.)

It was, however, the Yom Kippur War of 1973 which precipitated the crisis. The war involved the Arabs using their control over oil supplies as a weapon to force other states, including the Nine, the United States and Japan, to bring pressure to bear on Israel. Supplies of oil were reduced, and in the case of the Netherlands (and the US) supplies of Arab oil were totally cut off. This precipitated a crisis within the Community, since the threat was that if the other eight countries supplied the Netherlands and undermined the blockade they themselves were likely to be exposed to blockade treatment. The concept of a free market in oil and oil products within the Community was a major victim of the Middle East conflict. The answer of the Nine seems to have been not to call the bluff of the Arab oil suppliers by openly declaring their intention to supply the Dutch, but rather to adopt what may be termed a 'low profile' policy – it was anticipated, particularly by the French and British, that patient diplomacy would be more productive of a satisfactory resolution. It is noticeable that the Nine, in their November 1973 statement on the solution to the Israeli–Arab conflict, adopted a stance which was distinctly favourable to the Arab cause.

The use of supply cuts as a political weapon was accompanied by dramatic increases in the posted price of crude oil. Between 1 January 1973 and 1 January 1975 the price of Arabian light crude rose by more than 475 per cent (Weyman-Jones, 1986, p. 20). Initially this was taken to be a temporary problem – a device to secure a satisfactory settlement in the Middle East after which prices would return to normal. However, it soon transpired that these new price levels were to be maintained in the long term. The argument ran that this was a fair price – oil had not previously kept pace with the inflation in the price of industrial goods produced by countries in Western Europe, North America and Japan. It was the fact that major OPEC producers (the Middle East alone possesses about three fifths of the world's proven oil reserves) intended to maintain permanently this high price level which constituted the revolution in the facts facing energy policy-makers in the Nine. At the same time the view gained ground that the whole world was in any case moving into a period of energy shortage – even oil had a limited life as a major source of energy. It should be added that some of the factors which had helped to create the glut of oil in the sixties were no longer operative. For example, the US was now a net importer of oil.

This was not the final episode in the shift to a new reality in oil prices. In the late seventies a second oil shock occurred which was coincident with the Iranian revolution. Between 1 January 1979 and 10 January 1981 Arabian light crude prices rose by 134 per cent. This oil, which had cost as little as $1.39 a barrel in 1970, was priced at $34 a barrel in 1981, while higher-quality crudes commanded as much as $41 on the Rotterdam spot market (Weyman-Jones, 1986, pp. 20–21).

At this point it is worth noting how well-founded the EC Commission's concern about import dependence – particularly dependence on the politically unstable Middle East – had been. Two wars – the Six Day War and the Yom Kippur War – had vindicated the fear of vulnerability. What had been less clearly foreseen was the possibility of being in the hands of a cartel in the shape of OPEC. Given the magnitude of the challenge, it was not unreasonable to expect that the Community would feel that it was best tackled by a common response. At last a common energy policy would emerge. What might its shape be? Did it indeed happen?

Clearly it was worth considering whether it was possible to match the monopoly power of OPEC by some form of equivalent buying (i.e. monopsony) power. If that was impossible it was at least important to create a dialogue between oil users and oil producers in which the need for security of supplies and price moderation and stability were top of the agenda.

A prime feature of the common policy would presumably be a drive to become less energy-intensive and in particular to become less dependent on imported energy – most notably oil. The price rise itself would contribute to such an end, as it could induce a shift to other cheaper energy sources including indigenous supplies and it would create an incentive to save energy. It would also be possible to stimulate such a shift and saving further by imposing a tax on imported energy. Indeed a proposal for a Community tax was made in 1979. This idea had a number of virtues, as apart from giving rise to a shift and to saving it was also argued that the plan would reduce the price received by OPEC producers,[1] would provide an own resource for the Community budget and, by inflating the price of British North Sea oil, would help to compensate for the UK's budget imbalance.

Clearly it was important to develop indigenous supplies of energy. One source was solid fuel, of which the most obvious was coal. Here we must note the fundamental change which had taken place. The facts of the sixties were that oil was getting cheaper and coal dearer, in absolute and relative terms. A central feature of energy policy was the subsidizing of coal, and the emphasis in Community policy was on the harmonization of subsidies to avoid distortions,

1. Economic analysis predicts that the imposition of an indirect tax will *normally* raise the price to consumers but lower the price received by producers.

at least gross distortions, of competition. This did not prevent coal production in the Six from falling, contrary to what the West European coal producers (with their forecast of a world energy shortage in the mid seventies) wanted: coal production fell from 239 million metric tonnes in 1960 to 165 million in 1971. Nevertheless, the policy of subsidization helped to limit the decline of coal production and the associated increasing dependence on imported energy. In the new circumstances, a policy designed to stabilize, and if possible to increase, the output of coal was likely to be on the agenda. Financial aid from the Community in order to make the coal industry more efficient and thus to enable it to increase its penetration of the market was very worthy of consideration.

It would be necessary to stimulate the use of other indigenous sources of energy. There was an obvious need for a substantial exploration programme in order to find more oil, more natural gas and more hydro-electric power in Europe. A massive investment would also have to be made in the actual process of extraction. There was also a need to consider largely unexploited renewable sources such as solar energy, geothermal energy and wave power. Here again a substantial research and development programme was called for. If more domestic energy sources were to be developed in Europe it could be argued that it would be necessary to safeguard such supplies from undercutting. For example, North Sea oil was a high-cost source of energy which could be undermined if, deliberately or otherwise, the world price of oil were to drop. Investment in the extraction of oil etc. was likely to be encouraged if a floor price was guaranteed. This was also likely to be a precondition for a willingness to share energy in an emergency.

Atomic power as a basis for producing electricity is an obvious alternative to imported oil. This, however, raised the question of foreign dependence. Uranium has to be imported, and in the past some producers (notably Canada) had refused to export it. However, the world market was sufficiently well-supplied, with some producers being tied to member states, so that the import dependence factor was not regarded as a matter for great concern. It should also be pointed out that continued access to imported uranium supplies was only a problem in the case of the existing generation of nuclear reactors. The new generation of fast breeders only require an initial priming of uranium. Thereafter they work on plutonium and produce further plutonium via a recycling process. Thus they constitute a kind of renewable energy source. There is one major problem attached to uranium and plutonium reactors, namely accidents, as Three Mile Island, in the US, and Chernobyl, in the USSR, were to prove. Plutonium is a particularly nasty substance, and there is an added security risk in that, with the aid of quite elementary technology, it can be used to produce hydrogen bombs. Both these factors mean that there is a real problem of public acceptability. In the longer term it will, probably be possible to produce electricity by atomic fusion rather than fission, but that is still a long way off.

A common energy policy would also call for the creation of emergency procedures and facilities for dealing with situations such as a reduction or cutting off of external supplies. Such procedures would involve methods of sharing and reducing the use of short supplies. The holding of adequate stocks of oil and coal would also be a crucial facility. The 1968 decision to hold stocks of oil equal to 65 days' consumption (later raised to 90 days) was undoubtedly well conceived.

Clearly it was important that every effort should be made to diversify the geographical source of imported energy supplies. This was crucial in the case of oil but was also important in the case of natural gas. Coal was much less of a problem.

The Community's response has been a fourfold one, consisting of

(a) the adoption of Community energy targets and balance sheets;
(b) the implementation of policies which give rise to the rational use of energy;
(c) the elaboration of emergency procedures; and
(d) the use of all the Community's financial instruments to provide grants and loans to the energy sector with the aim of reducing import dependency.

We will consider them in that order.

Quite quickly after the 1973 shock, the Community decided to introduce targets designed to reduce dependency on imported oil. Thus in 1974 the Commission called for a series of policy initiatives which would reduce the imported component of energy consumption from approximately 60 to 40 per cent. Late in 1974 the Council of Ministers adopted a Resolution on the objectives of Community energy policy for 1985. It set the somewhat more conservative target of changing the pattern of energy demand and supply so that by 1985 the Community's import energy dependence would fall from 63 per cent (the actual figure for 1973) to below 50 per cent and if possible to 40 per cent. At the Bremen summit of 1978, the Heads of State and of Government added another element to the 1985 objectives when they agreed that oil imports in that year should be held down to the 1978 level. The process of producing objectives has been a continuing aspect of Community energy policy. Table 18 shows the 1985 energy objectives for 1995. It is important to stress that the purpose of these objectives was to set member states a collective target which, if achieved, would ensure that by 1995 the Community energy situation was secure. The action necessary to fulfil these targets lay with the member states, although Community financial assistance could help – see below. If member states failed to act in conformity with the plan then in the final analysis there was nothing to compel them to mend their ways. The Commission would, of course, monitor trends and would draw the Council of Ministers' attention to any signs that the Community was drifting off the target path.

The data in the two left-hand columns of Table 18 indicate that between 1985 and 1995 Community primary energy demand would rise from 1,048 million tonnes oil equivalent (Mtoe) to 1,138 Mtoe. All the components of energy demand would rise except for oil (item 1(a)) which would fall by 14 Mtoe. Items 2(a) to 2(d) indicated the likely growth of domestic supplies. There were some obvious shortfalls. Community oil production would drop – a reflection of North Sea trends. This was one reason why net oil imports (item 3) would rise from 336 Mtoe to 357 Mtoe. Natural gas production would likewise fall and the gap would have to be bridged by increased imports – some of it via the pipeline from Russia. Solid fuel production would have to rise, and there would have to be a very big increase in nuclear power. Without the planned growth of these two items, the position on net oil imports would be correspondingly worse. If the targets were met then oil consumption would be kept down to 40 per cent of total energy consumption. Clearly the public acceptability of nuclear power was a crucial factor.

As we indicated earlier, Community energy policy does not merely consist of drawing up targets. An important feature of the

Table 18. Community[1] primary energy balances 1985 and 1995 (million tonnes oil equivalent)

	1985	1995[2]	1995[3]
1. Total primary demand	1,048	1,136	1,205–1,255
Components of total primary demand			
(a) Oil	484	470	520–560
(b) Natural gas	184	190	195–205
(c) Solid fuels	238	287	265–295
(d) Nuclear	124	165	179–185
(e) Hydro, etc.	18	24	22–23
2. Total domestic production			
Components of domestic production			
(a) Oil	148	113	100
(b) Natural gas	126	110	not estimated
(c) Solid fuels	173	196	not estimated
(d) Nuclear	124	170	179–185
3. Net oil imports (i.e. 1(a)–2(a))	336	357	420–460

Notes: 1. Including Spain and Portugal.
2. Forecasts made before the fall in oil prices in 1986.
3. Assuming the low oil prices of 186 continue to operate, thus increasing demand and reducing domestic production.
Source: EC Commission, Energy in Europe, No. 6, 1986, p. 17.

policy has been the encouragement of rational use of energy. This has partly manifested itself in the form of measures to encourage energy saving. For example, the Council in 1979 adopted a Recommendation on the improvement of the thermal efficiency of buildings. Money has also been voted for demonstration projects on energy saving – see below. The other aspect of rational use of energy has been concerned with energy pricing. The Council of Ministers has on several occasions endorsed the principle of realistic energy pricing – this really implies that prices should be based on marginal cost. According to the Commission such correct pricing will:

– further energy efficiency and conservation by ensuring that consumers' decisions are based on prices which take full account of the costs of energy supply;
– lead to effective decisions on fuel choice, again by ensuring that

consumers take account of real costs in their investment and purchasing decisions;
- similarly, help to ensure optimal allocation of each particular fuel according to its value in each type of use;
- promote security of energy supply by assuring the necessary revenues to underwrite investments in production or long-term supply contracts. (EC Commission, 1984b, p. 3)

The third strand of the common energy policy is concerned with emergency measures. The decision of the community to hold oil stocks equal to 90 days' consumption has already been mentioned. Member states must also ensure that electricity producers maintain sufficient stocks at thermal power stations to ensure a supply of power for at least 30 days. In 1976 the Council agreed to a mechanism for sharing scarce oil supplies in an emergency, and in 1977 this was followed by agreement on methods of reducing oil usage in times of difficulty. At the Rome Summit of 1975 the UK appeared to secure the Community's agreement to a minimum floor price for oil. This would ensure the survival of North Sea oil in the face of a fall in the world price. However, the European Council does not make Community laws and no decision on this topic was subsequently taken by the Council of Ministers.

Fourthly, we need to note that the Community's financial mechanisms – the Community budget, the New Community Instrument and the European Investment Bank – have between them channelled large amounts of grant and loan money into the energy sector. Thus the Community budget has made a large number of grants towards demonstration projects concerned with energy saving, the development of renewable energy sources and the promotion of alternatives to oil and gas (both of which are heavily imported). The budget has also met 80 per cent of the cost of the JET (Joint European Torus) project. This is concerned with atomic fusion which we mentioned earlier. If successful, it will in the very long run provide abundant supplies of relatively safe energy. JET is actually organized as a joint undertaking in accordance with Articles 45 to 50 of the Euratom Treaty. The balance of the investment has been subscribed by the member states, Switzerland and Sweden. The borrowing powers of the New Community Instrument and the European Investment Bank have between them been heavily involved in financing the rational use of energy and the development of non-imported sources of energy – e.g. atomic power.

In the late eighties and early nineties two additional elements were injected into the Community's approach to the energy problem. One derived from the fact that the concept of a single European market, as envisaged in the Cockfield Report of 1985 (see Chapter 5), did not concern itself explicitly with energy matters. The Commission, however, recognized that a single Community market for energy could make a valuable contribution to the effective operation of European industry and that indeed some of the costs of 'non-Europe' owed their existence to internal barriers to trade and competition in the energy market. Therefore in 1988 the Commission addressed to the Council of Ministers a working paper surveying the obstacles to the free and undistorted movement of goods and services in the Community energy market, stressing points for action. The overall approach was endorsed by the Council of Ministers.

The Commission envisaged that the removal of the remaining barriers would create more competition in the energy market. This in turn would reduce energy prices and therefore increase the competitiveness of the Community's energy-using industries on the world market. The removal of barriers would also give rise to valuable complementarities and by increasing greater flexibility in the choice of energy available to particular users would actually add to the security of supply. Some of the proposed measures were similar to those envisaged in respect of other sectors – e.g. the need to address the problems posed by (a) differing national technical standards, (b) public procurement practices, (c) fiscal factors and so forth. Some, however, were peculiar to the energy field, e.g. the need for rationalization and transparency in energy costs, prices and tariffs and the desirability of pressing ahead with infrastructure network improvements. In respect of the latter the Commission stressed the need to adopt a European perspective in the planning and design of gas pipelines and the benefits to be derived from cross-frontier electricity interconnection.

The other, and quite crucial, new feature of the late eighties and early nineties was that in the devising of energy policy a new consideration became quite dominant. Previously energy policy had been concerned with factors such as the need for cheap energy and the, sometimes conflicting, desirability of ensuring the security of its supply. Now, however, discussions of energy policy had to take account of the associated environmental impact. Relatively local impacts in, for example, the form of acid rain had long been recognized. But in the late eighties and early nineties the concern with the environment took on a global character as attention was focused on the potential threat posed by the 'greenhouse effect'. This process derived from the 'greenhouse gases' such as sulphur dioxide, nitrogen oxides and, crucially, carbon dioxide. These, though not uniquely, are byproducts of fossil fuel combustion which is at the heart of much energy generation. They derive from stationary combustion sources (e.g. power stations) but also from transport.

The need to take account of the environmental impact was reflected in the forecasting work inaugurated by the Commission in 1988 which was concerned with likely energy trends up to the year 2010. These were preliminary studies designed to provide a basis for a new set of energy objectives going beyond the year 1995 (see above). Various scenarios were considered and, significantly on this occasion, much attention was given to the likely trend of emissions. Scenario I was based on the assumption that the Community would remain on a steady but unspectacular growth path up to 2010. It also assumed that energy policy and associated attitudes would remain unchanged. If that was the case sulphur dioxide emissions from fossil fuel use would fall by 70 per cent, nitrogen oxides would fall by a more modest 20 per cent but, and ominously, carbon dioxide emissions would grow steadily.

Given the growing international concern about the greenhouse effect, this trend in carbon dioxide emissions suggested to the Commission that a continuation of the current approach to energy policy was unacceptable. This reappraisal had two consequences.

First, in 1990 the Council of Ministers decided to attempt to frame an agreement on the stabilizing of carbon dioxide emissions within the Community. The UK had already publicly committed itself to stabilizing such emissions at the 1990 level by 2005. This was at variance with the rest of the Community, which looked to the year 2000 as the target date. Eventually, and in preparation for the World Climate Conference to be held in Geneva, the Community agreed to allow the UK until 2005 and decided that the rest of the

Community would make a bigger effort so that the Community as a whole would still achieve the stabilization at the 1990 level by 2000. This it pledged to do in November 1990 at Geneva although the agreement entered into by the 128 participating countries did not specifically define a timetable. The US was not willing to make specific commitments until it was sure it could meet them.

Second, and flowing from this commitment, was a need to rethink energy policy. This the Commission did in a Communication to the Council of Ministers in 1990 entitled *Energy and the Environment* (EC Commission, 1990b). The Commission laid major emphasis on the need to control carbon dioxide emissions by achieving greater energy efficiency and better energy conservation. To this end it promised an Action Programme (SAVE) concerned with measures relating to improved energy efficiency. Also it recommended continued support for JOULE type non-nuclear research programmes concerned with better energy conservation. A THERMIE programme was indeed approved by the Council of Ministers designed to run from 1990 to 1994. This promised financial support for energy technology research designed (a) to achieve more rational use of energy, (b) to develop renewable and non-polluting energy (e.g. solar, wind, geo-thermal, hydro-electric) sources, (c) to develop cleaner uses of coal and other solid fuels. Fiscal factors could also assist. Energy saving would arise from the price increases which would flow from the incorporation of social costs in energy prices (i.e. from fully internalizing pollution externalities). In the long run demand might be reduced by introducing some form of carbon dioxide tax. Rather delicately the Commission also drew attention to the non-greenhouse consequences of nuclear power, and to the benefits of energy substitution, i.e. the use of natural gas which is lower in sulphur dioxide and carbon dioxide emissions than coal.

While it is possible therefore to point to some significant developments in the field of energy policy, it is also necessary to point out that no instruments similar to the price support mechanisms of the CAP have been introduced. In earlier days the idea of a Community imported-energy tax was considered but dismissed. It will be interesting to see whether the idea of a tax designed to discriminate against energy sources which are heavy on carbon dioxide emissions has any greater success.

By way of postscript it should be added that although Maastricht

Treaty Article 3 included, amongst the Community's objectives, measures in the field of energy, in practice the new competences and powers contained in the subsequent articles did not include any relating to energy. The Commission will continue to act on the basis of present powers and in 1996 the omission of energy will probably be addressed.

9

REGIONAL AND SOCIAL POLICY

Introduction

The reader of Chapters 4 and 5 could be forgiven for forming the view that the EC is essentially an exercise in economic integration based on the economics of Adam Smith. That is to say, the course of economic events is to be determined purely, or largely, by the play of free trade and free competition. The word largely is perhaps more appropriate since the CAP is hardly a product of free-market thinking! However, the EC is not purely Smithian. Within the *present day* Community there are provisions designed to counteract and compensate for the effects of competition – notably these include the European Regional Development Fund, the European Social Fund and, more recently, the Cohesion Fund. While their capacities are limited, they do at least represent a recognition of the need to provide a balanced approach to the integration problem.

Regional policy

Rationale

Let us begin by asking what arguments have been adduced in favour of regional policy within the context of the European Community. The reader will at once recognize that the above question has been framed in a way which leaves open the question whether regional policy ought to be at national level, Community level or both. Some clues as to what the answer may be will, however, be found below.

A major justification has been that large disparities existed when the Community of Six was created and that disparities have continued to exist. For example, Professor Levi Sandri, writing in 1965 but referring to 1958, indicated that the *per capita* income of the most favoured region in the Community (Hamburg) was about seven times that of the least favoured Italian region (Calabria) (Levi

Sandri, 1965). It was no doubt with this in mind that the preamble to the *original* Rome Treaty included a declaration that the contracting parties were:

anxious to strengthen the unity of their economies and to ensure their harmonious development by reducing the differences existing between the various regions and the backwardness of the less favoured regions.

It was also because of this that the treaty explicitly called for the creation of the European Investment Bank (EIB) and that first on the list of the bank's objectives was the provision of loans for the assistance of the less-developed regions. Without that requirement, Italy would have found the EC a less attractive prospect – we say more about the Bank below. Subsequent enlargements only served to continue the state of disparity. This was clearly the case when the UK, Ireland and Denmark joined the Community. Thus the Commission pointed out that, taking an average of the years 1977, 1979 and 1981, gross domestic product per working person in various Danish regions was in the range of either 100–115 per cent or 115–130 per cent of the Community average, whereas in the various British and Irish regions it was either 70–80 per cent or less than 70 per cent of the Community average (EC Commission, 1984c, p. 2). Greek, Spanish and Portuguese membership brought into the Community regions whose living standards (on a *per capita* gross domestic product basis) were for the most part less than 72 per cent of the Community average (EC Commission, 1984c, p. 10). One of the main Community instruments for dealing with the regional problem is the European Regional Development Fund (ERDF). The Commission has pointed out that Article 3 of the 1984 ERDF regulation declared that the Fund's prime purpose was:

to contribute to the correction of the principal regional imbalances within the Community by participating in the development and structural adjustment of regions whose development is lagging behind and in the conversion of declining industrial regions. (EC Commission, 1986, p. 5)

Clearly, the absence of a commitment to correct regional imbalances would severely undermine Community solidarity and would discourage weaker economies from participating in any further advance towards economic and political unity.

Up to now we have been discussing the regional inheritance of the Community. But in addition we have to take account of the fact that Community membership can itself give rise to regional problems: when a country becomes a member it has to conform to the rules concerning external protection (tariffs and quotas), and these may give rise to structural changes which manifest themselves in a regional form. For example, a member state has to replace its external protection by the common external tariff together with the CAP external protection régime. Quantitative restrictions may also have to be modified. If the Community arrangements are more protective than the old national ones then domestic activities will flourish, but if the Community system is less protective, then third-country competition is likely to give rise to the contraction of certain sectors. Community membership will also require the dismantling of all forms of protection against partner economies. Relatively efficient industries will then expand, but the relatively inefficient will be forced to contract. The actual way in which all these adjustments manifest themselves will vary from economy to economy, but the possibility that they can have an adverse regional impact is not in doubt. If the effect of membership was to cause an overall deterioration in the balance of payments, then monetary measures (e.g. an exchange-rate depreciation) might be necessary. While they may bring the external account back into balance, it does not follow that the economy will be able to escape from industrial adjustments which have regional implications.

This, of course, is a transitional justification for regional policy. Nevertheless it has to be recognized that since the early seventies the Community has been in a constant state of transition as UK, Danish and Irish membership was followed by Greek and then by Spanish and Portuguese membership. Now we have to cope with the ex-EFTA states and looming on the horizon are the economies of Central and Eastern Europe. Moreover the need to cope with the competitive effects which may derive from dismantling protection has continued to be relevant as the single European market after 1992 and beyond has unfolded and residual forms of protection have been scaled down.

Harvey Armstrong and Jim Taylor have pointed out that Community membership can also give rise to problems in border regions (Armstrong and Taylor, 1985, p. 230). They distinguish between external and internal borders. External border areas (i.e. those at the periphery of the Community) may, prior to the creation of the customs union, have traded heavily with contiguous third-country economies. However, when Community protection régimes are instituted, those trading opportunities may be significantly reduced. Thus areas of West Germany bordering the German Democratic Republic (GDR) were forced to re-orient trade away from the GDR to the rest of the EC. Following the reunion of the two Germanys this problem has disappeared. Internal border areas are those which are external when member states are separate but which become internal to the EC when member states form a customs union. Such areas may have made a good living out of border formalities and processes, but such opportunities should disappear as the single European market finally emerges.

Another factor which has received considerable attention has been the possible tendency for industrial activity to gravitate towards the centre of the Community to the detriment of regions at the periphery. A glance at the map of gross domestic product *per capita* by region clearly demonstrates the existence of a central block of economic activity and prosperity which stretches from south-east England, Denmark and the Netherlands in the north, through central and north-east France and much of Germany (other than certain eastern regions) to south-east France and northern Italy. Economists point to the pulling power of industrial locations at the centre. First, they draw attention to economies of scale – i.e. the lower unit costs which *individual* firms enjoy as a result of producing large outputs. Since the bulk of the consuming public is close at hand, transport costs will be low. This in turn keeps prices low, which stimulates demand and in turn gives rise to scale economies. Secondly, economists have identified certain external economies – i.e. economies which depend on the size of the output of an industry (as opposed to the output of an individual firm). Thus, when an industry concentrates in a region it stimulates the emergence of firms within the region which benefit the industry. Firms may set up to process the industry's byproducts or to supply it with specialist financial and commercial services. Transport and other costs may, however, mean that only firms in the centre will be able to benefit to the full from these facilities. Thirdly, economists have identified certain agglomeration economies which arise from the general concentration· of economic activity in a region. Thus transport and telecommunications facilities may emerge which are only viable if used very intensively. These polarization factors may be accompanied by counterbalancing dispersal forces – i.e. industry might be driven out towards the periphery as a result of the shortage and consequent high price of land and labour. However, the general view seems to be that without a powerful regional policy centralizing forces will tend to predominate.

Another set of reasons why regional policy has been deemed to be necessary is connected with the adverse regional impacts which can arise from Community policies. One of the main reasons why the ERDF was set up was because it was felt to be an indispensable concomitant of the plan to achieve EMU by 1980 (see Chapter 7). The argument appeared to run as follows. Suppose that industrial unions in the UK sought Community pay levels, but at the same time UK productivity lagged behind that of the Community. The UK would become uncompetitive in the Community market – exports would tend to fall and imports to rise. Both these factors would tend to create unemployment. Prior to the union this problem could be alleviated by a devaluation. But once EMU was achieved this line of policy would be precluded. Exchange rates would quite possibly be fixed prior to the creation of a common currency. Within the Community the UK, for example, would be placed in the same position as Northern Ireland currently is within the UK. Northern Ireland has not been able to alleviate its unemployment problem by making its goods more competitive in the UK market by means of a devaluation against Great Britain. It has in fact had to rely on generous levels of regional aid in order to offset its locational disadvantages. Equally, within the union the UK would have to rely on Community aid.

Significantly, this kind of justification for a Community regional policy re-emerged following the decision in 1989 to press forward with the creation of EMU. The 1989 Delors Report (see Chapter 7) drew attention to the need to press ahead vigorously with a regional policy designed to narrow productivity differentials within the Community. Spain in particular latched on to this aspect of the EMU plan and demanded a transfer of resources to the poorer states as a condition for acceptance of the EMU proposal. This in due course led to the decision at Maastricht to set up a Cohesion Fund (this is discussed below). The Cohesion Fund was in fact part of a second package of resource transfers to poorer member states, the latter had achieved a previous transfer thanks to the Economic and Social Cohesion provisions of the Single Act (see Chapter 3).

Regional problems can of course arise as a byproduct of policies other than monetary union. Thus if the CAP is modified in a way which hits certain kinds of farms (e.g. small ones) or the producers of certain products (e.g. milk), then regional problems may arise if such farms are, or the production of such products is, concentrated in certain areas. The offer by the Community in 1992 in the GATT to cut farm subsidies (the Blair House accord – see Chapter 11) also had significant adverse regional implications. Then again a decision to enlarge the Community can have a very considerable impact on certain regions. The admission of the Iberian members was, for example, expected to hit the Mediterranean regions of the Community quite hard – particularly the producers of Mediterranean agricultural products. It was because of this that aid schemes in the form of Integrated Mediterranean Programmes were agreed. Under these programmes the Community planned to spend 6600 million ECUs over a seven-year period which began in 1986. About 4100 million ECUs were to come from the Community budget – the other 2500 million ECUs would take the form of loans from the European Investment Bank and the New Community Instrument. These loans could attract interest subsidies. The aim was to improve the production of crops not in surplus, to modernize and restructure fishing fleets, to create new industrial, service, and tourist activities and to promote training schemes.

A Community regional policy can also be justified on the grounds that it can make national policies more effective. For example, it can prevent competition between member states in the giving of aids. As we noted in Chapter 4 when discussing state aids, such competition may enable the richer countries to outbid the poorer ones in attracting footloose investment, and it may mean that aid is not concentrated in the regions where it will produce the maximum benefit. A Community regional policy may also facilitate the coordination of national efforts – a problem region may in fact straddle national frontiers. Community regional policy could of course take the much more radical form of transfers from the richer to the poorer members of the Community. We discussed that idea in

Chapter 4 when we considered possible longer-term developments of the Community budget.

Community regional instruments – the first phase

When we consider policies such as agriculture and transport, we see that there were separate Titles (i.e. groups of articles relating to a policy problem) within the Rome Treaty devoted to these subjects. The Titles called for common policies (in some cases detailing their nature) and provided powers for their implementation. But the *original* Rome Treaty contained no separate Title relating to the regional problem and made no explicit call for a common regional policy.

There were, and still are, provisions scattered throughout the treaty which bear upon the regional dimension, the most important of which is Article 92 relating to state aids. The general posture of Article 92 has already been discussed in Chapter 5. Basically it says that aids for regional development may be permitted (this is a derogation from the general principle that state aid is prohibited) and that the Commission shall exercise a general supervisory role. As we saw in Chapter 5, the Commission has used its powers under Articles 92 to 94 to control the level of regional aid and also the kind of aid instruments which may be employed. In the first case, grant ceilings have been prescribed for the various regions, and in the second, aid instruments have themselves been subject to scrutiny.

Article 92 therefore seems to suggest that the original role of the Community in the area of regional policy was to be largely negative. The Commission would vet aids, but it would not be involved in the giving of them – the latter would be a national responsibility. Ironing out the initial regional disparities and coping with the regional impact of integration was a job for the member states. But in fact this view is only partly true. Even in the earlier days three institutions had been established whose assistance had some impact on the regional problem. One of these was the European Investment Bank. This was established under the provisions of Articles 129 and 130 of the Rome Treaty. The EIB was devised to grant loans and guarantees on a non-profit-making basis within the Community for (according to Article 130) the following purposes:

(a) projects for developing backward regions;
(b) projects for modernizing or converting undertakings; or for developing fresh activities called for by the progressive establishment of the common market, where such projects by their size or nature cannot be entirely financed by the various means available in the member states;
(c) projects of common interest to several member states which by their size and nature cannot be entirely financed by the various means available in the individual member states.

Originally, the activities of the EIB were confined to the territories of the member states, but subsequently its sphere of operations was widened to cover countries which had come to have association or other agreements with the Community. These currently include Turkey;[1] African, Caribbean and Pacific (ACP) countries – these are ex-colonial dependencies of the original Six and the UK; certain Overseas Countries and Territories (OCTs),[2] a group of Mediterranean countries – the Maghreb Countries (Algeria, Morocco and Tunisia), the Mashrek Countries (Egypt, Jordan, Lebanon and Syria) plus Israel, Cyprus, Malta and Yugoslavia. More recently the EIB has been required to provide loans to facilitate the recovery of East European economies – notably Poland, Hungary, the Czech and Slovak Republics, Romania and Bulgaria. In 1990 the European Bank for Reconstruction and Development (EBRD) was established for the same broad purpose. The EIB as well as the EC became founder members, and the EIB undertook to supply 3 per cent of its capital and to take a seat on its board.

The subscribers to the EIB are the member states. The capital subscribed by them in 1992 amounted to 57.6 billion ECUs, of which about 8 per cent was actually paid up. The unpaid capital acts as a guarantee. Although some of the resources are thus provided by the Twelve, the bulk is raised by borrowing on the international capital market. In addition there are three other sources of funds. One is the New Community Instrument (NCI), or Ortoli Facility, which we mentioned in Chapter 3. Although the Commission uses this mechanism to raise money on behalf of the Community, the funds are made over to the EIB. The other two sources are the

---

1. Greece, Spain and Portugal also received assistance prior to full membership.
2. Not yet independent.

Table 19. EIB financing[1] 1988–92

	Total	%
Loans from EIB own resources and guarantees		
Within the Community	63,715.7	93.7
Outside the Community	3,201.4	4.7
Total	66,917.1	98.4
Financing provided from other resources		
Within the Community	497.6	0.7
Outside the Community	605.0	0.9
Total	1,102.6	1.6
Grand total		
Within the Community	64,213.3	94.4
Outside the Community	3,806.4	5.6

Note: 1. Million ECUs.
Source: EIB, *Annual Report 1992*, Luxembourg, 1993, p. 11.

Community budget and direct financing by the member states.

The EIB has been engaged in lending on a very considerable scale (see Table 19). Between 1988 and 1992 it extended loans and guarantees amounting to 66,917 million ECUs. Most of the money – 94 per cent – was devoted to internal purposes. The great bulk of the internal assistance was devoted to the development of backward regions by way of infrastructure and productive enterprise investments. In 1992, for example, loans for regional development amounting to 11,793 million ECUs absorbed nearly 70 per cent of the EIB's own resources. Some 90 per cent of these regional development loans were concentrated on priority regions characterized by lagging economic development, serious industrial decline or rural backwardness. The bulk of this regional assistance was indeed enjoyed by seven states – Italy, Spain, Portugal, Greece, Germany, the United Kingdom and France.

While it is legitimate to regard the EIB as a regional policy instrument, it is important to note that regional assistance normally takes the form of capital grants, rebates of interest, subsidies to inputs, etc. Clearly this kind of activity is outside the scope of the

EIB, which has to lend at interest. However, the fact that the EIB has an AAA credit rating, the highest there is, means that it can borrow on keen terms and reflect those keen terms in the interest rates it charges to its customers.[1]

Two[2] other bodies also made a contribution (and indeed continue to do so). One was the European Social Fund, which we shall discuss in more detail later in this chapter. The Fund makes money available for a variety of purposes including the training of young people and the retraining of unemployed workers. The other fund which has made a contribution has been the EAGGF. It has, for example, contributed towards the cost of programmes designed to improve the incomes of hill farmers in certain less-favoured regions. We should also note that the Brussels Commission has since 1967 been responsible for operating the relevant provisions of the Paris Treaty. Redevelopment policy has consisted of loans made available to develop new sources of employment in areas where employment in the coal and steel industry has contracted. Readaptation policy has been directed towards making grants to tide workers over until they could find new jobs, to assist with resettlement and to contribute to the cost of retraining.

From the inception of the EC, the Commission strove to develop a system whereby it could play an active and positive role in dealing with the regional problems of the Community. The Action Programme of 1962, and the Memorandum on Regional Problems of 1965 (with its stress on development poles such as that created at Taranto-Bari), were expressions of that concern. It was not, however, until 1969 that the Commission came into the open with the idea that it should itself play an active part in the process of aid-giving and not just be concerned with negative controls (under Article 92) and studies of the general problem. In documents

1. Whilst we are considering the role played by the EIB, it is convenient to note that at the Edinburgh European Council meeting in December 1992, as part of its declaration on promoting recovery in Europe, the Council invited the EIB to set up a temporary lending facility of 5 billion ECUs. This was not specifically for regional development but for the financing of Trans-European Networks in transport, telecommunications and energy, other projects in these sectors as well as environmental projects.

2. For completeness we should note that the EMS has also given rise to interest subsidies on EIB and NCI loans. These were directed to Italy and Ireland and were designed to enable them to cope with the challenge posed by participation in the EMS exchange rate mechanism.

attached to the 1969 Memorandum on Regional Policy (EC Commission, 1969c) it proposed the creation of a Regional Development Rebate Fund which would make grants by way of abatements of interest on loans for regional development purposes. This particular proposal was not implemented, but in the same year another proposal was made which eventually led to the creation of the ERDF. We are of course referring to the Hague Summit of 1969, which called for the creation of EMU by 1980. The Werner Committee, in its final report of 1970 (EC Commission, 1970), recognized that Community-financed regional interventions would be necessary, but it did not describe in detail the exact reasons why. We have, however, already considered the kind of thinking which almost certainly lay behind the Werner proposal. The next step occurred in 1972 at the Paris Summit, when the British, who were just about to enter, were successful in pressing for the establishment of what came to be called the ERDF. Whilst the kinds of consideration just referred to inspired this move, undoubtedly there was another motivating factor at work. As we saw in Chapter 3, the terms of entry secured by the UK were such that, compared with other members of the Community, its ultimate contribution to the Community budget was likely to be high in relation to the benefits it was likely to receive. The idea of a regional fund financed from the Community budget was therefore seen as a means of correcting the imbalance – that is to say it was expected that, given the problems of its economy, the UK could look forward to being a major beneficiary. The regional fund would do for the UK what the EAGGF had done for the agricultural surplus producers! The ERDF formally came into operation on 1 January 1975, and its operations between then and 1988 are summarized in Table 20.

During the life of the ERDF the rules governing its operation have changed on several occasions but it would not greatly add to an understanding of it if we were to laboriously summarize its key features. The finance for the ERDF was drawn from the Community budget; as we noted earlier the ERDF, the ESF and Guidance allocations under the EAGGF constituted what came to be called the Structural Funds. Regional development grants from the ERDF were designed to assist investment in industrial, service, handicrafts and infrastructure projects, which were located in regions scheduled by the member states themselves for regional assistance. Moreover

Table 20. ERDF operations 1975–88

Commitment appropriations[1]

Year	Total	Annual increase (%)	Share of Community budget (%)
1975	257.6[2]	—	4.8
1976	394.3[2]	53.1	5.6
1977	378.5[2]	− 4.0	4.9
1978	581.0	53.5	4.6
1979	945.0	62.7	6.1
1980	1 165.0	23.3	6.7
1981	1 540.0	32.2	7.3
1982	1 759.5	14.3	7.6
1983	2 010.0	14.2	7.6
1984	2 140.0	6.5	7.3
1985	2 289.9	7.0	7.5
1986	3 098.0	35.3	8.6
1987	3 311.0	6.9	9.1
1988	3 684.0	11.3	8.1

Notes: 1. Million ECUs. 2. 300 million UA in 1975, 500 million UA in 1976, 500 million UA in 1977 – all converted to ECUs at January 1978 rate.
Source: EC Commission, *European Regional Development Fund Fourteenth Annual Report*, 1990.

the money was to be used for projects that were assisted by the member states. ERDF assistance provided only a proportion of the funds involved – typically 50 to 55 per cent. Whilst the bulk of the money took the form of quotas allocated to individual member states, a limited amount was kept back for non-quota specific Community measures. This programme financing took various forms – for example it might be allocated to deal with a problem which affected more than one territory – normally such assistance involved the territories of two or more member states. A key feature of the ERDF was the principle of additionality which, alas, the UK tended to ignore. Additionality meant that the grants from the ERDF should be additional to the spending of the member state. The UK tended to reduce its regional spending by a corresponding amount whereas it should have maintained its spending so that aid from the Fund actually added to the intensity of the overall UK regional effort.

The Single European Act

The Single Act led to a reconsideration of the role of the ERDF and the arrangements made have broadly continued since then. The reader will recall from Chapters 1 and 3 that the Act involved an element of bargaining between the more-developed and the less-developed members of the Community. In return for accepting the intensified industrial competition implied by the completion of the internal market, the poorer members of the Community demanded some form of compensation. In part this took the form of an amendment to the Rome Treaty. A new Title was inserted headed Economic and Social Cohesion. A series of supporting articles were also added. While they did not in so many words call for the creation of a Community regional policy, they did declare that the aim of the Community should be to reduce disparities between various regions and the backwardness of the less-favoured regions. In the original Rome Treaty these were merely grandiose aspirations laid out in the preamble. As a result of the Single Act they were brought into the main body of the Treaty. Going along with this, the reader will recall from Chapter 3 that the Community budget settlement of 1988 laid down that the structural funds should grow. Indeed structural spending in 1993 should be twice that of 1987. Moreover structural spending should be concentrated on the poorest regions. Spending on them should also double.

This in turn led to a further redesign of the ERDF which came into effect in 1989. This redesign is part of a more general reconsideration of the combined role of the structural funds and the EIB. (The reader will recollect that the Single European Act expressly called for a close coordination of the work of the structural funds). Five priority objectives were laid down as follows, and entrusted to particular funds:

(a) Objective 1 – the promotion of the development of those regions which were lagging behind (ERDF, ESF and EAGGF Guidance section).
(b) Objective 2 – the conversion of regions affected by serious industrial decline (ERDF and ESF).
(c) Objective 3 – the combating of long-term unemployment (ESF).

(d) Objective 4 – the occupational integration of young people (ESF).

(e) Objective 5 – the promotion of rural development in the light of the reform of the CAP (EAGGF Guidance section, ESF and ERDF).

The reader will note that recent lending by the EIB (see above for details of loans in 1992) has reflected the objectives for the ERDF.

It was decided that while the ERDF would pursue objectives 1, 2 and 5, ERDF appropriations would mainly be used in respect of objective 1 – i.e. regions lagging behind. Indeed the fund would be allowed to devote up to 80 per cent of its resources to this end. Regions eligible for support under objective 1 would enjoy assistance up to 75 per cent of the cost of projects and equal to at least 50 per cent of the public expenditure involved. It was decided that only the following would qualify as objective 1 regions:

(a) In Spain – Andalusia, Asturias, Castile–Leon, Castile–La Mancha, Ceuta and Melilla, Valencia, Estramadura, Galicia, Canary Islands, Murcia only.

(b) In France – overseas departments and Corsica only.

(c) Greece – the whole country.

(d) Ireland – the whole country.

(e) In Italy – Abruzzi, Basilicata, Calabria, Campania, Molise, Apulia, Sardinia, Sicily only.

(f) Portugal – the whole country.

(g) In United Kingdom – Northern Ireland only.

These objective 1 regions are areas where the GDP per capita is less than 75 per cent of the Community average.

In 1993, in connection with the 1993 to 1999 Community budget programme, the rules were modified in a variety of minor ways. The definition of the objectives were redefined. For example, objective 1 was extended to include investment in the fields of education and health. Also objectives 3 and 4 were amalgamated with objective 2 and a new objective 4 was introduced designed to facilitate the adaptation of workers to industrial changes and changes in production systems. It was also agreed that the list of areas qualifying as objective 1 regions should be modified. In the UK Merseyside and the Highlands and Islands were added. The new German

Länder arising from reunification were also now included, as were Hainaut (Belgium), Cantabria (Spain), Flevoland (Netherlands) and the arondissements of Valenciennes, Douai and Avesnes (France). Seventy per cent of Structural Fund spending would be directed towards these objective 1 regions.

The Cohesion Fund

The reader will also recollect that in the lead-up to Maastricht, Spain led the pack of poorer countries in demanding yet a further transfer of resources. In the Maastricht Treaty this demand was acceded to. A Cohesion Fund was to be established. The beneficiaries would be those countries whose GNP per capita was less than 90 per cent of the Community average. This meant Spain, Portugal, Greece and Ireland. Grants from the Fund (financed from the Community budget – see Chapter 3) would be designed to support Trans-European Network and environmental projects. The Fund entered into operation in 1993.

Committee of the Regions

This is a convenient point to remind the reader that the Maastricht Treaty created a new institution – the Committee of the Regions. It consists of representatives of regional and local bodies, and has an advisory status. It can be expected to provide an important input into the appraisal of Union regional policy in the coming years.

Social policy

Social policy has proceeded in two phases. The first phase covered the period from 1958 until the negotiations leading to the Single European Act. During this period some modest – and the emphasis must be on the word modest – steps were taken towards the development of Community social policy. Such progress as was made was particularly noticeable in the period following the Paris Summit of 1972 when the Heads of State and of Government called for a Social Action Programme (see below). The second phase relates to the period from the Single Act negotiations to the present.

During this period social policy has assumed a much higher profile and has been a source of considerable controversy.

The First Phase and the Action Programme

There were four strands to Community social policy during this period. Then, as now, the first was contained in Article 2 of the old Rome Treaty, which laid down the tasks which the Community had to achieve. These were said to be the promotion of

> ... an harmonious development of economic activities, a continuous and balanced expansion, an increase in stability, an accelerated raising of the standard of living ...

A major preoccupation of the EC is the enlargement of the Community cake. Such an enlargement has social as well as economic implications. The question of the distribution of the cake, and in particular the question of the level of social services and the like, was largely left to the member states in the first instance. In the longer term the influence of harmonization would be felt; this is discussed below.

Then as now the second strand of social policy related to factor mobility. As we have already noted, under the Rome Treaty social policy is not confined to those spheres of activity which involve financial hand-outs. It also covers those policies which enable people to better themselves by virtue of the removal of restrictions on their freedom. The establishment of conditions in which, for example, a worker can move from one member state to another without loss of social security benefits and so forth is an act of social policy. In a significant number of individual cases such opportunities almost certainly provide a more powerful means of social improvement than mere doles to the unemployed. The subject of freedom of movement of labour and the right of establishment have, however, been dealt with in Chapter 6, and we shall not discuss them in any great detail here.

The third aspect of social policy was to be found in Articles 117 to 122. Their central theme is social improvement and social harmonization. Article 117 looks to the need to promote a better standard of living. The latter is to be defined broadly and thus takes in not only wages and salaries but also many other social factors. Article

118 indicates that these social factors include matters relating to employment, labour law and working conditions, basic and advanced vocational training, social security, prevention of occupational accidents and diseases, occupational hygiene, the right of association, and collective bargaining between employers and workers. The essential message of Articles 117 and 118 was that it was desirable that social standards should rise and that *pari passu* they should be harmonized. For the most part no specific targets were set and no timetables were laid down. Nevertheless, it was assumed that harmonization would progressively occur, partly as an inevitable byproduct of the creation of the Common Market, partly by virtue of the opinions produced by the Commission and partly by virtue of the Commission bringing the member states together to study social policy issues. Specific powers to act were conspicuous by their absence. However, two qualifications are appropriate. First, the Article 100 harmonization directive process might in certain cases be invoked since Article 101 declares that harmonizing directives can be adopted when discrepancies between the laws and practices of different member states distort competition. Having said that, it has to be admitted that in the period prior to the Single European Act, Article 100 harmonization was based on unanimous voting in the Council of Ministers. Given the disposition of the UK government under Margaret Thatcher and her successor to favour a hands-off approach to many employment and social problems, progress was likely to be difficult. Second, as we will see below, equal treatment of men and women was a specific requirement under the treaty and a basis for action was clearly provided.

The reader will have noticed that social security is one of the factors in the above list. The harmonization of it was a feature of the negotiations leading up to the Paris and Rome Treaties. The reason for this was that within the Six employers bore a heavy burden of social security contributions. Because the burden on French employers was particularly severe the French Government attempted, at the time the Paris Treaty was being negotiated, to include provisions for the immediate harmonization of social costs of production. In practice, the High Authority was not given the power to harmonize social conditions, and Article 3 merely refers to the general intention to harmonize conditions in an upward direction. In negotiations leading up to the Rome Treaty the issue was again raised by the French. They argued that the higher rate of social security contributions – very approximately 50 per cent on top of wages – raised their costs of production and placed them in a competitively vulnerable position. They also cited other examples of exceptional burdens, such as the law on equal pay for equal work and paid holiday schemes. Once again the French did not succeed in obtaining an explicit agreement to harmonize social security burdens within a given timespan.

With regard to the question of equal pay for equal work, it should be noted that the French secured what they no doubt regarded as a success. Article 119 of the Rome Treaty required that during the first stage each member state would introduce the equal pay for equal work system. The reason why the French pressed the equal pay for equal work point is obvious enough. In industries where the wages of women were raised above the level they normally would have been in the absence of the law governing equal pay, French industry would be at a competitive disadvantage in relation to member states which did not have such a law. The general espousal of equal pay under the Treaty therefore amounted to agreeing to the proposition that equalization would remedy distortions which would otherwise be caused by different legal provisions. It should, however, be pointed out that equal pay is a social and not an economic principle. Even if equal productivity is forthcoming this does not justify equal pay. According to conventional wage theory, the productivity of workers relates only to the demand side of the labour market. An entrepreneur will be prepared to take on a different quantity of labour at each wage rate, the actual amount being determined by the rule that the marginal revenue product of labour should be equal to the wage rate. Given equal productivity of male and female operatives an entrepreneur would be indifferent as between the two. However, on the supply side at each and every wage rate the amount of female labour offering itself might be significantly different from the amount of male labour on offer. The absolute equalization of wages paid to males and females could therefore give rise to the unemployment of female labour. This loss would have to be set against the elimination of distortions discussed above.

The fourth strand of Community social policy related to the European Social Fund (ESF). Like the EIB, which we discussed earlier, the creation of the ESF was specifically foreshadowed in Article 3 of the Rome Treaty. The basic treaty provisions were to be found in Articles 123 to 128. In the original Rome Treaty the task of the ESF was declared to be the retraining and resettlement of the unemployed and the maintenance of jobs while enterprises in difficulties changed their activities. However, the role of the ESF was re-cast from time to time and the last detailed constitution prior to the Single European Act was laid down by the Council of Ministers in 1983.

The Fund, as now, was fed by the Community budget. By 1986 Fund spending was about 7 per cent of total Community budget spending. The budget reimbursed up to 50 per cent, but in some cases 55 per cent, of certain forms of national expenditure. The eligible forms of spending were as follows. First, there was that concerned with vocational training and guidance. Secondly, the ESF could grant subsidies for up to one year for job creation of young or long-term unemployed. These jobs had to offer stable prospects. Thirdly, the Fund could help to meet the expenses incurred in connection with geographical mobility of workers. Finally, the ESF could assist in the provision of services and technical advice concerned with job creation. In 1983, in order to make the Fund more effective, the Council of Ministers decided that 75 per cent of ESF spending should go towards training and employment of the under-twenty-fives. It also decided on a geographical concentration of expenditure. Seven zones were designated as having an absolute priority. The under-twenty-fives did not get all the money. The Council emphasized that, in respect of the rest of the Fund spending, priority should be given to (a) assistance for the unemployed (especially long-term), (b) women wishing to return to work, (c) handicapped persons who wanted to work, (d) migrant workers, (e) workers who needed to retrain because of technological change, and (f) persons working in the field of employment promotion.

The Paris Summit of 1972 was significant for its concern with what may be termed the 'image' of the Community. The Summit noted that economic expansion was not an end in itself: social considerations were also important. Disparities in living conditions should be reduced, and this should be achieved with the participation of all the social partners. The quality of life as well as the standard of living should be improved, particular attention being given to intangible values and to the protection of the environment. All this has been described as giving the Community a human face – to replace the faceless economic machine centred in the Berlaymont Building in Brussels. The Summit called for an action programme, and the Commission subsequently obliged by publishing in 1973 its Social Action Programme. The document contained a long list of areas where action was needed, some being matters of priority; we shall not attempt to list them here. The programme of action, in a somewhat amended form, was accepted by the Council of Ministers in January 1974. The detailed actions fell into three categories – those related to the attainment of full and better employment; provisions concerning the improvement and upward harmonization of living and working conditions; measures which would increase the involvement of management and labour in the economic and social decisions of the Community, and of workers in the running of their firms. We shall not attempt to review all the achievements which arose out of this new initiative but merely highlight a few of the significant steps.

On the employment front, a good deal of attention was devoted to the plight of young people. In 1976 the ministers of education adopted a resolution concerning measures to improve the preparation of young people for work and to facilitate their transition from education to working life. In the following year the Commission addressed recommendations to the member states on the vocational preparation of young people under twenty-five who were unemployed or threatened with unemployment. In 1978, following a declaration of the European Council at Bremen, the Council of Ministers took a new step when they extended ESF funding to include the creation of new jobs for unemployed persons under twenty-five. An important institutional development occurred in 1977 with the opening in Berlin of the European Centre for the Development of Vocational Training.

The Community was quite active in respect of the improvement of living and working conditions, notably in the case of women. In the case of equal pay for equal work the Commission found that the member states had been dragging their feet. Therefore in 1975 the Council issued a directive requiring the principle to be adopted within one year. In 1976 there followed another directive on the principle of equal treatment for men and women as regards access to employment, vocational training and promotion and in respect of working conditions. In 1978 a directive was also adopted on the subject of equality of treatment for men and women in matters of social security. The Community has also sought to achieve a stronger protection of all workers' interests. In 1975 the Council adopted a directive on the approximation of laws concerning mass dismissals. In 1977 it issued a directive on the approximation of laws relating to the safeguarding of rights of employees in the event of transfers of undertakings or parts thereof. In 1980 a directive was also adopted on the protection of employees in the event of the insolvency of their employer. In 1975 the Commission addressed a recommendation to the member states on the subject of the length of the working week and paid holidays. Important institutional developments include the setting up of the European Foundation for the Improvement of Living and Working Conditions, in Dublin in 1976, and the decision of 1974 to establish the Advisory Committee for Industrial Safety, Hygiene and Health Protection.

The Community had much less to show on the participation and industrial democracy fronts. The Commission put forward a proposal for a fifth directive on the approximation of national company law. This was designed to give workers a say in the running of companies. However, it failed to find favour with the Council of Ministers. Long ago the Community proposed to establish, side by side with national laws, a system of Community law which would enable a European Company or *Societas Europea* to be formed. This too envisaged worker representation but also failed to find favour with the Council of Ministers. Mention must also be made of the Vredeling initiative, named after the Commissioner who proposed it in 1980. This directive was designed to set up formal employee information and consultation procedures in certain companies in the Community. It met with strong opposition both in its original and subsequently watered-down versions. Employers objected to both. Trade unions objected to the second version but liked the original one. It was not proceeded with.

The impression which emerges is that by about 1980 much of the steam had gone out of the social action programme other than in those areas concerned with tackling the unemployment problem. It was the growth of the latter which increasingly held the centre of the stage. Within the Twelve, unemployment was 8.7 million in 1980, but by 1985 it was more than 16 million. A good deal of the work of the Council of Ministers was concerned with making recommendations about approaches to various aspects of the unemployment problem. To a large extent the implementation of these proposals was in the hands of member state governments.

The Second Phase and the Social Charter

Several background influences helped to shape policy during this period. One was the concept of *L'Espace Social* – which literally means social space or social area. This concept was not new – the idea of a European Social Area had been put forward by the French President in 1981. In 1985 it was taken up by Commission President Jacques Delors. He appears to have seen it as a natural complement to the idea of completing the internal market by 1992. His argument was that some degree of equality in social standards was desirable, otherwise in the increasingly competitive environment those countries with lower standards of social protection would undercut those who sought to provide higher standards. In other words, Delors was drawing attention to the possible danger of 'social dumping'.

Another influence was associated with the idea of social dialogue – in this case a dialogue between the two sides of industry. Here, too, Delors was much to the fore when in 1985 he organized the Val Duchesse talks. Val Duchesse, a château in Belgium, was the location for a series of discussions on socio-economic issues in which the major participants were the European Trade Union Confederation, the Union of Industries of the European Communities and the European Centre of Public Enterprises. Then we have to take account of the concept of a People's Europe. That is to say there was a need to develop the kind of policies which had real practical significance for the person in the street and would bring home the contribution which the European Community could make to his or her wellbeing. This task was assigned to the Adonnino Committee to which we referred in Chapter 1 when discussing the origins of the Single European Act. Its reports covered a variety of topics but high on its list of future actions was the need to provide for greater freedom of movement for individuals.

Finally there was the Cockfield single European market concept. While many of the proposed measures were not social in character, those concerned with company law had a distinct bearing on the issue of employee participation in industry.

The social measures which actually emerged during the second phase were as follows. First, as we indicated in our discussion of regional policy, the Single European Act introduced into the Rome Treaty provisions concerned with economic and social cohesion. This had implications for the ESF. As we have already noted, these additions to the treaty stressed the need for a closer coordination of the activities of the ESF, the ERDF and the EAGGF Guidance Section. The Community budget agreement of 1988 shifted more resources to the structural funds (ESF and ERDF) and required them to focus their aid on the poorer member states. The reader will also recollect from our discussion of regional policy that specific roles were identified for the various funds – see page 305 for the tasks assigned to the ESF.

Secondly, the Single Act added two new articles to the section of the Rome Treaty concerned with social policy. New Article 118A required member states to pay particular attention to encouraging improvements, especially in the working environment, as regards the health and safety of workers. The member states should aim to harmonize conditions but not at the expense of improvements already made. In other words, the old upwards harmonization process should continue. The necessary harmonization directives would only require a qualified majority vote in the Council of Ministers. New Article 118B emphasized the idea of social dialogue – to this end the Commission was required to develop such a dialogue at the European level which could, if the two sides considered it desirable, lead to relations based on agreement. It should be added that the Val Duchesse talks continued although they tended to produce joint opinions rather than binding agreements and legislative obligations. Nevertheless they served to improve relations between the social partners.

The Single European Act, in committing the Community to complete the internal market by the end of 1992, also placed on the agenda a number of proposals which had social significance. Notable among these were measures relating to free movement of labour and the professions. The Commission also highlighted the need to make progress on the fifth company law directive and on the subject of the European Company Statute.

Significant as these developments were, they can hardly be said to have constituted a revolution in Community social policy. By contrast the Social Charter was *potentially* altogether more significant. It did not proceed directly from the Single Act but, as in the case of EMU, it can be argued that the seeds were sown in the preamble to the Act. The latter contained an important statement of principle by affirming that member states accepted the fundamental rights of citizens contained in the *Convention for the Protection of Human Rights and Fundamental Freedoms* and the *European Social Charter*. Both of these were products of the Council of Europe but their contents, particularly those of the second document, provided a potential foundation upon which to build a whole series of rights under the Rome Treaty.

Signs that this could happen were increasingly apparent in subsequent summit communiqués. Thus the Hanover Summit of June 1988 merely stressed 'the importance of the social aspects of progress towards the objectives of 1992'. But the Rhodes Summit later that year went further in emphasizing that the completion of the internal market could not be regarded as an end in itself but part of a larger design which involved maximizing the wellbeing of all within the European tradition of social progress. The summit communiqué also indicated that the Heads of State and of Government looked to the Commission for proposals based on the Social Charter of the Council of Europe. At Madrid they went yet further by declaring that the same emphasis should be placed on the social as on the economic aspects of the single market – they should be developed in a balanced manner. A preliminary draft of the Social Charter was also discussed. Matters came to a head at Strasbourg later that year. The Social Charter was tabled and approved by eleven of the twelve member states – the UK declined to subscribe. Mrs Thatcher had already made known her preference for deregulation rather than more regulation and state interference when she spoke at the College of Europe at Bruges in September 1988.

The Community Charter of Basic Social Rights for Workers, to give it its full title, took the form of a solemn declaration but one which did not have the force of law. According to Commissioner Vasso Papandreou it sought to establish a European social model which would guarantee that the search for greater competitiveness and efficiency was paralleled by simultaneous and equal advances in the social field.

The Charter enshrined the following rights and freedoms for Community citizens – in particular for workers, whether employed or self-employed.

(a) The right to freedom of movement. Here the emphasis is on the right to move to other countries and take up occupations on the same terms as nationals.

(b) The right to employment and to fair remuneration for that employment.

(c) The right to improved living and working conditions. Here the emphasis is on the idea that the completion of the internal market should be accompanied by harmonization of social conditions while the improvement is being maintained.

(d) The right to adequate social protection.

(e) The right to freedom of association and collective bargaining.

(f) The right to vocational training. Every worker has a right to continue vocational training right through his or her working life.

(g) The right of men and women to equal treatment. This extends beyond pay to access to jobs, education, training, career opportunities and social protection.

(h) The right to worker information, consultation and participation.

(i) The right to health and safety protection at the workplace.

(j) The right to the protection of children and adolescents. This includes a minimum working age of sixteen and rights to such things as vocational training after leaving school.

(k) The right of elderly persons to retirement pensions which provide a decent standard of living. Those not entitled to a pension should nevertheless be entitled to a minimum of social protection.

(l) The right of disabled persons to take advantage of specific measures especially in the fields of training and occupational and social integration and rehabilitation.

We have already noted that the Social Charter did not have the force of law. Rather it took the form of a declaration. At first sight it appeared not to be capable of being made binding under Community law. If it was to be implemented, the initiative would have to come from each member state acting individually within its own legislature. However, the situation was more complicated than that for three reasons. Some Charter topics did fall within the competence of the Community. Also in some cases the Commission could endeavour to argue so. Additionally the principle of subsidiarity enabled the Community to act when the aims to be achieved could be more effectively attained at Community as opposed to member state level. Having said that, it was necessary to recognize that the Commission in its proposals could not exceed the powers which were laid down in the Rome Treaty as amended by the Single Act.

The real problem is summed up in the last sentence. The Commission followed up by proposing an Action Programme which would set in motion the task of putting the Charter into operation. But here it was bound to encounter the problem that the Rome Treaty (as amended by the Single Act) was inadequate to the task, particularly in the light of continued British hostility. Thus when it put forward a draft proposal on working hours it was constrained to argue that this was really a health and safety measure, thus enabling it to take advantage of the majority voting procedure which applied in that area of policy. This was bound to provoke UK opposition. Equally old Article 100 did enable the harmonization power to be applied when laws, regulations and administrative actions in member states directly affected the creation of the single market. Since such laws, etc., could be social in character, it followed that the harmonization process could be applied to social matters. But we also have to remember that new Article 100A (introduced under the Single Act) excluded from the new majority voting arrangement matters relating to *the rights and interests of employed persons*! Thus unanimity was still required and the UK could impose a veto or water it down as the case demanded.

As a result relatively little progress was made in implementing the Charter. As Phillipa Watson has pointed out, the crux of the problem was a lack of adequate powers to fulfil the objectives of the Charter (Watson, 1993, p. 486). In a working paper addressed to the subsequent IGC (which gave rise to the Maastricht Treaty) the Commission blamed the lack of progress on:

the wide gap between the powers available under the current legal bases and the ambitions set out in the Charter and the new constraints arising from the completion of the internal market.

What was needed was a basic revision of the social policy section of the Rome Treaty. Hence the ultimate Protocol and Agreement on Social Policy of the Maastricht Treaty. This course of events was dictated by lack of adequate Treaty powers but was also, at least in part, the product of UK hostility to Community endeavours in the social sphere. In the IGC negotiations the UK continued to resist the incorporation of the Social Charter in the Rome Treaty, i.e. that the law-making powers contained in the social chapter of the Rome Treaty should be significantly extended and that this should be coupled with substantial use of qualified majority voting. The result was an untidy and very un-communautaire arrangement which essentially granted the UK an opt-out.

Much ink has been spilt in regard to the legal status of the Protocol on Social Policy and the attached Agreement. The general impact has been admirably summarized by Whiteford (Whiteford, 1993, p. 204). She points out that the preamble to the Protocol indicates that the provisions of the Agreement are without prejudice to the Rome Treaty. In other words the old eleven states agreed to exhaust the possibilities of the Rome Treaty before having to resort to the Agreement. The Agreement, however, enabled the eleven to make decisions which the twelve (i.e. including the UK) would not be able to agree to. Under the Agreement measures are divided into two categories. Category one are those decisions concerned with:

(a) improvement in particular of the working environment to protect workers' health and safety;
(b) working conditions;
(c) the information and consultation of workers;
(d) equality between men and women with regard to labour market opportunities and treatment at work;
(e) the integration of persons excluded from the labour market;

and these will be subject to qualified majority voting under the 189c process. Category two involves those decisions that relate to:

(a) social security and social protection of workers;

   (b) protection of workers where their employment contract is terminated;

   (c) representation and collective defence of the interests of workers and employers, including co-determination;

   (d) conditions of employment for third-country nationals legally residing in Community territory;

   (e) financial contributions for promotion of employment and job-creation;

and these will subject to unanimous decision, Council acting in consultation with Parliament and Ecosoc. The UK will not take part in the legislative process and will not be bound by the results of it. This UK reluctance is, of course, a product of Conservative Party thinking and was signalled by Margaret Thatcher in her famous Bruges speech. It was not supported by either of the main opposition parties and it is reasonable to assume that any change in political control in the UK would mean that the opt-out would be dropped.

In passing we should also note that the Maastricht Treaty has extended the Council of Minister's remit to include Public Health. Harmonizing powers are, however, excluded.

Education

The social policy actions discussed above have tended to focus on employment and the workplace. But a discussion of social policy also allows us to take into account the Community's impact on education, notably higher education. Space does not permit us to detail all the Community actions, but in order to give a flavour six will be highlighted. As early as the Messina conference of 1955 the idea of extending European integration into the fields of teaching and research was under consideration. At the Hague Summit of 1969 the Heads of State and of Government expressed interest in the idea of a European University. Thanks to pressure by the European Parliament, the European Institute at Florence was established in 1976 by a special convention signed by the Nine. It focuses on research and postgraduate teaching and is financed by the member states together with a subsidy provided by the Commission. The Community has for a number of years financed joint study programmes, which have involved student and staff exchanges between different member states. In May 1987 the ministers of education of the Twelve launched an intensified programme designed to increase such student and staff mobility in higher education, called ERASMUS. The Community has of course supported university-level research on a considerable scale. As we shall see in Chapter 10, the Community's science and technology programme, by being concentrated at the research end, has provided considerable funds to support research in higher-education institutes. The European Documentation Centres, financed by the Community, have also presented scholars with a valuable research facility. In 1989 the Community introduced with supporting finance a Lingua programme designed to improve the teaching and learning of foreign languages – the languages being those of the member states. In the same year it also approved the Jean Monnet project, which has provided support for higher-education posts relating to the teaching of European integration.

The Maastricht Treaty has had a significant impact on EC education policy. It should be noted that under the old Rome Treaty there was no specific mandate to make education policy. Education tended to creep in peripherally by virtue of the fact that the treaty did explicitly refer to vocational training. All this has now changed. Under Maastricht the Council of Ministers' remit now explicitly extends to education (and culture) although their powers are limited. For example, they cannot adopt harmonizing directives.

10

INDUSTRY, THE CONSUMER, FISHERIES AND THE ENVIRONMENT

Industrial Policy

Scope

The main focus of the first part of this chapter will be industrial policy in the EC. The industrial policy provisions of the ECSC treaty are significantly more *dirigiste*, and we will discuss them later. Industrial policy in the EC can be presented under six headings. (a) The first is concerned with the creation of a European industrial base. We have referred to this previously in terms of completing the single European market. (b) Considerable attention has been given to the need to facilitate business integration in the Community. This has given rise to a variety of proposals. One has related to the creation of a European company. Others have been concerned with measures which would facilitate cross-frontier mergers, and other forms of cross-frontier cooperation, and which would better enable parents and subsidiaries to organize themselves on a Europe-wide basis. In connection with the above, emphasis has been laid on the need to deal with the specific legal and fiscal impediments to cross-frontier arrangements. The desire to make business integration a reality has also led to proposals for the harmonization of national company laws. (c) The Community has also been concerned to encourage the development of Small and Medium-Sized Enterprises (SMEs) and to enable them to play a bigger role in the single market. (d) There has been a long-standing, and in recent years a growing, concern about the technological gap between the EC and countries such as the US and Japan. Suggestions as to how the Community could catch up have taken two forms. One has been highly *dirigiste*. For example, the EC should treat its high-tech sector as an infant industry which should be protected from import competition until it could stand on its own two feet. The less *dirigiste* approach has been to propose that individual states are too small to mount the necessary R & TD efforts across the board. Rather, critical areas should be identified and national R & TD efforts should be pooled. This could also involve cooperation with non-EC states. (e) Specific policies have been devised to deal with problem industries which have been encountering structural difficulties. (f) More recently, industrial policy has been concerned with the need for greater competitiveness.

The policy emerges – slowly

We have to begin by recognizing that there was no call for an industrial policy in the *original* Rome Treaty. There were, however, provisions scattered through the Treaty which related to aspects of industrial policy, and in the early days the Commission had to rely on them for a number of policy proposals. The word proposal is very relevant here, because this is a field of activity where the ratio of draft directives (concerned with the internal market and business integration) to those actually adopted was for many years, to say the least, extremely high.

It is also true to say that up to 1970 the prime concern of the Six was to construct the Community as it was envisaged in the 1957 Treaty. As we noted in Chapter 1, it was only when the twelve-year transition period had come to an end that the Community could afford to give consideration to further goals, and one of these was industrial policy.

An important step was taken in 1970 when the Commissioner concerned with industrial affairs, Guido Colonna, put forward a memorandum on industrial policy. The memorandum was an ambitious document. First, it envisaged the creation of a single European market or base. Secondly, it emphasized the idea of companies organizing themselves on a European scale. For this to happen certain legal developments were called for including the adoption of a European Company Statute, the approximation of national company laws, the introduction by all member states of legislation relating to corporate groups, and the possible introduction of new forms of business cooperation. On the fiscal front there was a need to eliminate the discriminatory tax treatment accorded to cross-frontier mergers when compared with that applied to internal amal-gamations. The third part of the memorandum was more *dirigiste* in character. The Commission, recognizing the need for the Community to catch up on matters of technology, saw the trans-national firm as being the vehicle which would enable this to be achieved. It therefore suggested that the Community should introduce development contracts with a priority being given to firms that were willing to carry out technological development on a trans-national basis. The reader should appreciate that although the EC had been in existence for twelve years, businesses had been remarkably slow to merge across frontiers. Section four emphasized the importance of economic adaptation – new industries would have to be developed to create new jobs as existing industries declined. The emphasis was laid on the new industry element, and stress was placed on the importance of labour mobility, the application of new technologies and the improved effectiveness of business management. The specific techniques to be applied to industries in decline were not discussed, although the need to deploy the resources of the Community (e.g. those of the ESF) so as to facilitate change was referred to. We shall see that in due course the detailed problems involved in coping with industries in decline or in difficulty became a major preoccupation of Community industrial policy. The fifth and final section called for the extension of Community solidarity into the field of external relations.

The memorandum was discussed by the Council of Ministers, but considerable difficulties were encountered. While the French were willing to contemplate a *dirigiste* approach, the Germans in particular favoured a free market as opposed to an active industrial policy. However, at the Paris Summit of 1972 the Commission was supported by the Heads of State and of Government. The communiqué at the end of the summit called for the establishment of a single industrial base, a concept for which the UK claimed some credit, the elimination of barriers of a fiscal and legal kind which hindered mergers and closer links between firms, the rapid adoption of the European Company Statute, and the promotion on a European scale of firms which were competitive in high technology. The communiqué also referred to the transformation and conversion of declining industries under acceptable social conditions – a reference no doubt to the use of Community instruments such as the ESF and the newly agreed ERDF. Reference was also made to the need for fair competition within and outside the Community – this seemed to pick up the point made in the fifth section of the Colonna Report.

In 1973, in the light of the Paris Summit, the Commission submitted a new memorandum on industrial policy. It was a toned-down version of the Colonna memorandum, and on the basis of it a programme of future action was adopted by the Council of Ministers later that year.

The year 1972 was also important for internal scientific and technological collaboration. The Paris Summit communiqué expressly called for a common policy in the field of science and technology. There duly followed in 1973 a Commission memorandum setting out a scientific and technological policy programme which stressed the need for (a) coordination of national science and technology policies; (b) joint execution of projects of Community interest; (c) a more effective flow of scientific and technical information; (d) technology forecasting, and (e) the creation of an effective organizational structure – the latter was a crucial element. Early in 1974 a programme of action on these lines was adopted by the Council of Ministers.

Unfortunately, the progress that the Community made towards achieving these goals was rather disappointing. Actions which helped towards the creation of a European industrial base did follow, as we have seen in Chapters 4 to 6. But the fact that in 1985 the Commission in the Cockfield Report was able to draw attention to a host of proposals that had not been adopted, and that according to the Single European Act the internal market would not be created until 1992, indicated that much more needed to be done. We shall discuss these matters in this chapter only briefly, as the nature of what has been done and needs to be done has already been indicated in Chapters 4 to 6. In respect of business integration, a variety of proposals were tabled by the Commission, but as yet only limited progress has been achieved. We discuss this topic in more detail below. In the case of science and technology, the Community did subsequently devote relatively limited amounts of budget resources to R & TD purposes but not on a scale calculated to prevent the technological gap from widening and certainly not enough to cause it to narrow. In the early eighties, however, the need for a more dynamic response to the technological challenge posed by the USA and Japan led to an important reappraisal of Community R & TD policy and this was reflected in changes contained in the Single European Act. We also discuss this below. The Communities also adopted policies in respect of industries experiencing structual difficulties, and we round off our account of industrial policy by considering four cases.

European industrial base

A single European market or base has been deemed desirable for two general reasons. First, it permits a greater exploitation of economies of large-scale production and distribution than would be possible within the confines of individual national markets. Secondly, the existence of the larger market means that enterprises in each individual national market are no longer shielded from the full blast of competition from enterprises located in other member states and this stimulates greater efficiency and innovation. Before the Single European Act the creation of such a European industrial base had proceeded but in a half-hearted fashion. It is true that tariffs and quotas had indeed been eliminated in respect of goods (see Chapter 4). Also, a start had been made on getting rid of non-tariff barriers to trade (see Chapter 5). But significant failures to act were evident in the field of NTBs and in some cases the processes for dealing with them were extremely cumbersome. A failure to act was particularly evident in the field of services – e.g. banking, insurance and air passenger transport – where systems of regulation, national but sometimes international in character, excluded entry to domestic markets. Thus relatively little had been done in banking and insurance (see Chapter 6) and virtually nothing had been achieved in air transport (see Chapter 8).

The 1992 programme, inaugurated by the Single European Act, was a response to this highly unsatisfactory situation in which markets continued to be divided. It was particularly unsatisfactory because national industrial markets, for example, were relatively small. Thus the West German market, the largest European market for industrial goods, is less than half the size of that of Japan and less than a quarter that of the US. The signatories to the Single European Act recognized that only a true single Community market would be of a size and kind which would provide the economies of scale in production, research and innovation, and the stimulus to competition necessary for survival on the world stage.

The actions which have been and are being taken to create such a base are many and we will confine outselves to a few of the main ones. In the case of goods, the problem of differences in technical standards which inhibited cross-frontier trade, and the procedures for dealing with them, had to be addressed. As we have seen, a more streamlined approach has been adopted (see Chapter 4). The Commission emphasized the need to deal not just with traditional products (e.g. foodstuffs) but also with high tech sectors (e.g. information technology and telecommunications). In areas such as telecommunications, standardization and equipment compatibility are essential. To this end, the Community in 1988 helped to set up the European Telecommunications Standards Institute in order to give a boost to standardization in the telecommunications industry.

Equally important in order to provide for greater scale economies and competition was the need to tighten up public procurement rules and to open up public purchasing in sectors where no directives had been introduced. Thanks to the single market programme, the rules have indeed been revised, and in 1990 agreement was reached on the bringing of hitherto exempt sectors within the ambit of specific Community public purchasing rules. Significantly, telecommunications was one of the previously exempt sectors.

In the case of services, the actions needed were largely concerned with modifying domestic and international systems of regulation which precluded enterprises from establishing themselves in other member states, prevented them from selling services across frontiers and in the case of airlines prevented entry and competition on inter-state routes. In the case of banking and insurance, the approach adopted has been based on a combination of harmonization of supervisory rules and mutual recognition of national systems of regulation (see Chapter 6). The approach adopted with airlines was to apply the rules of competition to inter-state airline operation, to allow airlines to make competitive fare offers on inter-state routes (which could not be blocked by rivals in other states) and progressively to abolish rules which restricted access to routes and rigidly, on a bilateral basis, shared traffic between the incumbent national flag fliers (see Chapter 8).

The concept of the single industrial base also called for developments in the field of intellectual and industrial property – patents, trademarks and copyrights. Differences in the laws concerning these matters have meant that enterprises have not treated the common market as a single environment for their economic activities. The Cockfield Report therefore called for a decision on the long-standing proposal for a Community Trademark. Considerable advantages would flow from such a development as enterprises could obtain by a single application a trademark covering all member states. In the case of patents a Community Patent Convention (not to be confused with the European Patent Convention) was signed in 1975 and it too looked forward to a simplified system for obtaining Community-wide patent protection. Unfortunately the Cockfield Report had to admit that it has not entered into force. Fortunately the outstanding problems were ironed out at the very end of 1989. The Convention was duly signed and later ratified by national parliaments. Other industrial property developments followed. For example, in 1993 the Council of Ministers adopted Regulation on the Community trade mark. This was designed to enable companies to adapt their activities to the dimensions of the European single market since a single trade mark registration will cover all member states.

Business integration

In the early days of the Community great stress was laid upon the need to create larger firms. Data was assembled to prove that in a number of important industries the size of firm in the Community was significantly smaller than in the US. This, it was argued, put the Community at a disadvantage, since there are economies of large-scale production and distribution which might only be fully reaped by large firms, and in addition R & TD was an activity characteristic of large enterprises and beyond the means of small ones. Although this view was evident within the Community, it would be dangerous to say that it was the Community view (if such a thing can in any case be said to exist). The idea that bigger firms were desirable was most strongly held by sections of industry. For example, the Community's federation of national industrial associations, the UNICE, was strongly in favour of it and so was the

Patronat Française. The French Government was particularly favourable to the greater-size thesis. A prime aim of the Fifth Plan was to reduce the number of independent enterprises by creating larger groups. In some cases it was envisaged that only one or two firms should constitute the industry. The Commission, on the other hand, seemed in the earlier days to take a more cautious view. Clearly the larger market provided the possibility of greater size without the problems of concentration which would arise at the national level. Cross-frontier mergers would also help to cement the Community together, and international companies with subsidiaries in several member states were extremely adept at providing mobility of capital (and know-how) which the Rome Treaty obviously sought to achieve. But the Commission's original stance was guarded – the aim of the policy was not simply the pursuit of larger firms but the introduction of greater neutrality in respect of those factors which determined firm size. It aimed to eliminate those factors which artificially encouraged or impeded concentration.

The Commission focused particular attention on the fields of taxation and company law as ones in which conditions of neutrality should be brought about. In the fiscal field, an obvious distortion was the artificial stimulus to vertical concentration presented by multi-stage or 'cascade' type of turnover taxes. Originally, these existed in all the member states of the EC except France, being particularly prominent in Germany. As we have seen, the 'cascade' system involves imposing a turnover tax upon raw materials, semi-finished products, or bought-in component parts every time they are sold by one firm to another. The result is that the taxes imposed in the earlier stages of manufacturing a product that passes through several stages are compounded in the final selling price of the product, which is thus higher than it would be but for the multiple incidence of tax. Under these circumstances, it is not surprising that industries in Germany should have chosen to avoid this multiple incidence wherever possible by vertical integration. In a completely vertically integrated concern that extends right back to the sources of raw materials, taxes are imposed only once at the final stage of production. The implications for the economy as a whole of this artificial inducement to vertical concentration are that the real economic advantages of specialization are less likely to be achieved, since the firm is encouraged to spread its activities for purely fiscal reasons, and vertical integration may in some circumstances make it possible for a vertically integrated concern to embarrass its non-integrated competitors, even if they are more efficient, by denying them raw materials, components or markets. The Commission always held, therefore, that the solution to this problem lay in the adoption of the value-added system which had been operational in France. This form of tax neither encouraged nor discouraged verti-cal concentration, and this is one reason why the Community adopted VAT.

The other area where, as we have seen, the Commission sought to make progress was in the field of cross-frontier mergers and cross-frontier business organization.

In respect of cross-frontier mergers two types of problem arose – one fiscal, the other legal. Let us take the fiscal points first. For a true merger to occur, a legal liquidation would have to occur in one country followed by a legal reconstruction in another. Unfortunately, when a company was liquidated, some countries imposed a liquida-tion tax on the difference between the book value and the actual value of the company's assets. In addition, in most countries capital gains arising at the time of liquidation were subject to taxation. If the tax liability was substantial, it might make the cost of an amalgamation prohibitive. Within each of the member states of the EC, therefore, the fiscal authorities made certain concessions to companies in these circumstances, perhaps by levying the tax at a reduced rate or by permitting the payment to be phased over a number of years. But this understanding attitude on the part of the authorities usually vanished when cross-frontier amalgamations were under consideration. In particular, the possibility of phasing the tax payment over a number of years became unattractive to the official mind when the company on which the tax was levied was due to disappear from the national scene. Thus economically desirable mergers might be impeded.

It is also important to note that fiscal problems arose when companies were organized on the basis of a parent in one state and subsidiaries in others. Quite simply, the problem was one of double taxation. In addition to corporation tax, member states would also deduct a withholding tax from dividends remitted across frontiers from a subsidiary to the parent.

On the legal side, the impediments to cross-frontier mergers were often quite stark. Dutch law, for example, did not provide for mergers between domestic companies, so mergers with companies in other member states were quite clearly impossible. German law too posed a problem, since it precluded mergers between German and foreign companies.

To deal with the legal problems of cross-frontier mergers, three developments were originally proposed. The first was an international convention on mergers which would modify national laws so that international mergers were possible. Such a draft convention was submitted to the Council of Ministers in 1973 but was later abandoned in favour of a directive aimed at harmonizing national company laws so as to facilitate cross-frontier mergers. This tenth directive has not yet been adopted. The second was to establish, side by side with national laws, a system of Community company law which would enable a European Company or *Societas Europea* to be formed. Such a statute was submitted to the Council as early as 1970. It too has not yet been adopted – in its proposals leading up to the Single European Act, the Commission looked to its adoption by 1990. Thirdly, nine company-law harmonization directives have so far been adopted. It should be noted that this harmonization process is complementary to the European Company Statute, because the less the differences between national laws the easier it would be for the member states to accept the statute. For example, German law allows workers to participate in the running of a German company (*Mitbestimmung* or co-determination) but not all national company laws adopt that principle. The Commission has proposed a fifth draft directive to deal with this problem. It has not yet been adopted. This failure to make progress is a reflection of the opposition of employers representatives in Ecosoc. UNICE has also indicated to the Commission that the proposal is unacceptable. It has argued that the proposed system would cut across and detract from existing national systems of consultation and slow down decision making. This, of course, is an area where social policy, following the Social Charter, and industrial policy interact.

Proposals to deal with the fiscal problems arising from cross-frontier mergers and from parent-subsidiary arrangements were put forward by the Commission as early as 1969! This is a good illustration of the stagnation which afflicted the internal market programme. The Cockfield Report emphasized the need to act and indeed in 1990 the Council of Ministers approved three measures which dealt with the kind of fiscal problems discussed earlier.

Subsidiaries will no longer be required to deduct withholding tax when making payments to parents – Germany has been allowed until 1996 to comply with this directive. Another directive provides that capital gains tax arising in connection with cross-border acquisitions will no longer immediately attract capital gains tax in the country of the target – the tax can be deferred provided certain conditions are fulfilled. The third measure in the form of a convention was concerned with the establishment of a body to arbitrate in respect of transfer pricing disputes concerning companies operating in more than one member state. It will prevent companies from being taxed twice when disputes arise.

The reader will recollect that the Colonna Report referred to the desirability of introducing other forms of business collaboration which would foster cross-frontier cooperation. In 1973 the Commission submitted a draft regulation to the Council designed to create a European Economic Interest Grouping. This would not be a company as such but would provide a legal basis for cooperation. It would be available to persons as well as companies, would have a cross-frontier character and would be particularly helpful to small and medium-sized undertakings. A modified proposal was submitted in 1978, and this was adopted in 1985.

From what has gone before it will be apparent that some progress has been made on the issue of business integration. The positive achievements are a series of company law harmonization directives, three measures relating to the elimination of tax obstacles to cross-frontier arrangements, the creation of the European Economic Interest Grouping and the establishment of the Business Cooperation Centre. The latter was set up in 1972. It acts as a marriage bureau for small and medium-sized firms and advises them on the economic, tax and financial aspects of cross-frontier cooperation and integration. The Business Cooperation Centre is now part of a system of information flows which include 226 Euro-Info-Centres (and correspondence centres) together with the confidential European Business Cooperation Network.

SMEs

Over a long period the Community has been anxious to encourage SMEs. A variety of initiatives have been launched. Efforts have been made to consult SMEs in regard to new legislation, emphasis has been laid on the need to avoid placing undue regulatory burdens on them, training schemes have been introduced in order to prepare them for the single market and so on. In its 1991 Communication to Council on European industrial policy for the 1990s, the Commission has emphasized the key role which such enterprises can play in improving the performance of the Community economy. In 1993 the Council of Ministers adopted a Decision on a multiannual programme of Community measures for enterprise in which the needs of SMEs were highlighted. At the Edinburgh meeting of the European Council in December 1992 the EIB was invited, as part of its own activities, to set up a temporary loan facility and at the subsequent 1993 Copenhagen summit meeting the EIB was requested to extend the scope of the facility to include SMEs. The European Council also agreed to provide interest rate subsidies. At Edinburgh the European Council requested the EIB to set up as a separate legal entity a European Investment Fund. One of its objectives was to be financial assistance, primarily in the form of loan guarantees, to SMEs.

Science and technology

In the light of the 1974 programme of action in science and technology, the Community did devote limited amounts of budget resources to R & TD. However, by the early 1980s the Community had begun to realize that it was suffering from a loss of competitiveness on world markets and that a more dynamic response to the technological challenge posed by the US and Japan was needed. In 1981 the Commission addressed a communication to the Council of Ministers on the need to develop a genuine European dimension in responding to this challenge and that appropriate financial instruments should be devised to support such an initiative.

Two alternative strategies were suggested. When the European Council met at Copenhagen in 1982, the Commission presented a package of proposals designed to establish Europe as a world industrial power. First, it called for the removal of barriers within the Community in order to generate greater efficiency through competition and scale economies. This was not new or controversial. Secondly, and very controversially, it argued that protection would be necessary for at least five years if European advanced-technology industries were to attain international levels of competitiveness (Pearce and Sutton, 1985, p. 5). In 1983 the French Government reacted in a similar way when it produced a memorandum which called on the one hand for protection, on infant-industry grounds, and on the other for collaborative R & TD and the opening up of public procurement. The French were also critical of the way in which domestic anti-trust policy frustrated the cross-frontier mergers which were necessary if the competition of the US and Japanese industrial giants was to be challenged successfully. This was in fact a reaction to the proposed merger between Thomson-Brandt of France and Grundig of West Germany, which was forbidden by the German cartel office. The French were critical because they felt that the West Germans were looking at competition in too narrow a context. If national markets were protected then mergers between firms which were previously competitors could be dangerous. But in the more open trading environment of today there was plenty of outside competition to keep merged firms on their toes.

This protective approach did not commend itself to the Community as a whole. Instead, the approach adopted has been based on the following ingredients. (a) The areas of technology where the Community is at risk need to be identified. (b) Having identified them, the Community should seek to meet those R & TD challenges on a collaborative basis. This the Community has done – see, for example, the ESPRIT programme below. (c) The proportion of the budget's resources devoted to Community R & TD efforts should be increased. At the Fontainebleau Summit of 1984 this was agreed. (d) Community collaborative activities should be set within multi-annual framework programmes. This too has happened. The first ran from 1984 to 1987. The second ran from 1987 to 1991. The third, which overlapped with the second, ran from 1990 to 1994. The fourth, which runs from 1994 to 1998, has been allocated 12,000 million ECUs with the possibility of an extra 1,000 million ECUs. (e) R & TD collaboration should concentrate at the research end since otherwise it risked being attacked by competitors such as the US on the grounds that EC products were being subsidized. (f) R & TD cooperation should also include cooperation with other European countries. (g) The Rome Treaty should more explicitly address itself to the research and technological challenge. A little more needs to be said on these last two points.

The idea of collaboration with other European countries is not in fact new. A body known as COST (Committee on European Cooperation in the Field of Scientific and Technical Research) was established by the Council of Ministers as far back as 1970. It has been a vehicle for involving other European countries in collaborative research projects on a case-by-case basis. COST comprised nineteen European countries. Between 1970 and 1985, fifty-five cooperative projects were carried out within the COST framework. What the American and Japanese challenge did was to place even greater emphasis on the urgency of achieving such wider European collaboration. In 1985 a European Technology Conference was held in Paris, and this in turn gave rise to EUREKA. This body brought together the Twelve, six EFTA countries and Turkey. Its object was to increase the productivity and competitiveness of European industry on the world market by means of cooperation in the field of advanced technology. In contrast to the Community's own research efforts and those of COST, which are largely concerned with pre-competitive research, EUREKA was concerned with projects which are closer to the market. EUREKA therefore tends to involve collaboration between firms, whereas Community research tends to focus more on universities and public-sector research bodies.

The idea of injecting an explicit commitment to research and technology in the Rome Treaty was a product of a memorandum which the EC Commission addressed to the Milan Summit in 1985. The memorandum was entitled *Towards a Technology Community* (EC Commission, 1985c). It was endorsed by the European Council and became one of the background documents which led to the Single European Act. As a result of the latter, the Rome Treaty was amended. A new Title VI[1] was added which was headed Research and Technological Development. The ensuing articles stated that the Community's aim should be to strengthen the scientific and technological base of European industry and to encourage it to become more competitive at the international level. To this end the Community would encourage firms, universities and research

1. Following Maastricht this is now Title XV. The decision system is broadly the same.

centres in their research and technological development activities. It would also help firms to exploit the Community's internal market through the opening up of public contracts, standardization and the removal of fiscal and legal barriers to cooperation. Although the multi-annual R & TD framework programmes would be decided on the basis of unanimity, individual items would be decided by majority vote. This was a most important development.

We turn now to the Community's internal R & TD efforts. These are divided into two main categories – direct and indirect. Direct action is carried out by the Community's own Joint Research Centre. Indirect action consists of projects which are carried out under contract by universities or industrial firms. Generally, the Community will pay half the cost – the rest being put up by the contractors.

The following are three examples of the more important indirect programmes. We mentioned the Joint European Torus (JET) project when discussing energy policy. It is concerned with nuclear energy produced by fusion as opposed to fission. As an exception to the rule, the Community contribution in this case was 80 per cent. Another programme which has attracted considerable publicity has been the European Strategic Programme for Research and Development in Information Technology (ESPRIT). This arose out of the Commission's investigations into areas where the Community was falling behind the USA and Japan. Information technology was agreed to be such an area. As a result, a ten-year programme was launched in 1984 involving twelve major European companies, hundreds of small and medium-sized firms as well as research centres and universities. The first five years were planned to cost 1500 million ECUs, of which 50 per cent would come from the Community budget. During the second phase of ESPRIT, funding has been increased to 3200 million ECUs. Another project, entitled Research and Development in Advanced Communications Technologies for Europe (RACE), was launched in 1985. This is concerned with the development of the technological base for a network of integrated broad-band telecommunications systems using optical fibres. Between 1985 and 1986, the research priorities were defined. Between 1987 and 1992 the precompetitive research work was to be carried out, and between 1992 and 1996 the actual equipment would be developed. Others include food science and technology

(FLAIR), industrial and material technology (BRITE/EURAM), energy (JOULE) and marine science and technology (MAST).

Collaborative ventures such as these, and several more could be cited, are clearly a major feature of the Community's approach to the problem of strengthening its position in the international technological race. But they do not constitute the whole of R & TD policy. We also have to take account of the way in which other aspects of Community policy have been adjusted in favour of R & TD activity. Thus, as we noted earlier (see Chapter 4), block exemption from the cartel prohibition of Article 85 has been allowed for certain forms of joint R & TD agreements between otherwise independent firms. The Commission has also recognized that while patent licensing and know-how licensing agreements may compartmentalize the Common Market, they do also contribute to the transfer of technology. Therefore under certain circumstances such agreements have been granted block exemption status. We have also noted that while Article 92 prohibits state aids, the Community has recognized that such aid for R & TD purposes can be approved. The broad conditions that are necessary for it to be acceptable are discussed in Chapter 4.

Problem industries

In the post-transition period, a new element began to emerge in industrial policy. The Community was forced to address itself to what may be termed problem industries, that is to say industries which had begun to exhibit structural weaknesses or greater structural weaknesses, often as a result of foreign competition, although the recession which began in 1974 aggravated the situation. Four industries have frequently featured in this context – textiles, synthetic fibres, shipbuilding and steel.

It should be emphasized that while industries may be in difficulty, and while chronic excess capacity may exist and a need to slim down and modernize may be apparent, the Commission is not empowered to step in and carry out the rationalization process. This latter role has to be discharged by the firms themselves, no doubt aided and encouraged by governments. That does not mean, however, that the Commission is powerless to act. It can in fact intervene in two ways. (a) It can control state aids in order to ensure that they are directed towards restructuring as opposed to merely propping up inefficient structures which have no prospect of longer-term viability. (b) It can also control imports from outside the Community, thus giving the industry a breathing space within which to adjust. In the case of the steel industry, which comes under the more *dirigiste* Paris Treaty, the Commission can also intervene in order to set a limit to internal competition and ruinous price wars – again the object is to give the industry a breathing space.

In the case of textiles, the Commission began to define its policy as early as 1971. In that year it published its *Framework for Aid to the Textile Industry* (EC Commission, 1971). The Commission recognized that the textile industry would have to face a situation in which it was increasingly open to cheap imports. Production within the Community was likely to shrink. It was equally likely that member states would seek to protect their industries by giving aids. These, if uncontrolled and uncoordinated, would distort competition within the Community. The Commission therefore laid down a series of rules which not merely sought to prevent internal distortions but were designed to facilitate the orderly readaptation of the industry. In issuing these rules, the Commission was not in any way seeking to indicate that aid-giving was necessary, but it did recognize that in certain acute situations it might be inescapable. What it did say was that aids which merely consisted of subsidies to price were unacceptable – they would merely prop up industries which in fact might have no prospect of independent viability. In so far as aids were permitted, they should not add to capacity – there was likely to be too much already. Rather, aids should reduce existing excess capacity (thus giving the remaining capacity a chance to survive) and should facilitate diversification away from the areas of acute competitive pressure. Aids to existing activities were to be permitted, but they should be designed to enable the industries to become competitive. Had the last element not been present, the rules would have been exclusively designed to facilitate the contraction of the industry. The aid rules were revised in 1976, but some of the essential features of the 1972 system were retained. Thereafter, the Commission continued to monitor aids. By 1985 the Commission was able to report that substantial restructuring had taken place, that the industry had largely regained the competitiveness required for its survival and that it could no longer be regarded as a crisis industry. Clearly, the Commission was signalling that it would therefore be disposed to regard aid-giving as unjustified.

On the external side, the original posture of the Community towards textile imports from the third world was quite generous. This was reflected in the Arrangements Regarding International Trade in Textiles, more familiarly known as the Multi-Fibre Arrangements (MFA), the first of which was negotiated in 1973 and ran until the end of 1977. It related not only to textiles but also to fibres and clothing. The parties to it were the developed countries such as the EC, US and Japan, which were major markets for the above products, and a large number of supplier countries which for the most part could be called developing or newly industrializing countries (NICs). It did not allow the penetration of developed industrialized markets to proceed in a totally unregulated manner but did, subject to certain exceptions, allow for a liberal growth in imports of 6 per cent a year.

However, by 1977, when the negotiations for the second MFA were beginning, the mood of the importing countries had changed. The penetration of the NICs and recession had taken their toll. The attitude of the EC and the other importing parties stiffened. Discussions within the EC in 1976 revealed considerable pressure at national level for a more restrictive arrangement. In the event, although the second MFA (to run until the end of 1981) maintained the import growth ceiling at 6 per cent, it also provided for a 'most-sensitive product' range where there was to be virtually no growth. Just how restrictive this could be was demonstrated by the UK, where the most-sensitive product range accounted for 61 per cent of imports. The third MFA, which ran from the end of 1981 until the end of July 1986, continued the much tighter approach, but in the latest MFA, which ran until the end of 1994, a somewhat more relaxed stance was evident. Nevertheless import quotas continued to exist and, following the completion of the internal market, these now take the form not of national quotas but of a Community quota which is also managed by the Community. As a result of the Uruguay Round of trade negotiations it was agreed in 1993 that these import restrictions would be phased out over a ten year period.

In the case of synthetic fibres a critical excess-capacity problem emerged in the 1970s. The problem was so acute that in 1977 the Commission requested member states to refrain from giving any aid that would have the effect of adding to synthetic fibre capacity. Aids were, however, approved where they would reduce capacity. The industry also endeavoured in 1978 to eliminate the intense competition by securing approval for a cartel agreement designed to share out the market according to the level of deliveries made by each firm in 1976. Arrangements were also made for sharing any increase or decrease in demand. This episode illustrates the obstacles which any such scheme is likely to encounter given the pro-competition ethos of the Rome Treaty. While the industrial affairs directorate of the Commission was willing to sponsor the scheme, the competition directorate was opposed. Later the competition directorate indicated that it was possible to condone an agreement restricting competition provided it aimed solely to achieve a coordinated reduction of capacity, did not otherwise hamper independent decision-making, was not accompanied by unsuitable devices such as price fixing and quotas and was not hampered by state aids which preserved excess capacity. In 1984 an agreement to cut capacity which apparently met these criteria was approved. Nevertheless it should be regarded as an exceptional decision – it is difficult to resist the conclusion that the exemption did not conform to the rigorous criteria laid down in Article 85 (3).

Shipbuilding has for many years been a problem for the Community. In this case the difficulties began before the 1970s but the depressed conditions in that decade served to exacerbate them. The problem stemmed originally from what was called an 'aid rush' in which during the sixties countries outside the Community sought to build up their shipbuilding sector by granting subsidies. Member state governments had little alternative but to follow suit and the Commission recognized that this was likely to cause distortions of competition within the Community. It therefore sought to impose uniform aid ceilings which would prevent unfair competition within the EC and would compensate for the disadvantage suffered by virtue of aids given outside the EC. There have been seven such directives to date – the latest came into effect in 1991 and by virtue of it aid in 1992 was limited to 9 per cent of the selling price of a vessel.

In 1979 the Commission did endeavour to persuade the Council of Ministers to adopt a somewhat more *dirigiste* approach to the shipbuilding problem. In that year it addressed a Communication to Council proposing a scrap-and-build programme for ocean-going ships. A one-for-one (in terms of compensated registered tons) scrapping and building arrangement would have increased the orders flowing into Community shipyards but equally obviously it would not have made any contribution to reducing the excess capacity in the existing shipping fleet. A reduction of the latter was desirable since it would raise freight rates and would therefore increase the incentive to shipowners to order new ships. In order to achieve these objectives the Commission therefore proposed a two to one scrapping to building ratio with the possibility of Community involvement in the financing of the scheme. The Commission thus envisaged an arrangement which had a threefold virtue – it would create more work for the yards, it would eliminate surplus shipping capacity and it would modernize, and thus increase the competitiveness of, the Community's ocean-going fleet. Unfortunately the scheme was not adopted.

Iron and steel is an industry for which the Community has a special responsibility because, along with coal, it is, as we noted earlier, subject to the special régimes laid down under the Paris Treaty. Specific rules and procedures, described below, are prescribed which effectively call for competition but impose conditions in respect of price, output and investment decision-making.

We will discuss these before turning to an account of the way in which they were employed to deal with the structural difficulties first encountered during the 1970s.

(a) Cartels and Dominant Positions are subjected to control in ways broadly similar to Articles 85 and 86 of the Rome Treaty. A specific power to control mergers (including a requirement to notify) is provided.[1]

(b) Rules are laid down which govern the pricing offers which can be made. These rules call for price publicity. Prices must also be related to a geographical basing point, and quotations to customers take the form of the publicized basing point price plus transport costs (the latter are supposed to be transparent, i.e. publicized and thus known to all possible suppliers) from the basing point to the

1. Such antitrust rules also apply to coal.

customer. There is, however, considerable scope for competition. Under conditions of boom, steel firms will probably be able to charge the full basing point price plus transport cost. But if there is a recession in sales they can align their prices down. They can indeed align them down to *match* the lowest delivered price which any other producer within the Community could offer. Such an offer does not have to be made – it is sufficient that it could be made. In other words, knowing all the basing point prices of all other producers and knowing the transport charges of all other producers to the customer in question, any particular producer can push his quotation down to the lowest of those theoretically possible delivered prices. It is of course always open to a producer to notify a cut in his own basing point price, in which case he can make lower offers. Equally well, if some producers notify cuts in their basing point prices then other producers have more scope to align down to match them. Here we are referring to internal alignment – competition against other Community offers. In addition Community producers can align down to meet (actual) offers from non-Community sources. This is referred to as external alignment. During recessions, the Community steel industry has proved to be highly competitive. List prices have been cut and the alignment possibility has been used to the full as Community producers scrambled to obtain a share of diminished Community orders; this has been particularly noticeable when the export market has also been depressed. They have also competed vigorously against non-Community offers which in depressed world market conditions have come in at low, even artificially low, price levels.

(c) In conditions of manifest crisis the Commission can step in and fix prices, production quotas, etc. In other words, although price competition, subject to rules, is to be the order of the day, if it gets out of hand intervention is possible with a view to limiting the price fall. Given that before the Second World War the European steel industry was cartelized and had little experience of competition, it is hardly surprising that when faced with the prospect of free competition it should be felt prudent that a safety net be provided.

Procedures, which can also be viewed as a safety net, are prescribed for investment. Here the fear presumably was that free competition might lead to the creation of excessive productive capacity with a consequent possibility of ruinous pressure on prices.

Provision was therefore made for the exercise of official influence on the volume and direction of investment. A forecast of the likely evolution of demand is made, and the Commission then attempts to keep investment in productive capacity in line with that development. This is referred to as the General Objectives system. Excessive investment can be discouraged (but not prevented) by adverse official opinions on reported projects and by the withholding of a Community contribution to investment financing.

As we have observed, the Community steel industry proved to be highly competitive, much more so than the UK industry, which was shielded from internal competition – it operated price-fixing cartels, took the officially prescribed maximum prices (under the old Iron and Steel Board) as minima, or was nationalized. Not surprisingly, the Community steel industry was stimulated to increase efficiency. Thus in 1976 the West German industry required 18 man hours to produce a tonne of steel while the UK figure was 30. But on the other hand, although relatively efficient by UK standards, the steel industry of the old Six did not keep pace with developments in countries such as Japan. In 1976 the Japanese industry needed only 4 man hours to produce a tonne of steel!

From 1974 onwards, the steel industry of the Nine was in difficulties. The recession in the Community, and in the world market, greatly intensified internal competition. Community producers also had to contend with low offers from outside (e.g. Japan). During the height of the recession prices on occasions fell between 30 and 50 per cent below list levels, and the industry worked at as little as 60 per cent of its production capacity.

All this led the Community to introduce measures to deal with the factors which were driving companies towards bankruptcy. (In 1977 the British nationalized industry was reported to be losing getting on for £2 million per day.) This first led the Commission in 1976 to introduce the Simonet Plan. Henri Simonet was then the Commissioner responsible for steel. The plan began to operate at the beginning of 1977 and consisted of voluntary cooperation between the Commission and producers, whereby delivery programmes were suggested which would in effect prevent the market from being swamped, thus helping to pull prices back up. In 1977 Viscount Etienne Davignon took on the industrial portfolio. Under his guidance more drastic measures (called the Davignon Plan) were introduced. In the spring of 1977 (under Article 61 of the Paris Treaty) prices were prescribed for concrete reinforcing rods, and guidance prices were also laid down for a number of laminated products. Then in January 1978 minimum prices were also prescribed for merchant bars and coils, and for the first time steel stockholders were required to obey these minima. The Commission also negotiated agreements with foreign steel-supplying countries whereby they were required to restrain their exports to the Community market. In the interim, minimum reference prices were laid down for steel coming into the Community, and a penal duty was placed on shipments sold below these minimum levels.

All this served to improve the profitability of the steel industry. In 1978 and 1979 prices improved. However, in 1980 the voluntary restraint on output collapsed. There was a scramble for orders, prices fell and the Commission was forced to declare a manifest crisis and impose mandatory output and sales quotas. The Commission had in fact assumed a monopolistic control of the industry.

Not surprisingly, the difficulties of the steel industry led member states to grant aids to their industries. As in the case of textiles, the Commission has had to control these. In 1981 the Commission persuaded Council to adopt a new aid code. Undertakings benefiting from aids had to be engaged in implementing a systematic and specific restructuring programme. Such programmes should lead to an overall reduction in production capacity and should not add to capacity in areas for which there was no growth market. Aids should be progressively reduced – the code envisaged the final phasing out of aid-giving by the end of 1985. In the interim, the Commission was given the task of supervising the application of the code.

In fact the Commission did decide that from the end of 1985 a new aid code should operate. This prohibited all operating aids and all aids intended to finance investment. However, aid towards protection of the environment, for R & TD and for closures was to be permitted but under strict conditions. In 1985 the Commission also persuaded the Council to make a start on removing the quota system which had been instituted back in 1980. This however proved to be a long drawn-out process since the Commission had to try to persuade producers to accept cuts in production capacity so that free competition without quotas would produce profitable price levels. Eventually cuts were promised and it was decided that quotas should end in 1990.

However, this return to free competition in steel, which had disappeared in the nineteen seventies, did not long survive. The recession of the early nineteen nineties soon led to a price collapse and not surprisingly subsidies were once more being demanded by the uncompetitive producers. In 1993 the Commission agreed to subsidies but demanded capacity cuts in return – the old story. It also wanted the non-aided sector to agree to cuts so that in total at least 19 million tonnes of capacity would be closed down. Understandably the more efficient producers did not respond kindly to this proposal. The promised cuts fell short of target and in 1994 the plan was virtually given up as dead. However a controversial interpretation by the Commission of the aid rules enabled the Italian government to agree to some capacity cuts which were expected to produce overall a cut of 16 to 17 million tonnes. The non-aided producers regarded the Italian offer with much scepticism since they looked for closures and clearly suspected that the aid would not really get rid of excess capacity for good. In November 1994 the Commission once more decided to abandon its restructuring plan.

Maastricht and After

Two developments need to be added. Whilst the original Rome Treaty contained no industrial policy competence, all that has now changed. As a result of the Treaty on European Union a new Article 130 has been added which in effect adds an industrial policy competence to the Rome Treaty. However, too much should not be made up of this change. It does not appear to provide the basis for a *dirigiste* industrial policy. The new article emphasizes the desirability of open and competitive markets and expressly precludes any measures which distort competition. Measures agreed in the Council of Ministers will require unanimity and significantly must be in support of actions taken by member states.

The industrial policy concerns of the Community have in recent years given increasing prominence to the problem of maintaining the competitiveness of European industry. The Eurosclerosis which has affected the Community since the nineteen seventies has been defined in terms of a relative decline in economic performance as well as a failure to make progress with closer economic and political union. It has been recognized that European industry has lost competitiveness, that the rate of growth has slowed down and that unemployment has risen cycle by cycle. This prompted the European Council at Copenhagen in 1993 to commission Jacques Delors to produce a white paper on Eurosclerosis. The result – *Growth Competitiveness and Employment* (EC Commission, 1993) noted that the role of the Community was a limited one. Rather it was up to member states to review and modify their approaches to education, vocational training, labour laws, employment and redundancy practices, provisions relating to geographical mobility, their social security system and the ways in which such systems heaped non-wage costs on employers, etc. Nevertheless, the Community had a contribution to make. First, the single market programme needed to be completed and implemented. Second, R & TD activity needed to be strengthened. Third, Trans-European Networks might not create a vast number of jobs but they would add to efficiency, as would information highways. Both these have been studied and indeed a programme of transport networks was approved in June 1994.

The Consumer

A specific policy-making competence relating to consumer protection was not contained in the original Rome Treaty. That did not mean that consumer protection dimension did not feature in the Council of Ministers' legislative agenda. For example, in Chapter 5 we referred to the directive on product-related injury. But such consumer protection measures were incidental – they arose as part of the need to create a level playing field within the competitive single market. The Maastricht Treaty has changed all this. Article 129a has been inserted in the Rome Treaty. It calls upon the Community to contribute to high level of protection not only via single market measures of the kind just referred to but also via any kind of measure which protects the health, safety and economic interests of consumers.

Fisheries

A discussion of industrial policy provides as relevant a location as any for a brief review of policy in respect of the fishing industry. A common fishing policy has been on the agenda for a long time, but it was not until 1983 that final agreement was achieved. Having said that, we should also note that the original Six were able to achieve a common position as early as 1970. Regulations were adopted, operative from the beginning of 1971, which were based on the principle of free and equal access for all EC fishermen to Community fishing waters and a free market for fish within the Community. Exceptions were, however, provided. The Six in fact managed to put this agreement together rather conveniently, in that four countries with significant fishing interests were about to join. Indeed, the fact that something of a *fait accompli* seemed to exist was one reason why Norway finally decided not to join. Arrangements were, however, made for the three new members. These included a general exclusive six-mile zone for fishermen of the coastal states, together with a twelve-mile exclusive zone in some areas. But unless the common fishery policy was reviewed these exclusive areas would become Community waters after 1982. This was not an acceptable long-term solution as far as the new members were concerned – they were giving up a lot and getting little in return.

There was therefore scope for possible future discord, but for a time the focus of concern switched to the international level. Between 1974 and 1976 the third United Nations Conference on the Law of the Sea (UNCLOS III) was in session, and in its deliberations the question of the extension of national fishing limits to 200 miles figured prominently. Prior to the conclusion of UNCLOS III, some of the Nine were in favour of going ahead with such an extension. It was, however, decided to await the conclusion of the conference. In fact, a binding international agreement failed to emerge from the final session and, following the Canadian, Norwegian and US announcements to the effect that they intended to extend their limits to 200 miles, the Community decided to do likewise. This agreement, reached at The Hague in October 1976, was also partly precipitated by threats of unilateral action, most notably from the UK. The extension was to take effect from the beginning of 1977. The Commission was also charged with carrying on negotiations with non-members. Clearly, in the absence of specific agreements the 200-mile limit would exclude countries which had previously fished in what was now being referred to as the Community pond. If they were to be allowed to fish then questions arose as to how large a catch they could be allowed and whether they would reciprocate in respect of their own waters. The Commission identified three categories of third-country negotiations. There were countries where reciprocity was possible, e.g. Iceland and Norway. There were countries with little or no interest in Community waters but with possible surpluses in their own waters to which access might be allowed, e.g. US and Canada. Finally there were those who had an interest in the Community pond but had little to offer in return, e.g. Eastern European states.

By 1976 the internal problem now began to loom again. Was it really going to be a Community pond with completely free access or would states be able to enjoy exclusive zones permanently? Alternatively, or perhaps in conjunction with such an arrangement, would the Community opt for some overall catch, perhaps reduced on conservation grounds, which would be allocated between states on a percentage basis? Since the common 200-mile limit meant that countries such as the UK and Ireland lost access to important fishing grounds (e.g. Iceland), what, if any, kind of compensation would be allowed within the pond allocation?

The UK set out by regarding the 12-mile limit as quite inadequate. Its initial policy stance was to demand a 100-mile exclusive zone, although this was subsequently dropped to 50 miles. Subsequently, the idea of a solution based purely on exclusive zones was given less emphasis, and more attention was paid to the idea of an absolute catch level divided into national quotas. In late 1977 the Commission suggested possible quotas, the UK figure being almost 30 per cent. This did not match her demands (45 per cent), which in part reflected her desire for compensation for lost access elsewhere.

In the final analysis, the agreement which was achieved in 1983 consisted of a mixture of zones and quotas. The Common Fisheries Policy (CFP) had four main ingredients and had much in common with the CAP. These four ingredients related to access to fishing grounds, devices for conserving fish stocks, measures to influence fish prices (and therefore the incomes of fishermen) and financial assistance towards improving the structure of the Community fishing fleet.

In respect of access to the market, the CFP allowed member states to retain limits of up to twelve miles for their own fleets and for other fishing nations which enjoyed historic rights in the twelve-mile zone. Beyond this zone all waters within the 200-mile limit were in principle open to all Community fishermen. However, a conservation box was placed around the Orkneys and Shetland Isles, and fishing for potentially endangered species there was subjected to limited licence arrangements.

In order to conserve fish stocks a variety of devices were introduced. Total Allowable Catches (TACs) were calculated for various species. Some of these catches were allocated to non-EC states who enjoyed fishing rights in Community waters. The rest of the TACs were divided into national quotas. These national quotas rose or fell according to the state of fish stocks. In addition a variety of other measures were brought to bear by way of conservation. These included minimum mesh sizes for nets, minimum landing sizes for fish and bans on the catching of certain species. In December 1990 in areas of the North Sea concentrations of immature cod were such that it was decided to require boats to stay in port for eight days in each month.

The implementation of the CFP lay with each member state but in addition the Community employed inspectors to see that the member states were playing by the rules! The Commission set guide prices for fish and below them were withdrawal prices. When prices fell to around withdrawal levels supplies could be withdrawn from the market. The Community budget provided finance (a) to compensate for such withdrawals, (b) to cover the cost of storage or conversion to other uses and (c) to provide export refunds.

Community finance was available for structural improvements in fishing. The emphasis was on modernization and withdrawal of capacity on a temporary or permanent basis. Recently, generous assistance has been made available to assist in the contraction of capacity – an essential feature of the conservation programme.

In 1992 the CFP was reformed. Basic features such as TACs, quotas, the 12-mile band, the Shetland box, etc. were retained. But certain new features were introduced in 1993 including the inauguration of a fishing licence scheme and new and tightened-up monitoring arrangements.

The environment

Before we proceed any further it is important to recognize that the Community's approach to the environment has had, and continues to have, both an international and an internal aspect. The account below is concerned with what may be termed internal issues. But in addition the Community has in recent years been drawn into international discussions on the global environment. We touched on some of these issues earlier when we recognized that the need to control the emission of carbon dioxide is now acting as a major constraint on the formulation of the Common Energy Policy (see Chapter 7). The Community has also been involved in international discussions concerning the depletion of the ozone layer caused by the release of chlorofluorocarbons (CFCs) and halons, although other substances such as carbon tetrachloride and methyl chloroform are also understood to have the same effect. The Community is a signatory to the Vienna Convention on the ozone layer, the Montreal Protocol on CFCs and the 1990 London and the 1992 Copenhagen amendments thereto. The Council of Ministers adopted appropriate Regulations in 1988, 1991 and 1992. More recently the Commission had taken the view that the Community should adopt a progressive approach to phasing out, and in 1993 proposed that CFCs should be phased out by 2016 and that production and consumption of methyl bromide should be reduced by 25 per cent by 1996.

Following the signing of the Rome Treaty increasing emphasis was laid on environmental issues in terms of pollution, other forms of degradation of the environment and the exhaustion of resources. On the face of it, however, the treaty contained no explicit reference to these kinds of issue and appeared not to provide the Community with a power to act in such matters. Nevertheless the Community did go on to develop an environmental policy. This followed the Paris Summit of 1972 when the Heads of State and of Government called for the introduction of such a policy. But how were the directives that emerged justified in legal terms?

The justification was twofold. The Community was from time to time forced to deal with environmental issues which arose in connection with the approximation or harmonization of national laws under Articles 100 and 101. For example, member states impose rules concerning the emission of exhaust gases by motor cars. To the extent that these differ from state to state, cross-frontier trade in cars could be inhibited. Inevitably, in such cases the harmonization of national laws involved the Community in making decisions on the question of pollution standards. In addition Article 2 of the original Rome Treaty outlined in a broad way the tasks of the Community which included 'a continued and balanced expansion' and 'an accelerated raising of the standard of living'. It was therefore argued that action on environmental issues was a necessary part of such a programme. Once this was accepted then Article 235 was ready to hand to enable the Community to take whatever *additional* powers were necessary to achieve environmental objectives. Not everyone was happy with this broad interpretation but it was never fundamentally challenged.

All this was transformed by the Single European Act, which inserted a new Title into the Rome Treaty expressly concerned with the environment. The new Article 130r declared that Community action in relation to the environment should seek to preserve, protect and improve the quality of the environment, contribute to the protection of human health and ensure a prudent and rational utilization of natural resources. It went on to say that preventive action should be based on the principle that the polluter pays and that in developing policies account should be taken of the potential benefits and costs of action or inaction. Action on the environment was based on the unanimity requirement in the Council of Ministers. However, an environmental measure that was connected to the creation of the single market was to be based on the Article 100a system which, as we noted earlier, allowed for qualified majority voting. The Maastricht Treaty reaffirmed the Community competence in environmental matters but has added a number of complications. First, Article 130r was revamped and now declares that actions on the environment shall aim at a high level of protection – previously this only applied to environmental actions connected with the single market. Second old Article 130s has been replaced by a new Article 130s which provides for a variety of possible decision-making mechanisms – e.g. the Council may operate in cooperation with, may co-legislate with or may merely consult, the Parliament. The Single Act imposed a subsidiarity requirement on the Community when contemplating environmental measures. This does not reappear in Article 130r. But this is not significant because subsidiarity under Maastricht is a general principle and does not need to be reiterated in respect of each policy competence.

Community environmental policy has generated some tensions between the member states and between individual member states and the Commission. While the dedicated environmentalist would regard it as desirable that all pollution should be eliminated, most economists do not take such a view. Rather they aim for the optimum degree of pollution – in other words it may be necessary to accept the existence of some pollution. Some pollution is acceptable because beyond a point in the clean-up process the benefits to be derived from getting rid of a bit more pollution are less than the costs of getting rid of it. In the early days there appeared to be some possibility that some states were in favour of proceeding towards the extreme position of eliminating all the pollution that it was technically feasible to eliminate. On the other hand, the UK adopted a different stance which essentially boiled down to the economist's view that the costs and benefits had to be weighed against each other. In the end, something like the economist's view prevailed at Community level and following the Single European Act a weighing of costs and benefits is quite clearly the required approach.

When pollution is under consideration the economist's approach is to say that it should be dealt with by internalizing the (disbeneficial) externality. A logical way to do that is to impose an appropriate level of tax on the polluter – we are assuming that it is possible to place a monetary value on the disbeneficial effect which is sustained by the rest of society. In practice, the imposition of taxes is not the approach normally adopted in the Community. Rather, the Community tends to proceed by way of imposing standards – i.e. in respect of emission levels or in terms of the effect on the environment. The reader will note that the Polluter Pays Principle (PPP) is now enshrined in the Rome Treaty. This is not a new development in Community thinking – its adoption goes back to 1973/74. The adoption of PPP is often taken to imply an acceptance of a tax-based solution. But in the case of the Community it means no more than that the costs of controlling the pollution are borne by the polluter. In other words the polluter will not receive subsidies to enable it to conform. The 1974 Communication by the Commission on this subject did, however, envisage some exceptions. Such a general approach is not necessarily optimal.

National differences have also surfaced in respect of the standards to be attained by anti-pollution activity. One approach is to lay down uniform emission standards. But the alternative is to set standards by reference to the impact that pollution has on the quality of the environment. In the end the member states have usually been given a choice.

The first environmental action programme was introduced in 1973, while the fifth runs from 1992 to 2000. The Community has introduced approximately 500 environmental measures. It would be boring in the extreme to attempt to list them all, so we will indicate the main developments. A considerable list of measures has been introduced which is designed to combat water pollution. Two approaches have been adopted. Minimum-quality standards for receiving water have been set depending on the water's final use, such as drinking or bathing. Directives have also been designed to prevent the discharge of dangerous substances which because of their toxicity and persistence pose a major threat to health and the environment. Cadmium and mercury are just two of the dangerous products for which specific directives have been introduced. The UK was notorious for its failure to come up to standard in respect of both drinking and bathing water. The Community has also produced a raft of directives concerning noise levels in relation to household appliances, hydraulic diggers, tower cranes, lawn mowers, aircraft and replacements for motorcycle exhausts. A significant programme of action has been set on foot to curb air pollution. Air quality standards have been set, with guide and limit values for sulphur dioxide, lead and nitrogen oxide. Rules have also been introduced concerning product quality. A directive was issued which fixed the maximum sulphur content for gas (but not heavy fuel) oil and another set a limit to the lead content in petrol. The clean car initative has included not only measures to encourage lead-free petrol but also to reduce the level of pollutants contained in vehicle exhaust gases. Directives have been introduced controlling the marketing and use of dangerous chemicals and other substances including asbestos, PCB and PCT. Standards have been devised in relation to the management of waste and the transport of hazardous wastes. In 1990 the Council adopted two directives setting precise guidelines for the contained use of genetically modified organisms and their release into the environment.

Two relatively recent decisions need to be highlighted. The first was the 1990 agreement to set up a European Environmental Agency. In 1993 it was decided that it should be located in Copenhagen. The second is the key principle, contained in the fifth action programme, that environmental considerations must no longer be regarded as peripheral. They must be absolutely central in all policy making – hence the environmental dimension of the McSharry reform of the CAP.

11

GLOBAL TRADING RELATIONSHIPS

The European Communities have some form of trade or economic cooperation agreement with virtually every country in the world. The purpose of this chapter is to review the various categories of relationship. Before we do so it is instructive to consider Table 21 where the structure of the Communities' trade both internal and external is set out.

The structure of Community trade

Roughly 60 per cent of the foreign trade of the Twelve in 1992 was intra-EC trade and it thus follows that trade with the rest of the world constituted the remaining 40 per cent or so of total foreign trade. The Twelve collectively had a modest trade deficit with the rest of the world. EFTA was the major trading partner in the industrialized world, followed by the US and Japan. The Twelve had a trade deficit with all three. The deficit position relative to the US has fluctuated. Before 1984 the Communities were in deficit with the US. This turned into a surplus, but in 1989 it was back in deficit and remained so in 1992. The deficit with Japan is large and persistent and we shall return to this issue later. The Communities were broadly in balance with developing countries as a whole. They were modestly in deficit with the countries of Eastern Europe but markedly in deficit with state trading countries – in practice this means mainly China. Looking at specific country groups within the extra-EC trade category, we note that the Twelve had a surplus with the Mediterranean basin, and deficits with OPEC, ASEAN and Latin America. The OPEC deficit was less than in some previous years.

Table 21. The Trade[1] of the Twelve in 1992

	Imports from	Exports to	Balance[4]
World	1 207 269	1 136 487	− 70 782
Intra-EC	719 595	700 832	—
Extra-EC	487 674	435 655	− 52 070
of which			
Western industrialized third countries	287 800	239 867	− 47 933
of which			
EFTA	111 616	107 698	− 3 918
US	86 766	73 905	− 12 861
Japan	51 508	20 505	− 31 003
South Africa	9 097	5 420	− 3 677
Australia	4 709	6 348	+ 1 639
Developing countries	145 717	152 818	+ 7 101
of which			
ACP[2]	17 955	17 047	− 908
Overseas countries and territories	1 734	9 426	+ 7 511
Central and East European countries	24 159	22 997	− 1 162
State Trading countries	17 537	7 726	− 9 811
of which			
China	16 780	6 850	− 9 930
Trade with specific country groups included in extra-EC category			
Mediterranean basin	41 163	45 392	+ 43 229
OPEC	42 743	42 010	− 733
Latin America	24 505	20 050	− 4 455
ASEAN[3]	22 403	19 278	− 3 125

Notes:
1. Million ECUs.
2. Lomé Convention countries – i.e. ex-colonial dependencies.
3. Association of South-East Asian Nations.
4. Exports minus imports.

Source: Statistical Office of the European Communities, *External Trade Monthly Statistics*, 1994, no. 8–9.

The Common Commercial Policy

Following Maastricht, the Rome Treaty (Articles 110, 112, 113 and 115) requires the EC to develop a Common Commercial Policy (CCP) – which should aim to contribute to the harmonious development of world trade and to the progressive removal of barriers. The centre-piece of the CCP is the Common External Tariff (CET). As we indicated in Chapter 4, all member states must apply the CET – unilateral changes are ruled out. In any GATT (General Agreement on Tariffs and Trade) negotiations concerned with the level of the CET, the negotiating mandate will be laid down by the Council of Ministers. The actual negotiations will be carried out by the Commission, which will be advised by a special committee set up by the Council. The final agreement will be ratified by the Council. The CCP also requires member states to bring their *quantitative* restrictions into line, and negotiations about quantitative limits (e.g. the Multi-Fibre Arrangements discussed in Chapter 10) are conducted by the Commission, on behalf of the members, against a similar organizational background. Following the single market these quotas are now Community quotas. The CCP also requires the member states to establish common principles in respect of (a) the systems under which aid is given in relation to exports to third countries (some implementing steps have been taken), (b) export policy (see Chapter 4 for an account of the New Commercial Policy Instrument) and (c) protection from unfair import competition (see Chapter 4 for anti-dumping rules, etc.).

Let us look a little more closely at the centre-piece – the CET. At the end of the Second World War, when the major economic powers were seeking to devise a new world economic order, they envisaged two international bodies. One was to deal with monetary matters, the other was to be concerned with trade. The IMF was the product of the first aspiration. It was anticipated that an International Trade Organization (ITO) would be responsible for the second. In fact the ITO never came into being. Nevertheless, negotiations concerning tariffs were held in Geneva in 1947, and these led to the signing of the GATT. The GATT system has continued to be the focal point of international trade bargaining. GATT gave rise to rules concerning international trade matters. These required that tariff bargaining should be based on reciprocity and should not give rise to discrimination. The latter was particularly important in the context of EC trade policy. It implied that if a country offered to cut its import duties on goods coming from country A, then it should also apply that treatment to all other countries – this is called most-favoured-nation treatment. The reader may wonder how the Community was able to form a customs union and still stay within GATT rules. Obviously, a customs union is discriminatory – import tariffs on partner goods are eliminated but are maintained on goods coming from third countries. The answer to that question is quite simple. GATT provided an exception in the case of customs unions (and free-trade areas). Various rules were devised, including the requirement that in the case of a customs union the CET should on the whole be no higher than the general incidence of the duties which the parties had imposed prior to the union. The EC drew attention to the fact that the CET was based on an arithmetical average of the previous national duties and that therefore it had not breached GATT rules.

If the EC had left matters at that then there would be little more to discuss. As far as tariffs are concerned we would merely have to record that all non-members have had to face the CET. In fact, matters did not end with a non-discriminatory CET. Rather, the EC chose to conclude a variety of trade agreements in which different groups were treated differently, and within given groupings (e.g. developing or industrialized economies) different treatments were accorded. To the evolution of this situation we now turn.

Part Four Association

The Part Four Association provisions are to be found in Articles 131 to 136. They were devised in order to accommodate the interests of the dependent or formerly dependent territories of the member states. Countries which benefited from Part Four Association arrangements came to be the most favoured third countries.

During the negotiations leading up to the Rome Treaty, the French vigorously pressed the idea of associating overseas territories. The Spaak Report (Spaak, 1956) made no mention of them, and it was only at the Venice meeting of foreign ministers in May 1956 that France, by making association a condition of going ahead with the scheme for a common market, got the subject on the agenda. The French had good reasons for taking this line. First, they regarded the overseas territories as an extension of France, but a customs union of the Six would definitely discriminate against them. Secondly, France bore a considerable burden both in the form of aid and relatively high prices for colonial raw materials. It felt that the Six should be placed on a more equal footing by taking on part of the financial responsibility. This was further emphasized by the fact that countries such as Germany were investing in commercial enterprises in the French dependencies and therefore derived much advantage from French expenditure on the necessary infrastructures. The overseas dependencies were listed in Annexe IV and included French West Africa, French Equatorial Africa, the French Trustee territory in the Cameroons, Madagascar, a range of other French overseas settlements and Togoland, the Belgian Congo and Ruanda Urundi, the Italian Trustee territory of Somalia and Netherlands New Guinea. The Netherlands Antilles was added in 1964.

The original basis of association was concluded for five years. Thirty-one countries were covered – all of them dependencies. These latter were referred to as Overseas Countries and Territories (OCTs). The broad thrust of the association arrangements, which had a double character, was as follows. The Community undertook to reduce its tariffs on goods coming from the dependencies in line with internal tariff disarmament. This was a vital concession in so far as the primary products supplied by non-associated states faced the Community's common external tariff. The dependent territories were required to reciprocate but could, however, retain protection needed for their development, industrialization or revenue, provided they extended to all member states the preferences they had previously extended to the mother country. The Treaty also brought into existence the European Development Fund (EDF) which was to channel aid to the associated territories. Such EDF aid is a notable feature of association under Part Four. The Six agreed that over the first five years they would make available $581.25 million. France and West Germany subscribed $200 million, Italy $40 million, Belgium and the Netherlands $70 million each and Luxembourg $1.25 million. French territories obtained no less than $511.25 million of this aid. It should perhaps be added that owing to administrative and technical difficulties there was a considerable delay in disbursing this money.

By 1960 many of the OCTs had become independent, and a new basis for association was required. Therefore in 1961 and 1962 negotiations took place, and these in turn led to the Yaoundé Convention. Yaoundé I ran from 1 July 1964 and Yaoundé II came into force on 1 January 1971. The signatories of the former were eighteen in number and were described as the Associated African States and Madagascar (AASM). In Yaoundé II the eighteen were joined by Mauritius. Trade and aid arrangements were also devised in respect of the remaining OCTs. Broadly speaking, Yaoundé I and II were concluded on the following lines. Tropical products entered the Community free of duty. In some cases where competition arose, duty-free quotas were prescribed. In the case of industrial products, preferential access to the EC was allowed but they might be subject to quotas. There was no requirement for the AASM to reciprocate in respect of the Community's exports – they could if necessary introduce or maintain protective duties and quotas. Aid was also provided. Under Yaoundé I, 666 million UA was made available by the EDF together with 64 million from the EIB. Under Yaoundé II, the aid level was raised to 828 million UA from the EDF and 90 million from the EIB. In addition an institutional framework, including a Council of Ministers, was established.

Inevitably, the preferences granted to the associated states gave rise to criticism. The Latin American states in particular called upon the EC to abolish its preferential system, and as a result the EC agreed to reduce the CET on tropical products from third countries generally. As a consolation, the AASM were allowed to benefit from a reduction in the defences enjoyed by Community agricultural producers under the CAP. The AASM too began to find the Yaoundé system less beneficial. This arose from the fact that the Community decided to grant preferential access to other groups. In 1971 it introduced the General System of Preferences (see below), and from 1972 it decided to develop a global Mediterranean Policy (see below). It was partly in order to compensate for these changes that the Community decided to step up the level of convention aid.

As Yaoundé II neared its end, the question of its successor fell due for consideration. Two factors suggested that the formula was in need of modification. First, there was the decline in the value of preferential access – a point we have just made. Secondly, as a result of the 1973 enlargement a lot of other ex-colonial dependencies were now in the queue for association benefits – i.e. those of the UK.

The solution was the Lomé Convention of 1975, which was hailed as a breakthrough in the relationships between the developed and the developing. Negotiated under Article 238, it brought together the nineteen AASM – the original Yaoundé states plus Mauritius – and twenty-one less developed Commonwealth countries. In addition there were five outsiders and Guinea, thus making forty-six in all who collectively were called the African, Caribbean and Pacific States (ACP). Lomé I was followed in 1981 by Lomé II, and in 1986 Lomé III entered into operation. Lomé IV, which takes in 69 countries collectively constituting more than a third of the UN, was signed in December 1989. It will run for ten years from 1990 although the Financial Protocol covered only the first five years and is negotiable thereafter.

What are the essential features of the present Lomé system? First the ACP states enjoy tariff preferences for their exports to the Community. Indeed, over 99 per cent of the ACP exports entering the Community market do so free of tariff. It should be mentioned that the ACP countries depend on the Community market for some 40 per cent of their exports, most which are primary commodities. While this sounds generous it has to be recognized that there have been exceptions to this liberal treatment. We are of course referring to products covered by the CAP. These have been subject to protection – limits on the quantities imported, the imposition of import duties, exporters required to impose export taxes, etc. The Community, on the other hand, points in its defence to the fact that a quota of sugar is purchased at a guaranteed price. This is intended to compensate ACP cane sugar producers who would otherwise suffer as a result of the UK joining the Community and demand being diverted to EC beet sugar sources. The Community also argues that under Lomé IV access for agricultural products has been improved. For example, the overall quota for beef and veal imports has been increased and ACP exporters will no longer be required to levy an export tax in return for the 90 per cent cut in levies accorded by the Community. All the Community requires in return is non-preferential and non-discriminatory most-favoured-nation treatment – a concept we discussed earlier.

The other main aspect of Lomé IV is concerned with aid. The new convention has made available 12,000 million ECUs for the period 1990–95. This is a 20 per cent increase in real terms compared with Lomé III. The EDF will provide 10,800 million ECUs and the EIB will provide 1,200 million ECUs in loans. The EDF contribution will consist of 7,995 million ECUs in grants, 825 million ECUs in risk capital, 1,500 million ECUs for STABEX and 480 million ECUs for SYSMIN. The latter two require some further explanation.

STABEX was introduced under Lomé I. Under this arrangement, funds are provided for ACP countries to cover shortfalls in earnings brought about by fluctuations in the price or output of agricultural products exported to EC countries. There is also a provision whereby countries which by virtue of their geographical position do not have the EC as a main outlet can have their exports to all destinations taken into consideration. The number of commodities covered by the STABEX scheme was progressively increased, and under Lomé IV forty-nine are covered. STABEX aid usually takes the form of grants, but in the case of the more developed ACP states it may consist of interest-free loans. SYSMIN (Special financing facility for ACP and OCT mining products) was introduced under Lomé II. It is directed towards ACP states which are heavily dependent on mining exports to the Community and is designed to remedy harmful effects on their incomes caused by serious temporary disruptions affecting the mining sector. Assistance in this case usually takes the form of loans.

To these existing special instruments has been added a new mechanism for rapid economic assistance. It has a funding of 1,150 million ECUs – it is included in the EDF total above. The new mechanism is designed to enable the Community to help to preserve social stability and to make a significant contribution to any necessary structural adjustment policies.

A number of OCTs still exist – e.g. St Helena, the Netherlands Antilles and New Caledonia. Similar types of arrangement have been made for them.

As we have indicated, the ACP states and OCTs enjoy a privileged status. They do not of course constitute the whole of the developing world. Nor do they take in all the developing countries of the Commonwealth – the reader will not have noticed any reference to India or Pakistan, to cite but two examples.

Association under Article 238

So far, the discussion has been about the association provisions which were designed in the first instance for the benefit of the colonial dependencies of the Six. In addition, Article 238 provides for association generally. The Community may indeed conclude with a third country, with a group of third countries or with an international organization an agreement which gives rise to an association involving reciprocal rights and obligations. We will illustrate this possibility with respect to two sets of countries within the Mediterranean Basin and EFTA.

The Mediterranean policy is an interesting one because it has concerned developing countries who have enjoyed relatively privileged access to the Community market even though they did not fall into the same ex-colonial category as the ACP. The Commission put forward proposals for a global Mediterranean policy in September 1972, and the policy was agreed in principle at the Paris Summit in October that year. The Council of Ministers agreed on the main guidelines the following month.

The essential features of the Mediterranean policy in its most generous form were to be as follows. The Mediterranean countries would enjoy tariff-free entry to the Community market for their industrial goods. The Community would not demand reciprocity but would be content with most-favoured-nation treatment. Agriculture would have to be treated in a different way, since the CAP precluded free access for imported agricultural produce. However, tariff reductions could be accorded to imported Mediterranean agricultural produce. But this concession would in practice be a limited one, since the most important form of protection was minimum import prices, and that would not be dropped. Financial assistance in the form of grants and loans, together with other forms of cooperation, would be made available.

The Maghreb agreement of 1976 (Algeria, Morocco and Tunisia) and the Mashrek agreement of 1977 (Egypt, Lebanon, Jordan and

Syria) were examples of the above approach. It should be noted, however, that recession and foreign competition forced the Community to impose restrictions on imports into the Community. While some of these related to products which were not of importance to Mediterranean producers, some, such as textiles, were. Even if the quotas were generous, they were bound to inhibit plans for industrial development based on the expectation of absolutely free access.

These Mediterranean agreements may however prove to be only an interim phase in the relationship of the Communities to their southern neighbours. In October 1994 the Commission launched a plan which envisaged a new relationship similar to that of the European Economic Area agreement with EFTA (see Chapter 1). Full membership is not, of course in prospect.

- The other group of Mediterranean countries to whom brief reference must be made includes Malta, Cyprus and Turkey. All three are involved in association agreements. All three are aspirants for full membership. Turkey however faces a threefold problem. First, it is economically backward and whilst this has not proved to be an obstacle in the past, it does create difficulties when it arises in a relatively populous state such as Turkey. Second, while the Cyprus issue is unresolved Greece will block Turkey's full membership. Third, the European Parliament has been critical of Turkey's record on human rights and will oppose Turkey's membership until it is satisfied on this issue. The applications of Malta and Cyprus are on the table and will be addressed after 1996. The Cypriot application is not likely to be resolved until the problem of the division of the island has been satisfactorily addressed.

The position with respect to EFTA has already been covered in Chapter 1. Most of the original members of EFTA have now become full members – i.e. the UK, Denmark, Austria, Finland, Sweden and Portugal. Norway, Iceland and Leichtenstein have remained in the EEA. Switzerland continues with the free trade relationship it established as an EFTA member when the UK and Denmark deserted the fold in 1973.

Outsiders – the developing world

Not all developing countries have enjoyed the same privileged access to the Community as those who have participated in Lomé and in the Mediterranean arrangement. Earlier we pointed out that countries in Latin America had been particularly vociferous in calling for an end to the preferential system operated by the EC. At the second United Nations Conference on Trade and Development (UNCTAD) in 1968, the Six showed a general willingness to shift ground. This brings us face to face with the idea of a generalized preference system, which was raised at the first UNCTAD in 1964. The general implication of this idea for the Community was that it should give a generalized preference to developing countries rather than be selective. If developing countries were to expand their output of manufactured and semi-manufactured goods, they would need outlets in the markets of developed countries. The outlets would in fact take the form of a tariff preference for developing countries in respect of these goods – that is to say, in the case of the EC it would levy a lower rate of duty on imports from developing countries than from developed ones. At the second UNCTAD the idea of generalized preferences was formally accepted and the rich nations agreed to make offers.

Negotiations followed, and a generalized preference plan was worked out. In March 1971 the Six agreed that in July 1971 it would introduce generalized preferences. They were in fact to run for ten years. In December 1980 the Council of Ministers agreed to extend the arrangement for a further ten years – 1981 to 1990 – and to modify the conditions.

Under the Generalized System of Preferences (GSP), imports into the Community from developing countries were exempted from customs duties, although the quantity of goods was not unlimited but was subject to ceilings or quotas. The Commission has explained (a) that the GSP was generalized in that the preferences were granted by the majority of industrialized countries, (b) that the preferences were non-discriminatory, (c) that they were autonomous (did not have to be negotiated), and (d) that they were non-reciprocal.

While the GSP sounded fine in principle, it clearly was not a substitute for the more generous access arrangements which had been accorded to other groups. Robert Hine, in a very penetrating study of EC trade arrangements, has argued that it was a very disappointing exercise. This he says was a result of an amalgam of factors. First, the impact was small because of the exclusion of some products from the scheme. Secondly, in respect of products which were included, strict quantitative limits were applied to the tariff-free treatment – this was obviously bound to be so in the case of 'sensitive' products such as textiles where the Multi-Fibre Arrangement was at work. Thirdly, a high share of the benefits tended to go to a relatively small group of the better-off NICs. Fourthly, the scheme was complex in operation – unnecessarily large stocks had had to be held, and some countries were not ultimately able to benefit from the scheme (Hine, 1985, pp. 196–211).

The scheme was again renewed – this time until 1994, when the Commission put forward new proposals for its operation from 1995 to 2004. Some of the modifications contained in the new proposal will hopefully make it more beneficial for developing countries.

The Community has also established cooperative contacts with both South-East Asia and Latin America. In the case of the former, it concluded its first cooperation agreement with the Association of South-East Asian Nations (ASEAN) in 1980. The members of ASEAN are Indonesia, Malaysia, the Philippines, Singapore and Thailand. Apart from some limited financial aid, and other forms of cooperation, the main element of the arrangement is the possibility of benefiting from the GSP. The Community has also concluded cooperation agreements with individual countries – e.g. Sri Lanka. In the case of Latin America, the Community signed cooperation agreements as early as 1983. In 1990 an economic and political dialogue between the Community and Latin American states was institutionalized under the Rome Declaration of 20 December of that year.

The Community is a substantial provider of Food Aid. The idea of food aid for poorer countries originated in 1967. It arose out of the Food Aid Convention which was created as part of the Kennedy Round of GATT tariff negotiations. Community food aid efforts, as distinct from member state efforts, began in 1969. In 1993 this assistance took the form of gifts of cereals, vegetable oil, milk powder and sugar. Some of this aid is routine, some is designed to deal with emergencies in various parts of the developing world.

Outsiders coming in

Until 1989 trading relationships between the Community and the Central and Eastern Europe Countries (CEECs) were extremely limited. Sectoral trade agreements on textiles, steel and meat products had been made with some CEECs prior to the establishing of diplomatic relations. Romania was the only Council for Mutual Economic Assistance (CMEA) country with which the EC had a *general* trade agreement, concluded in 1980. A general agreement had also been concluded with Yugoslavia in 1970 but it was of course outside the CMEA. However the revolutionary events in Central and Eastern Europe changed all this. The two Germanys were reunited on 3 October 1990, with the heads of State and Government agreeing that this could be accomplished without a revision of the treaties.

Of extreme importance was the decision of the Group of Twenty-Four Countries (G24) to set on foot an aid package. This decision emerged from the Western Economic Summit held in Paris in 1989. It gave rise to Operation Phare. The Commission was given the task of coordinating this economic assistance. The Phare programme became operational in 1990 for Poland and Hungary and was subsequently extended to cover all the CEECs including Slovenia but not the other states of the former Yugoslavia. The purpose of Phare was to support the process of economic restructuring and encourage the changes necessary to build a market-orientated economy and promote private enterprise. A big aspect of the Phare programme is privatization. For example, it pays for the Polish Ministry of Privatization.

The grant money made available under Phare has been accompanied by loan monies from various sources. The EIB has been authorized to extend its investment activity to Poland, Hungary, the Czech Republic, Slovakia, Romania and Bulgaria. The Community has guaranteed these loans. The ECSC can also make loans to the CEECs for restructuring the steel and coal industries and has earmarked monies for this purpose.

Operation Phare also gave rise to the establishment of the European Bank for Reconstruction and Development (EBRD). It opened for business in London in April 1991. Its aim is 'in contributing to economic progress and reconstruction ... to foster the transition towards open market-oriented economies and to promote private and entrepreneurial initiatives in the Central and Eastern European countries committed to and applying the principles of multi-party democracy, pluralism and market economies.' The

Bank's capital, 10,000 million ECUs, was initially to be provided by forty-two shareholders: forty countries, the European Community and the European Investment Bank. The Community, the member states and the EIB were to hold 51 per cent of the Bank's capital, and the Community, represented by the Commission, was to have one governor and one member on the board of directors. The ERBD is able to make or guarantee loans to enterprises in the private sector, but also for infrastructure improvements and to state-controlled enterprises being privatized or managed according to the principles of free competition. It is also able to invest in or finance investment in the capital of such enterprises. Up to 40 per cent of bank finance is for the public sector, the other 60 per cent of its funds is destined for the private sector.

A series of Trade and Cooperation Agreements were concluded with most of the CEECs. Such an agreement was signed with the former Czechoslovakia but not separately with the Czech Republic and Slovakia. The agreement with the former Yugoslavia is no longer in operation but an agreement was signed with Slovenia in 1993. The agreements were subsequently replaced by association agreements referred to as Europe Agreements.

These Europe Agreements (which are similar but not identical) were bilateral, i.e. between the Community and the country in question. They aimed to establish bilateral free trade in industrial products, but were asymmetrical in that in each case the Community undertook to remove protection more quickly than the individual CEECs partner. Substantial protection was, however, to remain for a group of sensitive industrial products. This has attracted some criticism and had led to concessions on the part of the European Communities. Agricultural trade was mostly excluded from liberalization. The Communities can impose voluntary export restraints (VERs) and have already done so in respect of some CEECs exports.

There are provisions for the right of establishment, freedom to supply services and free movement of labour. It would however be a mistake to assume that the latter provides for unrestricted movement of workers. Rather the agreements confirm existing agreements limiting the number of workers authorized to work in the European Communities. In the second five years of the ten-year period the Association Council can examine ways of increasing labour movement. There are also provisions relating to capital movements and currency convertibility in order to enable investment to take place and goods, etc., to be paid for.

An important feature of the agreements is the insertion of competition rules and limits on state aids to industry. Financial cooperation is also covered and the Phare programme is incorporated in the agreements.

There are political provisions. These open a so-called political dialogue. The agreements seek to support the new political orders in the CEECs and to facilitate their integration into the community of democratic nations.

The key question which they pose is that of ultimate membership of the European Union. The Europe Agreements 'only recognize that the final objective of the CEECs is to become EU members' (Baldwin, 1994, p. 125). However, the 1993 Copenhagen summit accepted that if they desired full membership, they should have it. But there were qualifications. One related to the ability of the Union to absorb them – and that is where the real problem arises.

The burden on the Community budget of a Visegrad[1] enlargement would be very considerable. This is partly because of their agricultural structures (they are relatively dependent on agriculture). As a result CAP spending would have to rise markedly. Additionally because of their low incomes, combined with a total population of 64 million, structural spending would also escalate. If the Visegrad states enjoyed similar terms to those presently existing in the European Union, Baldwin argues that there would have to be a 60 per cent rise in Community budget contributions of the current (1994) members (Baldwin, 1994, p. xvii). Adding other CEECs members would make matters worse. Reducing the generosity of current spending programmes would be a possible solution but would be violently opposed by the poorer current European Union states. Denying the Visegrad members access to CAP and structural spending would amount to second-class citizenship and would be offensive to them. Incidentally, Baldwin identifies two other potential problems. First, the CEECs as full members could attempt to use their voting power to screw even more resources out of the European Union. Second, migratory flows, though not necessarily vast, could cause problems by being concentrated in particular areas.

1. The Visegrad states are Poland, Hungary, the Czech Republic and Slovakia.

The structural-spending problem is of course partly due to the fact that the European Union was able to grant generous terms to its poorer states because, relatively, their populations are not over-whelming. Adding the Visegrad Four would significantly change the pattern of rich versus poorer states, and *a fortiori* matters would be changed radically if all the CEECs joined.

Baldwin has suggested a solution which also deals with a weakness of the present European Agreements which, being bilateral, do not adequately deal with the need for liberalization in intra-CEECs trade. He suggests a staged process. The first stage would involve weaving the European Agreements into a single multilateral arrange-ment. At a later stage those who were in the vanguard of the reform movement could be admitted to an arrangement similar to the EEA, discussed above. Eventually the process of economic develop-ment would mean that their budgetary impact would render them less of a problem as full members. Whilst the issue of membership has thus far been largely viewed as economic, there is also a foreign policy and security aspect in respect of which progress also needs to be made.

Not surprisingly, the Visegrad Four want early membership (par-ticularly Hungary and Poland who have thrown their membership hats in the ring) and hope it will occur by the year 2000. A further group consisting of Bulgaria, Romania, Slovenia, Albania and the Baltic Three (Estonia, Latvia and Lithuania) declare that member-ship is a medium-term goal. The European Union has however set its eastward boundary so as to exclude Russia and the other ex-Soviet republics (with the exception of the three Baltic states). Russia and the ex-Soviet states have been offered Partnership and Cooperation deals – Russia and the Ukraine led the way in 1994.

The GATT, Japan and US

As we indicated in Chapter 4, the Community has not been reluctant to engage in GATT negotiations designed to reduce the level of the CET. The tariff reductions resulting from the Dillon Round (1961–2) and the Kennedy Round (1964–7) were discussed in Chapter 4. The Tokyo Round (1973–9) led to further cuts but was also impor-tant because it involved negotiations on NTBs. Codes of practice were agreed on technical standards, public procurement and subsidies, among other things. As a result, some modifications were made to EC directives concerning these matters – e.g. public procurement. In 1985 an international conference was held at Punta del Este in Uruguay, where it was agreed that a new round of negotiations should be launched. This came to be known as the Uruguay Round. It covered not only the conventional topics, such as tariffs and NTBs, but also agriculture. The CAP was therefore bound to come in for some close scrutiny. The negotiations also broke new ground by seeking to expand GATT activities to include intellectual property rights (patents, trademarks, etc.), trade-related investment measures and services. It was originally assumed that the Uruguay Round would be wrapped up by the end of 1991 but, as we indicated earlier in connection with the discussion of the CAP (see Chapter 8), it was delayed by disputes concerning agricultural surpluses and lack of food export opportunities to the Community and was only concluded in December 1993. We shall discuss its conclusions later.

The tariff reductions of the Tokyo Round could easily give rise to a mistaken impression of the international trade atmosphere in the 1970s and 1980s. They could be taken to imply that the period was one of trade liberalization. However, this was not so. It was in fact one characterized by what has been called the 'New Protectionism'. Whilst member states discussed tariff reductions and indeed instituted such measures, other and newer forms of protection were introduced. Some of the protectionist measures were discussed in Chapter 10 – e.g. the Multi-Fibre Arrangement and the restriction of steel imports into the Community. These were Community measures. But in addition there emerged a range of nationally negotiated (either by governments or industries) voluntary export restraints (VERs) whereby countries were asked to restrain their exports of particular goods to the Community. It has been argued that this form of protection exploited a grey area between what is legal and what is illegal under GATT rules (Hine, 1985, p. 259). Japan was a key target of such arrangements, and exports from Japan of cars, fork-lift trucks, colour TV sets and tubes, video-cassette recorders, motor cycles, audio-cassette recorders, quartz watches and machine tools were all subjected to this treatment. In addition, countries in Eastern Europe and countries such as Taiwan, South Korea and Brazil between them had to exercise restraint over exports of footwear, radios, cutlery, ceramics and TV sets (Pearce and Sutton, 1985, p. 44).

The trade relationship between the Community and Japan has been under particular strain because of the persistent and chronic trade imbalance between the two. As we saw in Table 21, Japan's imports from the EC in 1992 were only 40 per cent of its exports to it. The accusation has been levelled at Japan that it has failed to open its market whilst taking full advantage of the more open trading conditions in Western Europe.

Given this unfavourable trade balance, various courses of action were possible. Pressure could be put on the Japanese to open up their market. The results of exhortation were repeated promises but relatively limited action. Because of this the Community resorted to more aggressive tactics.

Firstly, in its 1992 programme for liberalizing financial services the Community sought to exercise leverage by imposing reciprocity conditions. Third-country banks (the Japanese being very much in mind) will be able to establish subsidiaries and enjoy the benefits of the enlarged market, provided their home country reciprocates with respect to Community banks.

Secondly, member states and the Community have put obstacles in the way of Japanese exports to the Community. VERs introduced by member states were followed by Community involvement in the same kind of activity. Thus in 1983 the Commission presented the Japanese Government with a list of commodities for which VERs had already been agreed. It asked for restraint in respect of them and also negotiated a VER in connection with video-cassette recorders. Cars have been a particularly sensitive issue. Despite repeated warnings by the Japanese Ministry of International Trade and Industry, Japanese car manufacturers have continued to increase their penetration of the Community market. By 1986 the figure had risen to 11.7 per cent. This gave rise to angry protests from EC car producers and to a demand in 1987 for a Community freeze on car imports. These car imports gave rise to a particular problem in the context of the single market programme since the latter threatened those countries which had introduced their own VERs on Japanese cars. The removal of internal barriers would mean that their VERs would be undermined by Japanese cars entering their markets by the back door from countries not operating VERs. A solution had to be found at Community level. What the Commission did was to enter into an agreement to the effect that import restrictions would be phased out progressively but only by 1999. This would give the EC industry time to adjust. The Commission also entered into an agreement with Japan whereby the latter would limit exports to the EC. In recent years a Trade Assessment Mechanism has been operating involving the Community and Japan.

Thirdly, the Community has sought to persuade the Japanese to set up full-scale manufacturing plants in Europe. In many cases the Japanese have done so because their goods, produced outside the Community, have attracted anti-dumping duties. To avoid this, they first of all transferred final assembly to Europe. This in turn provoked an attack on so-called screwdriver operations – this was accomplished by the imposition of local-content rules. The Commission's more recent strategy now appears to be to devise origin rules which focus on the transfer of technology since a local-content rule of 80 per cent can still allow Japanese producers to hang on to key technological processes.

Trade relations with the US have been difficult – indeed at times they have been extremely tense as the account of the Uruguay Round in this chapter and Chapter 8 indicates. Protectionist proposals debated in Congress in the mid-eighties indicated that the US might go on the offensive. Indeed this pressure ultimately reflected itself in the passage in 1988 of the Omnibus Trade and Competitiveness Act. The main objective of the Act was to open up foreign markets to US goods and to provide effective sanctions against those thought to be trading unfairly. Tension was also generated by the single European market programme which it was feared would lead to a Fortress Europe approach on the part of the European Community. American businessmen, like their EFTA counterparts, were concerned about being excluded from Community rule-making about standards, public procurement and the like. Community demands for reciprocity in financial services (see above in the case of Japan) and Community preference provisions in public procurement rules helped to sustain these fears.

It would be tedious to catalogue the long list of trade skirmishes which have occurred. We will highlight just two sectors.

The CAP, as we have already noted, has been a long-standing cause of conflict, since the growth of self-sufficiency within the

Community has reduced the scope for US agricultural exports to the Community whilst the subsidized sale of EC surpluses on the world market has reduced the revenues from US sales elsewhere. Both these effects have been illustrated by trade disputes in the 1980s. In late 1986 and early 1987 a dispute blew up over the effect of Spanish accession which led to variable import levies being placed on Spanish imports of maize and soya under the CAP. The US objected because the expected effect of this action was a reduction of US exports of these products to Spain. It therefore threatened to retaliate by imposing duties of 200 per cent on EC products including brandy, gin, certain white wines and cheese. At the end of January 1987 a compromise formula was found which averted a minor trade war. The EC undertook to purchase specified quantities of maize and other cereals from outsiders, including the US, and in addition it reduced import duties on twenty industrial items. In 1988 trouble flared up on the issue of the Community's threat to ban imports of US beef containing hormones. This related to a Council directive of 1985 banning the use of hormones in cattle rearing. American threats led the Community in turn to indicate that it would retaliate. Further tension was caused on the agricultural front by a US request to GATT to examine certain Community oilseeds arrangements following a complaint by the American Soybean Association. The sensitive nature of EC-subsidized exports is well illustrated by an episode in 1983, when the US Government signed two agreements with Egypt for the sale of large quantities of wheat flour, butter and cheese at subsidized prices. The Community took exception to these sales at a loss, as they were taking place in what is regarded as one of its traditional markets. In truth it was really a case of the US recovering by subsidized sales a market which had been previously captured by the EC by means of subsidized sales!

Steel has been the subject of trade disputes since 1982, when the US Department of Commerce initiated a series of anti-dumping and anti-subsidy investigations in connection with steel imported from Community countries. Two thirds of Community steel exports to the US were thereby put at risk. In December 1992 the US imposed anti-dumping import duties of up to 142 per cent – closing outright about 70 per cent of the US market to Community exports of flat steel products. Fortunately on appeal the US International

Trade Commission accepted that the domestic industry had not been injured in just over half the cases cited which meant that about 54 per cent of the volume of trade from the Community escaped these draconian penalties.

It was against this kind of turbulent background that the long drawn-out Uruguay Round of negotiations wound its way to conclusion in late 1993. The results were extremely important. A further round of international tariff cuts were agreed – in the case of the Communities a cut in the CET averaging between 37 and 38 per cent was conceded. It was also agreed that the Multi-Fibre Arrangement (see Chapter 10) should be dismantled. Over a ten-year period beginning in 1995 the quotas will be phased out and tariff levels reduced. Various kinds of barriers to trade in goods and also services were also addressed. Clearer rules have been agreed in respect of anti-dumping measures that will make it more difficult to use them for purposes of trade harassment. Agreements were also entered into which further developed procedures elaborated in the Tokyo Round. One agreement tightens up the use of subsidies and also makes it more difficult to use anti-subsidy actions for trade harassment. Another introduces better rules to ensure that technical norms, testing and certification procedures do not create unnecessary obstacles to trade. The developing countries were pressed into accepting rules that are designed to protect the interests of the owners of intellectual property – i.e. patents, trade marks and copyrights. An absolutely key feature of the final settlement was the solution to the acrimonious dispute over agricultural protection and practices. The breakthrough was the Blair House accord of November 1992. This will lead to a reduction of subsidized farm exports. Subsidized exports will be reduced by 36 per cent in value and 21 per cent in volume. As we noted earlier (Chapter 8) EC cereal prices will be brought close to world levels and support will switch away from export subsidies to direct income support, which hopefully does not have the old effect of encouraging more and more production. Finally, the participating states decided to set up a World Trade Organization (WTO). GATT itself, the agreements on intellectual property, the codes on dumping, all now come under the umbrella of the WTO. It also operates a disputes procedure. WTO formally came into existence in 1995.

12

CHALLENGES FACING THE EUROPEAN UNION

Structure

One of the major issues facing the Union in the run up to the second millennium and beyond is the question of the appropriate structure. As we saw in Chapter 1, the possibility of a two-tier Europe was identified by Leo Tindemans as early as 1975. Whilst some regarded this as an extremely un-*communautaire* development, it can be argued that this was an overreaction. There is much to be said for the view that those who wish to forge ahead should be allowed to do so. If the move forward proves beneficial, it is not unreasonable to expect that the laggards will in due course be induced to come on board by the prospect of sharing in the benefits or at least avoiding the disadvantages of exclusion. The Maastricht opt-out arrangements on EMU may prove to be temporary. It is difficult to imagine that on the monetary front the UK will wish to assume a *permanently* semi-detached role since apart from prestige considerations this could have adverse effects on the inward flow of foreign investment from Japan, the US and elsewhere. It would also be damaging to the City of London. Having said that, we should not ignore the fact that the Maastricht Treaty did formally embrace a two-tier possibility since following the convergence exercise the treaty admits of the possibility that there will be some who participate in the EMU but also others who will have a derogation.

Policy pronouncements in France and Germany in 1994 indicated that there was some political support for the idea of approaching further integration on a two- or three-tier (or two or three concentric circles) basis. Some of this may have been a bargaining tactic. In the three-circle plan the inner circle would consist of those countries who were enthusiastic and strong enough to forge ahead with further integration. This would include Germany and France and, presumably, the Benelux countries. The membership of the other two circles tended to vary from account to account. It seems likely that the next circle would take in current Union members who are less enthusiastic or lack the economic strength to forge ahead. The outer circle would include current outsiders, such as the CEECs.

The single market

The single market remains a problem for a variety of reasons. The uncomfortable truth is that despite the prominence given to the completion date of 1992, the single market is not yet a permanent reality for all kinds of reason. Firstly, various measures have yet to be introduced – this is most obviously the case in respect of the fiscal dimension. Some of the failure to make progress on fiscal matters must be ascribed to the British reluctance, in the Single Act negotiations, to allow majority voting on tax harmonization issues. Secondly, it is important that member states incorporate single market measures in their domestic laws. There has been a notable tendency for some states to lag behind in this process. Hopefully they will eventually come into line. However there then emerges a third problem – namely enforcement. Member state governments will always be tempted to grant aids to their lame duck enterprises and in their public procurement to favour home-produced goods. Equally cartels and other private restrictions of competition will emerge from time to time. For these reasons the single market is never going to be a *fait accompli*. There will be a constant need for vigilance on the part of the Commission and no doubt its legitimate interventions will from time to time be vilified as unwarranted meddling.

Respect for Community law

This enforcement aspect of the Commission's role brings us face to face with the problem of the need for member states to respect Community obligations right across the spectrum of economic and social actions. In 1994 a quite spectacular episode occurred in connection with the failure of certain member states to implement the requirements of Community law in respect of milk quotas which had been agreed in 1984 (see Chapter 8). As a result they had produced excess milk whereas farmers in law abiding states had been forced to slaughter dairy cows. The states in question were

Italy and Spain. The original fines imposed by the Commission were £2,000 million and £1,400 million respectively. Apparently both countries refused to pay the fines, arguing that their original quotas had been too low. The Commission then agreed to a retrospective increase in their quotas which had the incidental effect of reducing the size of over-production and therefore the fines. This was opposed by the UK which launched a Court of Justice case alleging that in granting the retrospective quota increases the Commission had exceeded its powers. In the end the UK agreed to drop its case when Italy and Spain finally agreed to pay reduced fines of respectively £1,520 million and £1,000 million. This episode underlines the importance of the Maastricht Treaty's tightening up of the Article 169/171 procedure which now enables fines to be imposed on governments who refuse to conform to Court of Justice rulings.

Fraud is another embarrassing problem which the Community has yet to effectively tackle. In November 1994 the President of the Court of Auditors drew attention to a list of transgressions in connection with the use of Community budget monies. The impression which emerges is that some member states are primarily interested in getting money out of the Community and are little concerned about what happens to it thereafter! This has two adverse effects: first, the money is not achieving the objectives for which it was intended and second, it demeans the whole of the European union venture and provides excellent ammunition for all those who are opposed to it. Hopefully, at the Essen European Council meeting in December 1994 an effective start may have been made on the task of rooting out fraud. The European Council noted that the Council of Ministers on Justice and Home Affairs had reached agreement on penal sanctions in connection with the protection of the Community's financial interests. The European Council called upon the Justice and Home Affair ministers to agree on joint action or a convention during the first half of 1995. The Economic and Financial Affairs Council (Ecofin) was called upon to adopt an appropriate regulation on the protection of the Community's financial interests. Member states were required to report on the action they were taking in combating fraud. These reports would go to Ecofin and then to the European Council.

EMU

This is the next major step and throws up major issues. It seems unlikely that in the long-run a group of countries trading so intensively together will not move towards a single currency. However, all the signs are that the requirements of convergence (which Germany is bound to insist on) are such that full EMU will not occur in 1996 and that the earliest feasible date is 1999, and it may be later. This was the view of the President of the EMI in 1994. He also suggested that the final stage might be approached in two phases. Exchange rates could be fixed irrevocably, and then there may be a substantial interim period before the single currency makes its appearance. The possibility that EMU will be approached on a variable speed basis seems highly likely, particularly if the Community embraces the economies of Eastern Europe. Whilst Maastricht appears to provide for an automatic transition in 1999, it is difficult to see how it can occur without an act of will on the part of those who propose to participate. Incidentally, whilst business favours a single currency, it is evident that the public is not enthusiastic, notably in Germany. One feature of the EMU programme that has been neglected is the absolute emphasis laid on price stability. In a stimulating article Mark Blaug has expressed astonishment at the degree to which governments, bankers and the public have been, in his words, persuaded to accept the dogma 'that inflation is the root of all economic evil and that price stability is the key to growth and full employment' (Blaug 1993, p. 399). His conclusion is that the costs of unemployment vastly exceed the costs of inflation.

We noted in Chapter 7 that the main objective of the ESCB within the context of EMU will be the preservation of price stability. To this end the Maastricht Treaty calls for central bank independence. It is however open to doubt whether the evidence that high degrees of independence are *associated* with low inflation rates means a great deal. Association does not imply causality or necessarily indicate the direction of causality. It may be that societies which value price stability tend to opt for central bank independence. It may also be that a society which fears inflation (e.g. Germany, for historical reasons) will favour a tight monetary and fiscal stance and that trade unions will recognize the paramount importance of not pricing themselves out of jobs. That being so, it follows that independence for the proposed European central bank organs may not produce price stability since they cannot look across the Community for the same social support that the Bundesbank has enjoyed within Germany.

Some further thought will have to be given to the Maastricht plan for EMU. Critics have pointed to weaknesses in the system. It can be argued that there is a built-in tendency towards deflation. Thus, if a country suffers a negative economic shock, economic activity and incomes fall. If that country is at, or close to, its public sector deficit limit then the decline in activity will tend to drive it over the limit since as incomes fall tax receipts will also fall and unemployment expenditure will have to rise. The country concerned will have to raise taxes, cut spending or both. But this response will not be offset in some other part of the Union. It has also been pointed out that under full EMU a country facing an adverse asymmetric shock has little capacity to do anything about it since it has been stripped of key monetary policy powers. There is a need to redesign the Community budget, endowing it with greater resources and rendering it capable of producing automatic and compensating inter-country fiscal flows. There is however little sign that this sort of thinking has made a great deal of progress at the highest levels.

Unemployment

This conveniently moves us on to the macroeconomic phenomenon of unemployment in the Community which is extremely high both within the Twelve and among the new ex-EFTA members. This problem has been attracting increasing attention within the Community. In Chapter 10 we noted that it gave rise to the 1993 White Paper, *Growth Competitiveness and Employment*. However, as we saw earlier the White Paper recognized that the role of the Community in dealing with lack of competitiveness and unemployment was limited. *A good deal would fall to the member states.* The factors that inhibited employment, etc., varied from state to state. They would have to review the ideas contained in the White Paper and appropriately address their own approaches to education, access to vocational training, labour laws, employment and redundancy practices, their provisions for geographical mobility, their social security benefit systems and the ways in which such systems heap non-wage costs on employers.

Nevertheless there was some scope for a Community contribution. The first was the completion and effective implementation of the single market. The second was the introduction and financial support of Trans-European Networks which, whilst they would not immediately have a major impact on unemployment, would make a valuable contribution to increased cohesiveness, efficiency and competitiveness. The third was the development of information highways – i.e. systems for the transmission of data throughout the Community which would make it possible to combine transmission of information, sound, text and images in a single high performance system. The fourth was the need to strengthen R & TD activity.

A series of Trans-European Network projects have been approved and more are in the pipeline. Also, as part of a drive to increase competitiveness, a high-level Legislative Administrative Simplification Group (Deregulation Group) began work in 1994. Its task is to monitor Community and national laws for over-regulation. The European Council at Essen in December 1994 also welcomed the Commission's intention to set up an international council of expert advisers on competitiveness. Clearly the message is getting through that increasing competitiveness is crucial – no doubt the UK will lay claim to a good deal of the credit for this development and will continue to resist those social policy proposals that it sees as undermining competitiveness.

Agriculture

Agriculture has always been high on the Community problem list and is unlikely to disappear in the coming years. It is too early to make a judgement about the effectiveness of the McSharry reforms. The Community budget financial perspective to 1999 indicates that expenditure on the CAP will continue to grow in real terms. But as a proportion of budget spending it will fall. On the positive side there is the prospect that, notably as a result of reduced export subsidies, it will be less offensive to outside food producers and that it will be more environmentally friendly.

Economic and social cohesion

Some commentators have also identified economic and social cohesion as an area of possible future concern, i.e. that regional imbalances may increase. However, the evidence, at least to date, is not discouraging. Button and Pentecost, taking the period from 1975 to 1988/89, have shown that there was convergence in terms of the growth rate of regional GDP. They do however report that unemployment rates have diverged 'although during the 1980s there is some sign of convergence to a higher level of unemployment as the EC economies faced economic recession' (Button and Pentecost, 1993, p. 9). Evidence has also been provided by Barro and Sala-I-Martin to the effect that the EC experienced convergent growth of GDP per capita over the period 1950–85 (Barro and Sala-I-Martin, 1991). Armstrong has pointed out that this study was largely confined to the more prosperous regions and excluded certain EC states. He has conducted the analysis on a broader basis, bringing the results up to 1990, and concluded that the findings lend support to the catch-up view of regional GDP per capita growth among EC regions (Armstrong, 1995).

Enlargement

A major problem for the future is the prospect of further enlargement. The Union is besieged by countries that wish to join. Apart from Cyprus, Malta and Turkey, there are the Visegrad Four together with at least six other East European countries. The Community must give high priority to devising solutions to the problems posed by this prospect, notably in the case of the CEECs. When the history of the post-war period is written, the key events will be the fall of the Berlin Wall, the collapse of the Communist system and the diminished threat posed by Russia. The Union, for its part, will be judged in significant measure by the helpfulness of its response to these developments.

Part of the problem is economic and financial. Quite simply, as we noted in Chapter 11, the direct budgetary cost of CEECs enlargement would be quite substantial. Added to this is the possibility that the CEECs might use their voting power to extract additional resources out of the richer members. Further problems could arise from uncontrolled migratory flows from the east. A solution on the lines of winding up current agricultural and structural spending would be strongly resisted by the poorer states of the present Union. Admitting the CEECs, but excluding them from the benefits of such funding, would turn them into second-class members. Baldwin's solution (see Chapter 11) consists of recognizing that full unqualified membership is a long way off – it will depend on economic development, reducing the size of the agricultural sector and raising income levels. In the meantime a relationship involving an intermediate but progressive status is called for, which keeps the long term goal in sight and fosters the movement towards it.

The Community's response so far appears to be a gradualist one not out of keeping with Baldwin's suggestion. The CEECs will be allowed to join if they so desire. However, at the Essen European Council in December 1994, whilst the political leaders of Poland, Hungary, the Czech Republic and Slovakia, Bulgaria and Romania were in attendance, no firm date for membership was promised. Instead, the strategy mapped out consisted of bringing the CEECs progressively closer. Beginning in 1995 a series of annual meetings from heads of state down would be inaugurated. These would be additional to the meetings that occur under the aegis of the European Agreements. Additionally, as part of the pre-accession strategy, the prospective members will have to prepare themselves for the internal market. The need for a structured relationship in respect of the CFSP and in respect of aspects of CJHA was also identified at Essen. CEECs enlargement clearly dominated the Essen Council and this bodes well for the future.

Enlargement also poses problems for the Union institutions. This issue needs to be set against the background that the Community of Twelve at Maastricht could by virtue of the EFTA and other enlargements end up as a Community of between twenty and thirty. This raises all kinds of issues such as the effectiveness of the Council of Ministers if every national delegation must have its initial say before the hard bargaining can begin. A *tour de table* of ten minutes per minister among thirty adds up to five hours of preliminaries! This worries some. But others do not see it as a problem since they envisage that groups of countries will select one state to be their spokesperson. More members means more seats in the European Parliament and poses the question of how to maintain efficiency in such a dramatically enlarged parliament. The size of the Commission has already spiralled up from seventeen to twenty thanks to EFTA enlargement, and threatens to get even larger although it is widely argued that the appropriate figure would be ten. A larger number of states and greater diversity seem to point to the need for more streamlined voting processes in Council and for a vigorous approach to the concept of subsidiarity. An awkward issue which is likely to come up is the disproportion between Council votes and national populations. Following the completion of the EFTA negotiations it was pointed out that Luxembourg had one vote for every 186,000 whereas Germany had one for every 8 million people.

Institutional reform

The decision making system of the Union, including the role to be played by the European Parliament in the light of the Delors democratic deficit argument, is bound to be closely scrutinized in the 1996 review. Inevitably those with federal aspirations will return to the attack. Such an attack would no doubt include proposals for greater use of majority voting on economic and social issues in the Council of Ministers, a power of initiative and a conventional co-legislative role for Parliament together with the bringing of the CFSP into the majority voting system. However, a federalist versus anti-federalist dominated agenda would be very stultifying and would do little to advance the Union's cause. Federalist inspired proposals would probably automatically provoke the veto of the UK and possibly others. It would be much more productive if the debate was conducted on different lines – i.e. how to make the Union system more effective and efficient particularly in the context of an expanded and probably expanding membership. To such a debate the UK could not avoid contributing constructively since it has been one of the keenest advocates of enlargement.

CFSP

A major problem area concerns the CFSP and its development into a common defence policy and a common defence. Here a number of issues arise. The first is the problem of the cohesiveness of the CFSP in the virtual absence of majority voting. Cohesiveness will be tested by greater numbers and greater diversity. A number of ex-EFTA members who previously valued their neutrality seem to have had no difficulty in accommodating themselves to the prospect of a CFSP. Will they find it so easy to come into line when major real-world issues have to be faced?

The question of the appropriate arrangements in relation to defence were a matter of dispute prior to Maastricht. Maastricht, however, achieved a resolution of this problem. The nine-member WEU would implement decisions and actions of the Union which had defence implications, but the policy of the Union had to respect NATO obligations. The Maastricht Treaty Declaration on Western European Union in effect opened WEU up to all Union members. The 1992 WEU Petersburg Declaration followed up by deciding that WEU membership should be more closely aligned with that of the Union, and in November Greece became a full member and Denmark and Ireland became observers. Trevor Taylor has pointed out that this aspect of the Maastricht Treaty could lead to a near-automatic expansion of NATO membership. He points out:

> Given the stated desire of the Central European States (Poland, the Czech Republic and Hungary) to join NATO, it is predictable that if and when they achieve EC membership they will ask also to be WEU members. Yet it would be potentially very awkward to have Europeans covered by the WEU but not the NATO guarantee, since this could mean (for instance) that WEU states could get involved to their east in a crisis in which the United States had no formal voice. The obvious solution would be to expand NATO along with the WEU, but this would require ratification by North American legislatures.
>
> (Taylor, 1994, p. 3)

The possibility of NATO membership for CEECs has been approached cautiously for fear of provoking right-wing reactions in Russia. The policy has consisted of inviting former Warsaw Pact countries to join Partnership for Peace arrangements, which allow for participation in NATO activities but fall short of full membership and do not involve an assurance of a NATO response in the event of an attack on such a cooperating member.

Trevor Taylor has pointed out that if the CFSP is to be credible, three further developments are called for. A strategy document is needed which identifies the key and pressing problems and *indicates how they might be tackled*. Secondly, the Union has been dangerously weakened by defence cuts and this process needs to be brought to an end. Thirdly, the Union members need to cooperate effectively on equipment.

Attention will also have to be given to the tasks assigned to the various bodies in Europe which have security and defence roles to play. For example, what kind of relationship should exist between NATO's Rapid Reaction Force and an expanded Franco-Germany brigade? Douglas Hurd (Hurd, 1994, p. 427) has also pointed out that a weakness of the old EPC machinery was that it did not provide for any forward-looking analysis and planning. He has observed that if the CFSP is to be successful, it will need, not a massive bureaucracy, but nevertheless a dedicated back-up and one that is separate from the Commission. He argues that the strengthened CFSP section of the Council secretariat will be important in this context. Whether this proves sufficient only the future will tell.

ABBREVIATIONS

AASM	Associated African States and Madagascar
ACP	African, Caribbean and Pacific Ocean Countries
ASEAN	Association of South-East Asian Nations
Benelux	Belgium, the Netherlands and Luxembourg Customs Union
CAP	Common Agricultural Policy
CCP	Common Commercial Policy
CEEC	Committee for European Economic Cooperation
CEECs	Central and Eastern European Countries
CET	Common External Tariff
CFP	Common Fisheries Policy
CFSP	Common Foreign and Security Policy
CJHA	Cooperation on Justice and Home Affairs
Comecon	Council for Mutual Economic Assistance
COPA	Committee of Agricultural Organizations (Comité des Organisations Professionelles Agricoles de la CEE)
Coreper	Committee of Permanent Representatives (Comité des Représentants Permanents de la CEE)
COREU	Correspondance Européenne
COST	Committee on European Cooperation in the Field of Scientific and Technical Research
EAGGF	European Agricultural Guidance and Guarantee Fund (FEOGA)
EBRD	European Bank for Reconstruction and Development
EC	European Community
ECB	European Central Bank
ECC	European Communities Commission
ECE	Economic Commission for Europe
Ecosoc	Economic and Social Committee
ECSC	European Coal and Steel Community
ECU	European Currency Unit
EDF	European Development Fund
EEA	European Economic Area
EEC	European Economic Community
EES	European Economic Space
EFTA	European Free Trade Association
EIB	European Investment Bank
EMCF	European Monetary Cooperation Fund

EMF	European Monetary Fund
EMI	European Monetary Institute
EPC	European Political Cooperation
ERDF	European Regional Development Fund
ERM	Exchange Rate Mechanism
ESCB	European System of Central Banks
ESF	European Social Fund
ESPRIT	European Strategic Programme for Research and Development in Information Technology
EUA	European Unit of Account
Euratom	European Atomic Energy Community
EUT	European Union Treaty
FEOGA	Fonds Européen d'Orientation et Garantie Agricoles
GATT	General Agreement on Tariffs and Trade
GDP	Gross Domestic Product
GNP	Gross National Product
GSP	Generalized System of Preferences
ICE	Istituto Nazionale per il Commercio Estero
IFTRA	International Fair Trade Practice Rules Administration
IGC	Inter-governmental Conference
IMF	International Monetary Fund
JET	Joint European Torus
JOULE	Joint Opportunities for Unconventional or Long Term Energy Supply
MCA	Monetary Compensating Amount
MFA	Multi-Fibre Arrangement
MTFA	Medium-Term Financial Assistance
NATO	North Atlantic Treaty Organization
NCI	New Community Instrument
NIC	Newly Industrializing Country
NTB	Non-Tariff Barrier
OCTs	Overseas Countries and Territories
OECD	Organization for Economic Cooperation and Development
OEEC	Organization for European Economic Cooperation
OOPEC	Office for the Official Publications of the European Communities
OPEC	Organization of Petroleum Exporting Countries
R & TD	Research and Technological Development
RACE	Research and Development in Advanced Communications Technologies for Europe
SAVE	Action Programme for Increased Energy Efficiency
SEA	Single European Act

SEDOC	Système Européen de Diffusion des Offres et Demandes d'emploi et de compensation internationale
SMEs	Small and Medium – sized Enterprises
SYSMIN	Special financial facility for ACP and OCT mining products
TENs	Trans-European Networks
THERMIE	Programme for the Promotion of European Energy Technology
TVA	Taxe sur valeur ajoutée
UA	Unit of Account
UN	United Nations
UNCTAD	United Nations Conference on Trade and Development
UNICE	Industrial Confederation of the European Community (Union des Industries de la Communauté Européenne)
VAT	Value Added Tax
VER	Voluntary Export Restraint
WEU	Western European Union
WTO	World Trade Organization

REFERENCES

Armstrong, H. A. (1995), 'Convergence Among European Community Regions 1950–1990', *Papers in Regional Science*, forthcoming.

Armstrong, H., and Taylor, J. (1985), *Regional Economics and Policy*, Harvester Wheatsheaf.

Baldwin, R. E. (1994), *Towards an Integrated Europe*, Centre for Economic Policy Research.

Barro, R. J. and Sala-I-Marin, X. (1991), 'Convergence across States and Regions', *Brookings Papers*, Vol. 1.

Blaug, M. (1993), 'Public Enemy No. 1: Unemployment not Inflation', *Economic Notes Monte dei Paschi di Siena*, vol. 22, no. 3.

Bloomfield, A. (1973), 'The Historical Setting' in Krause, L. B. and Salant, W. S. (eds), *European Monetary Unification and its Meaning for the United States*, Brookings Institution.

Bowles, R. and Jones, P. (1992), 'Equity and the EC Budget; A Pooled Cross-Section Time Serves Analysis', *Journal of European Social Policy*, vol. 2, no. 2.

Button, K. and Pentecost, E. (1993), *Testing for Convergence of the EC Regional Economies, Economics Research Paper*, no. 93/5, (Department of Economics, Loughborough University of Technology).

Coffey, P., and Presley, J. R. (1970), 'Monetary Developments within the European Economic Community: 1970 – A Year of Achievement', *Loughborough Journal of Social Studies*, no. 10, November.

Dahlberg, K. A. (1968), 'The EEC Commission and the Politics of the Free Movement of Labour', *Journal of Common Market Studies*, vol. 6, no. 3, pp. 310–33.

E. Commission (1992), *Third Survey on State Aids in the European Community in the Manufacturing and Certain Other Sectors*, OOPEC.

E. Commission (1993), 'Growth, Competitiveness and Employment', *Bulletin of the European Communities*, no. 6, OOPEC.

EC Commission (1969a), *Memorandum on the Coordination of Economic Policies and Monetary Cooperation within the Community*, COM (169), 50.

EC Commission (1969c), 'Memorandum on Regional Policy', *Bulletin of the European Communities*, no. 12, OOPEC.

EC Commission (1970), 'Economic and Monetary Union in the Community' (Werner Report), *Bulletin of the European Communities*, Supplement no. 7, OOPEC.

EC Commission (1971), *Framework for Aid to the Textile Industry*, SEC (71) 2615 final.

EC Commission (1972a), *First Report on Competition Policy*, OOPEC.

EC Commission (1972b), *Fifth General Report*, OOPEC.

EC Commission (1973), *Second Report on Competition Policy*, OOPEC.

EC Commission (1975a), *Ninth General Report*, OOPEC.

EC Commission (1975b), *Report of the Study Group, Economic and Monetary Union 1980* (Marjolin Report), DOC 11/675/3/74.

EC Commission (1976a), 'European Union' (Tindemans Report), *Bulletin of the European Communities*, Supplement no. 1, OOPEC.

EC Commission (1976b), *Tenth General Report*, OOPEC.

EC Commission (1977a), *Eleventh General Report*, OOPEC.

EC Commission (1977b), *The Role of Public Finance in the European Communities*, vols. 1 and 2 (MacDougall Report), OOPEC.

EC Commission (1981a), 'Report from the Commission of the European Communities to the Council pursuant to the mandate of 30 May 1980', *Bulletin of the European Communities*, no. 1, OOPEC.

EC Commission (1982), *Sixteenth General Report*, OOPEC.

EC Commission (1983), *The Future Financing of the Community*, COM (83) 10.

EC Commission (1984b), *The Application of the Community's Energy Pricing Principles in Member States*, COM (84) 490 final.

EC Commission (1984c), *The Regions of Europe*, European File 15/84, OOPEC.

EC Commission (1985a), *Completing the Internal Market*, COM (85) 310 final.

EC Commission (1985c), *Towards a Technology Community*, COM (85) 530 final.

EC Commission (1986), *Eleventh Annual Report (1985) to the Council by the Commission: European Regional Development Fund*. COM (86) 545 final.

EC Commission (1988a), *Report on Economic and Monetary Union in the European Community* (Delors Report), OOPEC.

EC Commission (1988b), *Research on the 'Cost of Non-Europe'* (Cecchini Report), OOPEC.

EC Commission (1989), *First Survey on State Aids in the European Community*, OOPEC.

EC Commission (1990a), *Second Survey on State Aids in the European Community in the Manufacturing and Certain Other Sectors*, OOPEC.

EC Commission (1990b), *Communication from the Commission to the Council on Energy and the Environment*, COM (89) 369 final.

EC Council of Ministers (1970), 'The Problem of Political Unification'

(Luxembourg Report), *Bulletin of the European Communities*, no. 11, OOPEC.

EEC Commission (1961), *Memorandum on the General Lines of the Common Transport Policy* (Schaus Memorandum), VII COM (61) 50 final.

EEC Commission (1962a), *Report of the Fiscal and Financial Committee* (Neumark Report), Brussels.

EEC Commission (1962b), *Programme for the Implementation of the Common Transport Policy*, VII COM (62) 88 final.

EEC Commission (1965), *Concentration by Firms in the Common Market*, SEC (65) 3500.

Foley, P. (1993), 'Reforming the ERM', *Lloyds Bank Economic Bulletin*, no. 174 (June).

Goodhart, C. (1993), 'ERM and EMU', *LSE Financial Markets Group Special Paper*, 58 (November).

Hine, R. (1985), *The Political Economy of European Trade*, Wheatsheaf.

HMSO (1971), *The United Kingdom and the European Communities*, Cmnd 4715.

HMSO (1975a), *Membership of the European Community*, Cmnd 5999.

HMSO (1975b), *Membership of the European Community: Report on Renegotiation*, Cmnd 6003.

Hurd, D. (1994), 'Developing the Common Foreign and Security Policy', *International Affairs*, vol. 70, no. 3.

Kruse, D. C. (1980), *Monetary Integration in Western Europe: EMU, EMS and Beyond*, Butterworths.

Levi Sandri, L. (1965), 'The Contribution of Regional Action to the Construction of Europe', *Third International Congress on Regional Economics*, Rome.

Llewellyn, D. T. (1983), 'EC Monetary Arrangements: Britain's Strategy', in A. M. El Agraa (ed.), *Britain Within the European Community: The Way Forward*, Macmillan.

Lundgren, N. (1969), 'Customs unions of industrialized West European countries', in G. R. Denton (ed.), *Economic Integration in Europe*, Weidenfeld & Nicolson.

OEEC (1956), *Europe's Growing Needs of Energy – How Can They Be Met?* (Hartley Report).

Palmer, M., Lambert, J., Forsyth, M., Morris, A., and Wohlgemuth, E. (1968), *European Unity: A Survey of the European Organizations*, Allen & Unwin.

Pearce, J., and Sutton, J. (1985), *Protection and Industrial Policy in Europe*, Routledge and Kegan Paul.

Presley, J. R. (1974), 'Progress Towards European Monetary Union', *Economics*, vol. X, part 3, winter 1973/4.

Spaak, P. H. (1956), *Comité Intergouvernmental créé par la Conférence de*

Messine, Rapport des chefs de délégation aux Ministres des Affaires Étrangères (Spaak Report).

Taylor, T. (1994), 'West European Security and Defence Cooperation: Maastricht and Beyond'. *International Affairs*, vol. 70, no. 1.

Tsoukalis, L. (1977), *The Politics and Economics of European Monetary Integration*, Allen & Unwin.

van Ypersele, J. (1979), 'Operating Principles and Procedures of the European Monetary System', in P. H. Trezise (ed.), *The European Monetary System: Its Promise and Prospects*, Brookings Institution.

Watson, P. (1993), 'Social Policy After Maastricht', *Common Market Law Review*, vol. 30.

Weyman-Jones, T. G. (1986), *Energy in Europe: Issues and Policies*, Methuen.

Whiteford, E. (1993), 'Social Policy After Maastricht', *European Law Review*, vol. 18.

Wyplocz, C. (1994), 'The EMS Crisis: Please Save the Maastricht Treaty', *The ECU for European Business*, no. 15 (February).

FURTHER READING

ARCHER, C., and BUTLER, F. (1992), *The European Community Structure and Process*, Pinter.

ARMSTRONG, H., and TAYLOR, J. (1992), *Regional Economics and Policy*, Harvester Wheatsheaf.

ARTIS, M. (1994), *The Economics of the European Union*, Oxford University Press.

BAINBRIDGE, T., and TEASDALE, A. (1995), *Penguin Companion to European Union*, Penguin

BALDWIN, R. E. (1994), *Towards an Integrated Europe*, Centre for Economic Policy Research.

BELLAMY, C. W., and CHILD, G. D. (1991), *Common Market Law of Competition*, Sweet and Maxwell.

BUTTON, K. J. (ed.) (1991), *Airline Deregulation International Experiences*, David Fulton.

CAFRUNY, A. W., and ROSENTAL, G. G. (1993), *The State of the European Community*, Longman.

CANZONERI, M. B., GRILLE, V., and MASSON, P. R. (1992), *Establishing a Central Bank*, Centre for Economic Policy Research.

CAMPS, M. (1964), *Britain and the European Community 1955–1963*, Oxford University Press.

CECCHINI, P. (1988), *1992: The European Challenge*, Gower.

DE GRAUWE, P., and PAPADEMOS, L. (eds) (1990), *The European Monetary System*, Longman.

DIEBOLD, W. (1959), *The Schuman Plan*, Praeger.

GIOVANNINI, A., and MAYER, C. (eds), *European Financial Integration*, Centre for Economic Policy Research.

GROS, D., and THYGESEN, N. (1992), *European Monetary Integration*, Longman.

HANNEQUART, A. (1992), *Economic and Social Cohesion in Europe*, Routledge.

HENDERSON, R. (1993), *European Finance*, McGraw-Hill.

JOVANOVICH, M. N. (1991), *International Economic Integration*, Routledge.

KRUSE, D. C. (1980), *Monetary Integration in Western Europe: EMU, EMS and Beyond*, Butterworths.

LUDLOW, P. (1982), *The Making of the European Monetary System*, Butterworths.

McLACHLAN, D. L., and SWANN, D. (1967), *Competition Policy in the European Community*, Oxford University Press.

MAYES, D. (1993), *External Implications of European Integration*, Harvester Wheatsheaf.

MONTAGNON, P. (1990), *European Competition Policy*, Pinter.

NICHOLL, W., and SALMON, T. (1993), *Understanding the New European Community*, Harvester Wheatsheaf.

NIELSEN, J. U-M., HENRICH, H., and HANSEN, J. D. (1992), *The Economic Analysis of the EC*, McGraw-Hill.

NUGENT, N. (1991), *Government and Politics of the European Community*, Macmillan.

PINDER, J. (1991), *European Community: The Building of a Union*, Oxford University Press.

SWANN, D. (1983), *Competition and Industrial Policy in European Community*, Methuen.

SWANN, D. (ed.) (1992), *The Single European Market and Beyond*, Routledge.

SWANN, D. (1996), *European Integration in the Nineties*, Edward Elgar.

TEAGUE, P. (1989), *The European Community: The Social Dimension*, Kogan Page.

THATCHER, M. (1988), *Britain in Europe*, Conservative Political Centre.

WALLACE, W. (ed.), *The Dynamics of European Integration*, Pinter.

WEYMAN-JONES, T. G. (1986), *Energy in Europe: Issues and Policies*, Methuen.

WINTERS, L. A. (1993), *European Integration: Trade and Industry*, Centre for Economic Policy Research.

WISE, M., and GIBB, R. (1993), *Single Market to Social Europe*, Longman.

WISTRICHT, E. (1991), *After 1992 the United States of Europe*, Routledge.

INDEX